SPATIAL TRANSFORMATIONS

This book examines a variety of subjective spatial experiences and knowledge production practices in order to shed new light on the specifics of contemporary socio-spatial change, driven as it is by inter alia, digitalization, transnationalization, and migration. Considering the ways in which emerging spatial phenomena are conditioned by an increasing interconnectedness, this book asks how spaces are changing as a result of mediatization, increased mobility, globalization, and social dislocation. With attention to questions surrounding the negotiation and (visual) communication of space, it explores the arrangements, spatialities, and materialities that underpin the processes of spatial refiguration by which these changes come about. Bringing together the work of leading scholars from across diverse range disciplines to address questions of socio-spatial transformation, this volume will appeal to sociologists and geographers, as well as scholars and practitioners of urban planning and architecture.

Angela Million is Professor of Urban Design and Urban Development at Technische Universität Berlin, Germany.

Christian Haid is Senior Researcher at the Habitat Unit, Technische Universität Berlin, Germany.

Ignacio Castillo Ulloa is Research Assistant and Lecturer at Technische Universität Berlin, Germany.

Nina Baur is Professor for Methods of Social Research at Technische Universität Berlin, Germany.

The Refiguration of Space

Based on the premise that what is social always takes on a spatial form, this series explores the changes wrought in the relations of human-beings to spaces and their spatial practices by current social transformations, conflicts, crises and uncertainties. Welcoming studies from disciplines across the social sciences, such as sociology, geography and urban studies, books in the series consider the ways in which people (re-)negotiate and (re-)construct special orders according to a common pattern of 'refiguration', a process that often involves conflict and is frequently shaped by phenomena such as mediatization, translocalisation and polycontexturalisation.

Series Editors

Hubert Knoblauch is Professor of Sociology at Technische Universität Berlin, Germany.

Martina Löw is Professor of the Sociology of Planning and Architecture at the Technische Universität Berlin, Germany.

Titles in the series

Spatial Transformations
Kaleidoscopic Perspectives on the Refiguration of Spaces
Edited by Angela Million, Christian Haid, Ignacio Castillo Ulloa, Nina Baur

For more information about this series, please visit: https://www.routledge.com/The-Refiguration-of-Space/book-series/ROS

SPATIAL TRANSFORMATIONS

Kaleidoscopic Perspectives on the Refiguration of Spaces

Edited by Angela Million, Christian Haid, Ignacio Castillo Ulloa, Nina Baur

LONDON AND NEW YORK

First published 2022
by Routledge
2 Park Square, Milton Park, Abingdon, Oxon OX14 4RN

and by Routledge
605 Third Avenue, New York, NY 10158

Routledge is an imprint of the Taylor & Francis Group, an informa business

© 2022 selection and editorial matter, Angela Million, Christian Haid, Ignacio Castillo Ulloa, Nina Baur; individual chapters, the contributors

The right of Angela Million, Christian Haid, Ignacio Castillo Ulloa, Nina Baur to be identified as the authors of the editorial material, and of the authors for their individual chapters, has been asserted in accordance with sections 77 and 78 of the Copyright, Designs and Patents Act 1988.

The editors would like to recognize the work of Zoya Solovieva (pre-editing), Zachary Mühlenweg (proofreading) and Christian Sander (editorial assistance).

The Open Access version of this book, available at www.taylorfrancis.com, has been made available under a Creative Commons Attribution-Non Commercial-No Derivatives 4.0 license.

Trademark notice: Product or corporate names may be trademarks or registered trademarks, and are used only for identification and explanation without intent to infringe.

British Library Cataloguing-in-Publication Data
A catalogue record for this book is available from the British Library

Library of Congress Cataloging-in-Publication Data
A catalog record has been requested for this book

ISBN: 978-0-367-47720-2 (hbk)
ISBN: 978-1-032-11453-8 (pbk)
ISBN: 978-1-003-03615-9 (ebk)

DOI: 10.4324/9781003036159

Typeset in Bembo
by Apex CoVantage, LLC

Cultural center Comedor San Martín del Once in the neighborhood of La Balanza, Lima, Peru, 2019.

Photographer: © Eleazar Cuadros Choque. Source: Archivo CCC / Coordinadora de la Ciudad (en Construcción)

This book has been funded by the Deutsche Forschungsgemeinschaft (DFG, German Research Foundation)—project number 290045248—SFB 1265.

CONTENTS

List of contributors ... x

1 Navigating spatial transformations through the refiguration of spaces ... 1
Angela Million, Christian Haid, Ignacio Castillo Ulloa, and Nina Baur

PART I
Spatiality and temporality ... 15

2 The refiguration of space, circulation, and mobility ... 17
Martina Löw and Hubert Knoblauch

3 Spatial occupation—destruction—virtualization: types, categories, and processes of a crucial factor in social life ... 28
Karl-Siegbert Rehberg

4 The historicity of the refiguration of spaces under the scrutiny of pre-COVID-19 São Paulo homeless pedestrians ... 46
Fraya Frehse

5 Spatiotemporal entanglements: insights from history ... 60
Susanne Rau

6　Slow movement on the slope: on Architecture Principe's theory of the *oblique function* and the role of circulation in architectural and urban design　72
Christian Sander

PART II
Spatiality, social inequality, and the economy　85

7　'Open borders': a postcolonial critique　87
Gurminder K. Bhambra

8　The centrality of race to inequality across the world-system: old figurations and new reconfigurations　97
Manuela Boatcă

9　Spatial transformations in world-historical perspective: towards mapping the space and time of wealth accumulation　109
Roberto Patricio Korzeniewicz and Corey R. Payne

10　Infrastructures for global production in Ethiopia and Argentina: commodity chains and urban spatial transformation　120
Elke Beyer, Lucas-Andrés Elsner, and Anke Hagemann

11　Separate worlds? Explaining the current wave of regional economic polarization　136
Michael Storper

12　Spatial transformations and spatio-temporal coupling: links between everyday shopping behavior and changes in the retail landscape　151
Elmar Kulke and Nina Baur

PART III
Digitization and visualization of space　167

13　Network spillover effects and the dyadic interactions of virtual, social, and spatial　169
Marco Bastos

14　Talking to my community elsewhere: bringing together networked public spheres and the concept of translocal communities　181
Daniel Maier, Daniela Stoltenberg, Barbara Pfetsch, and Annie Waldherr

15 Annotating places: a critical assessment of two hypotheses on
how locative media transform urban public places 192
Eric Lettkemann and Ingo Schulz-Schaeffer

16 Representational and animatic corporeality: refiguring bodies
and digitally mediated cities 204
Gillian Rose

17 Refiguring spaces: transformative aspects of migration
and tourism 216
Stefanie Bürkle

PART IV
Imagining, producing, and negotiating space **241**

18 Ontological security, globalization, and geographical
imagination 243
Ilse Helbrecht, Janina Dobrusskin, Carolin Genz, and Lucas Pohl

19 Where we turn to: rethinking networks, urban space,
and research methods 258
Talja Blokland, Daniela Krüger, Robert Vief, and Henrik Schultze

20 Reconfiguring the spaces of urban politics: circuits,
territories, and territorialization 269
Jennifer Robinson

21 Appropriating Berlin's Tempohomes 285
Ayham Dalal, Aline Fraikin, and Antonia Noll

22 "I spy with my little eye": children's actual use and
experts' intended design of public space 294
Ignacio Castillo Ulloa, Angela Million, and Jona Schwerer

Index *310*

CONTRIBUTORS

Marco Bastos is the University College Dublin Ad Astra Fellow at the School of Information and Communication Studies and senior lecturer at City, University of London. He has held research positions at the University of California at Davis, Duke University, the University of São Paulo, and Goethe University Frankfurt. He is the author of *Spatializing Social Media: Social Networks Online and Offline* (Routledge, 2021) and principal investigator in the Twitter-funded project "The Brexit Value Space and the Geography of Online Echo Chambers." His research leverages network science and computational methods to explore the intersection of communication and critical data studies.

Nina Baur is Professor for Methods of Social Research at Technische Universität Berlin and principal investigator in the subproject "Knowledge and Goods: Consumers' and Producers' Spatial Knowledge" (A03) of the Collaborative Research Center "Re-Figuration of Spaces" (CRC 1265) funded by the German Research Foundation (DFG). Furthermore, she is Director of the "Global Center of Spatial Methods for Urban Sustainability" (GCSMUS), board member of the Research Committee on Historical Sociology (RC56) of the International Sociology Association (ISA), and managing editor of the journal *Historical Social Research* (HSR). Her research fields include social science methodology, process sociology, spatial sociology, and economic sociology (including sociology of consumption and sociology of work).

Elke Beyer is an urban researcher and professor of international urbanism based at the Habitat Unit, Institute of Architecture, Technische Universität Berlin. She taught theory and history of architecture at Technische Universität Berlin and ETH Zurich, where she also completed her PhD. She was a research associate in the project "Shrinking Cities," Berlin, and at the Leibniz Institute for Research on Society and Space, Erkner. Her research fields include transnational production spaces, architecture and planning of the post-WW2 era in Europe, and global knowledge transfer in architecture and urbanism.

Gurminder K. Bhambra is a professor of postcolonial and decolonial studies at the School of Global Studies, University of Sussex. Previously, she was a professor of sociology at the University of Warwick and has held visiting positions at EHESS, Paris; Princeton University; University of Brasilia; REMESO, Linköping University; Linnaeus University; and CES, University of Coimbra. Her publications include *Connected Sociologies* (Bloomsbury, 2014) and the award-winning book *Rethinking Modernity: Postcolonialism and the Sociological Imagination* (Palgrave Macmillan, 2007).

Talja Blokland is an urban sociologist who has held the Chair of Urban and Regional Sociology at Humboldt-Universität zu Berlin since 2009. She is the principal investigator in the subproject "The World Down My Street: Resources and Networks Used by City Dwellers" (C04) of the Collaborative Research Center "Re-Figuration of Spaces" (CRC 1265) funded by the German Research Foundation (DFG). She has worked at Yale University, the University of Manchester, and various Dutch universities. Her publications include *Urban Bonds* (Polity, 2003), *Community as Urban Practice* (Polity, 2017), and various articles on race and ethnicity in the city, poor neighborhoods, urban violence, gentrification, urban middle classes, and neighborhood relations and everyday interactions.

Manuela Boatcă is a professor of sociology with a focus on social structure and globalization and is Head of School of the Global Studies Program at the University of Freiburg. She was a visiting professor at IUPERJ, Rio de Janeiro, from 2007 to 2008, and professor for the sociology of global inequalities at Freie Universität Berlin from 2012 to 2015. Her publications include *Global Inequalities Beyond Occidentalism* (Routledge, 2016) and *Decolonizing European Sociology: Transdisciplinary Approaches* (co-edited with E. Gutiérrez Rodríguez and S. Costa; Ashgate, 2010). Her work focuses on world-systems analysis, postcolonial and decolonial perspectives, gender in modernity/coloniality, racialization, and the geopolitics of knowledge in Eastern Europe, Latin America, and the Caribbean.

Stefanie Bürkle is a Berlin-based artist and professor of visual arts at Technische Universität Berlin. Her artistical practice includes painting, photography, and video installations. In her artistic research projects, she explores topics such as stages, artificial worlds, facade architecture, and placemaking. Collaboratory projects with the DLR (Germany's research center for aeronautics and space), the Fraunhofer Institute Adlershof, and the National Academy of Science in Washington DC, among others, allow her projects to link art and science in order to rethink common perceptions of the city and spatial contexts, while providing new readings of surface projections and the hidden spaces behind them.

Ignacio Castillo Ulloa is an architect as well as a research assistant and lecturer at the Chair of Urban Design and Urban Development, Institute of Urban and Regional Planning, Technische Universität Berlin. He is a research associate in the subproject "Education: The Spatial Knowledge of Children and Young Adults (and Its Application) in Planning Contexts" (A02) of the Collaborative Research Center "Re-Figuration of Spaces" (CRC 1265) funded by the German Research Foundation (DFG) and the scientific coordinator for the "Global Center of Spatial Methods for Urban Sustainability" (GCSMUS). His research interests include uneven socio-spatial development and alternative disruptive (local) practices that counteract it; critical urban research; and the use of Lacanian theory to explore interrelations among planning theory, research, and practice.

Eleazar Cuadros Choque is an architect, photographer, and founding partner of the Lima-based architectural studio *Coordinadora de la Ciudad (en Construcción)* (2016–2019) and the non-profit organization CITIO (*Ciudad Transdisciplinar*) (2008–2015). He works as a freelancer architect and has designed and built several public projects (particularly skateboarding parks) in different Peruvian cities. He has won and taken part as a judge in various photography contests, such as "Lima Foto Libre," organized by the *Centro de La Imagen* and the Lima Biennale (2012), and "Foto Ensayos," organized by the INVI Institute at the University of Chile (2018). He has delivered workshops on urban photography throughout Peru and Latin America and writes the blog *Presbicia del Andar* (2013) about urban imaginaries through photography.

Ayham Dalal is an architect and urban planner holding a PhD in architecture with distinction from Technische Universität Berlin. He is a research associate in the subproject "Architectures of Asylum: Appropriation Processes in Refugee Accommodation" (A04) of the Collaborative Research Center "Re-Figuration of Spaces" (CRC 1265) funded by the German Research Foundation (DFG). Ayham is also a research fellow at Institut français du Proche-Orient (Ifpo) in Beirut and Amman. His research focuses on the intersections between space, urbanization, displacement, and migration.

Janina Dobrusskin is a PhD student in cultural and social geography at Humboldt Universität zu Berlin and research associate in the subproject "Geographic Imaginations: People's Sense of Security and Insecurity in a Cross-Generational Comparison" (A01) of the Collaborative Research Center "Re-Figuration of Spaces" (CRC 1265) funded by the German Research Foundation (DFG). In this position, she conducts research in Germany and Singapore on the political role played by emotions and affects in geographic imaginations and related notions of belonging. She worked as a research assistant in the development of Berlin's Competence and Advice Center against Discrimination on the Housing Market. Her research focuses on urban geography (social inequalities, housing), feminist geography, and migration/border regimes.

Lucas-Andrés Elsner is an urban planner and geographer educated at Technische Universität Berlin and the University of Münster. He is an associate member in the Collaborative Research Center "Re-Figuration of Spaces" (CRC 1265) funded by the German Research Foundation (DFG). Since 2018, he has been based at the Habitat Unit, Institute of Architecture, Technische Universität Berlin, where he is currently working on a joint project with the University of Lagos and the University of the Witwatersrand, Johannesburg, on graduate education in the urban fields of sub-Saharan Africa. His research focuses on the relationship between uneven spatial development, transport infrastructures, and global production relations.

Aline Fraikin is an urban planner holding a master's degree in urban and regional planning from Technische Universität Berlin. Since 2018, she has been part of the subproject "Architectures of Asylum: Appropriation Processes in Refugee Accommodation" (A04) of the Collaborative Research Center "Re-Figuration of Spaces" (CRC 1265) funded by the German Research Foundation (DFG). Her research interests lay in the field of urban sociology, particularly migration and its impact on cities.

Fraya Frehse is a professor of sociology at the University of São Paulo, where she coordinates the "Center for Studies and Research on the Sociology of Space and Time" (NEPSESTE) and acts as a lead partner of the "Global Center of Spatial Methods for Urban Sustainability" (GCSMUS, Technische Universität Berlin). She is an alumna of the Alexander von Humboldt Foundation, research fellow of the Brazilian National Research Council, and life member of Clare Hall College (University of Cambridge). Her research mainly addresses urban theory; space, everyday life, and history; space and time in sociology; body, public space, and urbanization (in Brazil); urban mobility; urban inequality/poverty; cultural heritage; urban visual culture; and sociology of everyday knowledge.

Carolin Genz is a postdoctoral research fellow and lecturer in cultural and social geography at Humboldt Universität zu Berlin and a research associate in the subproject "Geographic Imaginations: People's Sense of Security and Insecurity in a Cross-Generational Comparison" (A01) of the Collaborative Research Center "Re-Figuration of Spaces" (CRC 1265) funded by the German Research Foundation (DFG). As an urban anthropologist in the intersecting fields of human geography and urban studies, she is constantly developing ethnographic methods to capture the socio-spatial constitution of urban practices. Moreover, she engages in research on practices of urban resistance, housing, and the production and appropriation of space, questioning how and under which conditions civil actors can publicly engage in the transformation processes of urban civil society.

Anke Hagemann is currently a professor of international urbanism at Technische Universität Berlin. She was an interim professor for urban planning at Brandenburg University of Technology Cottbus-Senftenberg and a researcher in the project "Transnational

Production Spaces" at the Institute of Architecture, Technische Universität Berlin. She taught urban design and architecture theory at ETH Zurich, the University of Stuttgart, HafenCity University Hamburg, and Technische Universität Berlin. Her doctoral thesis investigates the spatial division of labor in Istanbul's clothing industry.

Christian Haid, architect and urban sociologist, is Assistant Professor at the Chair of International Urbanism, the Habitat Unit, and a lecturer in the Urban Management program at Technische Universität Berlin. He is an associate member of the Collaborative Research Center "Re-Figuration of Spaces" (CRC 1265) funded by the German Research Foundation (DFG) and founder of Poligonal Office for Urban Communication. Previously, he was a lecturer in urban sociology at Humboldt-Universität zu Berlin and in urban design at Leibniz University Hanover. He was a researcher in the EU FP7 project "DIVERCITIES: Governing Urban Diversity" at Helmholtz Center for Environmental Research, Leipzig. His research interests include critical urban studies, postcolonial theories, urban informality, diversity, and uncertainty in urban planning.

Ilse Helbrecht is a full professor of cultural and social geography at Humboldt Universität zu Berlin (since 2009) and principal investigator in the subproject "Geographic Imaginations: People's Sense of Security and Insecurity in a Cross-Generational Comparison" (A01) of the Collaborative Research Center "Re-Figuration of Spaces" (CRC 1265) funded by the German Research Foundation (DFG). She was the director of the Georg-Simmel Center for Metropolitan Studies at Humboldt Universität zu Berlin (2014–2019). In 2018, she was honored with the Caroline von Humboldt Professorship, and in 2019, she received the Thomas Mann Fellowship from the German Federal Government. Her research topics include urban geography, cultural and social geography, urban governance, and housing/homeownership.

Hubert Knoblauch is a professor for general sociology at Technische Universität Berlin and principal investigator in the subproject "Centers of Coordination: The Polycontexturalization of Power in Control Rooms" (B02) of the Collaborative Research Center "Re-Figuration of Spaces" (CRC 1265) funded by the German Research Foundation (DFG). Furthermore, he is spokesperson for the CRC 1265 and speaker of the Research Network on Social Theory (RN29) in the European Sociological Association. He has been, among others, guest professor at the University of Vienna and professor of sociology at the University of Zurich. His major research areas include sociological theory, sociology of religion, communication and knowledge, and qualitative methods.

Roberto Patricio Korzeniewicz is a professor and associate dean for faculty affairs (College of Behavioral and Social Sciences) at the University of Maryland, College Park (USA). His book *Unveiling Inequality* (Russell Sage Foundation, 2009), co-written with Timothy Patrick Moran, won the 2010 Best Book Award of the Political Economy of the World-System Section of the American Sociological Association. His current research focuses on global patterns of income inequality, social stratification, and mobility https://socy.umd.edu/facultyprofile/korzeniewicz/%28roberto%29-patricio.

Daniela Krüger is a PhD student in the Department of Urban and Regional Sociology at Humboldt-Universität zu Berlin and research associate in the subproject "The World Down My Street: Resources and Networks Used by City Dwellers" (C04) of the Collaborative Research Center "Re-Figuration of Spaces" (CRC 1265) funded by the German Research Foundation (DFG). In her PhD, she asks how the State cares in the unequal city and relates care theory to urban sociology and medical frontline work.

Elmar Kulke is Dean of the Faculty of Mathematics and Natural Sciences and Professor for Economic Geography at Humboldt-Universität zu Berlin. He is principal investigator in the subproject "Knowledge and Goods: Consumers' and Producers' Spatial Knowledge" (A03) of the Collaborative Research Center "Re-Figuration of Spaces" (CRC 1265) funded by the German Research Foundation (DFG) as well as co-speaker of the German Working Group on Geographical Retailing Research. He is the co-editor of the book series Geographische Handelsforschung (Geographical Retail Research) and the journal *DIE ERDE (THE EARTH)*. His research fields include locational changes in retailing/enterprise-oriented services and the development of global commodity chains, especially for fresh food articles.

Eric Lettkemann is a postdoctoral researcher in the Institute of Sociology at Technische Universität Berlin and research associate in the subproject "Locative Media: Inclusion and Exclusion in Public Spaces" (B04) of the Collaborative Research Center "Re-Figuration of Spaces" (CRC 1265) funded by the German Research Foundation (DFG). He earned his doctorate with a historical and sociological dissertation on the innovation biography of electron microscopy in Germany. He has worked on several topics in the field of science and technology studies, amongst them interdisciplinary work configurations, socio-technical assistance systems, and science communication.

Martina Löw is a professor of sociology at Technische Universität Berlin and principal investigator in the subproject "Smart Cities: Everyday Life in Digitalized Spaces" (B03) of the Collaborative Research Center "Re-Figuration of Spaces" (CRC 1265) funded by the German Research Foundation (DFG). Furthermore, she is spokesperson for the CRC 1265. From 2011 until 2013, she was president of the German Sociological Association, and she has worked as a visiting professor and held fellowships at universities in Gothenburg (Sweden), Salvador da Bahia (Brazil), St. Gallen (Switzerland), Paris (France), and Vienna (Austria). Her areas of specialization and research include sociological theory, urban sociology, space theory, and cultural sociology.

xvi Contributors

Daniel Maier is a postdoctoral researcher at Freie Universität Berlin and research associate in the subproject "Translocal Networks: Public Sphere in the Social Web" (B05) of the Collaborative Research Center "Re-Figuration of Spaces" (CRC 1265) funded by the German Research Foundation (DFG). His research interests include the theory and methods of social networks, computational methods of text analysis, political communication, and public health.

Angela Million, née Uttke, is an urban planner AKB/SRL and Professor for Urban Design and Urban Development. She is Director of the Institute of Urban and Regional Planning at Technische Universität Berlin and principal investigator in the subproject "Education: The Spatial Knowledge of Children and Young Adults (and Its Application) in Planning Contexts" (A02) of the Collaborative Research Center "Re-Figuration of Spaces" (CRC 1265) funded by the German Research Foundation (DFG). Furthermore, she is Director of the "Global Center of Spatial Methods for Urban Sustainability" (GCSMUS). Her research focuses on (participatory) urban design and *Baukultur*, with a special interest in multifunctional infrastructure development, cities as educational settings, children, and youth.

Antonia Noll is an architect currently pursuing a master's degree at Technische Universität Berlin. Since 2019, she has been part of the subproject "Architectures of Asylum: Appropriation Processes in Refugee Accommodation" (A04) of the Collaborative Research Center "Re-Figuration of Spaces" (CRC 1265) funded by the German Research Foundation (DFG). Her research focuses on shelter and the impact of urban environment on refugee camps.

Corey R. Payne is a PhD candidate in the Department of Sociology and the Arrighi Center for Global Studies at Johns Hopkins University. He studies the dynamics of historical capitalism, war-making, class struggle, and global governance.

Barbara Pfetsch is a professor of communication theory and media effects research in the Institute for Media and Communication Studies at Freie Universität Berlin. She is the principal investigator at the Weizenbaum Institute for the Networked Society in Berlin and in the subproject "Translocal Networks: Public Sphere in the Social Web" (B05) of the Collaborative Research Center "Re-Figuration of Spaces" (CRC 1265) funded by the German Research Foundation (DFG). She earned her PhD from the University of Mannheim and held positions at Berlin Social Science Center (WZB) and the University of Hohenheim. Her research and publications focus on comparative political communication, online communication and digital issue networks, and transnational and European public spheres.

Lucas Pohl is a postdoctoral research fellow in the Geography Department at Humboldt Universität zu Berlin and research associate in the subproject "Geographic Imaginations: People's Sense of Security and Insecurity in a Cross-Generational Comparison" (A01) of the Collaborative Research Center "Re-Figuration of Spaces"

(CRC 1265) funded by the German Research Foundation (DFG). He received his PhD in 2020 from the Institute of Human Geography at Goethe University Frankfurt with a dissertation elaborating on a psychoanalytic approach of urban ruination. In general, he works on the interstices between geography, philosophy, and psychoanalysis with a focus on social and spatial theory, built environments, and political action.

Susanne Rau has been a professor of spatial history and cultures at the University of Erfurt since 2009, a regular visiting professor at ENS Lyon and the CIHAM, France, since 2011. She is spokesperson for the "SpatioTemporal Studies" research group at the University of Erfurt and has published widely in the fields of urban history and on the theory, history, and anthropology of spaces. Currently, she is conducting a research project on the history of cartography in Europe and India and is spokesperson for the Humanities Center for Advanced Studies "Religion and Urbanity: Reciprocal Formations" (DFG-FOR 2779).

Karl-Siegbert Rehberg is a senior professor for social theory, history of sociology, and cultural sociology at Technische Universität Dresden. Amongst other things, he was president of the German Sociological Association (2003–2007) and a member of the Collaborative Research Center "Institutionality and Historicity" (CRC 537). He was a visiting professor or fellow at the Universities of Leiden (Netherlands), LUMSA (Vatican), Basel, Lausanne (Switzerland), Paris (France), Rome, Modena, Naples, Trento (Italy), Vienna (Austria), and Weimar (Germany). In 2011, he was awarded the scholar's prize by the Aby Warburg Foundation and the Chevalier de l'Ordre des Palmes Académiques. In 2013, he became an honorary member of the Sociology of Culture Section of the German Sociological Association.

Jennifer Robinson is a professor of human geography at University College London. Her book *Ordinary Cities* (Routledge, 2006) presented a post-colonial critique of urban studies. Her new book, *Comparative Urbanism: Tactics for Global Urban Studies* (Wiley-Blackwell, in press), proposes methodological foundations for global urban studies. Her earlier empirical research explored the history of apartheid cities and the politics of post-apartheid city visioning. Current collaborative empirical projects focus on the politics of large-scale urban developments (London, Johannesburg, Shanghai) and the transnational circuits shaping African urbanization (Accra, Dar es Salaam, Lilongwe).

Gillian Rose is a professor of human geography at the University of Oxford and a fellow of the British Academy and the Academy of Social Sciences. She is the author of *Feminism and Geography* (Polity, 1993), *Doing Family Photography* (Ashgate, 2010), and *Visual Methodologies* (Sage, fourth edition 2016), as well as many papers on images, visualizing technologies, and ways of seeing in urban, domestic, and archival spaces. She led the ESRC-funded project "Smart Cities in the Making: Learning from Milton Keynes"; her particular interest is how digital visualizations of many kinds mediate urban spatialities.

Christian Sander is an art historian and works at K LAB, a laboratory for contemporary communication of urban contents docked at the Institute for Urban and Regional Planning, Technische Universität Berlin. Before that, he was a curatorial assistant at Staatsgalerie Stuttgart and KW Institute for Contemporary Art in Berlin (8th Berlin Biennale for Contemporary Art). He wrote his PhD thesis at Freie Universität Berlin on the French group Architecture Principe (Claude Parent and Paul Virilio, Paris, 1963–1968). His areas of research include French architecture of the 19th and 20th century and the synthesis of art and architecture.

Henrik Schultze is a postdoc student in the Department of Urban and Regional Sociology at Humboldt-University Berlin and research associate in the subproject "The World Down My Street: Resources and Networks Used by City Dwellers" (C04) of the Collaborative Research Center "Re-Figuration of Spaces" (CRC 1265) funded by the German Research Foundation (DFG). His research interests include social constructions of belonging, social inequalities, and qualitative research methods.

Ingo Schulz-Schaeffer is a professor of sociology of technology and innovation at Technische Universität Berlin and principal investigator in the subproject "Locative Media: Inclusion and Exclusion in Public Spaces" (B04) of the Collaborative Research Center "Re-Figuration of Spaces" (CRC 1265) funded by the German Research Foundation (DFG). From 2008 to 2015, he was a professor of general sociology and sociological theory at the University of Duisburg-Essen. His recent empirical research in the field of science and technology includes the role of future concepts in technology development, distributed agency, crowdfunding as gift exchange, the social construction of human robot collaboration, and locative media.

Jona Schwerer is a sociologist and research assistant at the Chair of Urban Design and Urban Development, Institute of Urban and Regional Planning, Technische Universität Berlin. He is a research associate in the subproject "Education: The Spatial Knowledge of Children and Young Adults (and Its Application) in Planning Contexts" (A02) of the Collaborative Research Center "Re-Figuration of Spaces" (CRC 1265) funded by the German Research Foundation (DFG). His main research interests include urban sociology, sociology of space, and qualitative methods of social research.

Daniela Stoltenberg is a PhD candidate at Freie Universität Berlin and research associate in the subproject "Translocal Networks: Public Sphere in the Social Web" (B05) of the Collaborative Research Center "Re-Figuration of Spaces" (CRC 1265) funded by the German Research Foundation (DFG). Her research interests include digital public spheres, the relationship between communication and the construction of space, and computational research methods.

Michael Storper is a professor of economic geography at the London School of Economics; distinguished professor of regional and international development in urban planning at the UCLA Luskin School of Public Affairs; and researcher in the Center for European Studies and Comparative Politics (CEE) at Sciences Po, Paris. Among his most recent books are *The Rise and Fall of Urban Economies* (Stanford University Press, 2015) and *Keys to the City* (Princeton University Press, 2013). He is a corresponding fellow of the British Academy and has received the Regional Studies Association's Sir Peter Hall Prize for overall contribution to the field. His work centers on economic geography, cities, and globalization.

Robert Vief is a PhD student in the Department of Urban and Regional Sociology at Humboldt-Universität zu Berlin and research associate in the subproject "The World Down My Street: Resources and Networks Used by City Dwellers" (C04) of the Collaborative Research Center "Re-Figuration of Spaces" (CRC 1265) funded by the German Research Foundation (DFG). His research interests include school and residential segregation, neighborhood effects, use of infrastructures within cities, and quantitative and spatial methods.

Annie Waldherr is a professor of computational communication science at the University of Vienna and principal investigator in the subproject "Translocal Networks: Public Sphere in the Social Web" (B05) of the Collaborative Research Center "Re-Figuration of Spaces" (CRC 1265) funded by the German Research Foundation (DFG). She worked as an assistant professor at the University of Münster (2017–2020) and as a research associate at Freie Universität Berlin (2010–2016) and the University of Hohenheim (2006–2010). Annie studies the changing structures and dynamics in today's digitalized public spheres, combining computational and conventional empirical methods.

1
NAVIGATING SPATIAL TRANSFORMATIONS THROUGH THE REFIGURATION OF SPACES

Angela Million, Christian Haid, Ignacio Castillo Ulloa, and Nina Baur

From "turning to space" to thinking spatially

Over the course of the past three decades, space and spatial research furthering spatial thinking have become increasingly popular both within and—though in a more nuanced manner—beyond academic circles. By and large, it has been a gradual process of recognition that, "as many people have been saying, 'Space is hot'" (Bertsch and Sterne 1994; cited in Crang and Thrift 2000a, xi). Such weasel words eventually led to what came to be known as the "spatial turn," which, rather than emerging in the shape and form of "intellectual magnificence," put space at the core of critical analysis to shed light on economic, social, political, and cultural transformations to which the world is continuously subjected. Prior to the spatial turn, academic discourse typically affirmed space as an a priori external to human thinking and conceptualized space as a Kantian-absolute analytical category. As a result, jigsaw-like Euclidean conceptions of space emerged, underpinned by an understanding of space as a form of "outer sense," whereby objects are represented as existing outside of us—that is to say, "in space." Such static understandings of space were eventually rendered insufficient by the accelerating dynamics of spatial transformations such as globalization, progressively giving way to alternative approaches asserting that spatiality cannot be comprehended separately from its production. Moreover, humans do not just perceive and act within space as an immutable frame of reference; rather, by inhabiting, living, and all the while changing space, they render it relational (Lefebvre 1991; Massey 2005). In other words, far-reaching takes on contemporary phenomena must appeal to both social and spatial circumstances in order to move beyond the truism that "everything happens somewhere," for it is, in effect, the *where* what allows the *how* to be fathomed—the inextricable fusion of context and causality (Warf and Arias 2009; Baur 2018, 329–356).

Furthermore, several disciplines—above all, geography—were stripped of their epiphenomenal status. Concurrently, initiated by the pioneering works of Anthony Giddens (1979, 1981) and Michel Foucault (1980), efforts to interlace, for instance, a (concrete and descriptive) "geographical" with an (abstract and explanatory) "sociological" imagination started to flourish (Agnew and Duncan 1989, 1). Accordingly, a shift from "a sense of space as a practico-inert container of action towards space as a socially produced set of manifolds" took place, indicating not only that space cannot be envisaged "outside the realm of social practice" but also that "the ecology of thought is no longer seen as somehow standing outside of the spatial" (Crang and Thrift 2000b, 2).

From the mid-1980s onwards, space has been reasserted and emplaced within a multifarious, inter-, and transdisciplinary purview covering (and thereby making relevant) aspects such as everyday life, identity, and human subjectivity, which are integral to a coherent analysis of social life and lived experience. There have been insightful attempts to integrate the diverse strands of existing academic work. Diverse disciplines—such as geography, architecture, urban planning, philosophy, sociology, political sciences, anthropology, historical sciences, communication sciences, and many more—have either constantly been or are increasingly dealing with issues of spatiality and, in this context, have discussed space in their own particular manner—whether metonymically ("spaces of language"), introspectively ("spaces of the self"), socio-politically ("spaces of agitation"), culturally ("spaces of modernity"), or aesthetically ("artistic and architectural spaces").

Nevertheless, these preceding efforts to systematize spatial concepts have ended up indexing and, in consequence, replicating disciplinary boundaries. Furthermore, while the interest in space, spatiality, and spatial research has been steadily growing and spawning across fields of thought, there have rarely been any attempts either to identify convergences and intersections amid the variety of spatial conceptualizations or to synthetize modes of spatial thinking. Showing how fruitful intersecting and synthetizing would be is precisely the purpose of this book. More specifically, Martina Löw's (2016) conceptualization of relational space offers a conducive approach that illustrates how assorted understandings of space and/or forms of spatial inquiry could be astutely brought together. According to Löw (2016), space may be envisaged as relational arrangements in which actors, objects, and technologies are both placing and being placed. These arrangements, moreover, are based on two analytically distinct social processes: spacing—in other words, specific practices of placing—and synthesizing.

Building on similar theoretical considerations as well as empirical outcomes stemming from a variety of disciplines engaged with spatial research and thinking, the aim of this book is twofold: *opening spatial analysis and broadening the understanding of ongoing social processes as a whole*. In addition, a long-term goal, whereof this book serves as an initial stepping stone, is to develop an *empirically grounded theory of society that can best be defined as a "spatio-communicative figuration."* In this regard, moving from "turning to space" to "thinking spatially" plays a fundamental role in theory production, "not only in the ways that theory might apply to a spatially distributed world, but in the spatialities that allow thought to develop particular effectivities and intensities" (Crang and Thrift 2000b, 3). By concentrating on space as both the object and means of analysis and discussion, the book focuses on a key principle of the social order: exploring, first, various *social* transformations regarding their *spatial* dimensions and links; and, subsequently, restructured subjective actions, spatial knowledge, and spatial experience. On that account, spatial transformations are conceived not as abstract, unfathomable processes, but rather as processes of communicative actions and social practices embedded in people's everyday lives. What people experience, want, believe, know, do, and how they interact in turn engenders new institutions and novel forms of localization, interconnectedness, and spatially shaped (self-)experience.

In order to clearly present how the refiguration of spaces operates as an analytical angle, the structure of this book systematically follows a set of subthemes and questions. The assemblage of chapters in this book reveals, by and large, not only that space does not constitute a neutral entity existing a priori as regards its conception, but also how it is possible to delve into spatial transformations pointedly and discern or even contend their inherent intricacies.

Spatiality and temporality

It has long been known that space and time are intrinsically intertwined and neither concept can be thought of and written about without reflecting on the other. For example, spatial constructions change over time; humans interact in space and in certain times; it also takes time to move in and through space; and so on. Therefore, the assorted contributions in this book purposefully focus on both "the spatial" in general and *spatial transformations* specifically.

In order to discuss the specific entanglement of spatiality and temporality, it is necessary to reflect upon temporality first. As process theory has shown, two key concepts—duration and temporal pattern—are central when thinking about time (Baur 2005; Norkus and Baur 2020). "Duration" (*durée*; Braudel 1958) or "time layer" (*Zeitschicht*; Koselleck 2018) indicates that social processes differ in the amount of time they need to unfold: Whereas some phenomena must be examined over a long period, others need a more precisely delineated length of time. Heuristically, three types of duration can be distinguished (Baur 2005; Norkus and Baur 2020):

1   *Short-term social processes* unfold in moments, hours, or days
2   *Medium-term processes* ("*time of generations*") cover the memory of the living and usually cover years or decades
3   *Long-term processes (longue durée)* go beyond the memory of the living and cover centuries or millennia

In addition to a process's duration, its pattern over time is also important. To this effect, three basic *temporal patterns* of social change can be identified from a heuristic standpoint (Baur 2005; Norkus and Baur 2020):

1   *Trajectories* are social processes that are patterned in a systematic way or develop path-dependently

2   *Turning points* occur between different phases of a process or after abrupt changes such as innovations or crises
3   *Cycles* describe social processes that are characterized by repetition

Against this backdrop, authors in the first section discuss *how spatiality and temporality are entwined as well as what spatial transformations arise therefrom*.

Besides the abovementioned, more abstract considerations about space and time, a more specific question is what type of spatial transformations can be empirically observed over the course of history. Empirical evidence suggests that social change and spatial transformations are interlinked. For example, Norbert Elias ([1939] 1997) has shown that in Europe, ever since the middle ages, civilizing and nation-building processes have been mutually stabilizing, driving each other along established trajectories with typical trends and countertrends. Accordingly, Elias (1986) coined the concept of "figuration" to express that different scales—namely the micro level (Elias [1969] 2002) and the macro level (Elias [1939] 1997)—are intertwined, co-develop, and, within this process, (re-)produce social inequality by including ("insiders") and excluding ("outsiders") people (Elias and Scotson [1965] 2002). Following this line of thought, in this book, *Martina Löw* and *Hubert Knoblauch* kick off the debate on spatiality and temporality by arguing that the second half of the twentieth century marked a turning point, contending that the specific pattern whereby social and spatial transformations are interwoven has fundamentally changed. Within this *"refiguration of spaces"* (Knoblauch and Löw 2017; 2020; in this volume), three processes unfold in parallel:

1   The relations of spaces as social contexts of different activities, forms of communication, and societal functions are turning into a *polycontexturalization* of space. This means that, at both a particular and structural level, different arrangements of space are simultaneously put into effect. Individual and collective actors are thus faced with the challenge of having to cope with different spatial logics at the same time; a condition that adds to, as Fredric Jameson (1991, 44) sharply asserts, "the incapacity of our minds . . . to map the great global multinational and decentered communicational network in which we find ourselves caught as individual subjects."
2   Space is increasingly constituted in mediated forms spurred by hastily deepening advances in digital technologies of communication. Consequently, a *mediatization*—in the form of proactive and reflexive communicative acts unfolding on different scales and at different levels—arises and results in a simultaneity of digital and face-to-face interactions.
3   Humans, objects, and technologies are circulating more frequently, resulting in a *translocalization* and globalization of the economy, politics, culture, and everyday as well as urban planning/design practices. Hence, individual and collective actors and spaces, at variegated (geographically distant) locations, become progressively interconnected, coupled, and more interdependent alongside a prominent gain in the relevance of individual locations.

These processes in turn alter societies—and thereby typical patterns of social interactions—and, given that social and spatial changes are consubstantial, prompt spatial modifications (i.e. refigurations of spaces).

Therefore, Knoblauch and Löw's (2017; 2020; in this volume) concept of "the refiguration of spaces" emphasizes the overarching theoretical assumption of this book, namely that social transformations become particularly clear by looking at the restructuring of spaces and combining the knowledge, purviews, and research outcomes of diverse spatial disciplines. By concentrating on the effects of mediatization, mobility, and social dislocation in spatial transformations, contributions by other authors also aim at deconstructing the notion of refiguration of spaces—as a specific interpretative vehicle to explore spatial transformations—from different theoretical and empirical angles.

A first general criticism concerning spatiality and temporality, expressed in several chapters of this section, is that, conceptually, Knoblauch and Löw (2017; 2020; in this volume) restrict themselves to mid-term or even (in actual empirical research) short-term processes. However, when it comes to spatial transformations, many of the most important and conspicuous changes only unfold over extended periods, that is, in the longue durée. Likewise, all chapters in this section demonstrate, on the one hand, that the past lingers on well into the present and thereby impacts current communicative action (Knoblauch 2020) and, on the other hand, how to conceptually grasp, from different angles, the entanglements of spatial transformations occurring in and throughout diverse time layers.

Karl-Siegbert Rehberg illustrates not only that humans construct space but also that that space itself affects humans. To elucidate how physical space is shaping society and how this relates to social and power structures, he scrutinizes spatial transformations that have taken place since 70,000 BC. Rehberg's analysis reveals that the extent to which humans can construct and change space is much more limited than current social-science, spatial-planning, and spatial-design discourses suggest. By solely focusing on shorter-term processes, these discourses systematically underestimate the impact of physical space on social life.

Looking into the manners in which current communicative action (short-term processes) is influenced by historicity (long-term processes), *Fraya Frehse* introduces a four-step methodology inspired by Henri Lefebvre's (2001, 73–74) regressive–progressive method. Using homelessness as an empirical example, she demonstrates that the way homeless people in São Paulo (Brazil) produce space as part of their everyday life is influenced by both past communicative action and urban structure and topology. Against this empirical backdrop, Frehse criticizes Knoblauch and Löw's assumption of a transformative conversion from a somewhat dawdling past to a remarkably hastened present. In contrast, the refiguration of spaces seems to be less linear and much more complex: The production of space by homeless people indicates that new patterns of increasing mobility ("circulation") coexist alongside long-established patterns of (im)mobility.

Similarly, *Susanne Rau* departs from examples of people's experiences of space and time in everyday life and builds thereupon a theory of spatio-temporality, which allows scholars—in her particular case, historians—to comprehend the space–time connection. She argues that (modern) theories of space have to be integrated into the historical sciences, inasmuch as spatial studies also need to incorporate the perspective of the longue durée.

Finally, drawing on the work of the Architecture Principe group—namely Claude Parent and Paul Virilio—from the 1960s, *Christian Sander* gives an example of how a deeply spatial discipline (architecture) is shaped by temporality. According to the theory of the *oblique function*, the city is exclusively built with horizontal and inclined surfaces for pedestrians to circulate in order to drastically reduce the speed of movement. Circulation, Sander suggests, thereby becomes a principal organizational category in the transformation of space through time.

Spatiality, social inequality, and the economy

It is a well-known fact, especially in the social and political sciences, that the economy is a key factor in (re-)producing social inequality, inequity, discrimination, and exclusion. These interconnected phenomena obviously have a spatial dimension and manifest themselves on multiple scales. At a global level, the world-system is characterized by a global division of labor that reinforces (post)colonial divisions between the Global North and South. At a supranational and national level, regional disparities can be observed. At a community level, urban geographies of production as well as gentrification are discernible citywide.

There is strong empirical evidence to suggest that the relationship between spatiality, social inequality, and the economy is surprisingly stable in the long durée—powerful actors and locations consistently have managed to reproduce their advantageous position in the world-system over centuries. Hardly any war-related, economic, or political crisis manages to disturb this cycle of reproduction, and only rarely does a disadvantaged locality manage to upgrade its position (Heidenreich 2003). The chapters contained within this section explore possible reasons for this stability in order to identify ways of breaking the cycles of reproduction of social inequality and correspondingly bringing about social and spatial transformations. In doing so, the first chapters bridge the thematic gulf between the temporality and spatiality of social inequality and the economy. All chapters, moreover, find common ground by claiming that key actors reaffirming global inequality include states, other political players, and companies owned by transnational elites.

Gurminder K. Bhambra shows that current global inequalities were created during colonialism between the fifteenth and nineteenth centuries and, at the same time, criticizes the fact that economic analyses of long-term social change—such as the modeling of incomes over time—typically apply categories that implicitly reaffirm the logic of territorial thinking used by former colonial powers. Her historical sociological analysis reveals challenges for today, such as the need for concepts of differentiated citizenship and an ongoing acknowledgement of history "through forms of global distributive justice."

Also adopting a historical-sociological perspective, *Manuela Boatcă* argues that citizenship awarded by nation states is a category of social inequality in and of itself, dividing the world-system into cores, semi-peripheries, and peripheries. Consequently, Boatcă contends, citizens of peripheral countries not only suffer from economic deprivation but also, as a result, are racially stereotyped. The seemingly neutral capitalist economy is thus based on racism and global inequality and overlaid with populist, nationalist, fascist, and racist ideologies. Accordingly, increasing global inequality both within countries—represented by social class—and across countries—represented by citizenship—are driving spatial transformations, because the fastest way of improving living standards is to move from a *peripheral* to a *core* country. However, nation states privilege the very rich of any country by allowing them to move freely and keep the very poor from immigrating—thereby reproducing the structure of the world-system.

Roberto Patricio Korzeniewicz and *Corey R. Payne*, along with *Elke Beyer, Lucas-Andrés Elsner,* and *Anke Hagemann*, go beyond the analytical boundaries and apparent ubiquity of the nation-state by taking a closer look at how transnational economic elites manage to stabilize—or even increase—their wealth and thus contribute to either sustaining the world-system or triggering spatial transformations, depending on which strategy better serves their needs.

Roberto Patricio Korzeniewicz and *Corey R. Payne* show that, in the longue durée, political spaces and territorial boundaries have continuously changed. For rich families, these spatial transformations have brought about the issue of how to best preserve their assets. As the authors demonstrate, rich families met this challenge by engaging translocally as a key economic investment practice. The refiguration of spaces is therefore characterized by "interacting, longue durée geographies of social and political contestation, cooperation, and identity-formation that, precisely as a consequence of their very interactions, have constantly undergone change."

Investigating current economic actors' fluctuating roles and engagement in the process of establishing industries and logistics for global commodity production, *Elke Beyer, Lucas-Andrés Elsner,* and *Anke Hagemann* come to similar conclusions. Using the example of infrastructure and industrial development projects in Ethiopia and Argentina, which are implemented in cooperation with Chinese companies and financial institutions, the authors contend that novel transnational actor constellations are fostered. A commodity chain analysis reveals how different spaces of production and distribution are interlinked and how they generate uneven spatialities. Moreover, the authors indicate the intensive involvement in the financing, ownership, operation, or construction of the infrastructures based on global flows of commodities and argue that spatial transformation in certain territories can only be fully understood if examined from a transnational and relational perspective.

Up to this point, analyses have focused on the relationship of the nation state and transnational circulation on a global scale. In contrast, *Michael Storper* illustrates that social and economic inequalities are also apparent at a supranational level and take the form of increasing regional disparities, for example, at the very core of the world-system—the USA. Spatial economic polarization is, among other things, characterized by diverging qualifications, educational outcomes, labor force participation, and incomes. In addition, polarization of both political preferences and electoral choices is also perceptible in nationalist–populist and social liberalist–multiculturalist attitudes throughout various regions. Explaining these developments in their key mechanisms poses challenges for research on economic geography and regional and urban economy, which can only be solved through a multi-disciplinary approach that combines "micro-economic analyses of employment location, wages, the role of housing and amenities, skills and migration and place[s] them within a broad structural and developmental framework." This is ultimately a multi- and interdisciplinary effort. The stakes are high, because geographical polarization is a threat to social and economic stability and justice in the contemporary world.

Elmar Kulke and *Nina Baur* scale down the analytical scope by focusing on the urban economy and providing an additional explanation for the sluggishness of spatial transformations in the economy: the spatial and temporal coupling of institutions. Using the example of consumer–retailer interactions in West German cities, they show how consumers (demand side) combine shopping with other everyday activities and how retailers (supply side) couple their outlets with other retailers and social institutions. Further, the authors demonstrate not only how demand and supply are coupled together but also how such combination becomes embedded in the material urban structure, in turn slowing down spatial transformations.

Digitization and visualization of space

The next section turns to another key hypothesis of Knoblauch and Löw's (2017; 2020; in this volume) concept of the refiguration of spaces, namely that digitization drives spatial transformations. Hence, this section focuses on the function space performs in the formation of public spheres and their interaction with the digital and physical world. Additionally, several central questions are addressed: To what degree are actors and topics locally bounded or rather translocally influenced and connected? Does online communication influence the constitution of spaces offline? In what ways do actors push certain perceptions of spaces to advance their strategic goals?

In line with *Marco Bastos'* contribution, there is growing evidence that social media depend on physical spaces. The COVID-19 pandemic has even increased the interdependencies between online and offline social networks. Although they might seem unrelated at first glance, online and offline social activities reinforce each other. Furthermore, while social media interaction can develop without physical ties, interactions developed online can affect our perception of what is "real" offline and online. Bastos illustrates this by revealing that homophily is influenced by both online and offline social networks as well as the spatial dimensions of social media, which results from a tendency to associate oneself with other similar people.

Likewise, *Daniel Maier, Daniela Stoltenberg, Barbara Pfetsch*, and *Annie Waldherr* point out that digitization enables larger communities with shared imagination, interests, or experiences to become more translocal. In other words, although people move around the world much more than ever before, they can still relate to their groups at home via digital communication. Therefore, communities not only continue to be spatially rooted but also form translocally distributed social pillars for public spheres to enhance their strength through communication in social media. Moreover, digital communication regularly breaks up national territories and, at the meso level, reorganizes translocal communities and the relationship between the public sphere and space. The authors urge for research to incorporate the translocal as a key category to delve into social media communication. Their call resonates with planning, design, and policymaking circles, in which, though the power of Internet-based communication is widely acknowledged, the translocal potential and influence of communities has not been considered in the least.

Eric Lettkemann and *Ingo Schulz-Schaeffer* take a different stance at investigating how the digital and physical world are entangled by investigating whether the increasing use of locative media—such as Foursquare City Guide or Swarm—creates new inclusive public meeting places or reinforces urban segregation by creating exclusive places. Their study reveals that locative media encourage the exploration of unknown places and could therefore lead to a decentralization of social milieus in the public urban fabric. Urban data circulations thus result in a constant modification and recombination of communicative action in public space and, at least currently, practices of inclusion and exclusion seem to balance each other out.

Now, not only digital communication and data flows but also visual representations of space portray powerful spatial transformations and thereby modify and suggest distinctive spatial images and experiences, which may in fact alter the physicality of cities. *Gillian Rose* investigates how, in digitally mediated cities, people change their way of "looking at images of other people, on digital screens large and small, pictured in that city or another." She identifies a form of co-production of embodiments at the interface between different technologies that oscillates between representational and animated forms—best described as "animated embodiment." Whereas representational bodies denote existing social categories, animatic bodies are emergent, mobile, fluid, and mutating. Both constitute different organizations of urban space—in order to understand mediated cities, entanglements, transformations, and mixtures of urban circulations must be part of the equation.

Spatial transformations become visible in the photo essay by artist and researcher *Stefanie Bürkle*, who weaves together images of various places within different cultural settings to display the influence of migration and tourism on both space and individual spatial perception. The continued flow of images shows not only surprising links but also new compositional and content-related connections and transitions, which go well beyond the images themselves and between the depicted spaces. The photo essay comprises, altogether, a mode of spatial representation, which, far from solely artistic, is meant also as an animatic experience for the book's readers.

Imagining, producing, and negotiating space

The chapters in this book's last section explore how medium- and long-term spatial transformations have modified the relationship between humans and the production of space in contemporary society. To that end, a series of interlaced concepts—such as globalization, materiality, appropriation, affordance—are scrutinized, alongside the dynamics and logics of the production of physical space unfolding amid local–global tensions. Against this backdrop, the contributions grapple with questions such as: how the linking and coupling of spaces impact planning, construction, and appropriation processes; which alternative options for action and conflicts arise; the ways in which individuals cope with the notion of (in)security; and how multi-directionality forges new spatial knowledge and urban practices in addition to building new translocal alliances.

Since the 1970s, mounting economic exchange, migration fluxes, and communication technologies have not only amplified subjective uncertainty and insecurity but also paved the way for them to permeate identity politics. Consequently, political actors more often than not instrumentalize uncertainty and insecurity to legitimize their agendas and exert economic, political, and technical control over certain space—for instance, when designated "dangerous zones" in cities are put under surveillance to allegedly improve "security." Using Ronald D. Laing (1960) and Anthony Giddens' (1991) concept of "ontological security," *Ilse Helbrecht*, *Janina Dobrusskin*, *Carolin Genz*, and *Lucas Pohl* identify social practices that counteract the lack of ontological security, such as geopolitically positioning yourself (i.e. developing an understanding of the world by subjectively evaluating events happening all over the world), homemaking, and nature-related routines.

In line with such spatial strategies, *Talja Blokland*, *Daniela Krüger*, *Robert Vief*, and *Henrik Schultze* stress the importance of the neighborhood in mastering everyday life. The authors propose a research approach that takes into account not only subjective definitions of support needs but also from where and in what form support actually comes. This would eventually result in geographies of support that, sure enough, are also susceptible to the effects of mobility and digitization. Hence, in order to fully grasp spatial transformations at the neighborhood level, both local and translocal networks have to be analyzed, and spatiality, as pointed out by the authors, needs to be considered within network data studies, while factors other than proximity have to come into play.

Similarly, *Jennifer Robinson* argues that new territories of urban politics—including city-regions, operational landscapes, and large-scale development projects—cannot be fully understood without contemplating transnational actors and practices, circulating policies, and material and financial flows as key drivers of urban development. Robinson looks for the spatiality in urban policy action by making territories and territorializations of the politics an access key for analyses and theorization.

Ayham Dalal, *Aline Fraikin*, and *Antonia Noll* explore the tensions between urban inhabitants and policymakers as well as between long-term local residents and new migrants. The authors explore refugees' ability to adapt temporary homes gradually and thereby imbue them with "meaning beyond the [officially] envisioned planning." Refugees, the authors sustain, appropriate and reassign through subtle practices of forming soft and temporary spaces such as "hanging curtains, placing carpets, dismantling beds, assembling fridges, storing luggage, and relocating mattresses, chairs and tables." Refugees' material modifications constitute as much a political act as a spatial practice aimed at, somewhat stealthily, overcoming and undermining the arbitrariness of spatial regulations—which may even result in the erosion of disciplinary powers exerted through space.

In the last chapter of this section, *Ignacio Castillo*, *Angela Million*, and *Jona Schwerer* inquire into the discrepancy between experts' abstract conceptions and people's everyday uses of space in their study of children's "deviant" use of public space. Drawing on the concepts of affordance, relational space, spatial knowledge, and spatial pedagogization, public space is seen as an arrangement of multiple material objects and actors with varying degrees of spatial knowledge and physical qualities. The authors sustain that, whereas design and planning experts seek to assert a specific and ultimate purpose of public space's constitutive material elements (i.e. a spatial pedagogization), children subvert such efforts by "uncovering," through their intuitive actions, dormant affordances (i.e. a performative articulation of their spatial knowledge). In view of such a conundrum, the authors pose the question of how children's spatial knowledge, objectified in their uses of spatial arrangements, could be substantively integrated into the design process. Accordingly, the chapter deconstructs, as an empirical case study, the intervention of a public space on the outskirts of the city of Lima, which has followed a fairly unorthodox approach towards child participation and seems to have moved from a "prescriptive" to a "responsive" posture regarding the uses with which public space is to be instilled.

Towards an interdisciplinary scholarship of spatial research

The previously discussed overview of the sundry chapters comprising this volume illustrates the potential of multi- and interdisciplinary spatial research and spatial thinking—for both theory and practice. Overall, the contributions of this volume indicate that spatial transformations are characterized by three key aspects:

1   *Space-time entanglements*, which, though they are already comprehensible in the notions of "spatial transformations" and "refiguration of spaces," in order to fully understand them, it is important to keep in mind that spaces are refigured on different spatial scales—from specific localities and neighborhoods to cities, regions, and nation states, throughout the entire world-system—and that processes of refiguration unfold within different time layers. It is therefore especially important not only to carefully consider spatial transformations in the longue durée, but also to pay closer attention to the interactions of spatial transformations across different scales and time layers, as the patterns of refiguration become more specific and distinguishable.

2 *The processes of refiguration of spaces are characterized by power struggles*, and existing power relations contained therein are often reproduced and reinforced—perhaps the most conspicuous example being the postcolonial structures of inequality within the world-system. Several chapters direct a critical perspective towards the effects of spatial refigurations by concentrating either on the impacts of the economy of the spatial division of labor and social inequality or on spatial aspects of social inequality, inclusion, and exclusion. In doing so, they bring to the fore the upshots of the refiguration of spaces along the lines of class, gender, and ethnic relations and ask who is included or excluded, where, when, why, how, and to what effect. However, as powerless and disenfranchised as some actors—such as refugees and children—may seem, they are far from passive. They are fully capable of developing counterstrategies to undermine the very attempts at controlling them. *The power (im)balances and ensuing spatial practices among the different social groups in turn drive the process of refiguration of spaces.*

3 When looking into the manifold ways in which *offline and online public spaces are designed*, it needs to be taken into account that spaces are systematically related to and become entangled with one another. In this context, the entanglement of three fields needs to be taken into account more effectively in future planning and design processes:

  a Planning and appropriation of urban space
  b Translocal planning processes and procedures
  c The role of spatiality in online and offline public spheres

Examinations of spatial production consider the relationships and tensions between *planned space* and *appropriated space*, and thereby, implicitly, the interactions between (urban) planning, architecture, and people's interactions in everyday lives. In this context, the question as to how materiality, affordance, and refiguration of spaces are interrelated remains open. The contributions in this book reveal that planning processes and procedures can be tackled as a *translocally circulating planning practice* with similar expectations of spatial constitution and furnished with challenges on spatial production. Also, the ways and extent to which planning, in and of itself, contributes instrumentally to triggering the refiguration of spaces are explored, inasmuch as spaces in and beyond (the practice of) planning are conspicuously mediated through *visualizations*. Shedding light on the production of (new kinds of) imagery arguably reveals how spaces are refigured. Last but not least, the relationship between *spatial constitution* and *the public sphere* is examined. Based on the differentiation between diverse types of publicity in the literature, their spatial concepts are juxtaposed and compared to each other in terms of leading questions and empirical characteristics. The analytical gist, moreover, is the influence that processes of spatial constitution exert on the emergence and dynamics of distinctive sorts and forms of publics.

The inherent complexity of investigating these convoluted refigurations of spaces can be seen on the subjective plane, at the level of communicative actions and social practices and within institutional frameworks. To conduct, substantively, socio-scientific spatial research, in its broad sense, interdisciplinary cooperation is essential. This volume as a whole, along with each of the contributions, makes manifest that space, across the different disciplines covered, does not simply enable a relatively uncritical passive reflection on social phenomena, but rather constitutes both a *representational* and *constitutive* analytical strategy that allows bridges to be built across disciplines.

Acknowledgements

This research has been funded by the Deutsche Forschungsgemeinschaft (DFG, German Research Foundation)—project number 290045248—SFB 1265.

References

Agnew, John A., and James S. Duncan. 1989. "Introduction." In *The Power of Place*, edited by John A. Agnew and James S. Duncan, 1–8. London: Unwin Hyman.

Baur, Nina. 2005. *Verlaufsmusteranalyse*. Wiesbaden: VS Verlag für Sozialwissenschaften.

Baur, Nina. 2018. "Kausalität und Interpretativität." In *Handbuch Interpretativ forschen*, edited by Leila Akremi, Nina Baur, Hubert Knoblauch, and Boris Traue, 306–360. Weinheim: Beltz Juventa.

Bertsch, Charles, and Jonathan Sterne. 1994. "Personal Space." *Bad Subjects* 17, November.

Braudel, Fernand. 1958. "Histoire et sciences sociales: La longue durée." *Annales* 13 (4): 725–753.

Crang, Mike, and Nigel Thrift. 2000a. "Preface." In *Thinking Space*, edited by Mike Crang and Nigel Thrift, xi–xii. London: Routledge.

Crang, Mike, and Nigel Thrift. 2000b. "Introduction." In *Thinking Space*, edited by Mike Crang and Nigel Thrift, 1–30. London: Routledge.

Elias, Norbert. (1939) 1997. *Über den Prozeß der Zivilisation*. Frankfurt am Main: Suhrkamp.

Elias, Norbert. (1969) 2002. *Die höfische Gesellschaft*. Frankfurt am Main: Suhrkamp.

Elias, Norbert. 1986. "Figuration." In *Grundbegriffe der Soziologie*, edited by Bernhard Schäfers, 88–91. Opladen: Leske & Budrich.

Elias, Norbert, and John L. Scotson. (1965) 2002. *Etablierte und Außenseiter*. Frankfurt am Main: Suhrkamp.

Foucault, Michel. 1980. *Power/Knowledge*. Brighton: Harvester.

Giddens, Anthony. 1979. *Central Problems in Social Theory*. London: MacMillan.

Giddens, Anthony. 1981. *A Contemporary Critique of Historical Materialism*. Berkeley: University of California Press.

Giddens Anthony. 1991. *Modernity and Self-Identity*. Cambridge: Polity Press.

Heidenreich, Martin. 2003. "Territoriale Ungleichheiten in der erweiterten EU." *KZfSS* 55 (1): 1–28.

Jameson, Fredric. 1991. *Postmodernism, or, the Cultural Logic of Late Capitalism*. Durham, NC: Duke University Press.

Knoblauch, Hubert. 2020. *The Communicative Construction of Reality*. London: Routledge.

Knoblauch, Hubert, and Martina Löw. 2017. "On the Spatial Re-Figuration of the Social World." *Sociologica* 11 (2): 1–27. doi: 10.2383/88197.

Knoblauch, Hubert, and Martina Löw. 2020. "The Re-Figuration of Spaces and Refigured Modernity—Concept and Diagnosis." *Historical Social Research* 45 (2): 263–292. doi: 10.12759/hsr.45.2020.2.263-292.

Koselleck, Reinhart. 2018. *Zeitschichten*. Frankfurt am Main: Suhrkamp.
Laing, Ronald D. 1960. *The Divided Self*. Harmondsworth: Penguin.
Lefebvre, Henri. 1991. *The Production of Space*. London: Blackwell.
Lefebvre, Henri. 2001. "Perspectives de la sociologie rurale." In *Du rural à l'urbain*, edited by Henri Lefebvre, 63–78. Paris: Anthropos.
Löw, Martina. 2016. *The Sociology of Space*. New York: Palgrave Macmillan. https://doi.org/10.1057/978-1-349-69568-3.
Massey, Doreen B. 2005. *For Space*. London: Sage.
Norkus, Maria, and Nina Baur. 2020. "Time and Social Processes." In *SAGE Research Methods Foundations*, edited by Paul A. Atkinson, Sara Delamont, Richard A. Williams, Alexandru Cernat, and Joseph W. Sakshaug. London: Sage.
Warf, Barney, and Santa Arias. 2009. "The Reinsertion of Space in the Humanities and Social Sciences." In *The Spatial Turn*, edited by Barney Warf and Santa Arias, 1–10. London: Routledge.

PART I
Spatiality and temporality

2
THE REFIGURATION OF SPACE, CIRCULATION, AND MOBILITY

Martina Löw and Hubert Knoblauch

Introduction: social changes are spatial changes

"Re-Figuration of Spaces" is the title of our research consortium, which is designed to work for up to 12 years. When writing this text, the Collaborative Research Center (in German: "Sonderforschungsbereich") had only just started a year earlier, at a time when we could not have imagined what would ensue during the current corona crisis (which we will address in an afterword added during the editing of this article.) Any attempt to provide a semblance of empirical results would therefore be utterly premature at this point. We do not wish to start with a speculative catchline aimed at attracting public attention for the next two or three weeks. Rather, we prefer to sketch a notion of refiguration that can serve as a framework for a number of chapters within this volume. As this notion has already been outlined elsewhere in some detail (Knoblauch and Löw 2017; Knoblauch 2020; Knoblauch and Löw 2020a), our objective is to explain how it can be understood as a sensitizing concept for empirical inquiries on the current transformation of space not only for the contributions in this volume but also for future research relating to the consortium and its questions. With the notion of refiguration, we address the following questions: How do the current societal transformations and their ensuing conflicts, crises, and uncertainties affect the relationship between humans and spaces, their spatial practices, and the means they use to negotiate and construct spatial orders? How do changes in spatial practices and spatial formations transform society?

These questions presuppose some theoretical reflections on the social constitution and the communicative construction of space (see Löw 2016; Knoblauch 2020), of which we can only articulate the basic result: That space is the medium in which the transformation of any society or social change takes place. This holds even more true for contemporary society, which is characterized, on the one hand,

DOI: 10.4324/9781003036159-3

by functional differentiation, a vertical hierarchical order, and a tendency towards homogeneity and which, on the other hand, is often in tension with heterogeneity, heterarchies, and flat networks. The idea of refiguration is taken to describe the conflictual dynamic between these poles underlying societal transformation.

In this very short introduction, rather than outlining the general relational theory of space, we (1) sketch the notion of refiguration as a model for recent societal development. In the second part (2), we strive to delineate the approach to the questions of social and spatial transformation in our collaborative research group. As the title of the chapter suggests, we wish (3) to specifically inquire about the effects of mediatization of space on circulation and mobility. As refiguration is a sensitive concept, it is formulated in an abstract manner, thus leaving sufficient "space" and openness for specifications, modifications, and differentiations by means of empirical research.

In empirical research, we start from the methodological premise that what is social always takes on spatial forms. As much as this view came to be shared in the aftermath of the "spatial turn," it neglects the fact that current social changes and their ensuing conflicts, crises, and increasing uncertainties pose a common problem, namely that these crises, conflicts, and uncertainties affect the relationship between humans and spaces, their spatial practices, and the means they use to negotiate and construct spatial orders. We claim that a common pattern can be found in these transformations and conflicts, which we designate refiguration.

Refiguration

By refiguration, we mean that the social order of present-day societies results from two conflicting spatial logics based on two different dominant spatial figurations. While the notion of figuration builds on Elias' (1982) analysis of both societal and subjective changes in the civilization process, we use the term logic here in the sense of Bourdieu (1990) as a structural principle resulting from practicalities of action. To us, this praxeology depends on the spatial relations of (knowledgeable) bodies acting, interacting, and communicating with each other. Space is generally understood as a relational arrangement of living beings and social goods in places.

As Mol and Law (1994) suggest, one can clearly distinguish such logics from one another. Yet, the contemporary refiguration of society seems to be driven by the differentiation of institutionalized, specialized systems and the homogenization and centralization of bounded container spaces, which is probably best exemplified by the modern nation state. The second logic is characterized by relationality and refers to figuration represented by fluidity, hybridization, and transgression, sometimes symbolized by the network model. An important example of this may be the network society as suggested by Castells (2000). He links the rise of digitalization to a concept of network as a set of interconnected nodes at which different threads cross.

The notion of refiguration does not follow the linear argument implied in many globalization theories purporting that (late or postmodern) network society follows modern national society. Instead, it underlines the (1) persistence of these two dominant figurations (which are, of course, complemented by other spatial figurations, such as places and tracks), (2) the dynamics of conflict resulting from and caused by these figurations, and (3) the new forms, figurations, and spatial orders that result from these dynamics and are so often ignored by modernists and postmodernists, globalists and nationalists, structuralists and poststructuralists, and, more recently, unilateralists and multilateralists.

When addressing these encompassing dynamics, we refer to what Couldry and Hepp (2017, 57) call a figuration of figurations; that is to say, a model of society that covers the various orders within society. Changes in these figurations of figurations correspond to what Krotz (2001) has labeled a "megatrend." By refiguration, however, we want to avoid the implied container metaphor, which is still implicit in Elias' notion of the encapsulation of figuration.

As mentioned earlier, we understand refiguration as a process, which is caused and driven by the dynamics of conflict resulting from the spatial tension between dominant figurations and spatial logics. In order to understand the conflictual dynamics, we can juxtapose certain features within each figuration in an exaggerated, characteristic manner as follows:

This conceptual opposition is simply a way to grasp the dynamics of refiguration in a tentative and hypothetical manner, which should not be misunderstood as propagating refiguration to be a desirable state. Rather, we presume that the two figurations serve as a reasonable basis for studying empirical differences, similarities, and changes in socio-spatial forms, which make it possible to explain the reasons behind the social crises and subjective uncertainties we have been witnessing over the last decades. There is a quite conflict-laden polarity between the tendency towards transnationalization, for example in the European Union, and the emphasis on territorial borders in modern nation states, between the ethnic or cultural conceptions of purity (for example, in Poland) and multi-ethnicity or multiculturalism (for example, in France), and between the national rejection of regional autonomy (in Spain) and the provision of autonomy (for example, in Great Britain).

Spatial compression	Disembedding
Centrality	Polycentricity
Hierarchy	Heterarchy
Nationalization	Transnationalization
Boundaries	Transgression
Container	Relationality
Exclusion	Inclusion
Territory	Deterritorialization

DIAGRAM 2.1 Conflicting figurations and spatial logics

If we search for a recent example of the dynamics in the conflictual spatial figurations, the current corona crisis would seem to provide a natural experiment (which is elaborated in Knoblauch and Löw 2020b). In fact, the tension between territorial and network logics, between hierarchy and heterarchy, between limitation and delimitation, and between homogeneity and heterogeneity has been particularly acute during the corona crisis. Refiguration explains the simultaneity and tension of the corona crisis, which is essentially a global risk. Thus, it is quite remarkable that the global expansion has not been met with a *global* response, and even in Europe the national states have clearly overruled transnational cooperation. Instead, unilateral decisions to close the borders of national and even regional territories were made. Borders, for decades neither controlled nor fortified, were closed without prior notice or consultation between states, such as France and Germany. Not only have national territories been closed off, national citizens stranded outside their countries were quickly "brought home" in unprecedented "repatriation" actions.

This closure of territorial space is met with the opposing principle of mediating spaces by networks. Those who cannot meet face to face resort to video conferences. Those who cannot work in the office work at their newly established home office, and those who do not want to go out to eat order via an app and hope that the packages are as clean as the Internet. In the current hyper-compressed emergency order, digital space compensates for public presence, where music is played, groups meet, and games are played. But it also replaces the other functions of society: Universities are to be completely converted to digital communication, as is public administration. The home office allows the majority of other organizations to operate with digital communication technologies. Internet, emails, and the video conferences keep us in international circles, allowing us to launch initiatives, maintain bubbles of bounded communication networks, and establish new rituals.

The basic idea behind refiguration consists of the assumption of conflictual but interdependent dynamics between these different logics, or in a more metaphorical sense, refiguration denotes the forms resulting from the "energy" between these opposite poles of these two logics. Every logic is, of course, in itself heterogeneous. What was once called modern and what used to be called postmodern is in itself an array of different elements that can be investigated (in our case, by comparing different space studies). Moreover, Norbert Elias' idea of interdependencies allows us to add that these dynamics affect all social fields and society at all (micro, meso, and macro) levels, including the individual actors along with their knowledge, bodies, and emotions. We expect different expressions of refiguration in various societal spheres (i.e. economy, politics, arts, etc.) and levels (from the individual to an organization and cultural areas), as well as interdependencies between them. In addition, in non-Western societies, the lines of conflict may be quite different. Thus, in the "compressed modernity" of South Korea and likely China, we assume the refiguration to be driven by the conflict between a rapid process of economic and technological instrumentalism with its networked logic, on the one hand, and on the other by a familialism based on the container space model. Chang

(2010) calls this "individualization without individualism," supporting a specific East Asian form of nationalism, the reinvention of traditional values and kinship structures. Different lines of conflict may also be found in Muslim countries or Hinduist India—where conflict has been linked to religion—or, of course, South America and Africa. While the concept of refiguration is sensitive to these varieties of modernity, in the context of Western thinking, it allows us to adjust the epochal diagnosis in theories of modernization, globalization, and late and postmodernity.

Refiguration differs from a dialectical relation in that we do not assume that the conflictual poles are substituted (as Marx' dialectical materialism suggests) but, rather, are only changed and adopt new spatial forms. If their extreme characteristics come into direct contact with each other, this leads to changes, connections, or conflicts. The empirical studies are tasked with identifying these new forms so as to deduce the specific form of refiguration.

Refiguration of spaces

While there seems to be little doubt in social science discourse about the transformation of temporal structures and the acceleration of lives, communication, or markets, space has received much less attention when it comes to the diagnosis of contemporary society. Starting from the assumption that any social action finds its expression in space, we use the notion of refiguration of space to stress that the most diverging ongoing processes result in new figurations of space, such as the synthesis of virtual and real space in teleconferencing. To put it differently: Space is the medium of transformation for contemporary society as much as time. Therefore, the analysis of space provides an integrative starting point for the analysis of the emerging patterns of society.

If we focus on spatiality by using the concept of refiguration of spaces, we can see that the process of globalization is in conflict with the centralized figuration of the nation state with its bounded territory, clearly defined by enlightened cartography (Schlögel 2011), and characterized by its increased centralization of power, the monopolization of violence, and the differentiation of social structures. However, differences in spatial logics do not necessarily only result in conflict; territorial spatial forms (such as designated zones, camps, colonies, etc.) may co-exist, interlock with, or spread out alongside/over/beneath more fluid and more explicitly relational spatial assemblages (networks, layers, clouds, trajectories, etc.).

In similar terms, the homogenization of modern spaces, their clear functional differentiation (for example, modern cities divided into functional areas) or their vertical hierarchical order (e.g., in administrative architecture) is in tension with the heterogeneity of hybrid spaces, third or non-places, heterotopias, and the flatness of heterarchical orders so much underlined by theories of late, second, or postmodernity. The homogenizing top-down planning of smart cities in the Global South or in Asia, for instance, contrasts with the logic of networking and fluidity in the so-called smart infrastructure in the same countries. Similarly, the transgressive tendencies of transnationalism, cosmopolitanism, and world culture with its new virtual military conflicts, as institutionalized in the European Union for example, are confronted with the reaffirmation of principles of re-nationalization, the return of modern wars, and forms of regionalization that explicitly try to avoid the forms of adaptation postmodern theories call "glocalization."

This refiguration of society is articulated in fights over the meaning of spaces, in imaginary models of security and risk, and in processes of closure and exclusion, such as the erection of new frontiers, such as those between the UK and the EU, between Mexico and the U.S., or even between France and Germany during the corona crisis. These conflicts result in unpredictability and a lack of security and orientation. The most obvious transformation consists in what came to be known as globalization, meaning the increase in interdependencies and connectivity, such as the worldwide explosion of mobility, including groups of refugees, the circulation of commodities, free trade agreements between Japan and the EU, technical procedures and technologies, and the corresponding political, military, and legal strategies of control. At the same time, we are faced by opposing anti-globalizing tendencies such as Brexit, the abandonment of free trade agreements by the U.S. government, and "only eat local products" movements.

Translocalization, polycontexturalization, and mediatization

Refiguration can be tentatively characterized by three sub-processes, which function as sensitizing concepts for empirical investigations. The most well known of these concepts is that of translocalization. In using translocalization as a sensitizing concept, we assume that different places are increasingly linked, simultaneously increasing the relevance of constructions of locality because places are no longer assumed to be self-evident. For example, in our project on public space in the social web (coordinated by Barbara Pfetsch and Annie Waldherr, Pfetsch et al. 2019), we observed that U.S. politics is an important topic in the Twittersphere in Jerusalem (more important than in Berlin). The strong connection to U.S. topics seems to be driven by the Anglo-American population in Jerusalem, reflecting translocal ties.

The concept of polycontexturalization expresses our assumption that space, circulation, networks, and places, for example, are being connected in a new way by what we call communicative action (Knoblauch 2020). In the course of performing these embodied actions, more and more spaces, and potentially new spaces, are affected (or themselves affect these actions) and become effective at the same time. Take, for example, the massive change in control rooms (e.g., for the surveillance of crowds or monitoring mobility infrastructures). Control rooms constitute a paradigmatic form of modernity to control not only populations but also technological, natural resources, and risks. Surprisingly, digitalization with its assumed tendency towards networking and decentralization has not led to a substitution of spatially centralized control rooms, but rather has fostered the rapid integration of very different functionalities, such as water resources, health services, traffic, and electricity. The integration of different infrastructures into one local center and into a single control room connects a series of different spatial and material infrastructures that are not only observed by a scopic regime of multiple monitors and screens but also become relevant in contexts of actions—which take on what we believe to be a polycontextural character. This polycontexturalization, however, is not just a postmodern transgression of space; it appears to contribute to the bounding of certain spaces, such as smart cities, and to help accentuate the differences between urban and rural areas, nations and cultural areas, in a way conforming to our definition of refiguration.

In addition to translocalization and polycontexturalization, there is another concept that represents a major pillar for our understanding of refiguration: mediatization. Mediatization refers to the ways media and technology affect embodied communicative action, the relations constituted by them, and thus spatial structure. Its relevance can be easily understood if one recalls the substantial social transformation from oral cultures to literal cultures—in terms of settlements (cities) or political order (central power) (Soja 2011). One should also keep in mind that printing provided large masses of people with written and visual information (including maps very early on) several hundred years before the advent of the industrial society in England. Moreover, the electrification of industrial mass products and production in the 19th century was preceded by the dissemination of the telegraph, which made it possible to separate the means of communication and transport in a way that noticeably affected the spatial order immensely. In contrast to earlier spatial transformations, the current refiguration of space is related to and driven by the recent digital mediatization, which at the same time is a communication medium (computer). Digitalization has not led to the despatialization of society, as many had expected. Yet, digital mediatization quite obviously affects space, social action, and spatial imagination, as indicated by the study of locative media, such as dating apps, investigated in another research project (coordinated by Ingo Schulz-Schaeffer; Lettkemann and Schulz-Schaeffer, 2021). There is little doubt that late and postmodern visions, including the network society and its space of flows (see Castells 2015), have been countered by insights into the communicative power of the new media monopoles and their capacity to centralize information. These new communicative figurations are addressed by Couldry and Hepp (2017) as "deep mediatization." Digital media ubiquitously permeate the whole of society and increase interdependencies through their technical connectivity, extending processes of social communication locally by speeding up communication. Although digital mediatization quite clearly reshapes and substitutes the rather centralized and hierarchical order of mass media, it is not restricted to media communication. Being based on the revolutionary connection of information and communication technologies, digitalization is increasingly affecting every field of society.

It is not just the media system, as communication theorists assume, but all industries, technologies, and infrastructures that are refigured by digital mediatization. In the economy, for example, this becomes apparent in the production of commodities like 3D printing, their dissemination on the market, and their consumption (or combination of production and consumption, i.e. prosumption) in ways that have been labeled—somewhat one-sidedly—"digital capitalism," because most industries are still strongly tied to materiality.

However, mediatization also affects politics, sports, and, as we are currently seeing, science. By changing the relations between subjects as well as between subjects and objects, mediatization contributes to the refiguration of subjective aspects of space. Institutions as well as actors and subjectivities are being refigured, too: Research on the socialization of children suggests that while spatial environments were perceived as fairly homogeneous in the past, they are now increasingly experienced as isolated pockets of space (Zeiher and Zeiher 1994). Instead of one coherent unity, space appears as an accumulation of multiple interconnected, networked spatial fragments. These shifts are associated sometimes with increasing acts of vandalism in public spaces and an affinity for extremist positions (Heitmeyer 1996), but also with the revitalization of inner-city areas, as today's youth are out and about the city carrying mobile devices rather than sitting at home in front of the television.

Circulation and mobility

Mediatization visibly affects mobility and, consequently, the process we call "circulation" in that it can enhance and accelerate the movement of people, objects, and their communication in space, or it can intensify communication across space. Circulation refers to the way in which mobility creates spatial order and disorder. By circulation, we mean the movement of people, goods, signs, and technology between different places. Circulation is not an unsystematic, free flow of entities, but rather proceeds along orderly institutional paths, organizational fields, and social infrastructures with reliable transition points and follow-up operations. For example, food retailing is still strongly embedded in a city's built urban environment, and the corona crisis has revealed how strongly food production and retailing still depend on material infrastructures such as logistics. Nevertheless, even industries closely bound to materiality such as food production and retailing are affected by mediatization due to the increase in online retailing or the use of digitalization to improve logistics, for instance, thus resulting in complex new spatial forms (Baur et al. 2020).

If one thinks about the role of circulation in the refiguration of spaces, one quickly gets the impression that spaces of circulation are a consequence of social transformations. A closer look, however, shows that these trajectories (predefined paths of circulation, lines, routes of traffic) in which circulations occur have always been a necessary component of the construction of modern-day spaces. Routes, lines, paths, and tracks of various kinds (such as rivers, railway lines, public transport networks, motorways, footpaths) are the underlying material structures that have a propensity towards mobility, in homogenously designed urban spaces, for example.

Taking Le Corbusier's urban utopias as case studies, it is possible to understand how the contemporary city was consistently divided into spatially distinct, formally and functionally differentiated zones, and how the trajectory was implicitly established as a new leading figure, initially in urban planning (Vinken 2008).

Ulrike Jureit (2012) demonstrates in the context of the discovery of colonial space that this dynamic in modern society is not only visible in cities. Explorers, land surveyors, and adventurers followed clearly defined routes on foot or on horseback, with the clear intention of expanding the knowledge of space. In fact, the linearity of their routes transformed these paths into trajectorial space. The information gathered along the way flowed into a single map, with the spaces beyond the route remaining blank and thus perceived as empty space. The trajectorial space, which, in this case, is the precondition for the enforcement of territorial space, unfolds its pervasive logic of circulation, as postulated by Robert Venturi, Denise Scott Brown, and Steven Izenour (1977), in the form of the highway and automobile-driving subjects. It is evident in many newly founded cities outside Europe that an orientation towards roads, bicycle lanes, sidewalks, lanes for electric scooters, underground waste transportation systems, and information highways radically structures daily life.

The Korean city of Songdo, for example, which we are studying in various individual projects within the framework of our Collaborative Research Center (Löw and Stollmann 2018), stands out as a trajectorial space par excellence: With a target population of 70,000 (currently 35,000), the city boasts a number of eight-lane streets, assorted sidewalks that are several meters wide, and numerous cycle paths (although hardly any Koreans ride a bicycle). The shopping mall in Songdo was designed by the architect Minsuk Cho so that it could be easily crossed with electric scooters. Garbage is transported underground on conveyor belts and processed centrally. All these paths, lines, tracks, and routes that facilitate circulation, mobility, and displacement have not yet been sufficiently factored in as significant spatial areas in their own right in relevant research and theories (with the possible exception of research in urban planning departments). It is, however, trajectorial space (which also includes shipping and air routes) that organizes social coexistence and societal relations at the most fundamental level. The spatial analysis of Twitter networks demonstrates, for example, that statements of solidarity after terrorist attacks are sent not primarily from the region or from neighboring cities, but rather from cities with the most effective and lowest-priced flight connections to the attacked city (Lin and Margolin 2014).

Trajectorial spaces of circulation are especially relevant to the understanding of refiguration, since they literally "pave the way" out of the spatial homogenization of modern spaces with their clear functional differentiation or vertical hierarchical order right from the start. For Rudolph Schwarz, the general planner in the reconstruction of Cologne (after its destruction in WWII), for example, the transport system was a means to connect the homely city (a concept of place) to the world (a concept of translocality by circulation and trajectorial space).

In the very way that we conceive refiguration of present-day societies to follow two dominant conflicting spatial logics of "container" and "network" simultaneously, which are interdependent, circulation linked to territoriality is both part of modernity and a precondition for digitalized mediatization and deterritorialization. This becomes even more complicated if we return to translocalization.

Translocalization designates the linkage of different places. It does not necessarily mean the dislocation or even annihilation of place but instead can serve to boost the constructions of locality. From this perspective, places are simply no longer regarded as self-evident, and circulation forces us to develop an even stronger notion of place. We have to consider what is happening in Songdo and all over the world: If spaces of circulation and mobility become stronger, then we witness an increased emotional need to create spaces as networks of places (e.g., the reinvention of traditional Korean houses as meeting places and landmarks). Territorial spatial forms co-exist, interlock with, and spread out alongside, over, and beneath more fluid, more explicitly relational spatial networks, connections, and figurations. It is the very empirical task in our study of refiguration to answer the question: How do they do this? The forms of spaces (territorial space, trajectorial space, network space, etc.) are of interest for empirical spatial research, but the sociospatial aspect is best researched (in our opinion) with an emphasis on refiguration.

Conclusion

As mentioned at the beginning, the ideas presented here are not straitjackets but rather are considered sensitizing concepts. The refiguration of spaces, therefore, should be specified by means of the empirical studies conducted within the context of our collaborative research cluster as well as in neighboring research endeavors. The chapters in this volume constitute examples of such research. We also hope to learn from future research about the qualities and the range of the social transformations of space that we call refiguration.

Acknowledgements

This research has been funded by the Deutsche Forschungsgemeinschaft (DFG, German Research Foundation)—project number 290045248—SFB 1265.

References

Baur, Nina, Julia Fülling, Linda Hering, and Elmar Kulke, eds. 2020. *Waren—Wissen—Raum. Interdependenz von Produktion, Markt und Konsum in Lebensmittelwarenketten*. Wiesbaden: Springer VS.
Bourdieu, Pierre. 1990. *The Logic of Practice*. Stanford: Stanford University Press.
Castells, Manuel. 2000. *The Rise of the Network Society*. Oxford: Blackwell.
Castells, Manuel. 2015. *Networks of Outrage and Hope: Social Movements in the Internet Age*. Chichester: Wiley.
Chang, Kyung-Sup. 2010. "East Asia's Condensed Transition to Second Modernity." *Soziale Welt* 61 (3–4): 319–328. doi: 10.5771/0038-6073-2010-3-4-319.
Couldry, Nick, and Andreas Hepp. 2017. *The Mediated Construction of Reality*. London: Polity.
Elias, Norbert. (1939) 1982. *The Civilizing Process*, Vol. 2. Oxford: Blackwell.
Heitmeyer, Wilhelm. 1996. "Die gefährliche Zerstückelung von Zeit und Raum. Zu den Folgen wachsender sozialer Desintegration." *Frankfurter Rundschau*, September 26: 18.

Jureit, Ulrike. 2012. *Das Ordnen von Räumen. Territorium und Lebensraum im 19. und 20. Jahrhundert*. Hamburg: Hamburger Edition.
Knoblauch, Hubert. 2020. *The Communicative Construction of Reality*. London: Routledge.
Knoblauch, Hubert, and Martina Löw. 2017. "On the Spatial Re-Figuration of the Social World." *Sociologica* 11 (2): 1–27. doi: 10.2383/88197.
Knoblauch, Hubert, and Martina Löw. 2020a. "The Re-Figuration of Spaces and Refigured Modernity—Concept and Diagnosis." *Historical Social Research* 45 (2): 263–292. doi: 10.12759/hsr.45.2020.2.263–292.
Knoblauch, Hubert, and Martina Löw. 2020b. "Dancing in Quarantine: The Spatial Refiguration of Society and the Interaction Orders." *Space and Culture* 23 (3): 221–225. doi: 10.1177/1206331220938627.
Krotz, Friedrich. 2001. *Die Mediatisierung kommunikativen Handelns. Der Wandel von Alltag und sozialen Beziehungen, Kultur und Gesellschaft durch die Medien*. Wiesbaden: Westdeutscher Verlag.
Lettkemann, Eric, and Ingo Schulz-Schaeffer. 2021. "Lokative Medien: Inklusion und Exklusion in öffentlichen Räumen." In *Räume digitaler Kommunikation. Lokalität—Imagination—Virtualisierung*, edited by Thomas Döbler, Christian Pentzold, and Christian Katzenbach, 72–103. Köln: Halem.
Lin, Yu-Ru, and Drew Margolin. 2014. "The Ripple of Fear, Sympathy and Solidarity during the Boston Bombings." *EPJ Data Science* 3. doi: 10.1140/epjds/s13688-014-0031-z.
Löw, Martina. 2016. *The Sociology of Space. Materiality, Social Structures, and Action*. New York: Palgrave Macmillan.
Löw, Martina, and Jörg Stollmann. 2018. "Urbanität in Smart-City-Entwürfen und Stadtvisionen? Moderne Stadtentwicklung zwischen Songdo und Limerick." In *Urbanität im 21. Jahrhundert*, edited by Norbert Gestring, and Jan Wehrheim, 336–343. Frankfurt am Main: Campus.
Mol, Annemarie, and John Law. 1994. "Regions, Networks and Fluids: Anaemia and Social Topology." *Social Studies of Science* 24 (4): 641–671. doi: 10.1177/030631279402400402.
Pfetsch, Barbara, Daniel Maier, Daniela Stoltenberg, Annie Waldherr, Neta Kligler-Vilenchik, and Maya de Vries. 2019. "How Local is the Digital Public Sphere on Twitter? A Comparison between Jerusalem and Berlin." Paper presented at the 69th Annual Conference of the International Communication Association (ICA), Washington, DC, May 24–28.
Schlögel, Karl. 2011. *Mastering Russian Spaces. Raum und Raumbewältigung als Probleme der russischen Geschichte*. München: Oldenbourg.
Soja, Edward W. 2011. "Cities and States in Geohistory." *Theory and Society* 39 (3–4): 211–226. doi: 10.1007/978-94-007-0756-6_15.
Venturi, Robert, Denise Scott Brown, and Steven Izenour. 1977. *Learning from Las Vegas. The Forgotten Symbolism of Architectural Form*. Cambridge, MA: MIT Press.
Vinken, Gerhard. 2008. "Ort und Bahn. Die Räume der modernen Stadt bei Le Corbusier und Rudolf Schwarz." In *Räume der Stadt. Von der Antike bis heute*, edited by Cornelia Jöchner, 147–164. Berlin: Reimer.
Zeiher, Hartmut J., and Helga Zeiher. 1994. *Orte und Zeiten der Kinder. Soziales Leben im Alltag von Großstadtkindern*. Weinheim: Juventa.

3
SPATIAL OCCUPATION—DESTRUCTION—VIRTUALIZATION

Types, categories, and processes of a crucial factor in social life

Karl-Siegbert Rehberg

> It is not from space that I must seek my dignity,
> but from the government of my thought. . . .
> By space the universe encompasses
> and swallows me up like an atom;
> by thought I comprehend the world.
> —Blaise Pascal ([1670] 1958, Chapter VI:
> The Philosophers. Fragment 348)

Norbert Elias as methodological stimulator for the analysis of spatial transformations

Norbert Elias would have been pleased to contribute to the approach of analyzing the "refiguration of spaces" (Löw and Knoblauch in this book) because he was particularly proud of having "discovered" the significance of figurations for sociological analysis. Elias was deeply convinced that a focus on relational figurations was an integral yet missing key to recognizing and understanding causal relations and coherences within societies. This is why he developed a methodological approach to historical sociology that carried the spirit of the longue durée-orientated *Annales* School. Based upon his understanding of relationality and processuality within social relations, Elias ([1939] 1969, [1939] 1982) intended nothing less than to re-calibrate and re-establish sociological research.

Elias insinuated that historical and sociological sciences alike are habitually concerned with states—in the sense of static conditions, not of course in the political sense—instead of processes, without even differentiating according to the objects of their inquiry. In contrast to his idea, today's research mainly focuses on probabilities and contours of a possible "next society" (Baecker 2007). Even those require relating past events to the present in order to predict the future.

DOI: 10.4324/9781003036159-4

Following Elias's insights, in this chapter I address the beginning of spatial history and its interwoven myths of origin, corresponding mentalities, and strategies of entitlement (Rehberg 2014, 73–75, 257–286) to exemplify the interdependence between geo-physical spaces and culturally created ones. Both dimensions always act simultaneously as natural conditions of life and as objects of reorganization in conjunction with the interpretation of their associated magical, religious, commercial, ruler, or whatever. What matters most to me is the indispensable interplay of these different aspects over time, such that spatial effects always appear simultaneously both as perceived and interpreted realities, and as spatial designs and fantasies shaped by their materiality. The relevance of correspondence between physical effects of space and cultural influences on space becomes obvious when one analyzes spatial transformations in the longue durée. The fruitfulness of such a processual perspective is evident in the historical–sociological approaches of Max Weber, Norbert Elias, and many other authors, such as Edward P. Thompson, Michael Mann, Immanuel Wallerstein, Shmuel N. Eisenstadt, Stefan Breuer, or Fraya Frehse (in this book).

In his *History of Rome*, Theodor Mommsen's condensation of the connection between the natural and cultural power of spaces—for which he was awarded the Nobel Prize in Literature—becomes almost visual. Mommsen (1862) depicts the spatial relations formed and influenced by the Mediterranean in a quite revealing way:

> The Mediterranean Sea with its various branches, . . . alternately narrowed by islands or projections of the land and expanding to considerable breadth, at once separates and connects the three divisions of the Old World. The shores of this inland sea were in ancient times peopled by various nations belonging in an ethnographical and philological point of view to different races, but constituting in their historical aspect one whole. This historic whole has been usually, but not very appropriately, entitled the history of the ancient world. It is in reality the history of civilization among the Mediterranean nations; and, as it passes before us in its successive stages, it presents four great phases of development—the history of the Coptic or Egyptian stock dwelling on the southern shore, the history of the Aramaean or Syrian nation which occupied the east coast and extended into the interior of Asia as far as the Euphrates and Tigris, and the histories of the twin-peoples, the Hellenes and Italians, who received as their heritage the countries on the European shore.

From an early "Eastern" point of view (*ex oriente lux*), the Mediterranean was conceived of as "upper ocean of the dawn" and became a point of reference in a coordinate system consisting of "Europē" and "Asia," extended by a third part of the world, namely "Lybia" or "Africa" as described by Herodotus (Berger 1907). The hubris of Xerxes was dramatically staged in Aeschylus's *The Persians* (472 BC), while Herodotus (1920, 7.8C) bears witness to the Persian king's intention to expand his land by making "the borders of Persian territory and of the firmament of heaven be the same."

Even then a differentiation was achieved that simultaneously expressed a unity—not one of different countries but rather their connection and separation by the Mediterranean. The Mediterranean was already considered "*mare grande*" or "*mare nostrum*" in antiquity. That name was later used by Mussolini's fascist regime for the legitimation of its colonial engagements and was recently brought back into our awareness through the headlines about the criminally organized passages by refugees. This image of natural influences on spatial structures that are conversely modified by human interventions connects spaces of power with their original natural territory.

Interplay of the appropriation of physical space and the construction for large-scale territories in the longue durée

Migration in early human history

It may well be said that human history begins with *homo erectus* around 1.5 to 1.8 million years ago. As suggested by the Out-of-Africa theory, humans first migrated from East Africa to today's "Asia" about 50,000 to 70,000 years ago, before reaching "Europe" and "North America" later on. To understand the further development of these huge spaces, paleontologists rely on evidence of material culture, that is to say archaeological remains by means of which forms of settlement, production methods, and ways of life can be reconstructed (Parzinger 2016). The same is true for any other cultural traces like "works of art" (especially cave paintings), which began to emerge around 30,000 BC (Rehberg 2009). All of these indicators suggest that humans appropriate and configure space. More precisely, perhaps, they reveal a fundamental "openness to the world" ("*Weltoffenheit*") (Scheler [1928] 2009), which enables human beings to actively adapt their cultures to a wide variety of spatial and climatic conditions. Therefore, mankind is the only species—as Arnold Gehlen ([1940] 1988, 30) put it—that is not bound to a specific "climatic, ecological, etc. milieu," but is "viable all over the world, under the pole and the equator, on the water and the land, in the forest, swamp, mountains and steppes." In all these environments, humans can survive when succeeding in establishing their "second nature" by adapting to spaces as well as transforming them through cultural changes. This is profoundly constitutive for the basic concept of "culture" developed from settlement-based agricultural societies. The Latin word for "farming"—"*colere*"—does not simply mean the sowing and harvesting of crops but also implies the development of rites corresponding to the highly essential cultivation of soil. Therefore, possibilities and probabilities of survival have always been laid out in terms of spaces, which themselves were always reformed and redesigned in long-lasting and continuously ongoing processes.

Early empires

In order to outline the importance of migration and manorial land grabbing for spatial transformations, it is helpful to regard the earliest human migrations, which were driven by the search for habitats. The appropriation of spaces had been closely connected to large-scale, often nomadic migration, at least since 4000 BC. Since the settlement processes during the Neolithic, the spatial contacts between nomadic groups—mostly hunters and gatherers—and settled farmers had been extensive. Early rulers combined transcendent claims—namely that their empires were destined to include the "whole world"—with interconnections in the central areas of the Old World and stabilized them with trade (cf. Rehberg 2019).

A good example of how constantly unstable was this spatial control is the City of Babylon, which was continuously conquered, repeatedly destroyed, and rebuilt: dating back to its mythical period, there are Babylonian, Hebrew, Greek, and Persian narratives of Babylon's history. As the most significant state foundation in the Tigris–Euphrates region, Babylon came under Assyrian (8th century BC), Persian (6th century BC), Hellenic (4th century BC), and Parthian (2nd century BC) foreign rule. This famous metropolis for a time had more than 200,000 inhabitants and was said to be the largest city "in the world," flourishing numerous times in different periods, among them under the rule of Hammurabi (1792–1750 BC), Nebuchadnezzar (1140–1127 BC), Cyrus the Great (6th century BC), and Alexander the Great (4th century BC).

While nowadays, invisible power structures increasingly show themselves in an apparently "spaceless" mediality, in earlier history, rulers longed for and determined their respective ranks by subjugating the largest possible territories. The large-scale early empires that defined themselves as "global" also often claimed the divinity of their rulers or an omnipotence associated with their divine supremacy on earth. This can be seen as early on as in "old Babylonian times" in the "best known Ballad of Early Heroes," the lament of a mythical figure of divinity of the ancient Egyptian Hurrians (3rd until 2nd millennium BC):

> Where is King Alulu, who reigned for 36,000 years?
> Where is King Etana, the man who ascended to the heavens? . . .
> They are no longer engendered, no longer born,
> Like the remote heavens, I cannot overtake them,
> Like the deep netherworld, no one can know them,
> Life, in all its form, is but an illusion.
> *(Michalowski 2014, 165)*

In the Sargonian Empire (2334–2154 BC), the most powerful rulers named themselves the "Master of the Universe" (Michalowski 2014, 151). Fustel de Coulanges (1877, 231) shows that in ancient Rome—long before the "Axial Age" so recently and prominently rediscovered (Eisenstadt 1986)—the dignity of the priesthood emerged, and even in earlier times central rulers invoked the idea of their closeness to the divine—from which they derived their own divinity and drew the conclusion that they could dispose of the world (Michalowski 2014, 151; Rehberg 2019, 38–40, 49–52). This is reflected in a wide variety of ideas and formulas that signify requirements with regard to heaven: in the "Sumerian Kings List" (Michalowski 2014, 155–156) of the third dynasty (2112 to 2004 BC), "kingship was handed down from the heavens," a concept of self that was still evident in the Divine Right of Kings claimed by European monarchs. This concept simultaneously distinguished genealogically and spatially, as Naram-sin's (2273–2219 BC) claim to rule "extended to eternity" or the idea of a *"Roma eterna"*—albeit much later—exemplify. Typical metaphors for claims to world domination were images of a disposition of the whole space to the end of the world (Haubold 2013)—a rule over "four vertices" (Michalowski 2014, 155). Hammurabi (1793–1750 BC), the Babylonian "King of Justice," had a monumental legal code carved into stone in order to make his universal rule visible to everyone and, at the same time, appropriating not only space but also time by postulating that his "name be remembered favorably for all times in the Esaĝila temple in Babylon, which I love," whereby he also regarded his city as the "Center of the Universe" (ibid., 153–154). The Assyrian kings also sought to expand their empire "beyond the shores of the sea" (Rollinger 2014, 199).

Cyrus II, "the Great" (559–530 BC) and sixth king of the Achaemenid Empire (Holy Bible, Isaiah 44.28, 45.1; Daniel 10.1; Ezra, 1.1–2, 1.7–8, 3.7, 4.5, 5.13–14, 5.17; II Chronicles 36.22–23), constructed himself simultaneously as the descendent of a long genealogy of rulers and as the "king of the universe, mighty king, king of Babylon, king of Sumer and Akkad, king of the four quarters" and so on (Rollinger 2014, 191). The reign of Cyrus II was supposedly conferred on him by the God Marduk, whose name in the Old Testament means "Bel, son of the sun" and who in the course of history had changed from being the Babylonian city god to the father of the gods. Marduk appointed Cyrus as a just ruler, overlord, who called "all kings who sit on thrones, from all sectors of the world, from the upper sea to the lower sea" and from more distant districts to Babylon so that they could submit to him and kiss his feet. And yet, from a Jewish point of view, Marduk encountered an even more powerful deity—the tribal god Yahweh (Deutero-Isaiah 44, 23, and 45:1), who made Cyrus the tool of repatriation of the Jews held in Babylon (including the restoration of the temple in Jerusalem) and simultaneously confirmed his universal claim to rule. Similarly, when depicting the war campaigns to expand his empire, Darius (549–486 BC) announced that his empire extended to the shores of the sea that surround the world and claimed to have even conquered cities "beyond the sea."

This way of affirming dominion in ancient Mesopotamia and Persia persisted until the Habsburg Charles V (1500–1558), who was said to rule "the empire on which the sun never sets," a formula that was later used for the British Empire as well.

The process of conquests and appropriation of spaces and their ontological and practical importance started in Babylonian times and can also be observed in the Persian Empire (from 555 BC). Two hundred years later, Alexander the Great's cosmopolitanism strongly influenced the Hellenistic world's political and cultural landscape during the imperial expansion of Macedonia. The Roman Empire's expansion of its imperial territory roughly half a millennium later can be understood as the process of the organization of large-scale territories "as the successor of the great Empires of Old" (Yang and Mutschler 2008, 110). China and the Indian subcontinent can also be regarded as other formative examples for constructing large-scale territories.

Man's ability to symbolically interpret and process realities is intrinsically entwined with the materiality, controllability, and, more importantly, uncontrollability of spaces: as spaces can be both life-giving or life-threatening, chances of human survival are necessarily connected to the culturalization of spaces. There are two main strategies of securing and stabilizing control over large-scale domains:

Assimilation includes forms of habitual alignment with the cultural center—for instance, both Babylon and Hellenistic Greece allowed for the integration of immigrants with local elites (Stevens 2016). Rome granted citizenship to nationals of the conquered states because "the Romans . . . showed an unparalleled readiness to incorporate subalterns into the metropolitan political community" and allowed for creating a "truly trans-regional aristocracy" (Lavan, Payne, and Weisweiler 2016, 23). The "previously powerful" were often drawn from the periphery to the central court, often with an increase in symbolic prestige and a simultaneous loss of power—a strategy that was used up until the times of Louis XIV. Incidentally, the ability of formerly mobile groups to self-assimilate should not be underestimated. Think of the Vandals, who have become proverbial as barbarian destroyers of Rome, whose leadership classes imitated and mimicked Roman customs in a special way and even tried to overbid Roman habits during their kingships in Carthage (after 429 AD).

Alternatively, space can be appropriated using various forms of *subordination* (Lavan, Payne, and Weisweiler 2016, 1–28), for example through the use of satraps or representatives of the central power and equipping them with regional and local titles, which could also be associated with relative autonomy. In the latter case, the residents who could not be homogenized by the central power lived in a wide variety of spatial conditions, customs, and traditions. They were hierarchically subordinate, but often their linguistic and cultic peculiarities were tolerated and acknowledged by the rulers. Similar processes had already taken place in Babylonia and in Macedonian-dominated Hellenistic Greece, namely through the integration of local elites into the imperial order, often combined with an identity dominated by the center. It is therefore also possible to work out different forms of manorial world disposition, which are closely linked to the conquest and the configuration of space.

As rule over conquered areas is risky and mobile forces pose a threat, it is also possible to stabilize territories by waiving expansion or shifting towards guaranteeing internal order. Applied to Rome, the term "imperial" is an ambivalent one. Thus, one could say that Rome became "imperial" twice: for the first time when it expanded its rule over "almost all the inhabited world" (Polybius I. 1.5), so that after the destruction of Carthage (146 BC) "sea and land lay everywhere open to its way," and for the second time when Augustus ended the civil wars that had disrupted the Roman Republic and introduced a monarchical form of government (Mutschler 2008, 119). After unsuccessful campaigns against the "Teutons," Augustus founded the long-lasting "Pax Romana"—the pacification of the empire's interior became the central goal of imperial rule (cf. comparative studies on the Roman Empire and the Chinese Empire in Mutschler and Mittag 2008). In a similar way, China's later Ming dynasty (16th century) was characterized by a relative self-closure, which however is often overestimated: despite the "ideal of 'Great Unity'" and the idea of rule "All-under-Heaven," which emerged in the context of imperial unification in 221 BC, the Ming dynasty was also fragmented, comparable to a "multistate system" (Pines 2012, 11–16), and China never self-closed itself as much as Japan between the Tokugawa shogunate (1630s) and the forced opening of the country in 1853.

As already in the case of the Scythians (6th century BC) and the Parthians (4th century BC), the equestrian peoples from Northern Asia—such as the Huns and the Mongols in the 6th and 13th century AD—practiced expansive conquest for centuries. This was also the foundation of other struggles for great empires in the 8th century AD, including the Arab expansion from the Indus River to the Iberian Peninsula (711–719), which was finally halted by the Christian *Reconquista* of Andalusia. During its most intense phase in 1492, the violent displacement of the Arabs also resulted in the Jewish population being forced into exile. While the Germanic expansion into the Roman Empire is only perceived as the proverbial *Völkerwanderung*, the "Mongol storms" destroyed empires, such as in India where the Mughals installed indirect rule in the 16th century (comparable to later English colonialism). Later, between the 15th and the 18th centuries AD, the Turkish expansion continuously posed a challenging threat to the territories in Southeast Europe.

Land-based feudalism

Whenever hierarchical systems of land ownership emerged in agricultural societies, warrior elites would come into being and consolidate their power by establishing complicated formal relationships of granting protection and exploitation. This can be seen, for example, in the nomadic "overlapping" (*Überlagerung*; Gumplowicz 1905, 28) of early peasants. After the division of the Carolingian Empire, in the 10th century, the process of "feudalization" involved splitting up formerly integrated domains. Norbert Elias saw this as a starting point for century-long territorial struggles, which—at least in France—finally led to a new centralization of land ownership and a royal position of authority binding everyone. Elias ([1939] 1982, 104–116) called this the "monopoly mechanism," which—as a predecessor of the structures of modern statehood—led to a monopoly of tax collection and a standing military. As a consequence, claims of power were radicalized up to the point that Louis XIV enforced ceremonialization of his court in Versailles and thus paradoxically succeeded in separating the aristocracy from their land bases. In this way, agricultural land was merged into territories of sovereignty with complex internal structures.

Sociological system theorists in the tradition of Niklas Luhmann often overlook the fact that functional differentiations do not just exist in modern times. Instead, when combining the use of space with feudal stratification, societies have invented complex, highly differentiated and balanced systems (Rehberg 2017). Similarly, in his classic analysis of the feudal system, Marc Bloch ([1939] 1982) assumes that the specific structure of power relationships induced how space was distributed and what effect these distributions of space had. Similarly, Fernand Braudel ([1949] 1996) did not assume that the geological–geographical material properties of space determined how the Mediterranean was constructed as a connection of the Middle East, Africa, and Europe. Instead, this connection was socially constructed by powerful actors and mediated by social structures.

Colonialism

In the "Eurasian" context, all spatial categories changed again radically due to the discovery of the "New World" (as it was aptly named from the European perspective), ushering in global European colonialism. During this period, the Popes co-created a "landless," "meta-feudal" concept of a "universal lordship," which seems to confirm Georg Simmel's ([1908] 2009, chapter IX) argument that the state's attachment to land is opposed to the universal "spiritual rule" of the Roman Church. The Borgia Pope, Alexander VI, however, "lent" the newly discovered lands in South America to Spain and Portugal, making the "landless" church an actor beyond its ability to proselytize the pagan masses.

During the age of modern colonialism, the world was redistributed by Spain, Portugal, the Netherlands, later France, and, most pervasively, Great Britain, which "occupied the sea" (*Seenahme*), as Carl Schmitt ([1942] 1997, 47) hymnally described by quoting Sir Walter Raleigh:

> Whoever controls the sea controls the world's trade, and whoever controls the world owns all the treasures of the world and indeed the world itself.

Nation-building and geopolitics

When modern nations emerged—based on the rule over a demarcated territory and its inhabitants—new ideas of spatial exclusivity and the relationships between different states evolved. In science, this was reflected in new subdisciplines. For example, Friedrich Ratzel introduced "Anthropogeography" (1882, 1891) and "Political Geography" (1897). Both works naturally presuppose colonialism to be legitimate on the basis of racial categories. Ratzel (1897, 17) also links land-based states with the metaphor of a "living space" (*Lebensraum*) and argues that "every political entity seeks a connection to the ground." The appropriation of space was always about power differences. These power differences, which "naturally" (*naturwüchsig*), as Karl Marx would have said, and "necessarily," as Ratzel (1897) argued, linked conquest to colonization:

> The size of the space we think and plan into politically depends on the size of the space we live in. . . . The large space encourages bold expansion, the small one leads to tentative crowding.
> *(Ratzel 1897, 261, cited in Köster 1992, 126)*

Therefore, people would have to be educated toward expansion. Using these ideas, the Nazi regime later pushed the long history of spatial occupation to an extreme, and it was that kind of argument that Karl Haushofer—Ratzel's student and Rudolf Hess's confidant—used to justify Hitler's expansion plans. It is evident that the emerging modern nation states created new spatial competitions, which they justified using the semantics of past rule. For this purpose, Carl Schmitt—who was often described as the "Nazi's Crown Lawyer"—with stylistic bravery and dangerous acumen provided a legal justification for "large territories." From the perspective of fascist (and implicitly also Soviet) rule, Schmitt envisaged the rise of a new order that was linked to the old empires. In this view, Hitler's expansionism was meant to establish a new empire "of a thousand years" that was to determine the future of Europe and the world by breaking Britain's undisputed supremacy as the leading naval power—as Wilhelm II had already intended during the First World War.

When the European empires collapsed—the Russian Empire (1917), Habsburg Monarchy and German Empire (1918), the Ottoman Empire (1922) and 27 years later the British Empire (1945)—the mostly multiethnic and multicultural imperial domains dissolved and the number of nation states with nationalist delusions of grandeur increased even further. In the 20th century, ideologically founded "empires" re-emerged, such as the Soviet Union—which served as a multiethnic-state blueprint for working-class societies all over the world—or the fascist or National Socialist regimes. For example, Benito Mussolini tried to employ this kind of imperial strategy by cruelly conquering Abyssinia. The Allies' victory over Nazi Germany made reality of what Alexis de Tocqueville had already prophesied in 1835 (1961, 479)—namely that, according to a secret plan of the divine, the Russians and the Americans "each seems called by some secret design of Providence one day to hold in its hands the destinies of half the world." During the Cold War, both superpowers' priorities were no longer of an imperial nature but rather hegemonic: the Eastern Power dominated the "brother states," the United States the Latin American countries. After the Soviet Union collapsed, the number of nation states increased further to 193 members of the United Nations plus the Vatican, together with 12 controversial cases, resulting in a profound reorganization of European space as well.

Regardless, Ulrich Beck (2005, 7) was wrong when he claimed "Germany no longer exists; neither France, Spain, Italy, even Great Britain" and argued that imagining societies as contained by nation states was a model to overcome sociologically (Beck 1997, 49). I believe that for a long time to come, nation states will continue to provide institutions of political legitimation and mechanisms for translating transnational decision-making for their own political system. Incidentally, it seems to me that the term "world society," as based on Niklas Luhmann's (1975) very plausible initial consideration that there is a "logical" limit to human communication, is misleading. First of all, it implies the development from "empire" to "world-state." However, the strategies of world domination described earlier show that these ideas already existed in ancient times (Weisweiler 2016). Second, Luhmann implicitly assumes that a global society already exists today. Although the incomparably denser worldwide networks surely play a crucial role in shaping all current societies, this assumption seems problematic: the coronavirus crisis reveals the simultaneity of the *mondialization* of the spread of the virus and nationally distinct measures and fates of the people—validating the term "glocalization" coined by Roland Robertson (1994).

Interplay of social and sociological reflections on space

Making space invisible

Both "space" and "time" are key categories for defining humans' relationship to the world. Both are simultaneously physical a priori and socially constructed. Depending on the historical times and cultural contexts, sometimes one category is stressed more, sometimes the other. "Time" is always highlighted during times of fundamental social change. This is by no means only true for the modern age. For example, just think of the chiliastic "Third Reich" of Christ's return promised by Joachim of Fiore in the 12th century.

How the relationship between "space" and "time" is conceived is affected by the respective historical circumstances and *Zeitgeist*. It is characteristic for modern progressive societies and the way they self-reflect to dominantly treat "time" with a view towards a future to achieve anticipated goals, which starkly contrasts with past societies: with the exceptions of revolutionary turmoil or utopian visions of imagined futures, noble societies were oriented towards a genealogically affirmative past. All modernization theories are shaped by this manner of conceptualizing temporality. This fascination with the future is rooted in monotheistic religions, the secularizing enlightenment, and the associated changes in historical consciousness—Reinhart Koselleck (1972), for example, observed "a profound change in the meaning of classic *topoi*" in the *Sattelzeit* ("Saddle Time," 1750–1850) and made this the starting point for the historical analysis of semantic changes in a multivolume lexicon. According to Koselleck, since then, semantic changes of political and social terms have mainly been driven by a "temporalization of the categorical meanings" as well as their "politicization" and "ideologization."

During the Industrial Revolution, new means of transport and machinery accelerated social life, which evoked fears and anxieties from early on. In 1843, Heinrich Heine wrote: "Space is being killed by the railroad and we will be left with time alone" (quoted by Günzel 2010, 204). At the same time, rapid urbanization caused an explosion of space that at the same time can be conceived as a diminution of space: "With the advent of modernity time has vanished from social space," as Henri Lefebvre (1991, 95–96) put it. Other formulas claimed the "expulsion or erasure of time" and that "time has been murdered by society." This dominant subjugation of space combined with the technical media-induced suggestion that space was diminished or even destroyed may have contributed to the fact that the domination-related categories of space seem to have lost their prominence today. As a result, power relationships are hidden, too. While it was once indispensable to present power publicly, today power is increasingly becoming invisible (Rehberg 2014, 287–323), and this is reflected in the way the social sciences conceive "spaces," and therefore also "places," "territories," and "empires."

Concepts of space in social science

One of the key authors in the current sociological debates reflecting the relevance of space is Martina Löw (2001, 58–63), who—in reference to Georg Simmel—developed a relational sociology of space, emphasizing that space is constructed by "spacing" (Löw 2001, 158–161). Using this term, she describes placements based on perception, memory, efforts at synthesis, and the resulting abstraction processes. Simmel ([1908] 2009, chapter IX) had argued that no independent entities exist, since their social meaning lies precisely in the "structuring that is based on the soul," in other words, in the psychological function of a "synthesis of the space." That is why the term "place" is "purely sociological" and "absolutely nothing substantial or individual, but a mere form of relationship."

Elisabeth Holzinger (2007) systematically compares different concepts of space and shows that in different phases of the theoretical debate, gains and losses of space are asserted to different degrees. Often, theorists conceive new technologies and global media networks as an "end of space." Indeed, keywords like "globalization," "acceleration," "ubiquity," and "virtualization" reveal an "atmosphere of de-spacing" ("*Entraumstimmung*"). At the same time, theorists perceived the forecast "loss of distance" and "proximity" as threatening. "Technologies transcending space" (*Raumüberwindungstechnologien*) co-evolve with digital stock markets in the economy and a refiguration of the relationships between decentrality and centrality. Together, they drive the fear that "space will be killed."

Social theories also argue that industrialization in the 19th century induced a specialization of space—such as the separation of private spaces (the family, the home) from public spaces (workplace, political sphere), which in turn resulted in a "loss of proximity." Note that the current COVID-19 pandemic has induced a recapturing of private spaces or, more precisely, real-life private places for professional and commercial purposes. The "loss of proximity" also changes forms of familiarity with spaces. For example, in big cities with an urban sprawl on the outskirts, space is often experienced as many small and unconnected "islands."

Furthermore, extensive privatization poses a threat to solidarity or any kind of community. Arnold Gehlen ([1957] 1980, 59–65) predicted in 1957 that people would increasingly live from an "opinion as second-hand experience." Today, more recent theories take up this idea when they discuss people's increasing dependence on the omnipresence of the media, which in turn relates to all possible levels of experience and opportunities for action. In particular, humans are increasingly unable to influence larger-scale relationships. At the same time, the range of experiences conveyed by the media is expanding.

It is striking that the currently dominant concepts of communication seem to be completely aspatial, as exemplified by opposing theories such as those of Niklas

Luhmann and Jürgen Habermas and their respective adepts. Based on her analysis, Holzinger (2007, 62–66) proposes a typology of spatial terms with categories such as "material" versus "immaterial/abstract," "one-dimensional" versus "complex," "deterministic" versus "non-deterministic," "rigid" versus "process-based," and "absolutistic" versus "relational". Her extensive research led her to a rather one-sided conclusion: "Space is not something that exists in itself, but a process of permanent (re)-production" (66)—the self-evident human condition, that all perceptions are constructs of the perceived matter, stands in opposition to the equally true claim of independent space as an inherent force.

Changes in terminology on spatial control

In the first part of this chapter, I traced the relationship between societies and space in an historical sociological analysis. Why is this of any relevance for today's spatial sociology? I argue that humans are simultaneously exposed to spaces and actively create new spatial relationships, which they constitute by practices and experiences. The interplay of the two processes only unfolds in the longue durée.

This is not a new idea. Even in ancient Greece, the subjective constitution of spaces was a dominant theme. For example, when Aristotle reflected on human orientation, he granted reference to the cosmos as well as to different world models (Zekl 1992, 68). The permanent influence of spatial conditions on people's lives necessarily implies that the way the *animal symbolicum* (Cassirer 1972, 44) conceives space cannot be thought of anthropologically without taking humans' actions and sense-making into account. Humans also differentiate between spaces defined by their potentiality and specific locations (Rehberg 2006b, 45–47).

If the historicity of the relationality of actors and spaces is emphasized, then humans' corporeality comes into play in a specific way. Helmuth Plessner ([1928] 1981, 360–365, 181–187) explained this connection between humans' "eccentric positionality" and the resulting "spatiality" (*Raumhaftigkeit*) in his main anthropological work. Since the "spatial turn," the influence of (natural) spatial conditions on social and cultural phenomena have been brought into focus again, and Markus Schroer (2006, 176) reminds us that "space [shapes] our behavior and . . . puts his stamp on" us.

Strangely enough, this has been criticized on several occasions. I disagree: this is not "geodeterminism." Rather, relationality as a method should bear in mind that material or imagined space can have an effect. This does not mean that material space itself has no effect without being mediated by human interpretation, nor does it mean that material space is mere imagination. Instead, the challenge lies in understanding the interplay between the effective power of material objectivity and subjectivity. Due to living in cities built by humans, we may have lost our experience of the effects of natural space—and expressing this loss is often branded as outdated romanticization. Nevertheless, even today, when encountering our interdependencies with nature—for instance, in the high mountains, in the savannah, or in coastal regions at the mercy of the sea—the way we adapt to nature impresses our perceptions and affects our ways of defining, processing, and interpreting space.

It is well known that the Nazi regime not only killed millions of people and destroyed large parts of Europe, but also made many substantial words of the German language unusable, including *Nation* ("Nation"), *Heimat* ("homeland"), and *Raum* ("space")—which in contemporary German do not spark associations with the familiar land and soil of one's own origin but instead with the Nazis' spatial expansion projects, such as the "SS Plan East," which envisioned Aryanization (*Arisierung*), enslavement (*Versklavung*), and resettlement (*Umvolkung*). The imagery of this once murderous spatial policy is now used in populist and right-wing rhetoric to warn against the ethnic threat to its own people. This line of thought has a long tradition in the theme of a "shortage of space" (*Raumnot*) that made expansion seem a necessary task for Germany, which had been feeling enclosed in central Europe at least since the Thirty Years' War (1618–1648). While German lands were destroyed, some great European nations in the second part of the 17th century experienced their "Golden Ages," which caused an often conjured-up trauma. German philosopher and sociologist Helmuth Plessner ([1935] 1982, 17) even spoke in his book, *Die verspätete Nation* (with reference to German Nobel laureate in literature Thomas Mann's *Reflections of a Nonpolitical Man*), of Germany as a country that "missed" the 17th century. In post-war Germany, this resulted in avoiding all German terms related to space, corporeality, and race. Even in institutions that had to deal with demographic issues, the categories used in analysis cause suspicion and discomfort. When politicians talk about "space," they appear presumptuous, indeed revanchist. For example, the post-war dispute over the recognition of the Polish–German border conjured Hans Grimm's (1932) propagandistic motto "People without Space" or Carl Schmitt's *The Nomos of the Earth* ([1950] 2003) or *Land and Sea* [1942] 1997). In order to discuss topics that can only be mentioned using taboo words, contemporary Germans often use the English expressions as a detour to avoid a certain historically charged tone, for example, "community" instead of *Gemeinschaft*, "leader" instead of *Führer*.

Global versus local life

Although social science discourse on space has dismissed many essential spatial categories, the current densification of the world and increased interconnectivity have not resulted in one unified monolithic culture but rather in a cultural syncretism combined with different ideas and practices (Pieterse 1998, 101). It is therefore fruitful to speak of "globality" and differentiate between "globality" as a real fact, "globalization" as a process of acceleration, and "globalism" as a neoliberal market illusion created by capitalism (Beck 1997).

Describing society as having evolved into a "global class" (Dahrendorf 2000) that lives "everywhere" seems more like a superficial bird's-eye view from the perspective of transnational elites such as global players in the areas of diplomacy and transnational organizations, business, architecture or arts, and highly specialized natural scientists. For these elites, the world has actually shrunk.

Portable communication devices may even simulate this delimitation in the everyday life of the masses. Nevertheless, most people live locally—no matter how far they travel for their vacation trips with low-cost airlines. So, indeed, social life becomes more and more dense spatially and accelerates temporally. While at the beginning of cartographic representations fantastic monsters were needed to somehow enliven the blank spaces on maps, the blue planet can now be visualized right down to the last corner. In Google Street View, one can see streets and house facades. Using Google Earth, one can obtain an overview of landscapes or zoom into a living room. Above all, geographic information systems have been developed with multi-dimensional markings and layers of landscapes, integrating data about their history and much more. Transport, travel, and the imagination of personal accessibility to any place or territory at any time decrease spatial distance and thus create a feeling of a densification of the world, too.

In stark contrast to these processes, the worldwide right-wing populist movements, with their hate-fueling, contagious, and fearmongering rhetoric, have become the latest carriers of the call for an uprising of the "sedentary." Underlying this process is a class struggle because, at an objective level, social inequality has been increasing and the opportunities for overcoming it have been decreasing, while subjective values and aspirations are converging on a global scale (Rehberg 2006a).

Apocalyptical spatial materiality?

With the exception of the analysis of the Egyptian and Asian hydraulic cultures, scientists have rarely taken into account the role of ecological conditions of space for the rise and fall of great empires. However, at various periods, European intellectuals have projected their fears about uncontrollable influences over society onto the decline of Rome. They pointed out its decadence, decay of morals, extensive militarization, increasing contrasts between poor and rich, and failure as a state. One of the causes for the decline of this ancient empire was also the depletion of natural resources. Adam Ferguson, in 1766, or later Justus von Liebig, postulated that at all times it is the land that "holds human society together or drives it apart and makes nations and states disappear or makes them powerful" (Demandt 1984, 348). Alexander Demandt argued that depletion of the soil resulted in the impoverishment of free farmers over "plantation cultivation of large landowners with their troops of slaves," leading to increasing grain prices and finally to a population decline (ibid.). Georg Sigwart hypothesized in 1915 that the decline of Sparta, Athens, and Greece in general and the decline of Etruria, the Roman Republic, and the Roman Empire were all caused by the leaching of the soil, leading to "impoverishment, inflation and a reacting despotism" (ibid., 349). In this view, every culture that produces a desert eventually annihilates itself.

Today, in the—rather repentantly than proudly—so-called Anthropocene, most people are—at least abstractly—aware of the fact that nature increasingly seems to push back against being permanently forced into submission by humankind or, as the

Vulgate and Luther's Bible presented it, as a mission directly out of the mouth of the world's creator: to "subdue the world." Key terms of the anticipated ecological disaster include "global warming," "desertification," "acidification," "overfishing of the oceans," "destruction of rainforests," and many more. The United Nations estimates the livelihood of 1.5 billion people to be under threat, and humanity literally "is losing its footing" (Latour 2018, 13): climate is changing and will cause an increase in natural disasters, as has become noticeable in recent years, even in Central Europe.

These essentially humanmade phenomena require us to develop new perceptions and categories of spatial presence and perceptions, as nature intrudes into the virtual spaces of comfort provided to us by the media. One might think of the return of an unsolicited presence of space, which is no longer a symbol of great power but rather of a self-inflicted impotence. Jakob van Hoddis had already anticipated this in a vibrant expressionist manner in 1911 (1977):

World's End

From burgher's pointy head flies the hat.
In all quarters resounds hullaballoo.
Roof tilers plummet down and break in two.
Along the coasts—one reads—the floodings rise.

The storm is here, wuthering seas are hopping
Ashore to crush dams as if they were midges.
Most people have a cold that is not stopping.
The railway waggons tumble down from bridges.

Acknowledgements

For their contributions to this chapter, I wish to sincerely thank Martin Siebert, who translated the text, Richard Groß for copyediting, Zoya Solovieva and Zachary Mühlenweg for their language editing, and Stephen Mennell and Christian Sander for their thoughtful remarks. I also thank Carolin Thiele, Bettina Haßkamp-Böhmer, Rose Marie Schulz-Rehberg, Laura Förster, and Gerrit Morrin for their support and helpful suggestions. I would like to especially thank Nina Baur for her very constructive and committed editorial revision and stylistic advice, as well as the Dresden Latinist and China connoisseur Fritz-Heiner Mutschler for imparting important literature and valuable pointers regarding cultural comparisons between the ancient empires.

References

Baecker, Dirk. 2007. *Studien zur nächsten Gesellschaft*. Frankfurt am Main: Suhrkamp.
Beck, Ulrich. 1997. *Was ist Globalisierung? Irrtümer des Globalismus—Antworten auf Globalisierung*. Frankfurt am Main: Suhrkamp.
Beck, Ulrich. 2005. "Europäisierung." *Aus Politik und Zeitgeschichte* 34–35: 3–10.

Berger, H. 1907. "Europe." In *Pauly's Real-Encyclopädie der Klassischen Altertumswissenschaft*, Vol. 11, edited by Georg Wissowa, 1287–1310. Stuttgart: Metzler.

Bloch, Marc. (1939) 1982. *Die Feudalgesellschaft*. Frankfurt am Main: Propyläen.

Braudel, Fernand. (1949) 1996. *The Mediterranean and the Mediterranean World in the Age of Philip II*, 2 Vols. Berkeley: University of California Press.

Cassirer, Ernst. 1972. *An Essay on Man*. New Haven: Yale University Press.

Dahrendorf, Ralf. 2000. "Die globale Klasse und die neue Ungleichheit." *Merkur* 54 (619): 1057–1068.

Demandt, Alexander. 1984. *Der Fall Roms: Die Auflösung des römischen Reiches im Urteil der Nachwelt*. München: Beck.

Eisenstadt, Shmuel N., ed. 1986. *The Origins and Diversity of Axial Age Civilizations*. Albany: SUNY Press.

Elias, Norbert. (1939) 1969. *The Civilizing Process: Sociogenetic and Psychogenetic Investigations*. Vol. 1: *The History of Manners*. Oxford: Blackwell.

Elias, Norbert. (1939) 1982. *The Civilizing Process: Sociogenetic and Psychogenetic Investigations*. Vol. 2: *State Formation and Civilization*. Oxford: Blackwell.

Fustel de Coulanges, Numa Denis. 1877. *The Ancient City: A Study of the Religion, Laws, and Institutions of Greece and Rome*. Boston: Lee and Shepard/New York: Dillingham.

Gehlen, Arnold. (1940) 1988. *Man: His Nature and Place in the World*. New York: Columbia University Press.

Gehlen, Arnold. (1957) 1980. *Man in the Age of Technology*. New York: Columbia University Press.

Grimm, Hans. 1932. *Volk ohne Raum*, München: Langen-Müller.

Gumplowicz, Ludwig. 1905. *Ausgewählte Werke*, Vol. 1, edited by Franz Oppenheimer and Gottfried Salomon. Innsbruck: Universitätsverlag.

Günzel, Stephan, ed. 2010. *Raum. Ein interdisziplinäres Handbuch*. Stuttgart: Metzler.

Haubold, Johannes. 2013. *Greece and Mesopotamia: Dialogues in Literature*, Cambridge: Cambridge University Press.

Herodotus. 1920. *The Persian Wars*, Vol. III: Books 1–7. Cambridge: Cambridge University Press.

Hoddis, Jakob van (1911) 1977. *World's End*. Manchester: Carcanet New Press.

Holzinger, Elisabeth. 2007. "Raum verloren, Räume gewonnen—Veränderungstendenzen der räumlichen Organisation der Gesellschaft." In *Lebensstile, soziale Lagen und Siedlungsstrukturen*, edited by Jens S. Dangschat and Alexander Hamedinger, 51–70. Hannover: Verlag der ARL.

Koselleck, Reinhart. 1972. "Einleitung." In *Geschichtliche Grundbegriffe. Historisches Lexikon zur politisch-sozialen Sprache in Deutschland*, Vol. 1, edited by Otto Brunner, Werner Conze, and Reinhart Koselleck, XIII—XXVII. Stuttgart: Klett.

Köster, Werner. 1992. "Raum, politischer." In *Historisches Wörterbuch der Philosophie*, Vol. 8, edited by Joachim Ritter and Karlfried Gründer, 122–131. Basel: Schwabe.

Latour, Bruno. 2018. *Das terrestrische Manifest*. Berlin: Suhrkamp.

Lavan, Myles, Richard E. Payne, and John Weisweiler, eds. 2016. *Cosmopolitanism and Empire: Universal Rulers, Local Elites, and Cultural Integration in the Ancient Near East and Mediterranean*. Oxford: Oxford University Press.

Lefebvre, Henri. 1991. *The Production of Space*. Oxford: Blackwell.

Löw, Martina. 2001. *Raumsoziologie*. Frankfurt am Main: Suhrkamp.

Luhmann, Niklas. 1975. "Die Weltgesellschaft." In Niklas Luhmann. *Soziologische Aufklärung*, Vol. 2, 51–71. Opladen. Westdeutscher Verlag.

Michalowski, Piotr. 2014. "The Presence of the Past in Early Mesopotamian Writings." In *Thinking, Recording, and Writing History in the Ancient World*, edited by Kurt A. Raaflaub, 144–168. Chichester: Wiley Blackwell.

Mommsen, Theodor. 1862. *The History of Rome*, Vol. 1. Cambridge: Cambridge University Press.

Mutschler, Fritz-Heiner. 2008. "The Problem of 'Imperial Historiography' in Rome." In *Conceiving the Empire: China and Rome Compared*, edited by Fritz-Heiner Mutschler and Achim Mittag, 119–141. Oxford: Oxford University Press.

Mutschler, Fritz-Heiner, and Achim Mittag, eds. 2008. *Conceiving the Empire: China and Rome Compared*. Oxford: Oxford University Press.

Parzinger, Hermann. 2016. *Abenteuer Archäologie: Eine Reise durch die Menschheitsgeschichte*. München: Beck.

Pascal, Blaise (1670) 1958. *Pensées*. New York: Dutton.

Pieterse, Jan Nederveen. 1998. "Der Melange-Effekt: Globalisierung im Plural." In *Perspektiven der Weltgesellschaft*, edited by Ulrich Beck, 87–124. Frankfurt am Main: Suhrkamp.

Pines, Yuri. 2012. *The Everlasting Empire: The Political Culture of Ancient China and Its Imperial Legacy*. Princeton: Princeton University Press.

Plessner, Helmuth. (1928) 1981. *Die Stufen des Organischen und der Mensch*, Vol. IV of Helmuth Plessner. *Gesammelte Schriften*, edited by Günter Dux, Odo Marquard, and Elisabeth Ströker. Frankfurt am Main: Suhrkamp.

Plessner, Helmuth. (1935) 1982. Die Verspätete Nation, Vol. VI of Helmuth Plessner. *Gesammelte Schriften*, edited by Günter Dux, Odo Marquard, and Elisabeth Ströker. Frankfurt am Main: Suhrkamp.

Ratzel, Friedrich. 1882, 1891. *Anthropogeographie*. 2 vols. Stuttgart: Engelhorn.

Ratzel, Friedrich. 1897. *Politische Geographie*. München: Oldenbourg.

Rehberg, Karl-Siegbert. 2006a. "Die unsichtbare Klassengesellschaft." In *Soziale Ungleichheit, kulturelle Unterschiede: Verhandlungen des 32. Kongresses der Deutschen Gesellschaft für Soziologie in München 2004*, edited by Karl-Siegbert Rehberg, 19–38. Frankfurt am Main: Campus.

Rehberg, Karl-Siegbert. 2006b. "Macht-Räume als Objektivationen sozialer Beziehungen." In *Machträume der frühneuzeitlichen Stadt*, edited by Christian Hochmuth and Susanne Rau, 41–55. Konstanz: UVK.

Rehberg, Karl-Siegbert. 2009. "Kunst." In *Handbuch Anthropologie: Der Mensch zwischen Natur, Kultur und Technik*, edited by Eike Bohlken and Christian Thies, 359–363. Stuttgart: Metzler.

Rehberg, Karl-Siegbert. 2014. *Symbolische Ordnungen: Beiträge zu einer soziologischen Theorie der Institutionen*, edited by Hans Vorländer. Baden-Baden: Nomos.

Rehberg, Karl-Siegbert. 2017. "Differenzierungs-Transformationen gegen eine theoretisch verdeckte soziale Ungleichheit: Anmerkungen zu Niklas Luhmanns historisierender Systemtheorie." In *Un/Ordnungen denken: Beiträge zu den Historischen Kulturwissenschaften*, edited by Anne Gräfe and Johannes Menzel, 188–215. Berlin: Quintus.

Rehberg, Karl-Siegbert. 2019. "Herrscher als Typusfiguren der Verkörperung institutioneller Macht im Kampffeld von Spannungsbalancen." In *Die Macht des Herrschers: Personale und transpersonale Aspekte*, edited by Mechthild Albert, Elke Brüggen, and Konrad Klaus, 27–68. Göttingen: Bonn University Press.

Robertson, Roland. 1994. "Globalization or Glocalization?" *Journal of International Communication* 1 (1): 33–52.

Rollinger, Robert. 2014. "Thinking and Writing about History in Teispid and Achaemenid Persia." In *Thinking, Recording, and Writing History in the Ancient World*, edited by Kurt A. Raaflaub, 187–212. Chichester: Wiley Blackwell.

Scheler, Max. (1928) 2009. *The Human Place in the Cosmos*. Evanston: Northwestern University Press.

Schmitt, Carl. (1942) 1997. *Land and Sea*. Washington, DC: Plutarch Press.

Schmitt, Carl. (1950) 2003. *The Nomos of the Earth in the International Law of the Jus Publicum Europaeum*. New York: Telos Press.

Schroer, Markus. 2006. *Räume, Orte, Grenzen: Auf dem Weg zu einer Soziologie des Raums*. Frankfurt am Main: Suhrkamp.

Simmel, Georg. (1908) 2009. *Sociology: Inquiries into the Construction of Social Forms*, Vol. 2. Leiden: Brill.

Stevens, Kathryn. 2016. "Empire Begins at Home: Local Elites and Imperial Ideologies in Hellenistic Greece and Babylonia." In *Cosmopolitanism and Empire: Universal Rulers, Local Elites, and Cultural Integration in the Ancient Near East and Mediterranean*, edited by Myles Lavan, Richard E. Payne, and John Weisweiler, 65–88. New York: Oxford University Press.

Tocqueville, Alexis de (1835) 1961. *Democracy in America*. New York: Schocken.

Weisweiler, John. 2016. "From Empire to World-State: Ecumenical Language and Cosmopolitan Consciousness in the Later Roman Aristocracy." In *Cosmopolitanism and Empire: Universal Rulers, Local Elites, and Cultural Integration in the Ancient Near East and Mediterranean*, edited by Myles Lavan, Richard E. Payne, and John Weisweiler, 187–208. New York: Oxford University Press.

Yang, Huang, and Fritz-Heiner Mutschler. 2008. "The Emergence of Empire: Rome and the Surrounding World in Historical Narratives from the Late Third Century BC to the Early First Century AD." In *Conceiving the Empire: China and Rome Compared*, edited by Fritz-Heiner Mutschler and Achim Mittag, 91–114. Oxford: Oxford University Press.

Zekl, Hans Günter. 1992. "Raum, griechische Antike." In *Historisches Wörterbuch der Philosophie*, Vol. 8, edited by Joachim Ritter and Karlfried Gründer, 67–82. Basel: Schwabe.

4
THE HISTORICITY OF THE REFIGURATION OF SPACES UNDER THE SCRUTINY OF PRE-COVID-19 SÃO PAULO HOMELESS PEDESTRIANS[1]

Fraya Frehse

The implicitness of historicity

This chapter aims to contribute to the "refiguration of spaces" approach by critically addressing the concept of historicity on which it relies. Assuming historicity as a "time determination" based on links between past, present, and future events (Weidenhaus 2015, 24), the issue concerns the historicity that underlies this figurational approach to the so-called production of space, which in sociology summarizes the macro- and micro-social processes involved in the generation and/or regeneration of space as a set of bodily and materially mediated social relations (Frehse 2020, 3–4).

Since Karl Marx's pioneering conceptualization of societal historicity (Weidenhaus 2015, 194), various social scientists have developed their own approaches to the socially specific rhythms of historic change in different societies. If we, against the backdrop of this debate, consider that the refiguration of spaces was conceived as a "diagnosis of the present time" (Knoblauch 2017, 16–17, 381–398) that "makes it possible to explain the dynamics of contemporary societies" (Knoblauch and Löw 2017, 16), the historicity of the sociospatial process inquired by the approach becomes a conceptually unescapable issue.

So far, however, the historicity of the refiguration of spaces has only been addressed implicitly. By assuming the "acceleration of social life" as an overall empirical assessment, Hubert Knoblauch and Martina Löw (2017, 1) emphasize their conceptual commitment to Hartmut Rosa's (2005, 11) thesis on social acceleration as a historically speedier-than-before orientation of social change that particularizes "our present society." Indeed, Rosa's temporal diagnosis also corroborates alternative conceptualizations of the relationship between time and the production of space by authors who use the "refiguration of spaces" approach (Weidenhaus 2015; Christmann 2015; Knoblauch 2017).

DOI: 10.4324/9781003036159-5

A second indirect allusion to the historicity of the refiguration of spaces substantiates the conceptual construction of the approach. Its authors are interested in threefold spatial changes from the last fifty years regarding bodily and materially mediated communicative action amid specific post-war societal processes that social theory termed "modernity" and later "globalization" (Knoblauch and Löw 2017, 6–11). The multiplication of both contexts of meaning ("polycontexturalization") and the forms of communication ("mediatization") go alongside "the embedment of social units, such as families, neighborhoods and religious communities" into increasing physical and digital mobility circuits ("translocalization") (Knoblauch and Löw 2017, 11–14). Based on Norbert Elias' figuration concept, the authors propose that polycontexturalization, mediatization, and translocalization are processes of spatial *re*figuration, or the spatial transformation of the "centralized figuration" that characterizes "modern society" (Knoblauch and Löw 2017, 10).

Both implicit references to historicity suggest that the refiguration of spaces is a linear transformation of a relatively slow past into an accelerated present. It does not matter that "social acceleration" implies a possible "frantic standstill" (Rosa 2005, 460). Indeed, according to the authors of the "refiguration of spaces" approach, not even COVID-19 has changed the "general spatial pattern" in focus (Löw and Knoblauch 2020, 222), although "particularly the western world" will "witness a refiguration" of the "established 'interaction order'" (Goffman 1983) after quarantine (Löw and Knoblauch 2020, 224). Therefore, it is more precise to propose that the *model of historicity* implicit in the production of space from the 1970s is one of *poly-linear acceleration*. Its linearity is as multiple as the communicative actions through which spaces have been refigured.

In the wake of two former critical appraisals of approaches to historicity in the sociology of relational space from the 1950s (Frehse 2017; 2020), this chapter addresses the operational consequences inherent in the historicity model of poly-linear acceleration on the empirical reach of the "refiguration of spaces" approach. I argue that this model restricts the mobilization of the approach in empirical fields marked by *alternative* models of historicity. This especially applies to empirically given *patterns of spatialization implicit in social interaction*: their temporal immediacy is underpinned by a *plurality of social temporalities of a historical nature* that challenge the unicity of the poly-linear acceleration model.

In order to demonstrate this proposition within the limits of this chapter, I focus on Knoblauch and Löw's hypothesis on the increasing physical and digital mobility implicit in translocalization. I firstly confront this statement with a sociospatial phenomenon that has increasingly characterized São Paulo, the biggest Latin American city, precisely within the time span curtailed by the "refiguration of spaces" approach: homelessness. More specifically, in the second section, I apply a specific dialectical-cum-phenomenological methodology to the historicity implicit in the patterns of spatialization of bodily and materially mediated (non-)verbal interaction by specific homeless pedestrians in São Paulo's pre-COVID downtown streets and squares in order to depict what the underlying model of historicity discloses about the production of public space in the city. Hence, what comes to the conceptual forefront is a historically at the very least bitemporal process of dialectical space (*re*)production, which transcends the implicit poly-linear acceleration of the refiguration of space. This model conclusively signals to three contributions of this chapter for expanding the empirical plausibility of the "refiguration of spaces" approach.

Homelessness as empirical counterevidence to increasing mobility

Since the 1980s, rough sleeping has been added to the social–political, geographical, and sociological agendas in cities as diverse as Los Angeles, New York, London, Toronto, Paris, São Paulo, Singapore, and Melbourne. Given the continuously expanding urban palette, homelessness has become a worldwide issue (Bainbridge and Carrizales 2017), often in connection with other materializations of housing that policyholders qualify as "inadequate": temporary shelters, evictions, and "illegal campsites" (FEANTSA 2015). Particularly in São Paulo, roughly 45% of the almost 24,500 homeless people identified as such (2019), among the city's 12.5 million total inhabitants are demographically settled in the city's downtown district Sé.

International scholarship on the bodily dimension of homelessness—in other words, on the interference of simultaneously physical and symbolic human skills on the phenomenon at stake—often alludes to "mobility" in order to heighten the role played by physically moving through urban public places on a regular basis in characterizing homeless people (see, for example, Kawash 1998; Mitchell 2005; Frangella 2009; Blomley 2010). This conceptual association comes as no surprise if we remember that the homeless' mobility is often explained with the aid of empirical references to police repression against these people's daily physical presence in streets, squares, parks, and other places.

Given that "in recent decades" (Clarke and Parsell 2018, 1952) the surveillance and punitive practices in Anglo-American cities have co-developed with policies aimed at turning downtowns into "sites of consumption and leisure," it becomes conceptually tempting to pair the physical mobility implicit in homelessness with the historical increase in digital and physical mobility that is addressed by the "refiguration of spaces" approach—and hence, with its implicit model of poly-linear acceleration.

However, things are conceptually more complex when we focus on one definite bodily and material evidence of homelessness in the pre-COVID São Paulo downtown streets and squares during the shop opening hours: the "maloca" (Figure 4.1), a popular Brazilian label for for "indigenous hut," which is used by homeless people in Brazilian cities to identify their daily face-to-face gatherings in public places (Frangella 2009, 153, 184; Frehse 2013, 119–122; Robaina 2015, 328–330)—at least until corona entered the scene.

There are still no research data about these gathering-malocas in COVID São Paulo—meaning the time between the municipality's official closure of commercial and service establishments as well as parks (March 2020) and now (July 2020). But the pre-COVID central public places daily hosted uncountable gatherings of

FIGURE 4.1 Research clues of a *gathering-maloca* in São Paulo's cathedral square on a Wednesday afternoon, 20 April 2011

Source: Photo by Fraya Frehse/private collection

at least three homeless men, less frequently women, and more rarely children, surrounded by specific material goods. These ranged from plastic bags and backpacks, blankets and sometimes mattresses or pillows, to trolleys and buggies as well as second- or third-hand cardboard boxes and chairs from surrounding rubbish bins, in addition to second-hand clothes and accessories such as caps and sunglasses, umbrellas, shoes, and clandestine merchandise from the discreet clandestine fair ("feira do rolo") nearby (Frehse 2014, 254). All of this coexisted in these essentially symbolic places devoid of objective physical borders, which the homeless used to call malocas, together with low-cost variations of the sugar-cane drink "cachaça" and tobacco alongside marijuana cigarettes, cocaine stones, and crack pipes. It did not matter that mobile police stations lay only a few meters away, or that mobile policemen and women patrolled the sites daily amid the to and fro of other, more or less mobile pedestrians.

This empirical evidence undeniably challenges scholarly international commonsense about the prevailing physical mobility of homeless people in urban public spaces. The challenge becomes conceptually even more vexing when we consider that the number of regular homeless gatherings in São Paulo's downtown streets and squares was also remarked on in the first studies about begging and homelessness in the city. Until the 1970s, rough sleepers were socially labelled "beggars" (Stoeffels

1977) and physically remained in what have been referred to as spots ("pontos") of São Paulo's downtown public places. Individual begging (Stoeffels 1977, 123), rough sleeping (Vieira, Bezerra, and Rosa 1992, 49), resting, or "the earning of subsistence" (Simões 1992, 37) were safe due to group strategies (Stoeffels 1977, 123). Hence, it makes sense that in the early 1990s the spots were recognized as "the preferred gathering locales of the street population" (Simões 1992, 37).

All in all, what we observe is not increasing mobility but rather *persistent physical immobility amid mobility*. This state of affairs has persisted despite the fact that the São Paulo municipality abolished park benches and any other functional seating devices from downtown streets and squares in 2007.

Therefore, homelessness in pre-COVID São Paulo's downtown public places is clearly useful for the purposes of this chapter. As we will see with the aid of a four-step methodological approach that brings together Erving Goffman and Henri Lefebvre, the empirical assessment in focus contradicts the hypothesis of increasing mobility that underpins the "refiguration of spaces" approach due to the model of historicity implicit in the patterns of homeless interaction that become spatial in the malocas.

The production of space through the historicity implicit in the spatialization of interaction

My methodological sensitivity to what I term *spatialization patterns of social interaction* stems from Erving Goffman's analysis of the temporality and spatiality of face-to-face interaction (see Frehse 2020, 10–12). He focused in analytical terms on the (temporal) immediacy of (spatial) situations comprising bodily and materially mediated non-verbal and verbal conduct—in other words, communicative rules that are respectively forged in the individuals' "body idiom," put into action by means of material objects in places (Goffman 1963, 33–42), and shared by groups of "adherents" (Goffman 1967, 49). Thereby, this author drew sociologists' attention to the symbolic regularities involved in (non-)verbal interaction becoming spatial—and hence, for example, bringing to the conceptual forefront "regions" and "territories" (Goffman 1959; 1963; 1967; 1971; Frehse 2020; 2021; forthcoming/2021).

From this standpoint, the spatialization of interaction implies the temporally immediate production of various social orderings of space—or spatialities—within the spatial boundaries of social interaction—or situations (Frehse 2020, 8, 11). Hence, my search of spatialization patterns of interaction becomes operational: once the patterns of (non-)verbal interaction are analytically identified, we may address the spatialities that humans produce immediately by means of these same bodily and materially mediated interactions.

In this methodological step, the historicity of the spatialities of interaction enters the analytical scene—and Goffman leaves it. Although admitting that not everything that occurs (immediately) "*in* a situation" is "of" it, his focus was on the interactional dimension of what I term spatiality—in his words, the "*situational* aspect of a situated activity*" (Goffman 1963, 22; 1983, 2; original emphasis).

Therefore, it comes as no surprise that the historicity of interaction is absent from Goffman's work (Frehse 2020, 21), and also from recent international scholarship that mobilizes his space concepts (Frehse 2021).

But the historicity implicit in the spatialization of interaction remains underexplored in other current sociological strands as well. One relatively recent historical–sociological approach to historical transformations in patterns of interaction (Baur 2005, 100, 103–107) emphasizes the causality of timing, the form and duration of these changes rather than what is of interest in this chapter: the entanglements of historical temporalities within *the temporally immediate spatialities* of interaction. Nevertheless, even that approach remains rare in a scholarly landscape that usually privileges the temporal immediacy of interaction. The same applies to the debate on the production of space (Frehse 2020; for an exception, see Frehse 2017).

Subsidized by a former empirical demonstration that the historicity of the empirically inquired sociospatial processes influences their production (Frehse 2017), my specific statement here is that the historicity of the spatialities of interaction by the homeless pedestrians in São Paulo's pre-COVID malocas interfered by means of these homeless bodies with the production of space in the city's downtown—and hence also, in theoretical terms, with the sociospatial processes addressed by the "refiguration of spaces" approach. What remains open is the "how" of this interference.

In search of an answer, I again (Frehse 2014; 2017) turn to Henri Lefebvre's three-step regressive–progressive method (2001, 73–74). Although developed in the early 1950s, it remains unique in combining the ethnographic "description" of social relations and material elements in various empirical fields with the "analytical-regressive" depiction of their historical dates, or ages—in other words, the specific temporal moments of social history in which they emerged (Lefebvre 2001, 65–66). The aim is a "historical-genetic" interpretation of what their historically more or less contradictory temporal coexistence discloses in dialectical terms about wider social transformations—and particularly about phenomenological and historical trends in the "production of space" (Lefebvre 2000; Frehse 2020, 12–15). Given that homeless people are not subjects of historicity in Lefebvre's sense—which stems from Marx's reflections on the historicity of mankind—and that Lefebvre addressed neither social interaction nor its spatialities (Frehse 2017, 518), I freely adjust his method to my aim of describing, analyzing, and interpreting how the historicity of the spatialization patterns of social interaction interferes with the production of space.

Therefore, in theoretical terms, this interference is dialectical instead of causal. Without resorting to historical determinism, Lefebvre (2001, 22) argues that "the historical" persists and acts upon "the actual" everywhere, given that "the society in act, the result and product of the social activities" is "inscribed" in space through the mediation of (past) time. Hence, "the space generated by time is always actual" (Lefebvre 2000, 131). Methodologically, this implies privileging the analytical tool that I term *historical dating* rather than the pair chronology-timing, which is employed in historical sciences and historical sociology in search of causality chains

(Baur 2005, 81–83; Hergesell 2019, 56–58; Hergesell, Baur, and Braunisch 2020, 276–280).

As we will see from this point forward, the overall methodological outcome of this singular theoretical encounter between Goffman and Lefebvre is a regressive–progressive procedure that descriptively departs from (i) rules of (non-)verbal interaction in order to analytically depict (ii) their spatialities, whose historical dates may then (iii) be scrutinized with the aim of (iv) interpreting what the underlying historicity discloses about the production of space. When applied to my ethnographic fieldnotes and interview transcriptions about one maloca in particular that regularly took place in São Paulo's cathedral square (Praça da Sé) from February to July 2013, this approach evinces a peculiar *historical poly-temporality* that mediated the *bodily (re)production* of an immobile public space by the pre-COVID São Paulo homeless amid their own and other pedestrians' mobility in the city's downtown.

Step 1: descriptively identifying rules of (non-verbal) interaction

I was introduced to the sugar-cane drink maloca on the first day of my thirteen-month period of systematic fieldwork in the five major squares of downtown São Paulo during the shop opening afternoons (2–6 p.m.) on Mondays and Fridays. Based on (non-)verbal interaction with twenty-seven maloca members during participant observation of the maloca, and with ten members during in-depth interviews "in" the same setting, I grasped a social structure composed, on the one hand, of a nucleus ranging from three to eight homeless pedestrians (at least three men, at maximum five men and three women). They physically stayed on a regular basis either at or around one specific spot around the low walls that separated the square's gardened area from the cathedral's rectangular forecourt. On the other hand, the maloca comprised a periphery of mobile (ex-)homeless pedestrians, who used to visit the nucleus somewhat regularly (of the aforementioned twenty-seven pedestrians, ten were homeless and seventeen ex-homeless and/or loiterers). Visits occurred especially on Friday afternoons, when a samba circle ("roda de samba") enlivened the maloca with the aid of drums improvised out of cans and wooden or paper cardboard boxes. On workdays, the gathering regularly vanished from the square after 6 p.m. This was when the stores and government agencies started to close their doors and the public shelters started to open theirs. Hence, passers-by and *non-passers-by* (Frehse 2014, 252) such as the maloca members made their way to their (rough) sleeping places.

The social structure at stake became analytically visible to me due to *six* rules for what I have termed *body conduct* (Frehse 2017, 518). It was by means of these patterns that the reproduction of spatialized (non-)verbal interactions took place in the maloca, at least on workdays:

1   The gathering's bodily and material layout stemmed from the aforementioned temporally regular physical behavior of *immobility amid mobility*, which the maloca members shared in the square;

2   As for the maloca's access to (limited) material resources, a straightforward division of labor aimed at the *acquisition of food for all*. Twice a day, two nucleus members departed in order to either beg for food or to identify sources of collective food distribution;
3   There was a similarly straightforward *collective division of gains*. Any money obtained by the members was converted into cachaça or marijuana contributions to the maloca;
4   The *collective attempt to protect the members' individual stuff* peculiarly condenses the former three rules. The (only sparsely extant) personal belongings of each member were not to be touched by anyone, and the nucleus tried to defend them jointly—depending on their degree of soberness;
5   As for the maloca's intramural sociability, there was the *interactional valorization of identity labels regarding specific family members*. Each nucleus member had a family-role label: "father," "mother," "sister," "brother," "sister-" and "brother-in-law," and "mistress." Moreover, the maloca hosted a variety of these nuclear families (the members verbally informed me of at least four). By the same token, the maloca's female members verbally conveyed that they wished to be "married" to male members instead of being single—a condition they equated to socially despised prostitutes;
6   Regarding extramural sociability, there was the members' *(non-)verbal welcoming of (non-)passing-by visitors* like myself and other passers-by—but never the police! When arriving for the first time, visitors were invited to eat and drink for free, mainly at a Friday afternoon chicken barbecue that was improvised around the square's low walls with a whole chicken and a gas cooker.

Step 2: analytically identifying spatialities within the rules of interaction

As to the spatialities of the six patterns of body conduct, they are twofold:

1   *The (non-)everyday*: The maloca members mobilized the rules at stake in the temporal immediacy of situations that were reproduced at least on workdays. This circumstance suggests that their spatiality is "the everyday" as the spatial realm of socially repetitive and doxic uses of cyclic and linear rhythms (Frehse 2020, 8). Indeed, the maloca's physical size in the square also varied on a daily basis: its spatially systolic–diastolic feature repeated itself indefinitely. *Simultaneously*, however, these spatial repetitions did *not* follow cyclic or linear rhythms. Instead, they applied to the socially forged *propensity* for physical immobility amid mobility, for the collective search for food, for money gains, for the protection of belongings, and for socializing within the maloca's imprecise spatial borders. Temporal routines did not apply to the *factual effectiveness* of this propensity, which was completely arbitrary: the maloca's bodily and material reproduction depended on the individual degree of soberness to the also random repressive initiatives by the police. Therefore, I consider *the* dialectical *(non-) everyday* a decisive spatiality of the six rules of body conduct.

2   *The factual(-imaginary) social space of marginalization(-integration)*: In sociological terms, the rules suggest that each maloca member was factually alone within the joint marginal social space that encompassed them altogether due to common biographical traits (mental health conditions, family and migration background, socioeconomic poverty). At the same time, however, the patterns were framed within an alternative joint spatiality concerning the maloca members' positions in social space. Their factual social positions did not prevent them from imagining, that is to say, mobilizing their intrinsically human ability to symbolically produce images, which are "forms" of "the imaginary" (Lefebvre 1980, 240). From this theoretical viewpoint, the imaginary is one historically specific "relation between the (reflected, subjective) conscience and the real as such"—in other words, "the immediate" (Lefebvre 1980, 56, 42)—which is "mediated" in symbolic terms by the massive, industrially driven production of images that prevails in post-war capitalism (Lefebvre 1980, 56). Therefore, *the factual social space of social marginalization* that involves the maloca's members *simultaneously encompasses an imaginary dimension of social integration*: a large family that comprises indefinite smaller, nuclear families and acquainted visitors. This essentially symbolic space of belonging socially integrated the maloca members in a way that was denied to them by the social space where they were located in sociological terms due to social indicators. Both spatialities coexisted dialectically. It does not matter that the family compounds were contingent, stemming from affective affinities between daily (re)established heterosexual couples, solo members, and passing-by acquaintances. Under the aegis of such affinities, the rules of interaction between all of these pedestrians were quickly reordered within a categorial set of parenthood terms that bore its own sociospatial margins: "wives" despised female members "without a family" as being socially marginalized "mistresses."

Step 3: analytically dating the spatialities of interaction in historical terms

Regarding this methodological phase, a backward reading (Baur 2005, 84) of the corresponding social–scientific and historical literature is especially suitable:

1   As for the (non-)everyday, studies on various empirical objects implicitly offer empirical evidence of the historically persistent (non-)everyday routine of the poor in São Paulo's streets and squares: the experience of homeless children therein during the 1990s (Gregori 2000); the corporality of homeless adults during the 2000s (Frangella 2009); the bodily uses of this city's downtown streets and squares by pedestrians in different historical moments ranging from the colonial and slaveholding early nineteenth century to the 2010s (Frehse 2011; 2017; 2018a; 2018b); the historical contradictions implicit in conceptually mobilizing the everyday in order to understand the "conscience of the ordinary man" in early twenty-first–century Brazil (Martins 2008). These data testify to a historically long-standing routine that is made up of the temporally

and spatially aleatory character of at least two sociospatial traits of São Paulo's downtown public places, starting in the officially post-slavery late nineteenth century (i.e. as of 1888). I am referring, on the one hand, to police repression regarding social activities by the poor (street vending, loitering etc.) and, on the other hand, to the situational components implicit in these pedestrians' (non-)verbal interactions with other pedestrians and workers or inhabitants of the surrounding buildings.

These findings not only confirm that, as pioneered by Lefebvre (1968), the everyday is a particular historical product, which emerged in the modern late nineteenth-century capitalist world, but also indicate that the (non-)everyday of the maloca on workdays dates back in historical terms to *the late nineteenth century*.

2   As for the factual(-imaginary) social space of marginalization(-integration), crucial historical dating references stem from a wider anthropological debate about family structure and female identity among the poor in urban Brazil as of the 1980s (Corrêa 1982; Sarti 2003, 19). This literature addresses human types whose factual marginalized social space owes everything to the fact that they lack the means that assign power, wealth, and prestige to individuals in a capitalist society (Sarti 2003, 19–20). At the same time, the studies suggest that the maloca's imaginary large family of families and visitors can be accounted for by the spatially far-reaching role played by the family as a distinctive moral set of consanguinity and affinity relations among the urban poor in São Paulo's peripherical districts at least since the 1980s. Grounded on a patriarchal and hierarchical structure within which the "whole" prevails over its "parts"—the individual members (Sarti 2003, 20)—and in which the woman holds a subordinate position (Sarti 2003, 20), the family's symbolic reference is a hierarchical moral code that transcends the "house" (casa), which has been a referential social and physical space in Brazil since colonial times (for a summary, see Frehse 2013, 102). Comprising neighborhood and work relations, too, this code "expands to the outside, and configures a system of values that impacts the ways in which the poor conceive and face the social world" (Sarti 2003, 21).

In light of these references, the maloca's social space, which is factually marginalized and imaginarily integrated, originated in *the 1980s*.

Step 4: interpreting the production of space through the historicity implicit in the spatialities of interaction

Given that both historical dates refer to spatialities of (non-)verbal interaction, they necessarily interfered with the bodily and material layout of São Paulo's cathedral square during the first semester of 2013. During the maloca's existence, the immobility amid mobility that characterized that public place was *also* due, on the one hand, to a (non-)everyday invigorated by the temporal coexistence between the post-slavery nineteenth and the early twenty-first centuries; and, on the other hand, to a factual(-imaginary) social space constantly enlivened by values of the 1980s regarding poor São Paulo families.

Hence, we notice one entanglement of historical temporalities. The first one is more than a century old, whereas the second is aged almost forty years. Their empirical simultaneity in the same square conceptually suggests that the sociospatial phenomenon maloca bears a *bitemporal historicity model at minimum*—that is to say, a *historical poly-temporality*. Now we may at last address the "how" of the interference. The historicity model indicates that during the maloca's existence, São Paulo's cathedral square was *reproduced* in bodily and material terms, on workdays, by means of the *spatially productive* temporal coexistence of at least the late nineteenth and the late twentieth centuries within the temporally immediate interactions of the square's (im)mobile homeless pedestrians. If we follow Lefebvre's (2001, 74) suggestion that the historical–genetic interpretation of the previously dated structures depends on assessing their transformations against the background of the further (internal or external) development and these structures' subordination to the overall structures (Frehse 2017, 517), a methodologically tempting reference of such an overall process (Lefebvre 2001, 74) is the production of urban public space within the aforementioned societal processes addressed by the "refiguration of spaces" approach.

From this standpoint, the production of public space in pre-COVID São Paulo was a bodily and materially *r*eproductive process spurred, among other things, by two spatialities of interaction whose (temporally immediate) *production* (i.e. spatialization) was due to the historical poly-temporality of the (non-)verbal interaction of homeless pedestrians in public places such as Praça da Sé. It was a sociospatial process of a dialectical nature, indeed a *bodily (re)production* of space underpinned in historical terms by a time-span that ranged from the late nineteenth to the early twenty-first century, and which *temporally coexisted* with the poly-linear accelerated vigor of mobility that has refigured this very space along with several others since the 1970s.

Conclusion: the relevance of historicity

Hence, we may return to this chapter's original objective. In order to increase the empirical plausibility of the "refiguration of spaces" approach, it would be advisable to turn the historicity models implicit in the production of space into an analytical issue. My regressive–progressive approach to the historicity of the patterns of spatialization implicit in the social interaction of particular homeless pedestrians in the pre-COVID São Paulo downtown public places demonstrated in a synthetic way that (i) space is produced by means of spatialities of social interaction that bear *various* historical dates; (ii) *different* models of historicity may *simultaneously* underpin one and the same societal process of space production; (iii) *no societal process of space production* is *overarchingly linear in historical terms*. As a whole, these findings show that specific historicity models interfere in *various* ways with empirically given processes of space production, and hence with their conceptualization. The models implicit in the spatialized interactions that empirically underlay the (im)mobile sugar-cane drink maloca indicate a *dialectical (re)production* of a persistent (im)mobile public space rather than the *linear refiguration* of an increasingly mobile one.

In light of these conceptual outcomes, a second contribution of this chapter to the "refiguration of spaces" approach may come to the fore. It would be worth engaging with dialectical approaches to the production of space in greater detail. Whether or not the dialectical method is "unique in addressing the multiple determinations of what is concrete" (Martins 2013, 74) should be of interest to a theory that addresses the spatial dynamics of contemporary societies. The aforementioned three conceptual findings of my method, for instance, indicate an absolute historical diversity within the temporally both immediate and simultaneous production of coexisting diverse spaces. Alternative temporal patterns may thus conceptually emerge and enrich the figurational understanding of spatialization processes.

This chapter's third and last input into the refiguration of spaces particularly concerns the relationship between homelessness and the production of space. A historically sensitive approach to the spatialization patterns of social interaction offers alternative findings to this debate. Instead of a commonsensical "social problem," homelessness is a *sociospatial* process, a specific way of producing (public) space within the wider set of spatial changes of the last fifty years encompassed by the "refiguration of spaces" approach. In pre-COVID São Paulo, the vigor of the immobility amid mobility of the homeless testifies to the fact that surely for economic, *but also* for sociocultural reasons related to the historicity of the bodily (re)production of public space by homeless pedestrians, mobility as a spatialized pattern of interaction was never fully established among homeless people in the city.

But what can be said about post-COVID São Paulo? In light of the epidemiologic intensity of COVID in this city, we could at first glance expect that the city's daily (im)mobile gatherings of homeless pedestrians have disappeared, thus confirming the aforementioned *re*figuration of the established interaction order. However, things are again more complex than that. The sociopolitical combination of a long-standing social inequality with an unprecedented social-political irresponsibility, which has recently prevailed in Brazil, implies that the current São Paulo streets and squares are increasingly the home of whole families. Therefore, although new spatialization patterns of interaction are certainly underway, they are supported by vivid reproductive rules. Public space continues to be (re)produced bodily.

Note

1 This research received grants from the Brazilian National Research Council (from 2018), the Alexander von Humboldt Foundation (2019), and the Centre of Latin American Studies of the University of Cambridge (2020). All translations from languages other than English are my own.

References

Bainbridge, Jay, and Tony Carrizales. 2017. "Global Homelessness in a Post-Recession World." *Journal of Public Management & Social Policy* 24 (1): 71–90.

Baur, Nina. 2005. *Verlaufsmusteranalyse*. Wiesbaden: VS Verlag.

Blomley, Nicholas. 2010. "The Right to Pass Freely: Circulation, Begging, and The Bounded Self." *Social & Legal Studies* 19 (3): 331–350.
Christmann, Gabriela B. 2015. "Das theoretische Konzept der kommunikativen Raum(re)konstruktion." In *Zur kommunikativen Konstruktion von Räumen*, edited by Gabriela B. Christmann, 89–117. Wiesbaden: Springer VS.
Clarke, Andrew, and Cameron Parsell. 2018. "The Potential for Urban Surveillance to Help Support People Who are Homeless: Evidence from Cairns, Australia." *Urban Studies* 56 (10): 1951–1967.
Corrêa, Mariza, ed. 1982. *Colcha de Retalhos*. São Paulo: Brasiliense.
FEANTSA (Fédération Européenne des Associations Nationales Travaillant avec les Sans-Abri). 2015. "ETHOS Typology on Homelessness and Housing Exclusion." www.feantsa.org/spip.php?article120&lang=en.
Frangella, Simone. 2009. *Corpos Urbanos Errantes*. São Paulo: Annablume/FAPESP.
Frehse, Fraya. 2011. *Ô da Rua!* São Paulo: Edusp.
Frehse, Fraya. 2013. "A rua no Brasil em questão (etnográfica)." *Anuário Antropológico* 38 (2): 99–129.
Frehse, Fraya. 2014. "For Difference 'in and through' São Paulo: The Regressive-Progressive Method." In *Urban Revolution Now*, edited by Lukasz Stanek, Ákos Moravánszky, and Christian Schmid, 243–262. Farnham: Ashgate.
Frehse, Fraya. 2017. "Relational Space Through Historically Relational Time—In the Bodies of São Paulo's Pedestrians." *Current Sociology Monograph* 65 (4): 511–532.
Frehse, Fraya. 2018a. "On Regressive-Progressive Rhythmanalysis." In *Perspectives on Henri Lefebvre*, edited by Jenny Bauer and Robert Fischer, 95–117. Berlin: De Gruyter.
Frehse, Fraya. 2018b. "On the Everyday History of Pedestrians' Bodies in São Paulo's Downtown amid Metropolization (1950–2000)." In *Urban Latin America*, edited by Bianca Freire-Medeiros and Julia O'Donnell, 15–35. London: Routledge.
Frehse, Fraya. 2020. "On the Temporalities and Spatialities of the Production of Space." *SFB 1265 Working Paper No. 4*. doi: 10.14279/depositonce-9492.
Frehse, Fraya. 2021. "Erving Goffman's Sociology of Physical Space for Architects and Urban Designers." In *The New Urban Condition*, edited by Tom Avermaete, Leandro Medrano, and Luiz Recamán, 73–85. New York: Taylor & Francis/Routledge.
Frehse, Fraya. Forthcoming/2021. "Concepts of Space (Region, Territory, Frame)." In *Goffman-Handbuch*, edited by Robert Hettlage and Karl Lenz. Berlin: J.B. Metzler.
Goffman, Erving. 1959. *The Presentation of Self in Everyday Life*. New York: Anchor Books.
Goffman, Erving. 1963. *Behavior in Public Places*. New York: The Free Press/Collier-Macmillan.
Goffman, Erving. 1967. *Interaction Ritual*. New York: Anchor Books.
Goffman, Erving. 1971. *Relations in Public*. New York: Harper Colophon Books.
Goffman, Erving. 1983. "The Interaction Order." *American Sociological Review* 48 (1): 1–17.
Gregori, Maria F. 2000. *Viração*. São Paulo: Companhia das Letras.
Hergesell, Jannis. 2019. *Technische Assistenzen in der Altenpflege*. Weinheim: Beltz Juventa.
Hergesell, Jannis, Nina Baur, and Lilli Braunisch. 2020. "Process-Oriented Sampling." *Canadian Review of Sociology* 57 (2): 265–285.
Kawash, Samira. 1998. "The Homeless Body." *Public Culture* 10 (2): 319–339.
Knoblauch, Hubert. 2017. *Die kommunikative Konstruktion der Wirklichkeit*. Wiesbaden: Springer VS.
Knoblauch, Hubert, and Martina Löw. 2017. "On the Spatial Re-Figuration of the Social World." *Sociologica* 11 (2): 1–27. doi: 10.2383/88197.
Lefebvre, Henri. 1968. *La vie quotidienne dans le monde moderne*. Paris: Gallimard.
Lefebvre, Henri. 1980. *La présence et l'absence*. Paris: Casterman.

Lefebvre, Henri. 2000. *La production de l'espace*. Paris: Anthropos.
Lefebvre, Henri. 2001. *Du rural à l'urbain*, edited by Henri Lefebvre. Paris: Anthropos.
Löw, Martina, and Hubert Knoblauch. 2020. "Dancing in Quarantine: The Spatial Refiguration of Society and the Interaction Orders." *Space and Culture* 23 (3): 221–225. doi: 10.1177/1206331220938627.
Martins, José de S. 2008. *A Sociabilidade do Homem Simples*. São Paulo: Contexto.
Martins, José de S. 2013. *A Sociologia como Aventura*. São Paulo: Contexto.
Mitchell, Don. 2005. "The S.U.V. Model of Citizenship: Floating Bubbles, Buffer Zones, and the Rise of the 'Purely Atomic' Individual." *Political Geography* 24: 77–100.
Robaina, Igor. 2015. "Entre Mobilidades e Permanências." PhD diss., Universidade Federal do Rio de Janeiro.
Rosa, Hartmut. 2005. *Beschleunigung*. Frankfurt am Main: Suhrkamp.
Sarti, Cynthia. 2003. *A Família como Espelho*. São Paulo: Cortez.
Simões Jr., José G. 1992. *Moradores de Rua*. São Paulo: Pólis.
Stoeffels, Marie-Ghislaine. 1977. *Os Mendigos de São Paulo*. Rio de Janeiro: Paz e Terra.
Vieira, Maria A. da C., Eneida M. R. Bezerra, and Cleisa M. M. Rosa. 1992. *População de Rua*. São Paulo: Hucitec.
Weidenhaus, Gunter. 2015. *Soziale Raumzeit*. Frankfurt am Main: Suhrkamp.

5
SPATIOTEMPORAL ENTANGLEMENTS
Insights from history

Susanne Rau

Introduction

While there is much to be said for investigating the influence of current social processes (such as digitalization or globalization) on spatial arrangements, as sociologists Hubert Knoblauch and Martina Löw (2017) have set out to do, it is equally important to analyze the relationship between space and time or between spatiality and temporality. Spaces or spatial arrangements change in the course of transformation processes, but so too does the relationship between space and time.

Since it is not possible to tell the whole story of space-time in this context, I instead refer to the work of the "SpatioTemporal Studies" group, a research group at the University of Erfurt, and briefly outline its guiding principles. Furthermore, since the history of the interrelationship of space and time cannot be described in just a few pages, I will fall back on a few illustrative examples that show how space and time have been graphically and cartographically represented in their interrelation. The examples come from the European Middle Ages and the early modern period. These singular examples can at least serve to illustrate that even in the pre-modern age, there must have been—if not a theory of space-time—at least an awareness of the entanglement of space and time.

I will start with a counterfactual argument ("history without time?"), then move on to a short presentation of the ideas and ongoing research activities of the Erfurt-based "SpatioTemporal Studies" group before I discuss the pre-modern understanding of the relationship of spatiality and temporality, followed by some examples.

History without time?

A counterfactual argument should be considered first (Rau 2019, 40–41). What would history be without time? (The same question can, of course, also be asked

DOI: 10.4324/9781003036159-6

in relation to space.) In recent years, spatial theories and, in particular, Löw's (2001) sociology of space have been widely received in the historical sciences. Löw's relational approach has focused primarily on the constitutional processes of social spaces (operations of placement or "spacing" followed by operations of conceptual synthesis). The reception of the *spatial turn* in history has sometimes led to the paradoxical situation that spatial orders have been given priority over temporal ones.

With a more specific definition of space—as an organizational form of coexistence that makes synchronicity or simultaneity visible—we reach a point where we must ask what history we are actually writing when we continue to ignore temporal aspects such as succession, sequentiality, diachronicity, procedurality, or acceleration. It would of course be worth trying to write a history in a purely locative mode. But, as long as we human beings experience time as passing and spaces as changing, this would hardly make sense. We should thus continue to combine spatial aspects with temporal aspects.

Space, namely, cannot be understood at all in its complexity if we do not include the factor of time and multiple temporalities. This interrelatedness of spatiality and temporality can be founded both theoretically and practically in relation to our everyday lives, since we would not even be able to think or live in just one category or the other. Whoever wants to remain standing in just one place, to neither move nor change anymore? The same holds true for the historical subjects and the spatial phenomena under examination. When we take interest in historical subjects and their environments, practices, feelings, and interpretations in a comprehensive human sense, taking both dimensions into consideration cannot be avoided. If the intention is to capture subjects within their complex relations with their environment—and not, in other words, only through their spatial relation with their surroundings—everything suggests that we should call our considerations "historic-anthropological."

The second reason for choosing the designation "historic-anthropological" is that these relationships do not remain anthropologically constant but rather change over time, diachronically, and these changes are in no way simply linear. This perspective thus differs from many historical–geographic approaches inasmuch as time appears to stand still in these approaches, or because changes are represented as linearly homogeneous (for example, in a scheme of before/after). This can often be seen, for example, in topographic charts of cities in older history books.

A third reason for calling our approach "historic-anthropological" is that historicity also means taking into consideration the potential difference of spatial constructs and constellations in different cultures or contexts. However, this is not as yet sufficient to propose a thesis on the indivisibility of spatiality and temporality.

In creating and developing such methodological instruments, we need not start from scratch: various non-historical disciplines have already brought forth interesting approaches to this problem which we can use as a point of departure. For geography, the Swede Torsten Hägerstrand developed a time-geography in the early 1970s. Through the translation of his works into English, his approach has gained international recognition and was incorporated, not least, into the structuration theory of sociologist

Anthony Giddens (Giddens 1997, 168; Gregory 1984; Stjernström 2004). On the one hand, Hägerstrand (1970) engaged with large-scale geographies. Yet, on the other, he also examined movements of people in what he called "action spaces," defined as the set of spatial possibilities and limitations of action available to an individual. As a geographer, Hägerstrand set out to examine all spatial and temporal levels that play a role in the life of an individual—from their living quarters to the globe, from a single day to the span of their life. Temporalization of space can thus be examined from perspectives of limitation of use (of space), the specification of duration, or the elasticity of activities.

By contrast, the spatialization of time can be understood as the "patterning of time" by individuals who are in turn dependent on the distribution of spatial possibilities (Carlstein, Parkes, and Thrift 1978).

As can easily be seen, temporality is an important dimension of space, both theoretically speaking and in everyday life, then as now. The Erfurt research group therefore thinks of spatiality and temporality together, as will be briefly explained hereafter.

The "SpatioTemporal Studies" group

From a conceptual perspective, "SpatioTemporal Studies" assumes that, in everyday life, spatiality and temporality cannot be separated from each other in their constructedness. This interdisciplinary research group strives to provide new impulses in the theoretical debate on space in the social and cultural sciences as well as to promote the regionalization and historicization space and time. Its members come from the fields of history, literature, religious studies, geography, art history, philosophy, and theology.

Another focus lies in the spatial and temporal practices of historical actors and groups. As historians, we see as one of our tasks to historicize spatial theories and to discover spatiotemporal concepts and practices in times long before the so-called spatial turn—which is an empty shell, as it does not offer any agreed upon methodology or common language. We should therefore speak of "spatial turns," in the plural, instead. Either way, theories about and beyond the "spatial turn" have taught us that spaces are no longer regarded as something simply physically given (Lefebvre 1991; Werlen 1995–1997; Löw 2001), but rather as something socially constructed. Spaces are the result of negotiations and designs, and these take place in time. An example of this approach and interdisciplinary collaboration is the project on the spatiotemporality of imperial practices of governance and ruling. In the course of imperial aspirations, new space-time constellations have been not only created but also represented in a wide range of media since antiquity (Meyer, Rau, and Waldner 2017a). The positive echo of the conference "Spacetime of the Imperial" and the homonymic volume highlight the growing interdisciplinary interest in an integrated view on the history of spatial patterns and their dynamics (Kirchberger 2018; see also Dorsch and Vinzent 2018; Bauer and Fischer 2019; Schmolinsky, Hitzke, and Stahl 2019; for further volumes, see Dorsch et al. 2017–2020).

Another project on historical urban planning processes, conducted within the same framework a couple of years ago, also revealed the fruitfulness of such an integrated view, in the sense that it could further the understanding of a complicated spatiotemporal process—especially when taking into account that many spatial expansion projects have been discussed but never realized. This is probably still the case today, but it has not yet been applied to urban planning history. The study dealt with two major expansion projects in the city of Lyon in the 18th century (Rau 2013). The crucial point here is that one should not look only at the physical results of this process. Through a detailed analysis of historical sources (from architects, the city council, the Academy of Sciences, and travel reports) over a period of more than one hundred years, it was possible to demonstrate that the history of planning and process of shaping the urban periphery often resembled a dialectical movement of spatial visions and partial failure, entailing temporal setbacks that, in the end, led to a synthesis of the half-planned and half-unforeseen. Yet, many spatial theories, including those that emphasized the role of capital in the production of space, offer insufficient explanations of the complex spatiotemporality of urbanization processes. It was thus proposed against the backdrop of the Lyon projects—which were already doing much of what was happening in many European cities in the 19th century—that a description of processes of urban (meaning spatial) expansion must take into account such temporal phenomena as vision, retrospection, hope, and delay.

Theories and methods of cultural space-time

The main theoretical input for the Erfurt research group stems from Mikhail Bakhtin, Henri Lefebvre, and Michel de Certeau.

One of the most well-known models of spatiotemporality is the concept of the "chronotope," derived around 1940 from the ideas of Mikhail Bakhtin, which strives to find a modeling of space and time that is characteristic for a particular epoch or formation (Meyer, Rau, and Waldner 2017b, 4). Bakhtin understood chronotope to mean the "intrinsic connectedness of temporal and spatial relationships that are artistically expressed in literature." (Bakhtin 1981, 84–85)

Derived from mathematics and Einstein's theory of relativity, Bakhtin used the category to examine the relations of time and space in literature. According to Bakhtin, the two categories belong together, forming each other and structuring any narrative. Time only gives meaning to places and spaces in narratives (or novels). The chronotope is therefore somewhat like the condition of the possibility of a narrative. First developed for the analysis of narratives, the concept can be extended and applied to the changing spatiotemporal structures (of images) of the world and of humankind (Rau 2019, 96). That would not have been against Bakhtin's intentions, as he also saw himself as a cultural scientist.

To Henri Lefebvre, the group owes the emphasis on the historicity and culturality of spaces. In essence, Lefebvre expressed this through the following statement: "Every society . . . produces a space, its own space. . . . [example:] . . . the ancient city had its own spatial practice: it forged its own—*appropriated*—space" (translation from the French original text by Rau 2019, 28). Historicity in this context means that each time or epoch must be seen under its specific conditions. Besides historicity (as past temporality), Lefebvre (1991, 48) also defended a concept of processes and of epochal divisions, which was strongly influenced by Marxist historiography:

> The history of space cannot be limited to the study of the special moments constituted by the formation, establishment, decline and dissolution of a given code. It must deal also with the global aspect—with modes of production as generalities covering specific societies with their particular histories and institutions. Furthermore, the history of space may be expected to periodize the development of the productive process in a way that does not correspond exactly to widely accepted periodizations.

The new periodization or epochal classification claimed here must by no means follow Marxist historiography (such as: ancient slaveholder society, the medieval feudal society, modern capitalism, communism). Those who recognize Lefebvre's appeal will look for a periodization that turns the important changes in spatial constellations into epochal turns, which can vary from region to region.

The third favorite theoretician of the research group is Michel de Certeau, with his emphasis on stories and practices of space.

In his *Practice of Everyday Life*, published in French in 1990, Certeau writes that narratives "organize" places; they single them out and connect them with each other. He formulated the saying "every story is a travel story," a spatial practice (Certeau 2011, 115; Rau 2019, 70–73). Narratives, in other words, do not simply transpose steps into the level of language. They organize these steps, make the "journey," and create geographies of action. By combining syntax and practices, Michel de Certeau brought together spatial stories and spatial practices. This means, for example, if we describe a walk through a city, we are not simply describing a distance from one place to another, but rather are subjectively organizing an urban space and appropriating it, ensuring we can remember it and make it available to others.

These approaches from the social and cultural sciences dating back to the 20th century are also reflected in the semantic history and even have an older history.

Views from conceptual and semantic history

In most languages, the word combination "spatiotemporal" or "spatiotemporality" does not appear before 1900. Moreover, Albert Einstein was probably the first to provide a theory of "space-time" in which time, as a fourth dimension, is closely linked to the three dimensions of space. But this is physics (for a sociology of space-time, see Weidenhaus 2015). As far as everyday language is concerned, we find references in the Merriam-Webster dictionary where "spatiotemporal" is defined in two senses:

1 "Having both spatial and temporal qualities"
2 "Of or relating to space-time"[1]

According to the dictionary, which was founded in 1828, the first known use of the adjective "spatiotemporal" appeared in 1900, in the meaning of the first definition.

However, these findings do not necessarily mean that the notion or idea of an entanglement of space and time did not exist in earlier times. We can also find them in practices and in media such as tables and maps.

Although it may be quite clear that before the 20th century there was no theory of space-time (and also no notion of time as the fourth dimension of space), the history of language has left traces of the connection between space and time.

Thus, for example, "space" (*espace*) can be proven in the meaning of "duration" (*durée*) in French as early as the 12th century. In other words, if someone spoke about an extended time, or a period of time (from—to), they used the word "espace."

The adjective "geraum" exists in German, which was initially only used for spatial determinations. Since the 15th century, it has also appeared with a temporal meaning—as we still say today, "seit geraumer Zeit," which translates to "for quite some time." If this idea is expressed differently—for example, using the phrase "seit langem" ("for a long time")—one can assume that the speaker has a three- if not four-dimensional conception of duration.

Entanglements of space and time as reflected in historical discourse and media

Representations of the spatiality of time can also be found in the history of historiography and cartography. Time courses and stories were conveyed in not only text form but also in graphic representations of time. Basically, this began with the medieval annals, in which year after year the most important events were written down, which in principle must have evoked a linear course of time when reading (see Figure 5.1).

The chronicle of Eusebius was written at the beginning of the 4th century but was copied and amended several times during the Middle Ages. Thus, the graphic form of the history in tables, in which events of different empires are arranged in columns next to each other and listed in annual steps, was also handed down until early modern times.

In this tradition, European circles of scholars graphically represented time and history in the form of "tabulae," "tables historiques," "tables universelles," "chronological tables," "views of universal history," or "Tabellenwerke." These history tables and diagrams are often provided with vectors or at least suggest a temporal sequence through the viewing and reading direction. Above all, however, the temporalized events take up space: first of all, space on paper. In the figurative sense, however, time periods (alias duration) are symbolized again: time period of an event, time period of a reign, time period of an entire epoch or "empire," as expressed in

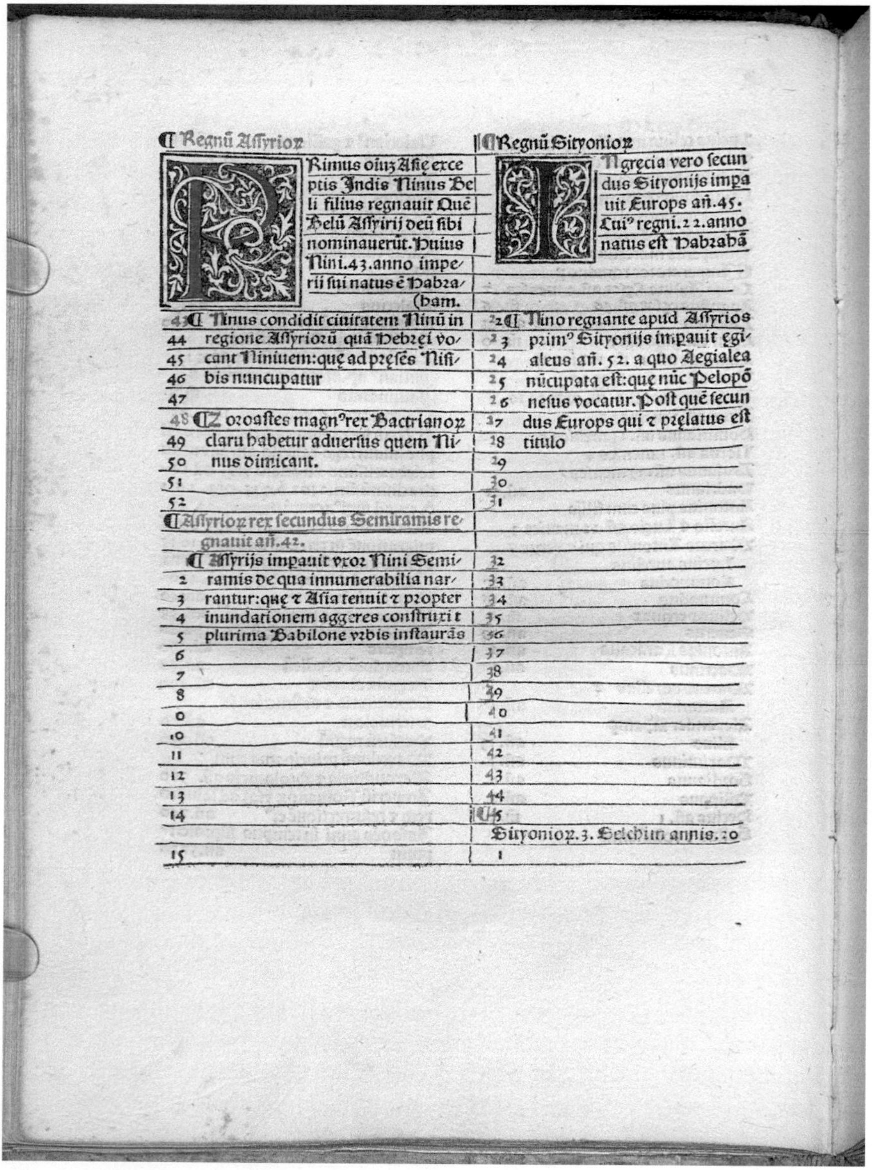

Regnū Assyriorꝫ

Primus oīuʒ Asię exceptis Indis Ninus Beli filius regnauit Quē Belū Assyrij deū sibi nominauerūt. Huius Nini.43.anno imperij sui natus ē Habraham.

43 Ninus condidit ciuitatem Ninū in
44 regione Assyriorū quā Hebręi vo-
45 cant Niniuem: quę ad pręsēs Nisi-
46 bis nuncupatur
47
48 Zoroastes magnꝰ rex Bactrianorꝫ
49 claru habetur aduersus quem Ni-
50 nus dimicant.
51
52

Assyriorꝫ rex secundus Semiramis regnauit aū.42.

Assyrijs impauit vxor Nini Semi-
2 ramis de qua innumerabilia nar-
3 rantur: quę ꝛ Asia tenuit ꝛ propter
4 inundationem aggeres construxi t
5 plurima Babilone vrbis instaurās
6
7
8
0
10
11
12
13
14
15

Regnū Sityoniorꝫ

In grecia vero secundus Sityonijs imperauit Europs aū.45. Cuiꝰ regni.22.anno natus est Habrahā

22 Nino regnante apud Assyrios
23 primꝰ Sityonijs imperauit Egi-
24 aleus aū. 52. a quo Aegialea
25 nūcupata est: quę nūc Pelopō-
26 nesus vocatur. Post quē secun
27 dus Europs qui ꝛ prelatus est
28 titulo
29
30
31
32
33
34
35
36
37
38
39
40
41
42
43
44
45
Sityoniorꝫ.3. Selchiu annis.20
1

FIGURE 5.1a Example for graphic representation of time as chronological table

Source: *Chronicon Eusebii, a sancto Hieronymo latine versum et ab eo, Prospero Britannico et Matthaeo Palmerio continuatum, editum cura C. L. Johannis Hippodami*. Venice: E. Ratdolt, 1483. Bayerische Staatsbibliothek München, 4 Inc.c.a. 290, fol. 14v and 15r.

Regnū Hebreorum.		Regnū Aegyptiorum.	Anni mūdi
Nbui° Nini imperio. Apud Hebreos nascit Habrahā: q̃ cū centū esset ānor genuit Isaac. Cui° Habrahe erat ann° pm°: tūc cū imperij Nini. 43. Habrabam an̄		Apud Aegyptios aūt. 16. potestas erat quā vocāt Dynastiā: quo tēpe regnabant Thebei q̃ pfuerunt Aegyptijs an̄. 190.	3184
1	Regnate Nino apud Assy	1	Nino regnāte apud Assy	3186
2	rios nouissimo ei°tpe nascit	2	rios Thebei Aegyptijs
3	Habrabam.	3	imperant.
4		4	
5		5	
6		6		3190
7		7	
8		8	
9		9	
10	Habrabā natione Chalde° primā etatem apud Chaldeos agebat.	10	
11		11	
12		12	
13		13	
14		14	
15		15	
16		16		3200
17		17	
18		18	
19		19	
20		20	
21		21	
22		22	
23		23	
24		24	
25		25	

FIGURE 5.1b (Continued)

the context of the concept of the four-monarchy or seven-empire doctrine. An example of this is the "Chart of History" by British polymath Josef Priestley, who designed the chart as teaching material for students and put on it—according to his claim—the entire history of the world with its most important events and localities (see Figure 5.2).

In contrast to Thomas Jefferson's "Chart of Universal History" of 1753, Priestley regularized the distribution of dates on the chart and oriented it horizontally to emphasize the continuous flow of historical time (Rosenberg and Grafton 2010, 120–121). In this sense, the historical chart is a space-time medium.

A further development of these chronological tables is historical maps, which sometimes also contain temporal information or are even converted into graphical form. These hybrid maps then combine geographic and temporal information. An early example of this is the "Carta istorica dell'Italia e d'una parte della Germania," drawn and published by Girolamo Andrea Martignoni in 1721 (see Figure 5.3).

Compared to Priestley's charts, Martignoni's historical maps used typical elements of a map—territories, bodies of water (oceans, lakes, rivers), geographic names—but less text than on the charts, together with a series of symbols and icons. But the rivers are not simply geographical elements. Especially on the upper map sheet, they represent the flow of time (Rosenberg and Grafton 2010, 108).

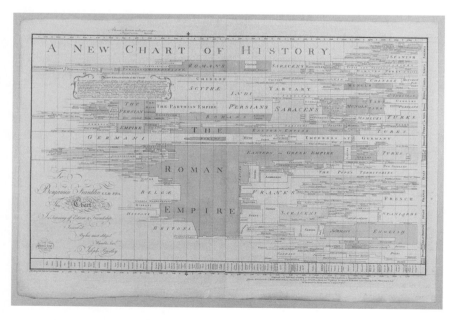

FIGURE 5.2 Example for graphic representation of time as spatialized charts

Source: Joseph Priestley. 1769. *A New Chart of History*. Wikimedia Commons, Public Domain. https://commons.wikimedia.org/w/index.php?curid=25092379

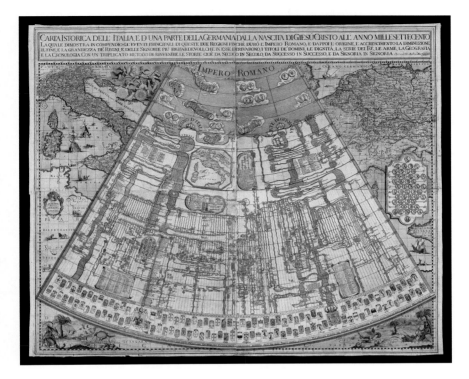

FIGURE 5.3 Example for hybrid map

Source: Girolamo Andrea Martignoni and Giovanni Petroschi. 1721. *Carta istorica dell'Italia, e d'una parte della Germania dalla nascita di Giesú Cristo all'anno millesettecento*. Rome. Institut Cartogràfic i Geològic de Catalunya (ICGC), RM.220396

Thus, these "rivers of time" on the historical maps depict the fact that history is in motion, that it itself changes geographical objects (e.g., the "Impero Romano" at the top of the map).

Conclusion

My starting point was that spatiality cannot be understood without temporality (the reverse is also true), because they are mutually dependent on and form each other. The demand of the various voices in the "spatial turn" to pay more attention to space and to analyze the constitutional processes of social space in a more differentiated way is certainly justified. However, this claim has also led in part to one-sidedness, such as the paradoxical neglect of temporality. With my considerations, I have attempted to show that this does not make sense from a historical–anthropological point of view, because people need spatial and temporal categories in their world relations, both for orientation and in retrospective description. The fact that it is only since Einstein that we have had a(n initially physical) theory of space-time should not prevent us from looking into history and other cultures and asking about their perceptions, practices, and representations of this relationship. My short contribution was only able to present a few highlights in this regard. Both conceptual history and various attempts to represent history graphically (in tables or on maps) bear witness to older efforts to think of space and time together and to represent them in their interdependence. Considering the multiple temporalities of space could also be a meaningful extension of the concept of "re-configuration of spaces," since it is used to investigate processes in the social world that are certainly not linear.

Note

1 Space-time, "a system of one temporal and three spatial coordinates by which any physical object or event can be located" (see www.merriam-webster.com/dictionary/space-time [8.2.2019]), appeared for the first time in 1910. Spatiotemporal: www.merriam-webster.com/dictionary/spatiotemporal#examples (8.2.2019). The entry "spatiotemporality" does not exist. For German language usage, see DWDS: www.dwds.de/. "Raumzeitlichkeit" appears only in the 20th century. No entry in the Wörterbuchnetz, a digital platform for historical dictionaries: www.woerterbuchnetz.de/cgi-bin/WBNetz/setupStartSeite.tcl. Only the Grimm contains the keyword "temporality" in the sense of transience.

References

Bakhtin, Mikhail. 1981. "Forms of Time and of the Chronotope in the Novel." In *The Dialogic Imagination*. Translated by Caryl Emerson and Michael Holquist, 84–258. Austin: University of Texas Press.
Bauer, Jenny, and Robert Fischer, eds. 2019. *Perspectives on Henri Lefebvre: Theory, Practices and (Re)Readings*. Berlin: de Gruyter.
Carlstein, Tommy, Don Parkes, and Nigel Thrift, eds. 1978. *Timing Space and Spacing Time*, 3 Vols. London: Edward Arnold.
Certeau, Michel de. 2011. *The Practice of Everyday Life*. Translated by Steven Rendall. Berkeley: University of California Press.
Dorsch, Sebastian, Bärbel Frischmann, Holt Meyer, Susanne Rau, Sabine Schmolinsky, and Katharina Waldner, eds. 2017–2020. *SpatioTemporality/RaumZeitlichkeit*. Book series. Berlin: de Gruyter. www.degruyter.com/view/serial/SPATIO-B?contents=toc-59654.
Dorsch, Sebastian, and Jutta Vinzent, eds. 2018. *SpatioTemporalities on the Line. Representations—Practices—Dynamics*. Berlin: de Gruyter.
Giddens, Anthony. 1997. *Die Konstitution der Gesellschaft. Grundzüge einer Theorie der Strukturierung*, 3rd ed. Frankfurt am Main: Campus.
Gregory, Derek. 1984. "Space, Time and Politics in Social Theory: An Interview with Anthony Giddens." *Environment and Planning D: Society and Space* 2 (2): 123–132.
Hägerstrand, Torsten. 1970. "What About People in Regional Science?" *Papers of the Regional Science Association* 24: 7–21.
Kirchberger, Ulrike. 2018. "Holt Meyer/Susanne Rau/Katharina Waldner (Eds.), Space-Time of the Imperial. (SpatioTemporality/RaumZeitlichkeit, Bd. 1.) Berlin/Boston, De Gruyter 2017." *Historische Zeitschrift* 307 (3): 753–755. doi: 10.1515/hzhz-2018-1510.

Knoblauch, Hubert, and Martina Löw. 2017. "On the Spatial Re-Figuration of the Social World." *Sociologica* 11 (2): 1–27. doi: 10.2383/88197.
Lefebvre, Henri. 1991. *The Production of Space*. Translated by Donald Nicholson-Smith. Oxford: Blackwell.
Löw, Martina. 2001. *Raumsoziologie*. Frankfurt am Main: Suhrkamp.
Meyer, Holt, Susanne Rau, and Katharina Waldner, eds. 2017a. *Spacetime of the Imperial*. Berlin: de Gruyter.
Meyer, Holt, Susanne Rau, and Katharina Waldner. 2017b. "'. . . *this smooth space of Empire* . . .' Introduction to Six Spatiotemporal 'Stabs' at Analyzing the Imperial." In *SpaceTime of the Imperial*, edited by Holt Meyer, Susanne Rau, and Katharina Waldner, 1–20. Berlin: de Gruyter.
Rau, Susanne. 2013. "The Urbanization of the Periphery: A Spatio-Temporal History of Lyon Since the Eighteenth Century." *Historical Social Research* 38 (3): 150–175.
Rau, Susanne. 2019. *History, Space, and Place*. Translated by Michael Thomas Taylor. London: Routledge.
Rosenberg, Daniel, and Anthony Grafton. 2010. *Cartographies of Time: A History of the Timeline*. New York: Princeton Architectural Press.
Schmolinsky, Sabine, Diana Hitzke, and Heiner Stahl, eds. 2019. *Taktungen und Rhythmen. Raumzeitliche Perspektiven interdisziplinär*. Berlin: de Gruyter.
Stjernström, Olof. 2004. "Theory and Migration: Towards a Framework of Migration and Human Actions." *Cybergeo: European Journal of Geography*. doi: 10.4000/cybergeo.3827.
Weidenhaus, Gunter. 2015. *Soziale Raumzeit*. Berlin: Suhrkamp Verlag.
Werlen, Benno. 1995–1997. *Sozialgeographie alltäglicher Regionalisierungen*, 2 vols. Stuttgart: Franz Steiner Verlag.

6
SLOW MOVEMENT ON THE SLOPE

On Architecture Principe's theory of the *oblique function* and the role of circulation in architectural and urban design

Christian Sander

Movement along the straight path or free exploration

In 1977, Paul Virilio's book *Speed and Politics* ([1977] 2006) was first published in France with the subtitle *Essai de dromologie* (Essay on Dromology). The term "dromology" is a neologism derived from the Greek word *dromos*, meaning race or racecourse. According to Ian James, the theory deals "specifically with the phenomenon of speed, or more precisely, with the way speed determines or limits the manner in which phenomena appear to us" (2007, 29). Broadly speaking, Virilio's main hypothesis is that modern means of communication and transport are based on military technologies, the speed of which is fundamentally changing the global political geography in the sense that it produces a hegemony of "real time" to the disadvantage of "real space" (Virilio and Lotringer [1983] 2008, 230). In a conservation with Sylvère Lotringer in the early 1980s, Virilio stated:

> Space is no longer in geography—it's in electronics. Unity is in the terminals. It's in the instantaneous time of command posts, multinational headquarters, control towers, etc. Politics is less in physical space than in the time systems administered by various technologies, from telecommunications to airplanes, passing by the TGV [French high-speed train], etc. There is a movement from geo- to chronopolitics: the distribution of territory becomes the distribution of time. The distribution of territory is outmoded, minimal.
>
> *(ibid., 126)*

To discuss the connection between space and time, Virilio repeatedly referred to physics, particularly to Albert Einstein's special theory of relativity, based on which Hermann Minkowski, at the beginning of the 20th century, developed his theory of four-dimensional space-time. Virilio was often criticized for his free handling of

DOI: 10.4324/9781003036159-7

scientific terminology; for example, he was one of the authors attacked by the physicists Alan Sokal and Jean Bricmont in their book *Intellectual Impostures: Postmodern Intellectuals' Abuse of Science*, first published in French in 1997 ([1997] 1998). In 1998, media scientist Kay Kirchmann published a "decidedly critical monograph" (1998, 7; own translation), in which he accuses Virilio of "methodical arbitrariness" (ibid., 9; own translation). However, he failed to look at Virilio's early work, which is not unimportant for an understanding of dromology. From 1963 to 1968, together with architect Claude Parent, Virilio formed the Architecture Principe group, which in its 1966 eponymous magazine—the group's manifesto—developed the theory of the *oblique function*. The idea was to design the building and the city exclusively using horizontal and inclined planes, on which the residents would have to exert themselves physically in order to get around (Figure 6.1). Architecture Principe's drawings show topographical architectural reliefs, so to speak, that were intended to generate new types of perceptual experiences and encounters.

In their contribution to this book, Martina Löw and Hubert Knoblauch emphasize the role of circulation in the refiguration of spaces. They point out the importance of traffic routes, for example, in Le Corbusier's utopian cities, which are divided into different functional zones by means of a geometric network of expressways. One

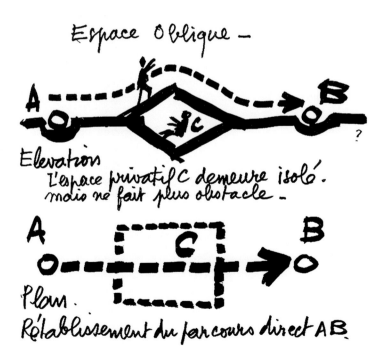

FIGURE 6.1 Claude Parent. Sketch illustrating the theory of the *oblique function*, the roof of the building becomes a pedestrian area, 1970

Source: Parent [1970] 2012. © Claude Parent Archives

can also think of the famous quote from *Urbanisme* (Urbanism), Le Corbusier's urban design treatise from 1925: "The curved street is the path of donkeys, the straight street the path of men" ([1925] 1994, 10; own translation). For the speed critic Paul Virilio, however, the geometric organization of urban space, together with mediatization, leads to an alienation of the city dweller from his environment; this involves a temporary climax in the spatio-temporal organization of global air traffic:

> when you look at Greek urban planning (the city of Miletus for example), colonial planning or that of the Roman camps, you see quite well that the roads are rectilinear. It's an organization of speed to drain the populations as fast as possible toward the city gates, toward the outskirts. A city is not simply a place where one lives, it's above all a crossroads. . . . This is why the airport today has become the new city. . . . People are no longer citizens, they're passengers in transit. . . . The new capital is no longer a spatial capital like New York, Paris, or Moscow, a city located in a specific place, at the intersection of roads, but a city at the intersection of practicabilities of time, in other words, of speed.
>
> *(Virilio and Lotringer [1983] 2008, 77–78)*

In November 1965, together with architecture critic Patrice Goulet, Claude Parent criticized Le Corbusier for making the pedestrian "a slave to the car" (1965, 2; own translation). With the *oblique function*, published a year later and focusing on the phenomenological body, the goal was to "reconnect" the city dweller with the physical urban space by forcing him to move around on foot. There should be no defined pathways on the sloping floors; in his short text "Pulsions" (Drives), published in July 1966 in the fifth issue of the *Architecture Principe* magazine, Parent writes:

> The oblique function allows for travel. Architecture becomes the support of displacement; the movement is freed from the constraint and precision of the distance traveled, and the choice of the itinerary is left open. No longer is there canalization or constraint, but distance crossed and conquered; the human fluid can pulse at his own rhythm, upheld by the spatial structure, yet independent of the formal organization of the support.
>
> *(Parent [1966] 1997b)*

The example of Architecture Principe's theory will be used in the following to further investigate the role of circulation, which refers to the movement of people in this chapter, in architectural and urban design. To do this, it is first necessary to take a look at the tradition of space-time in the first half of 20th-century architecture.

Streamline architecture and the city dweller's haste

The theory of four-dimensional space-time directly influenced the founders of modern art and architecture. In his book *Space, Time and Architecture*, first published in 1941, Sigfried Giedion writes about "unconscious parallelisms of method in science and art" (Giedion [1941] 1949, 14)—a statement that has already been put into perspective. The supposed space-time in art and architecture was mostly a matter of simplification or creatively misunderstood takeovers from the scientific debates of the time (Noell 2004, 308). Minkowski's theory was influential because the perception of space and time was indeed altered by the technical innovations of the 19th and early 20th centuries, especially modern means of transport. In 1914, architect Peter Behrens published the article "Einfluss von Zeit- und Raumausnutzung auf moderne Formentwicklung" (The Influence of the Use of Time and Space on the Development of Modern Form) in the yearbook of the *Deutsche Werkbund* (German Association of Craftsmen), which focused on city traffic.

This "development of modern form" became particularly evident in corner buildings. In reference to his redesign of the so-called Mossehaus in Berlin (Figure 6.2), to which he added additional floors and a new façade with a seemingly aerodynamic shape, Erich Mendelsohn stated in 1923:

> the building is not a disinterested spectator of the rushing cars and of the advancing and receding flow of traffic; rather it has become an absorbing, cooperating element of the motion. The building both visibly encompasses in its overall expression the high speed of traffic, where the tendency toward motion is raised to an extreme, and at the same time the balances of its forces soothes the frenetic pace of the street and of the passersby. . . . By dividing and guiding the traffic, the building, despite all tendencies of its own towards movement, becomes an immobile pillar amidst the turbulence of the street.
>
> *(Mendelsohn [1923] 1992, 28)*

FIGURE 6.2 Erich Mendelsohn, Richard Neutra, and Paul Rudolf Henning. Renovation of the Mossehaus, Berlin, 1921–1923

Source: Photograph: © Christian Sander, 2020

Thus, in order to "calm" the city dweller, according to Mendelsohn, one only has to balance the technologically enhanced speed with a "dynamic" architectural form. In his 1947 book *Vision in Motion*, in the subchapter "Speed" of the section "Space-Time Problems," László Moholy-Nagy explains that one must clearly distinguish between the perception that is influenced by a means of transport and the perception when walking ([1947] 1969, 245–246). Another subchapter of this section is called "Mobile Architecture," in which the artist allows himself to be carried away into calling it "space-time reality." For example, he claims that Walter Gropius and Martin Wagner "are advocating demountable, movable houses for future cities" and that there "are projects not only of movable but of moving houses too; sanitariums, for example, turning with the sun" (ibid., 256–257). In his book, Moholy-Nagy celebrates the artist as a pioneer of developments in the technical-scientific field; for example, artistic experiments with positive and negative forms would have provided the basis for the design of streamlined products (ibid., 58–61). However, Moholy-Nagy makes it clear that he rejects the inflationary use of the streamlined shape:

> The speed and motion of our period justify "streamlining." But streamlining was originally invented for moving objects and there is hardly any reason for an ashtray to be streamlined. Thus, when every product is blown up like a balloon—we have to fight against it, as formerly we did against the mechanical utilization of symmetry with which everything, in previous periods, could be made "harmonious and balanced."
>
> (ibid., 34)

All quotes from *Vision in Motion* that have been cited here were published in French in 1950 in the fifth issue of the second series of *Art d'Aujourd'hui* (Art of Today). The art magazine was in a way the publication organ of the Espace (Space) group, an association of artists, designers, architects, and engineers founded by the painter Félix Del Marle together with the artist and editor André Bloc to promote the synthesis of the arts in the reconstruction of France after the Second World War. Before meeting Paul Virilio, Claude Parent was a member of Espace, where he mainly worked with Bloc and the sculptor Nicolas Schöffer. The latter, because he called for the integration of technology into art, can be seen as the exemplary artist of the *Trente Glorieuses* (The Glorious Thirty), the years between the end of the Second World War and the mid-1970s, which were characterized by economic prosperity and technological progress. In 1965, Schöffer was one of the founders of the Groupe International d'Architecture Prospective (GIAP) and, as such, primarily concerned himself with his project on a *Ville cybernétique* (Cybernetic City). This city model adopted a number of elements from the radical projects of the interwar period, for instance the division of the city into functionally differentiated zones, such as work and living. According to Schöffer, "man, caught in a spiral of acceleration and accumulated efforts, feels the need to differentiate his working environment from that of his residence" (Schöffer 1969, 100; own translation). Of course, in such a city, with great distances between work and home, fast means of transport are needed: in the drawing of the *Ville résidence-dortoir* (Commuter Town) (Figure 6.3), which is a part of the cybernetic city project, cars race past the elevated apartment buildings, which Schöffer designed together with Parent in the mid-1950s.

Parent shared Schöffer's opinion that architects and artists alike should open up to the latest technical developments. In his article "Les corps en mouvement" (Bodies in Movement), published in 1960, the architect formulated this conviction by referencing the streamlined shape:

> It is said with enthusiasm in the art community that BRANCUSI'S sculptures preceded the appearance of aerodynamic forms. This fact, quite unverifiable, is extremely characteristic of what the world expects of the architect. It will be necessary to make the choice, to express it, to pronounce it by means of a form, which will no longer be only the consequence, the result of a sum of minor conditions, but rather an artistic choice, a choice on the part of a sculptor, who can act with the greatest degree of freedom, where the coefficient of penetration of a volume in the air will perhaps be one of the important elements guiding and exalting the research.
>
> *(Parent 1960, 6; own translation)*

FIGURE 6.3 Nicolas Schöffer. *Ville cybernétique, Ville résidence-dortoir (ville horizontale)*, around 1969

Source: Schöffer 1969. © VG Bild-Kunst, Bonn 2021

Parent had very large structures that are exposed to strong winds in mind. Nevertheless, his own preoccupation with aerodynamics was limited to means of transport; later on, in his article, he discusses the shapes of cars, planes, ships, and trains.

From the *oblique function* to dromology and the city of slow movement

The collaboration with Paul Virilio, who was critical of technology as early as the 1960s, marked a turning point in Claude Parent's work. In a 1997 text on the *oblique function*, Virilio criticizes Nicolas Schöffer's cybernetic city project, in which the buildings are equipped with helicopter landing pads:

> The heretical nature of this detour through the techniques of the body can be easily imagined, related to the problem of lodgings, that of a body having become *self-moving* again in contradistinction to prostheses of displacement of all sorts which had already invaded the city, waiting for the moment of the "cybernetic city" imagined at that time by Nicolas Schöffer.
> (Virilio 1997, 11)

At the beginning of this chapter, it was pointed out that Virilio regularly emphasized the supposed military origins in modern means of transport—in "prostheses of displacement"—and communication devices. As an excerpt from the 1978 essay "Le monument irréel" (The Unreal Monument) on Erich Mendelsohn's Einstein Tower in Potsdam shows, he also recognized it in streamline architecture:

> In the wake of the intensive production of **dynamic** (aerodynamic) **means of transport** by an arms industry that has essentially switched to the manufacture of means of transport and communication, architects have denatured the building, **a static means of transport**, in order to turn it into a dynamic (aerostatic) pseudo means of transport, as if the roofs and façades had suddenly turned into ship keels—recreating the ruins of this First World War, when the sky darkened with metallic thunder. Dramatic symbols of a disfigured, threatening space, the dissolution of the sky, and a premonition of those later storms in which the intense motorization of the crowds ultimately led to their deportation, in a "blitzkrieg" that saw Erich Mendelsohn flee from Nazi Germany after succumbing to the fateful lures of the Italian futurists.
> (Virilio 1978, 366–368; own translation)

Thus, Virilio did not criticize streamlining for being decorative, as László Moholy-Nagy did. Rather, he used it as a representative example to highlight the alleged ubiquity of military structures. In a 1995 conversation with architect Enrique Limon, he clearly separated the two phases of his theoretical work—the Architecture Principe manifesto and the dromological writings—and even dismissed his collaboration with Parent as "a kid's game": "Groupe Architecture Principe was about space and politics whereas the issue of speed is about time and politics, which opens a whole new vista of research" (Limon and Virilio 1995, 184). What is problematic about this clear separation of space and time, however, is that Virilio, like the above-mentioned modern architects and artists, repeatedly referred to the theory of four-dimensional space-time and thus to the mutual dependence of space and time. What distinguishes Virilio's considerations from the enthusiasm felt by artists such as Nicolas Schöffer for machine-produced space-time phenomena is not the separation of space and time but rather the radical criticism of the devaluation of space by the technically enhanced speed as it is developed in the arms industry and then introduced into everyday life. This conviction forms the theoretical basis for Virilio's "whole new vista of research."

The main difference between the Architecture Principe manifesto and dromology is in fact that the latter presents a cultural pessimistic perspective, whereas the former develops an alternative model of architectural and urban design. For Parent, his membership in the Architecture Principe group was no less important. While the architect in the 1950s followed Nicolas Schöffer in his technological zeal and in 1960 even pleaded for an aerodynamic design of the architectural form, in his text "Le temps mort" (Time Out/Moribund Time), published in March 1966 in the Architecture Principe manifesto, he suddenly advocated a city for pedestrians:

> The displacements in cities will be slow, their speed will be that of the pedestrian. The concern for speed will be found elsewhere, in other galaxies or in entertainment. Displacements necessary to life will become active. The notion of "wasted time" will disappear. Speed will no longer be necessary, nor a condition for survival.
>
> *(Parent [1966] 1997a, VI—VII)*

Not just because of the capital letters, "Le temps mort" could also be taken for a chapter from one of Virilio's dromological essays:

> We must first of all determine our position with respect to SPACE-TIME. Current thought in urban planning comes down to estimating geographical displacement in "units of TIME" instead of in units of linear measure proportioned to the displacement. We want nothing to do with this proposition based on "speed". We reject this view. Exploration in space invalidates and outdates the very notion of speed. In the new urban agglomerations, speed will not be considered a fundamental factor. It will no longer exist. As a result, the universe of aerodynamism will crumble.
>
> *(ibid., VI)*

Parent stuck to this anti-speed stance after his collaboration with Virilio; in his book *Entrelacs de l'oblique* (Interlacing the Oblique), a kind of catalogue raisonné of his own work published in 1981, he continued to imagine the city of the *oblique function* as a pedestrian city in which vehicles should only be used to transport patients or deliver goods (Parent 1981, 30). This can be read in a chapter entitled "Phénoménologie du mouvement oblique et potentialisme" (Phenomenology of the Oblique Movement and Potentialism), which once again reveals the influence of Virilio, who in several interviews emphasized the impact of Maurice Merleau-Ponty's phenomenological philosophy on his thinking (Armitage and Virilio [1999] 2001, 15 and 18). Yet, the oblique city remained utopian, and in 1969, one year after the Architecture Principe group split up, the Concorde embarked on its maiden flight, capable of flying faster than twice the speed of sound. According to Virilio, it engendered "a deregulation of distance which causes time-distances to replace space-distances" (Virilio and Lotringer [1983] 2008, 74).

Circulation translated into architectural form versus its fracturing by Architecture Principe

While Nicolas Schöffer's cybernetic city project, due to its geometric organization for the effective (fast) movement of vehicles, can be regarded in line with the urban utopias of the interwar period like Le Corbusier's city projects, the *oblique function* must be understood as a kind of phenomenological countertheory to this technophilic approach of urban design (Busbea 2007, 7 and 160–167). Thilo Hilpert put it very clearly: "As an artificial relief, the city [of the *oblique function*, C.S.] should remain a physical space for movement and be accessible on foot, such that an archaic relationship to space is maintained despite the technical age" (Hilpert 1997/1998, 54; own translation). But circulation, that is, the movement of people in this chapter, is not just involved in the organization of the city; it also influences the shape of our built environment. With the car came the idea to design the buildings lining the road according to the perception influenced by the speed of the vehicle, and computer-based design now allows for even more elaborate ways to translate circulation into architectural form. In the 1990s, architect Greg Lynn used animation software from the film industry to document data such as wind movement, car traffic, and pedestrian flows in order to develop an animation from which he could generate a spatial structure (Ruby 2002, 42–43). For the Yokohama International Port Terminal, Foreign Office Architects (Farshid Moussavi and Alejandro Zaera-Polo) worked with a "no-return diagram" (Figure 6.4), that is, "a field of movements with no structural orientation." For the architects, this diagram was their "first attempt to provide the building with a particular spatial performance" (Moussavi and Zaera-Polo 2002, 11). The resulting pier can be described as paths turned into architectural form.

Due to its variously inclined surfaces, the Yokohama International Port Terminal was repeatedly associated with the theory of the *oblique function* (Bideau 2002, 17; Simonot 2010, 167). However, in Claude Parent's drawings of the church of Sainte-Bernadette du Banlay (Figure 6.5), built by Architecture Principe in the central French city of Nevers in the 1960s, the arrows do not represent the movement of people in the building. Here, it is the architectural form that, in the architect's drawing process, moves to finally become a spatial structure in which one is forced to find one's *own* way. When Architecture Principe designed the church, Parent was influenced by Hans Scharoun, whose Philharmonie in Berlin, with its

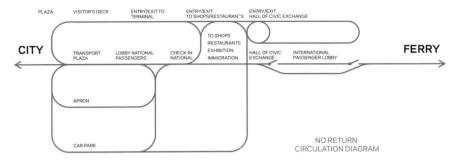

FIGURE 6.4 Farshid Moussavi and Alejandro Zaera-Polo (Foreign Office Architects, FOA). Yokohama International Port Terminal, no-return diagram, around 1995

Source: © AZPML

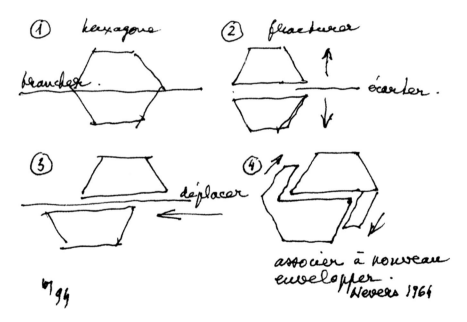

FIGURE 6.5 Claude Parent. Sketch illustrating the form-finding process for the church of Sainte-Bernadette du Banlay, built in Nevers in 1965/66

Source: Parent [1994] 2012. © Claude Parent Archives

highly complex plan, was built in the early 1960s. In a 1967 article, Parent writes about Scharoun's building: "In the interior spaces, one is at times faced with such a complex network of paths and circulation that one's attention is necessarily in a state of permanent alert" (Parent 1967, 38; own translation). It is this permanent alertness to our built environment that is taught to us in Architecture Principe's countertheory of the *oblique function*.

References

Armitage, John, and Paul Virilio. (1999) 2001. "From Modernism to Hypermodernism and Beyond." In *Virilio Live: Selected Interviews*, edited by John Armitage, 15–47. London: Sage.

Behrens, Peter. 1914. "Einfluss von Zeit- und Raumausnutzung auf moderne Formentwicklung." In *Der Verkehr*, edited by Deutscher Werkbund, 7–10. Jena: Eugen Diederichs.

Bideau, André. 2002. "Den Raum ergründen: Parent, Virilio und die Theorieplattform Architecture Principe." *werk, bauen + wohnen* 89 (11): 14–19.

Busbea, Larry. 2007. *Topologies: The Urban Utopia in France, 1960–1970*. Cambridge, MA: The MIT Press.

Giedion, Sigfried. (1941) 1949. *Space, Time and Architecture: The Growth of a New Tradition*. Cambridge, MA: Harvard University Press.

Hilpert, Thilo. 1997/1998. "Stadtvisionen der sechziger Jahre." *ARCH+* 139/140: 50–57.

James, Ian. 2007. *Paul Virilio*. London: Routledge.

Kirchmann, Kay. 1998. *Blicke aus dem Bunker: Paul Virilios Zeit- und Medientheorie aus der Sicht einer Philosophie des Unbewußten*. Stuttgart: Verlag Internationale Psychoanalyse.

Le Corbusier. (1925) 1994. *Urbanisme*. Paris: Flammarion.

Limon, Enrique, and Paul Virilio. 1995. "Paul Virilio and the Oblique." In *Sites & Stations: Provisional Utopias: Architecture and Utopia in the Contemporary City*, edited by Stan Allen and Kyong Park, 174–184. New York: Lusitania Press.

Mendelsohn, Erich. (1923) 1992. "The International Consensus on the New Architectural Concept, or Dynamics and Function." In *Erich Mendelsohn: Complete Works of the Architect, Sketches, Designs, Buildings*, 22–34. London: Triangle Architectural Publishing.

Moholy-Nagy, László. (1947) 1969. *Vision in Motion*, Chicago: Paul Theobald and Company.

Moussavi, Farshid, and Alejandro Zaera-Polo. 2002. "Design Evolution." In *The Yokohama Project: Foreign Office Architects*, edited by Albert Ferré, Tomoko Sakamoto, and Michael Kubo, 7–61. Barcelona: Actar.

Noell, Matthias. 2004. "Bewegung in Zeit und Raum: Zum erweiterten Architekturbegriff im frühen 20. Jahrhundert." In *Raum—Dynamik: Beiträge zu einer Praxis des Raums/Dynamique de l'espace: contributions aux pratiques de l'espace*, edited by Franck Hofmann, Stavros Lazaris, and Jens E. Sennewald, 301–314. Bielefeld: transcript.

Parent, Claude. 1960. "Les corps en mouvement." *Esthétique industrielle* 46: 5–26.

Parent, Claude. 1967. "Scharoun ou l'espace dynamique." *Aujourd'hui: Art et Architecture* 57/58: 38–39.

Parent, Claude. 1981. *Entrelacs de l'oblique*. Paris: Éditions du Moniteur.

Parent, Claude. (1966) 1997a. "Time Out/Moribund Time." In Claude Parent and Paul Virilio. *Architecture Principe: 1966 and 1996*, VI—VII. Besançon: Les Éditions de l'Imprimeur.

Parent, Claude. (1966) 1997b. "Drives." In Claude Parent and Paul Virilio. *Architecture Principe: 1966 and 1996*, XIV. Besançon: Les Éditions de l'Imprimeur.

Parent, Claude. (1970) 2012. *Vivre à l'oblique*. Paris: Jean-Michel Place.

Parent, Claude. (1994) 2012. *Le Carnet de la fracture*. Paris: Manuella Éditions.

Parent, Claude, and Patrice Goulet. 1965. "Le Corbusier: Architecture, urbanisme." *Aujourd'hui: Art et Architecture* 51: 1–95.

Ruby, Andreas. 2002. "Informierte Oberflächen: Kontinuität als Narration der Neunziger." *werk, bauen + wohnen* 89 (11): 39–45.

Schöffer, Nicolas. 1969. *La Ville cybernétique*, Paris: Tchou.

Simonot, Béatrice. 2010. "Claude Parent, présent dans la postérité/Claude Parent, Present in Posterity." In *Nevers: Architecture Principe: Claude Parent, Paul Virilio*, edited by Frédéric Migayrou, 162–169. Orléans: Éditions HYX.

Sokal, Alan, and Jean Bricmont. (1997) 1998. *Intellectual Impostures: Postmodern Intellectuals' Abuse of Science*. London: Profile Books.
Virilio, Paul. 1978. "Le monument irréel." In *Paris–Berlin, 1900–1933: Rapports et contrastes France–Allemagne*, 365–371. Paris: Centre national d'art et de culture Georges Pompidou.
Virilio, Paul. 1997. "Disorientation." In Claude Parent and Paul Virilio. *Architecture Principe: 1966 and 1996*, 7–13. Besançon: Les Éditions de l'Imprimeur.
Virilio, Paul. (1977) 2006. *Speed and Politics*. Los Angeles: Semiotext(e).
Virilio, Paul, and Sylvère Lotringer. (1983) 2008. *Pure War*. Los Angeles: Semiotext(e).

PART II
Spatiality, social inequality, and the economy

7
'OPEN BORDERS'
A postcolonial critique

Gurminder K. Bhambra

Postcolonial challenges to spatialisation

Our times are marked by the unprecedented attention given to the movement of people. This has been highlighted in recent years as a consequence of what is generally called the 'refugee crisis' in Europe. However, I prefer to see it as the crisis produced for refugees by our—that is, European—failure to abide by the norms and obligations set out in various international human rights treaties to which we are signatories. For all the attention—media and political—given to this movement of people, one would expect the ensuing numbers to be far in excess of the 0.31% increase in the total population in Europe that successful asylum applications have otherwise constituted over the last few years (Bhambra 2017a). Even if we were to add the numbers of those who come for what are termed 'economic' reasons, the movement of people in our contemporary times is far smaller and less significant in terms of its impact on land and local people than earlier movements. Here, I am alluding to the mass movement of Europeans from the seventeenth century onwards to what came to be known as the New World.

Indeed, across the nineteenth century and into the twentieth, over 60 million Europeans moved to the lands of others, far exceeding in scope and impact the numbers moving today (Miège 1993). Europe could, but for the most part chooses not to, absorb others into its societies; however, they were forced to give way to Europeans and to their domination over them. Yet, almost without exception, those writing on migration today do so without any reference to that earlier movement. Nor do they understand how it is part of the explanation of contemporary inequalities and, as such, would need to be part of any solution.

Even those commentators on public policy who see migration as the most effective way to address issues of global inequality—such as Branko Milanovic (2016)—do so through a presentist lens, which sees migration primarily in terms of the

DOI: 10.4324/9781003036159-9

problems posed by 'open borders' for the host societies. It is in this context that Milanovic (2016), formerly lead economist in the World Bank's research department, proposed in an op-ed in the *Financial Times* whether a trade-off might not be made between citizenship and migration to resolve this contradiction. He argues that while open borders are likely to be the most effective way of reducing global inequality, this would require a trade-off between citizenship and migration on the part of those moving; they might be allowed to move, but they should be denied citizenship and the associated rights.

In contrast, as I will go on to argue, the postcolonial challenge to the contemporary spatialisation of modernity requires us to consider the extent to which our current neoliberal times reproduce earlier colonial logics that facilitated movement for some while establishing hard borders for others. As Knoblauch and Löw (2017) argue, modernity can be seen in terms of violent processes involving the extension and enforcement of boundaries and the homogenisation of spaces and populations. The solution to the identified problems consequent to this spatialisation of the world does not, for me, rest on the idea of 'open borders', particularly as this is being conceptualised by some economists. Nor does it lie in the alternative promoted by those such as Wolfgang Streeck (2018) of a hostile environment for migration and refugee aid close to the source. Rather, it lies in a collective accountability that can only be met through a process of social democratic reparative action; that is, through a generalising of social democracy rather than the establishment of a nationally specific social democracy available to some but denied to others.

Global inequality, open borders, and differential citizenship

The idea that issues of global inequality can be addressed through the movement of individuals across open borders in conjunction with limiting the rights of those who move has been put forward by a number of economists and other scholars. Eric Posner and Glen Weyl (2014, np), for example, argue that 'the most powerful force to reduce inequality worldwide' is a system of 'open migration laws that are coupled, paradoxically, with caste systems'. They suggest that we look to the Gulf nations, which, by welcoming migrant workers, 'do more than any other rich country to reduce global inequality'. They recognise that migration to these countries is facilitated by limiting the rights of migrant workers in these authoritarian states; but suggest that 'reducing inequality will require uncomfortable tradeoffs'. Branko Milanovic (2016) similarly aligns himself with this position.

Milanovic (2018) sees the problems associated with the movement of people as resting in two phenomena. First, that globalisation has made knowledge of income differentials between countries better known and, relatedly, that transportation costs are much lower than was previously the case. Second, that there are increasing gaps in real incomes between wealthy countries and poorer ones. Milanovic (2018) argues that, whereas previously the locus of global inequality could be identified in class differences, as had been argued by Marx and Engels, it now rests in aspects of location. While the available datasets from the nineteenth century confirm Marx and Engels' assumptions about the 'similarity in the economic position of workers across the world' (Milanovic 2012, 126–127), Milanovic suggests that this changes by the early twenty-first century. At this point, he argues, inequality comes to be predominantly determined by geographical location and not economic class. That is, as he states, the poorest citizens in the richest countries have incomes higher than the richest citizens in the poorest countries. It is this income differential across locations that drives people to migrate because, as he argues, 'people can increase their incomes several fold if they migrate from a low mean income location to a high mean income location' (Milanovic 2012, 130).

As such, Milanovic (2016, np) claims that 'migration does more to reduce global poverty and inequality than any other factor', but that the problem with this solution is that the 'arrival of migrants threatens to diminish or dilute the premium [generally understood in terms of access to the welfare state] enjoyed by citizens of rich countries', who are then hostile to the new arrivals. In part, he argues, this is a consequence of those who are the poorest in rich nations being 'the biggest losers' of globalisation (Milanovic 2013, 202). The shift from the end of the twentieth century to the early twenty-first century saw real incomes rise for almost everybody globally, except for the very poorest 5% or those within the '75th and 90th percentiles of global income distribution, whose real income gains were essentially nil' (Milanovic 2013, 202). These people—on lower incomes in rich countries, whose income has not increased, but who are still part of the 25% of highest earners in the world—are presented by Milanovic as the 'nonwinners' of globalisation and as the people most likely to be threatened by and hostile to immigration. And whose hostility has been acknowledged as legitimate.

Milanovic (2018), somewhat inconsistently, concedes that there is only a slight negative impact on wages as a consequence of migration from poorer countries. This suggests that domestic policy rather than globalisation might explain the stagnant incomes of the 'nonwinners' of the West. However, it is the cultural impact that he treats as significant and requiring accommodation. That is, he suggests an approach is needed that would balance the economic needs of a country for migrants 'with the preservation of certain cultural norms' (Milanovic 2018), as if migrants necessarily disrupt those norms. This could be done by restricting migration to those workers who 'come to do specific jobs for a limited period of time' and who would then return to their countries of origin (Milanovic 2018). Another solution would be to restrict the citizenship rights of migrants in the countries of arrival and make them pay higher taxes given the benefits they gain by being granted entry to these countries. This, Milanovic (2016, np) argues, would 'assuage the concerns of the native population, while still ensuring the migrants are better off than they would be had they stayed in their own countries'.

Notice that the world's poorest are asked to pay taxation to support those within the 75th to 90th percentile, while the top 10th percentile appropriates the profit from their exploited labour and has experienced a significant reduction in their tax burden. It is the world's poorest who, as a price for their mobility, are asked to pay taxes for services for others—to which they themselves are denied access—as well as a further tax (or rent) for simply working in wealthier countries. This is Milanovic's compromise solution, which, he suggests, is 'in tune with globalisation but also with legitimate concerns for national heritage' (Milanovic 2018, np). As I will go on to argue, this compromise solution is only a solution in the context of accepting neoliberal norms and precepts as defining not only our contemporary times, but also our normative understandings.

Indenture as a 'choice' to reduce global inequality

Eric Posner and Glen Weyl (2014, np) state quite openly that 'Gulf states explicitly seek non-Arab, dark-skinned migrants so as to minimize the risk that nationals will sympathize, fraternize, or intermarry with migrants (who would then demand permanent residence, if not citizenship)'. Further, they suggest that migrants should be paid significantly lower wages than those typical of even low-paid workers in the host society. They must also be deprived of rights to organise and protest, and are to be delivered into a strict subordination to employers as indentured labour. While the exploitation of indentured labour will be to the benefit of employers (and some consumers) in the north, they claim that it will also be to the betterment of indentured labourers themselves, who are escaping the worse conditions they otherwise face 'at home'.

This, as I have argued with John Holmwood (Holmwood and Bhambra 2015) elsewhere, is a 'pro-slavery' argument for the free movement of unfree labour. Significantly, Posner and Weyl seem to repeat arguments last articulated in defence of Jim Crow policies in the southern states of the United States of America, specifically that slavery itself was relatively beneficial for transported Africans compared with the circumstances in Africa from which they came. Quite apart from the distasteful nature of the argument, its sociological or political naivety is also evident. They write as if the colonial process of enslavement had no impact upon the populations that were left behind in terms of their possibilities for subsistence and collective determination (see Manning 1983; Lovejoy 1989). 'Belonging', and with it the right to have social and political rights, is presented as a privilege of local (European and European-descended) citizens; migrants are displaced from where they belong and are to be offered no recognition or rights in the places to which they move.

This is exacerbated by Posner and Weyl's (2018) further proposal for relatively disadvantaged citizens in wealthy countries to be able to 'sponsor' or 'rent' migrants as a way of binding them to the overarching project of alleviating global poverty by providing them with a direct return. They explicitly advocate for a segregated system dependent on patronage and enforced through the maintenance of ascribed differences (see also Weyl 2016). Domestic capital should be free to exploit indentured labour, while migrant labour should be policed and prevented from claiming rights enjoyed by other citizens (though it is unlikely that local populations in the global North could be insulated from the effects of divided citizenship and merely enjoy the fruits of the indentured labour in the form of rent or cheap services). In effect, they implicitly recognise that enforcing cheap labour creates a windfall profit for those who can access it, but seeks to resolve that inequality by widening the pool of exploiters. This represents not so much a universal basic income as a racialised income supplement.

Such arguments are contingent upon the idea that the global North bears no collective responsibility for the conditions found in the global South. The issues are framed simply in terms of our charity and benevolence towards others in constrained circumstances with little reflection on how we may be responsible for the commission and maintenance of those very circumstances. Furthermore, it relies on the notion that, however constrained, indentured labour represents a 'choice'. The question that we must ask, however, is at what point does 'indentured labour' become so constrained that it represents enslavement? As Chris Bertram argues, such a posited solution 'distorts our moral understanding, specifically, our understanding of justice, to represent a pragmatic compromise with unjust attitudes as exemplifying what justice itself demands' (2019, 290). Further, denying rights to alleviate global inequality, he continues, 'when we could achieve the same outcomes by acting otherwise, involves the [active] commission of injustice' (2019, 295). Global inequality is not a natural condition that requires 'us' to address it through acts of willed generosity; instead, it requires a more thoroughgoing understanding of its production and our related obligations as a consequence of this shared and unequal history.

Histories of global inequality

There is a general recognition that the process of moving as a means of addressing issues of local impoverishment and inequality is not new. Yet, there is little discussion of how that migration—what used to be called in nineteenth-century German national economy 'emigrationist colonialism' (Smith 1980)—itself contributes to the process of creating the vast differentials between incomes on a global scale. Today, European and North American debates make no reference to colonialism and scarcely allude to that movement of people, for the most part Europeans, who, whether intentionally or not, come to be part of the project of settler colonialism and the processes of dispossession, elimination, and extraction that have significantly contributed to the specific configuration of contemporary inequalities.

Across the nineteenth century, as mentioned earlier, around 60 million Europeans left their countries of origin to make new lives and livelihoods for themselves on lands inhabited by others (Miege 1993). Each new cohort of Europeans was allocated land at the edges of the territory that had already been colonised. This was done in order to extend political control over contested border territories. In this way, Europeans from across the continent participated in the elimination and dispossession of the populations who were on that land and were thus complicit in the settler colonial project.

At least 7 million Germans moved to these lands—to what was to become the United States in the north and to Brazil and Argentina in the south—becoming, by the late nineteenth century, one of the largest immigrant groups in the north

(Bade 1995). Large-scale Polish emigration started in the period after the Franco-Prussian war, and by the turn to the twentieth century, over 2 million Polish people had moved to the Americas, with about 300,000 settling in Brazil, another settler colony, by 1939 (Zubrzycki 1953). Two million subjects of the Dual Monarchy of Austria-Hungary travelled to the Americas (Zahra 2016), as did over 8 million Irish people (Delaney 2000)—including a million as a consequence of the mid-century famine induced by British colonial rule. By 1890, nearly a million Swedes, one-fifth of the total Swedish population, were living in the lands colonised by (and as) the U.S. In addition, 13.5 million British people moved to white settler colonies across the globe (Fedorowich and Thompson 2013). National migration associations were set up to facilitate the movement of poor and unemployed Europeans to the New World and beyond. Those who left remitted money back, pointing to the ways in which the wealth accrued through colonial endeavours was directly linked to the development of the economy, and particularly local economies, 'back home'. European empires also taxed the peoples they dominated, appropriating not only a surplus for the management of the colony, but also a surplus for the building of state institutions in the metropole, what Milanovic calls the 'national patrimony'.

The movement of peoples, of such magnitude, is implicitly claimed to have been unproblematic and in some of the literature is called the age of 'free migration', referring to the 'open border' of the United States during most of this period. Milanovic, for example, suggests that the issue in terms of people's movement today, as compared to movements in the past, is that today 'the impediments are greater' (2012, 131); that is, there are walls, barriers, fortified borders, which there had not been in the past. This appears to suggest that the mass European movement of the nineteenth century occurred without any contestation. What is not accounted for in such a presentation is the preceding movement, also of Europeans, that had largely eliminated the prior populations of these lands to enable them to be seen as 'free soil', to use Weber's term (quoted in Mommsen 1984 [1959], 83, fn 56). The 'open border' of the United States might have been open on the eastern edge, but this was only as a consequence of Europeans having eliminated indigenous peoples and appropriated their lands. It was not 'open' prior to being made so through European colonisation.

As such, not only are European imperial powers implicated in the production of global inequalities, but also broader European populations who, by moving to these lands, consolidated the 'manifest destiny' of expansion at the expense of the prior inhabitants.

This earlier movement of people was different to contemporary migration not least because those who move across borders in the present live according to the rules and norms of the societies of the lands to which they come—this was not the case with Europeans moving to the lands of others. Those who moved in the age of 'free migration' are better understood as colonial settlers, and colonial settlers are not migrants even if much of the scholarship confuses them as such. To naturalise the historical processes of conquest and colonisation as 'migration' normalises and legitimates violence in the past as the condition for continued violence against others in the present (who bear that violence as their 'patrimony'). The violence of imperial rule and colonial settlement disappears from histories of the nation—happening, as it does, outside of the borders of the national state—at the same time as arguments about national sovereignty and national heritage are used to securitise borders in the present and to argue for differentiated citizenship for those with the temerity to move across them. Milanovic (and others, such as Streeck) argues for a legitimate national heritage and perceives problems in the integration of difference, yet it is colonialism itself that racialised difference and made it difficult to consider treating 'diverse others' as equals. On this, there is little to no comment.

European colonisation and the production of global inequality

Milanovic (2012, 132) is not unaware of Europe's long history of colonisation; it is just that he euphemises the process as one whereby Europe 'exported its people elsewhere'. As such, he does not seem to regard it as significant to the shaping of the world or to the establishment of inequalities within it. For example, he states that India, today, similar to China, 'is also recording high rates of growth and has also started from a very low baseline' (Milanovic 2013, 200). This is presented without any comment about the drain of resources that had occurred from India to Britain over two hundred years of colonial rule (Patnaik 2017) and the similar practices imposed upon China by the West to create the 'very low baseline'. Instead, in their modelling of incomes over time, economists use national categories to discuss territories that were in fact colonised. For example, Milanovic (2013, 205) writes that Marx's presentation of proletarians in different parts of the world—that is, 'peasants in India, workers in England'—sharing the same political interests was 'a broadly accurate description of the situation at that time'. This is because, he states, 'equally poor people of different nations faced equally rich people in their own' (Milanovic 2013, 205). This rather neglects to address the fact that peasants in India were not being exploited by rich people within their 'nation', as India was at that time under colonial rule exercised by Britain and the profits of exploitation were appropriated by the colonial power, and only partly by local elites.

This form of methodological nationalism—or what I have also called 'methodological whiteness' (Bhambra 2017b)—within the social sciences, while leading to inadequate scholarship in its own terms, also has pernicious consequences in the debates on migration and citizenship. Milanovic, for example, states that the reason poor migrants should not have access to full citizenship rights is because it would be viewed as unfair by local citizens whose 'citizenship premium' would be diminished. This is because, as he states, rich countries accumulate wealth and transmit it 'along with many other advantages, to the next generations of their citizens' (Milanovic 2013, 207). 'We take it as normal,' he suggests, 'that there is a transmission of collectively acquired wealth over generations within the same nation' (Milanovic 2013, 207) and for the enjoyment of its citizens. But, if as I have been arguing, European states were not constituted simply as nations, but as imperial powers, and that a significant proportion of what is presented as their national wealth historically is attributable to the coerced labour and appropriated resources of others, then what does it mean to argue for the protection of that wealth solely for one's own citizens? Notice, too, that Milanovic is also silent on the decline of that public capital through policies of privatisation.

The idea that most European countries were simply nations, generating wealth endogenously, is a fundamental misreading of the historical processes that produced Europe. Even those countries that are not explicitly regarded as having been colonial powers partook nonetheless in the wealth of the European colonial project through the involvement of their populations in emigrationist colonialism and through being the beneficiaries of 'colonial drain' (Patnaik 2017). The wealth that is claimed by nations in Europe has a much broader provenance and, if we were to accept this, then we might be persuaded to reconfigure our politics in the present such that addressing global inequality would not require a trade-off between social and political citizenship and migration. Even Milanovic (2018) recognises that there are other ways to address global inequality, including global redistributive schemes. He just does not believe that such a scheme would be feasible. I would argue, in contrast, that not only is such a scheme feasible and just, but also that it is the only way in which we can tackle the confluence of neoliberal and the increasingly authoritarian politics of the present.

Conclusion: for postcolonial reparative action

European colonialism was a collective and individual endeavour that established, determined, and perpetuated the forms of global inequality that continue to disfigure our contemporary world. Its address requires us to acknowledge the ways in which we benefit from this structuring of the world and act to resolve those structures in a fully inclusive and social-democratic, not a nationalist, way. The injustices that disfigure the world we share can only be addressed by acknowledging the histories that have produced them as well as the historiographies that have obscured them.

This requires reflection upon the past and what I call postcolonial reparative action in the present. Perhaps unconditionally accepting refugees, asylum seekers, and other migrants to Europe would mitigate the actions of earlier generations that have precisely made the places 'they' come from unliveable? Could rethinking and reformulating trade and other policies, which are entirely to Europe's advantage, be an act of reparative justice? Might relabelling 'aid' as 'reparations' create the space for conversations about how little Europe gives and how much of what is given returns to Europe anyway and facilitate the possibility of doing more?

Europe is the wealthiest continent on the planet. Its wealth is an 'inheritance' derived from the very same historical processes that have left other places in poverty. Migration is an inadequate solution to the problem of global inequality. The problem of global inequality has itself been configured as a consequence of earlier

European movements. The only effective solution to issues of global inequality is to acknowledge and address these histories through forms of global distributive justice.

References

Bade, K. 1995. 'From Emigration to Immigration: The German Experience in the Nineteenth and Twentieth Centuries.' *Central European History* 28 (4): 507–535.
Bertram, Chris. 2019. 'The Openness-Rights Trade-off in Labour Migration, Claims to Membership, and Justice.' *Ethical Theory and Moral Practice* 22 (2): 283–296.
Bhambra, Gurminder K. 2017a. 'The Current Crisis of Europe: Refugees, Colonialism, and the Limits of Cosmopolitanism.' *European Law Journal* 23 (5): 395–405.
Bhambra, Gurminder K. 2017b. 'Brexit, Trump, and "Methodological Whiteness": On the Misrecognition of Race and Class.' *British Journal of Sociology* 68 (S1): 214–232.
Delaney, Enda. 2000. *Demography, State and Society: Irish Migration to Britain, 1921–1971*. Liverpool: Liverpool University Press.
Fedorowich, Kent, and Andrew S. Thompson. 2013. 'Mapping the Contours of the British World: Empire, Migration and Identity.' In *Empire, Migration and Identity in the British World*, edited by Kent Fedorowich and Andrew S. Thompson, 1–41. Manchester: Manchester University Press.
Holmwood, John, and Gurminder K. Bhambra. 2015. 'Capitalist Dispossession and New Justifications of Slavery,' *Open Democracy*, July 3. www.opendemocracy.net/en/beyond-trafficking-and-slavery/capitalist-dispossession-and-new-justifications-of-s/.
Knoblauch, Hubert, and Martina Löw. 2017. 'On the Spatial Re-Figuration of the Social World.' *Sociologica* 11 (2): 1–27. doi: 10.2383/88197.
Lovejoy, Paul. 1989. 'The Impact of the Atlantic Slave Trade on Africa: A Review of the Literature.' *The Journal of African History* 30 (3): 365–394.
Manning, Patrick. 1983. 'Contours of Slavery and Social Change in Africa.' *The American Historical Review* 88 (4): 835–857.
Miège, Jean-Louis. 1993. 'Migration and Decolonisation.' *European Review* 1 (1): 81–86.
Milanovic, Branko. 2012. 'Global Inequality: From Class to Location, from Proletarians to Migrants.' *Global Policy* 3 (2): 125–134.
Milanovic, Branko. 2013. 'Global Income Inequality in Numbers: In History and Now.' *Global Policy* 4 (2): 198–208.
Milanovic, Branko. 2016. 'There is a Trade-off between Citizenship and Migration.' *Financial Times*, April 20.
Milanovic, Branko. 2018. 'Migration into Europe: A Long-Term Solution?' *Social Europe*, November 19.
Mommsen, Wolfgang J. 1984. *Max Weber and German Politics 1890–1920*. Translated by Michael S. Steinberg. Chicago: University of Chicago Press.
Patnaik, Utsa. 2017. 'Revisiting the "Drain", or Transfer from India to Britain in the Context of Global Diffusion of Capitalism.' In *Agrarian and Other Histories: Essays for Binay Bhushan Chaudhuri*, edited by Shubhra Chakrabarti and Utsa Patnaik, 277–317. New Delhi: Tulika Books.
Posner, Eric A., and Glen Weyl. 2014. 'A Radical Solution to Global Income Inequality: Make the U.S. More Like Qatar.' *The New Republic*, November 7. https://newrepublic.com/article/120179/how-reduce-global-income-inequality-open-immigration-policies.
Posner, Eric A., and Glen Weyl. 2018. *Radical Markets: Uprooting Capitalism and Democracy for a Just Society*. Princeton: Princeton University Press.

Smith, Woodruff D. 1980. 'Friedrich Ratzel and the Origins of Lebensraum.' *German Studies Review* 3 (1): 51–68.
Streeck, Wolfgang. 2018. 'Between Charity and Justice: Remarks on the Social Construction of Immigration Policy in Rich Democracies.' *Culture, Practice and Europeanisation* 3 (2): 3–22.
Weyl, Eric Glen. 2016. 'The Openness-Equality Trade-Off in Global Redistribution.' *The Economic Journal*, October 25. https://ssrn.com/abstract=2509305.
Zahra, Tara. 2016. *The Great Departure: Mass Migration from Eastern Europe and the Making of the Free World*. New York: W. W. Norton and Company.
Zubrzycki, J. 1953. 'Emigration from Poland in the Nineteenth and Twentieth Centuries.' *Population Studies* 6 (3): 248–272.

8
THE CENTRALITY OF RACE TO INEQUALITY ACROSS THE WORLD-SYSTEM[1]

Old figurations and new reconfigurations

Manuela Boatcă

Linking the increase in inequality and the reconfiguration of space

In its latest report, entitled "Time to Care," Oxfam International (2020) pointed out, as it has done several times in the past decade, that global economic inequality is out of control. Other global organizations and academic publications have also sounded the alarm about a rapidly polarizing world. Yet until rather recently, the fact that the inequality of wealth and income had increased since the 1980s within rich countries—notably the United States and Great Britain—only spurred debates about how social inequality was "bad for growth" (*The Economist* 2012). At the same time, news of the decline of income inequality in Latin America, viewed as the world's most unequal region for decades, increasingly made the headlines as "Gini Back in the Bottle" (*The Economist* 2012)—a pun on the Gini coefficient, a common measure for income inequality, and the hit song "Genie in a Bottle." The fact that the unprecedented changes had suddenly rendered the United States more unequal than much of Latin America further spurred debates on inequality in rich countries (Light 2013).

However, only a few voices pointed to how the increase in inequality worldwide was contributing to a reconfiguration of space and to the shifts this reconfiguration occasioned in charting elites and underclasses across cores and peripheries of the world-system. In world-system scholarship, the capitalist world-economy that emerged in the sixteenth century with Europe's colonial expansion into the Americas is the basic economic entity. It comprises a single division of labor in which different areas perform different economic tasks—typically, industrial production in the core, raw material production in the periphery and a mixture of the two in the semiperiphery. While the unequal division of labor ensures the steady transfer of surplus from the periphery to the core, the location of world areas

DOI: 10.4324/9781003036159-10

within the global division of labor shifts in time and mechanisms of surplus transfer change. The system develops as a whole in a "pattern of interplay between cyclical processes of expansion and contraction and the secular evolutionary processes that undermine the basic stability of the system" (Wallerstein 2000, 109), as competing strata, technologies, and institutions negotiate conflicting interests across the interdependent structural locations of core, periphery, and semiperiphery. Knoblauch and Löw (2020) have coined "refiguration of space" to refer to the transformation of the social order as a result of tensions and conflict between different social structures in a recent, "refigured modernity"; this represents, for world-system scholars, the very mode of functioning and underlying logic of the capitalist world-economy since the sixteenth century. Drawing on world-system scholarship, anthropologist Fernando Coronil referred to the most recent installment in this pattern of interplay as a refiguration of space, noting that

> While the gap between rich and poor nations—as well as between the rich and the poor—is widening everywhere, global wealth is concentrating in fewer hands, and these few include those of subaltern elites. In this reconfigured global landscape, the "rich" cannot be identified exclusively with metropolitan nations; nor can the "poor" be identified exclusively with the Third and Second Worlds. The closer worldwide interconnection of ruling sectors and the marginalization of subordinate majorities has undermined the cohesiveness of these geopolitical units. . . . The social tensions resulting from these processes often lead to a racialization of social conflict and the rise of ethnicities.
>
> *(Coronil 2000, 361)*

It is this reconfiguration of the global landscape through the unequal mobility of the very rich across cores, peripheries, and semiperipheries—rather than a spatial refiguration towards the centrality of the semiperiphery alone—that will constitute the focus of the present chapter. Coronil's call for a differentiated, basically intersectional analysis of inequality echoed the provocative formula that Immanuel Wallerstein used in his 1988 analysis of racism and sexism in the world-system in order to describe racialized social mobility under capitalism:

> Some groups can be mobile in the ranking system; some groups can disappear or combine with others; while others break apart and new ones are born. But there are always some who are "niggers". If there are no Blacks or too few to play the role, one can invent "white niggers".
>
> *(Wallerstein 2000, 350)*

In turn, in a long essay published in the *Journal of World-Systems Research* in 2017, titled "Moving Toward Theory for the 21st Century: The Centrality of Non-Western Semiperipheries to World Ethnic/Racial Inequality," Wilma Dunaway and Don Clelland argued for decentering the analysis of global ethnic/racial inequality that sees white supremacy as the sole cause of racism and bringing the non-Western semiperiphery[2] to the foreground instead. In world-system scholarship, the structural position of the semiperiphery has been credited with ensuring the survival of the capitalist world-economy since its inception—mostly because semiperipheral intermediate positions have served to placate the system's tendency towards polarization between an exploiting core and an exploited periphery. By preventing the unified opposition of the peripheral areas against the core, semiperipheries fulfilled not only a significant economic function in the capitalist world-economy but also, and first of all, the major political task of providing stability to the system, one region at a time. As Wallerstein put it in the wake of the 1970s economic crisis:

> The essential difference between the semiperipheral country that is Brazil or South Africa today and the semiperipheral country that is North Korea or Czechoslovakia is probably less in the economic role each plays in the world-economy than in the political role each plays in conflicts among core countries.
>
> *(Wallerstein 1979, 75)*

Drawing on this conceptualization of the semiperiphery, Dunaway and Clelland argue that future theory-building must pay particular attention to "the rise of the Asian semiperiphery, where two-fifths of the world's population is concentrated" (2017, 399). It is worth engaging at length with their arguments in order to illuminate both the benefits and the pitfalls inherent in the (over)emphasis of spatial reconfiguration more generally, and of the structural position of the semiperiphery in particular. Such overemphasis placed on shifts in the world-system hierarchy, I argue, obscures decisive dynamics—first and foremost racially mediated social and physical mobility across cores, semiperipheries, and peripheries.

The authors' starting point is the observation that "more of the share of the world wealth that once accumulated in the core and in the European semiperiphery is now being appropriated by nonwestern semiperipheries" (Dunaway and Clelland 2017, 408). The article offers much-needed empirical evidence against the recurrent catching-up development rhetoric that World Bank reports often derive from undifferentiated data on population size and economic growth in low-income countries. It also makes a strong case for a more differentiated analysis of hierarchies of oppression that would account for the diverse ethnic make-up of the transnational capitalist class as much as for the actions of non-Western states. The article thus strives to decenter Eurocentric perspectives by bringing non-Western semiperipheries to the forefront of social theory and by denouncing approaches centered on race as a universalization of Western knowledge. To this end, Dunaway and Clelland strongly emphasize the visibility of semiperipheries, yet underplay and even explicitly argue against the importance of white supremacy for an understanding of global inequality.

While I agree, and have previously argued myself that closer attention should be paid to semiperipheries in terms of their transformative potential, I consider the claim that non-Western semiperipheries exacerbate and even cause racial/ethnic inequality to be misleading. The data provided by Dunaway and Clelland do speak to the role of semiperipheries more generally (Western and non-Western) in lending stability to the system by replicating, mirroring, and disseminating racialized mechanisms of endless accumulation of capital at different levels in the structural hierarchy. Yet this does not amount to the non-Western semiperipheries' ability to overturn the racializing logic on which endless accumulation has been premised since the emergence of the modern/colonial world-system, and should not be mistaken for such.

In the following, I thus want to caution against what I think are three weak links in the argument about the role of semiperipheries in the increase of racial and ethnic inequality: mistaking visibility for causation, conflating the concept of race with the reality of racism (and its many historical and geopolitical configurations), and throwing the baby (white supremacy) out with the bathwater (Western knowledge).

I will limit my comments to two aspects. The first aspect is methodological and concerns the unclear unit of analysis that underlies Dunaway and Clelland's claim for the centrality of non-Western semiperipheries to ethnic/racial inequality. The second aspect is more substantive and targets the relationship between racism and the emergence, functioning, and reproduction of the modern/colonial world-system.

The unit of analysis: magnifying glass or methodological bottleneck?

In order to draw attention to the role of non-Western semiperipheries in causing and exacerbating ethnic/racial inequality, Dunaway and Clelland observe that

> greater wealth accumulation has not been accompanied by an end to ethnic/racial oppression in the core, nor has ascent to semiperipheral status led to less ethnic/racial exploitation in nonwestern societies.
>
> *(Dunaway and Clelland 2017, 412)*

South Africa is mentioned as an example where the dismantling of white rule has even led to a Black elite oppressing a Black majority. Together with the fact that the richest countries now include many non-Western states and that large numbers of non-Westerners have joined the capitalist class in recent decades, this is viewed as evidence against a global apartheid thesis—according to which white supremacy dictates the terms and amount of wealth accumulation:

> why did "white supremacy" not operate to prevent "nonwhite" interlopers from accumulating wealth between 1980 and 2015 that this racial dualism reserves to "western" countries? . . . Why did "coloredness" not prevent seven Third World countries from achieving GDPpc [gross domestic product per capita] that was 2.3 times greater than that of the United Kingdom in 1980?
>
> *(Dunaway and Clelland 2017, 412)*

Answers to the questions thus formulated seem to be possible only as blatant negations of the white supremacy theory. Yet this is due to the methodological bottleneck inherent in the questions themselves: on the one hand, their focus constantly shifts from structural positions within the world-system (core, semiperiphery) to national units (societies, countries) to regional constructs (the West, Eastern Europe, the Third World); on the other hand, these units seem to operate on their own, rather than as parts of the capitalist world-economy.

For non-Western semiperipheries to cause ethnic/racial inequality, mechanisms for the production and reproduction of difference would need to be available there that are unavailable elsewhere in the world-system, and that are somehow confined to that particular location. For South Africa to experience the dismantling of exploitation and segregation of the non-white majority after the end of apartheid, racism would need to have worked there independently of the racism built in the exploitative logic of the capitalist world-economy. Yet the very contribution of world-systems analysis to understanding global inequality consists in viewing capitalism as operating at the level of the entire world-economy, rather than in individual countries going through different stages of development. Shifting the unit of analysis from the nation-state to the world as a whole makes it possible to view inequalities as intrinsic to the world-economy, their increase in the longue durée as part of a secular trend, and their eventual disappearance as premised on a fundamental transformation of the entire world-system, not just individual units—whether countries, regions, or semiperipheries.

If we are to understand the ways in which racism produces ethnic and racial inequality in the world-system today, the unit of analysis for the questions we ask has to be the world-system as well. The so-called West is only "white," the allegedly post-Socialist Europe "white, but not quite," and the former Third World "colored" in relation to each other and in a world-system premised on a constructed notion of whiteness as the norm. In this sense, they are "large scale figurations," as Knoblauch and Löw observe, drawing on Norbert Elias' concept (Knoblauch and Löw 2020, 265). However, they are not new but instead date back five hundred years; their current reconfiguration does not change the systemic logic behind their creation. Indeed, Wallerstein's early engagement with the construction of race as a structural category in the African context does justice to both the systemic logic and the local fluctuations that operate to maintain white supremacy:

> Race is, in the contemporary world, the only international status group category. It has replaced religion, which played that role since at least the eighth century AD. Rank in this system, rather than colour, determines membership in the status group. Thus, in Trinidad, there can be a "Black Power" movement, directed against an all-Black government, on the grounds that this government functions as an ally of North American imperialism. Thus, Quebec separatists can call themselves the "White Niggers" of North America. Thus, Pan-Africanism can include white-skinned Arabs of North Africa, but exclude white-skinned Afrikaners of South Africa. Thus, Cyprus

and Yugoslavia can be invited to tricontinental conferences (Asia, Africa and Latin America) but Israel and Japan are excluded.

(Wallerstein 1979, 180)

The world-systemic lens has the advantage of a magnifying glass that puts into clear relief entanglements and interdependencies between seemingly unconnected and spatially distant areas. If we focus instead on the role of one structural location—in this case, the semiperiphery—in order to explain the functioning of phenomena such as racism and processes such as increasing inequality, which have a system-wide logic, we exchange the magnifying glass for a methodological bottleneck that prevents us from seeing both historical connections and present transformations.

Race in the modern/colonial world-system

However, Dunaway and Clelland further clarify their strong disavowal of white supremacy as an explanatory factor for racial/ethnic inequality. They argue that, while ethnicization and racism are built into the dynamics of the world-system, they operate at multiple levels across the structural positions of core, semiperiphery, and periphery, rather than as a racial dualism that pinpoints "whites" as the only perpetrators of ethnic and racial inequality (Dunaway and Clelland 2017, 418) across all tiers. They thus take the increasing racial and ethnic diversity of the transnational capitalist class in the past decades as a particularly strong indication of the ways in which non-Western semiperipheries will increasingly cause and/or exacerbate most of the world's ethnic/racial inequality in the twenty-first century. As much as 53% of the world's wealthiest capitalists today are not Westerners, Dunaway and Clelland point out. And yet, the authors note, globally visible outlets, such as Oxfam's 2016 report on the concentration of wealth in the hands of ever fewer billionaires, disregard this momentous change in the composition of this class.

This evidence, pointing to an unprecedented shift in the nationalities of the world's most recent billionaires, is indeed both striking and mounting. World-system scholars found that the number of billionaires in middle-income countries tripled in just six years despite the 2008 recession, with Brazil, Hong Kong, and India registering a twofold, Russia almost a threefold, and China a staggering twelvefold increase in their respective number of billionaires from 2006 to 2012 (Albrecht and Korzeniewicz 2018, 103). At the same time, global financial consultancies such as Arton Capital predicted that the billionaire population was going to grow nearly 80% by the year 2020, an increase of 1,700 billionaires, to which China and India were expected to contribute disproportionately (Arton Capital 2017). The newest data, which show Asia recording the fastest rise in billionaire numbers in 2019 and China alone accounting for 32 of the top 40 fastest growing high net worth cities for the period 2018–2023, seem to confirm these predictions.

Although Europe and North America remain the regions with the largest number of billionaires, such trends clearly render the Asian semiperiphery more visible with respect to its impact on global inequality—but they are neither caused nor exacerbated by the semiperiphery. Rather, they provide further evidence of the world-system's increasing polarization into an ultra-rich transnational class and an increasingly impoverished 99%: as calculated by Oxfam, since 2015, the richest 1% have owned more wealth than the rest of the world, while the number of individuals who held the same wealth as the bottom half of humanity has rapidly decreased from 388 in 2010 to 62 in 2016 and to only 8 in 2017 (Hardoon 2017). For 2019, Oxfam reported that the world's billionaires, only 2,153 people had more wealth than 4.6 billion people combined (Oxfam International 2020).

Nevertheless, it is misleading to treat the (relatively and absolutely) fast-growing but still relatively small group of non-Western billionaires as an indicator of changes in the role of the semiperiphery as a whole.

First, because even between 2006 and 2012, the period of the fastest increase in the number of ultra-rich non-Westerners for which there is data, the odds of becoming a millionaire were still twice as high for citizens of high-income countries than for citizens of middle-income countries that qualify as semiperipheries (Albrecht and Korzeniewicz 2018, 105).

Second, a large number of the semiperiphery's billionaires is made up of non-residents who either already have a second citizenship in a core country or are in the market for one, which is what makes them more interesting for global financial consultancies in the near future than they already are. The same financial recession that marked the shift towards more non-Western capitalists becoming billionaires after 2008 also saw the proliferation of investor residence and citizenship programs throughout the European semiperiphery (Western and non-Western). It thus became possible to acquire a European Union residence permit or a second citizenship with a sizeable investment in real estate or government bonds (Boatcă 2016). The main beneficiaries of such programs, implemented since 2010 in Hungary, Cyprus, Malta, Macedonia, Greece, Bulgaria, Lithuania, Spain, and Portugal, have been Chinese and Russian but also Lebanese and Egyptian investors, who thus obtain the right of visa-free travel to core countries, the citizenship of a Schengen-zone state (except in the case of Bulgaria, which is not part of the Schengen zone), and the right to reside and work anywhere in the European Union. None of these programs include strict residence requirements for their investor citizens. Investors thus use the rights they purchased as remote access to the wealth accumulated in Western core states, shielded from the majority of the world's population through Western core states' enforcement of borders, visa regimes, and citizenships. As summed up by Arton Capital:

> With more and more wealth being created in Asia, yet demand for residence in European territories being so high, this trend of UHNW [ultra high net worth] individuals seeking global citizenship will undoubtedly continue to grow.
> *(Arton Capital 2017)*

The boom in the number of non-Western capitalists seeking the advantages of residence and citizenship in the U.S. and Europe is therefore hardly a challenge to core dominance or white supremacy. Rather, their rising number points to the paramount role that race continues to play for a global stratification in which the "premium citizenships" of core Western states highly correlate with whiteness as a constructed norm; and to which only very wealthy non-whites have recently gained access through the commodification of rights in semiperipheral states that share a visa-free travel zone with core Western states. For wealthy non-Westerners, investment residence and citizenship of Western states constitute global social mobility as well as a means of "buying into" whiteness.

The European Union is the historic heir to Western colonial states (Böröcz and Sarkar 2005) whose wealth accumulation has been highly premised on a racialized division of labor and a structurally unequal distribution of resources to those racialized as non-white. The Henley & Partners Visa Restriction Index, produced by a private British consultancy in cooperation with the trade association for the world's airlines, IATA, ranks Japan, Singapore, and South Korea, followed by Germany, Denmark, Finland, France, Italy, and Sweden, in the top 3 passports worldwide on account of a total score of countries to which their citizens can travel visa-free (189, 188, and 187, respectively, out of a total number of countries of 219) (Henley and Partners 2019). Of these, only South Korea is a semiperipheral country. Most passport holders in Africa, the Middle East, and South Asia have scores below 70, while semiperipheral mainland China has a barely slightly higher score of 74—equal to that of Lesotho, and right below that of Namibia and Thailand. This explains why EU residence permits are extremely attractive to Chinese investors, and much more so than for Hong Kong investors, who—at least at the time of writing this chapter, amid changes in Chinese policies regarding Hong Kong—have access to 152 countries on account of holding "Special Administrative Region of China" passports—a reminder of residual colonial ties. The juxtaposition of the top 5 and the bottom 5 ranks on the index—only available for the 2018 ranking, and therefore slightly different from the 2019 numbers—makes the core-periphery divide in terms of global mobility particularly apparent.

It is thus even more misleading to view the ethnic and racial diversity of billionaires from semiperipheral countries as an argument against white supremacy. A growing number of Brazilian millionaires have increasingly sought either a U.S. green card, the investor citizenship of a Caribbean country still part of the Commonwealth, or European citizenship through descent from a European ancestor as a means of translating material wealth into global social mobility (Fellet 2016). Such capital-facilitated moves up the citizenship ladder are themselves ways of buying into whiteness, or what, in the context of racial inequalities in Brazil, has been referred to as "whitening with money" (Hasenbalg 2005). At the global level, these are strategies of eluding the ascription of citizenship to one's place of birth. As such, they belie the experience of the great majority of transnational labor migrants, for whom international migration in search of upward economic mobility entails the risk of downward racial mobility through reclassification as non-white.

The fact that race is used as a census category in few states and whiteness is seldom chosen as a means of self-identification, as Dunaway and Clelland observe, should not deceive us into denying the processes of racialization being replicated throughout the structural positions of the world-system. Nor should the fact that the word "race" does not exist in a majority of the dialects of Asian semiperipheries (Dunaway and Clelland 2017, 448) be taken to indicate the absence of whiteness as the constructed norm and racial stratification as a reality in Asia.

First, as scholarship on Orientalism, racism, and critical whiteness has repeatedly shown, prevailing norms—whether the West, Europe, heterosexuality, or whiteness—feature as unmarked categories (Hall 2006; Todorova 2005). Their normative character becomes visible through the simultaneous construction of difference—of the Orient as the non-West, of Eastern Europe as lesser Europe, of homosexuality as non-heterosexuality, and of Blackness as non-whiteness. All deviant categories thus constructed require naming, while their unmarked counterparts remain unnamed, unqualified, or unstressed. The label of "Europe" always includes both Western Europe and its white populations, but Eastern Europe needs to be specifically mentioned in order to be included in the term, while Black Europe needs to be argued, defended, and explained. In this context, the fact that the European East is often portrayed as "semi-Oriental" or "somehow Asian" not only serves to sanction Western Europe's position as the norm, but also to legitimate the—geographically untenable—continental division between Europe and Asia (Lewis and Wigen 1997). The vast regional inequalities and trade imbalances that Dunaway and Clelland observe in Asia are undeniable, yet they only prove that Asia as a whole is not an adequate unit of analysis, but a racialized, Orientalist construct. As critical geographers have long pointed out, the very fact that regional commonalities in Asia made it impossible to pinpoint an "Asian identity" is precisely what "has allowed Europeans to see the disproportionate diversity of the Asian 'continent' as a challenge for Asian civilization, rather than as a challenge to their own system of geographical classification" (Lewis and Wigen 1997, 37).

Second, the extent to which Asian societies are impacted by racialization as a deviance from whiteness becomes apparent, among other things, due to the fact that economies—as well as politics—of beauty have consistently privileged whiteness in ways that reinforce and reproduce colonial patterns of racialization despite the absence of explicit references to whiteness (Haritaworn 2016). Instead, what is often labeled the "Eurasian" or "Pan-Asian" look, considered more attractive than darker skin by a large majority of men and women across Asia, is associated with racial superiority, status, and higher income. It consequently fuels a booming cosmetics industry that thrives on skin-bleaching. Accordingly, four out of ten women surveyed in Hong Kong, Malaysia, the Philippines, and South Korea use skin-whitening products, the global market for which was "projected to reach $19.8 billion by 2018, driven by the growing desire for light-coloured skin among both men and women primarily from the Asian, African and Middle East regions" (Pe 2016).

Does all of the above amount to evidence for the existence of the "global racial dualism" that Dunaway and Clelland seek to disprove? Not necessarily. It certainly is not evidence for a "fixed racial axis of the world-economy" that "reduces the world's diverse people into two lumps that conceal massive ethnic/racial complexity" (Dunaway and Clelland 2017, 411). When attempting to see "beyond white racists and colonists" (Dunaway and Clelland 2017, 442), however, we need to take into account that, even if not all racists are white, racism in the world-system is premised on historically constructed and colonially enforced whiteness. In this context, whiteness is just as much a geopolitical category as it is a racial designation. The modern/colonial world-system piggybacked on previous forms of xenophobia and discrimination and incorporated them as part of the logic of endless accumulation, just as it incorporated older regimes of labor control, such as slavery, serfdom, and tenancy. In ancient China, India, and Japan, as well as in Europe, fair skin implied wealth and nobility, while darker skin signaled work in the field (Pe 2016). In Europe, medieval Christendom offered an entire apparatus of otherness formed by unmarried and learned women, heretics, Jews, and Muslims. Ella Shohat showed how European demonology prefigured colonial racism and sexism by drawing on the stock of Jewish and Muslim stereotypes "to characterize the savage, the infidel, the indigenous man as sexual omnivore and the indigenous woman as sexual object" (Shohat 2017, 333). The incorporation of the Americas into the emerging world-system entailed transforming such imperial differences into colonial ones, as well as inventing Europeanness, ethnicity, and race (Mignolo 2006; Quijano and Wallerstein 1992). Walter Mignolo points to the momentous shift operated by the translation of race into racism as part of the emergence of the capitalist world-economy by noting that:

> The link between capital accumulation and a discourse of devaluation of human beings was absent in co-existing sixteenth centuries empires like the Mughal, the Ottoman, the Aztec, the Inca, the Chinese and the emerging Russian one. The complicity between political economy and political theory, based on the racialization of human beings, languages, places, cultures, memories, knowledge . . . was the "novelty" of the sixteenth century and the historical foundation of the racial colonial matrix whose logic is still at work today.
> *(Mignolo 2006, 18)*

The coemergence of capitalism and the racial colonial matrix has provided the context for the global division of labor between cores, semiperipheries, and peripheries since the sixteenth century. Semiperipheries today are therefore (still) competing within a capitalist world-economy based on racism and inequality and their strategies are imbricated with nationalist, fascist, and racist ideologies recurrent throughout the system. But such ideologies neither originated with nor were enhanced by the structural position of non-Western semiperipheries. When we start paying closer attention to spatial reconfigurations in order to understand current or historical phenomena, we should therefore make sure not to gloss over the very logic according to which some of these reconfigurations took place. In the case of inequality under capitalism, as the Black Lives Matter movement has amply demonstrated in recent years, racism most certainly remains a paramount structuring principle and underlying logic.

Notes

1 This is a revised and expanded version of an article titled "The Centrality of Race to Inequality Across the World-System" and initially published in 2017 in the *Journal of World-Systems Research* 23 (2): 465–473. doi: 10.5195/jwsr.2017.729.
2 In the following, I will use Dunaway and Clelland's spelling of "nonwestern" only in direct references to their article. For more general statements, I will employ the more common spelling "non-Western" (countries, regions, semiperipheries).

References

Albrecht, S., and R. P. Korzeniewicz. 2018. "'Creative Destruction' From a World-Systems Perspective: Billionaires and the Great Recession of 2008." In *Global Inequalities in World-Systems Perspective. Theoretical Debates and Methodological Innovations*, edited by M. Boatcă, A. Komlosy, and H.-H. Nolte, 94–115. New York and London: Routledge.

Arton Capital. 2017. *A Shrinking World: Global Citizenship for UHNW Individuals*. Accessed February 24, 2020. www.artoncapital.com/documents/publications/Arton-Capital-Wealth-X-Report-web.pdf.

Boatcă, M. 2016. "Exclusion through Citizenship and the Geopolitics of Austerity." In *Austere Histories in European Societies. Social Exclusion and the Contest of Colonial Memories*, edited by S. Jonsson and J. Willén, 115–134. London: Routledge.

Böröcz, J., and M. Sarkar. 2005. "What Is the EU?" *International Sociology* 20 (2): 153–173.

Coronil, F. 2000. "Towards a Critique of Globalcentrism. Speculations on Capitalism's Nature." *Public Culture* 12 (2): 351–374.

Dunaway, W. A., and D. A. Clelland. 2017. "Moving toward Theory for the 21st Century: The Centrality of Nonwestern Semiperipheries to World Ethnic/Racial Inequality." *Journal of World-Systems Research* 23 (2): 399–464.

(The) Economist. 2012. "Gini Back in the Bottle: An Unequal Continent is Becoming Less So." October 13. Accessed March 2, 2020. www.economist.com/sites/default/files/20121013_world_economy.pdf.

Fellet, J. 2016. "'Compra' de cidadania caribenha vira opção para brasileiro que quer viver nos EUA." *BBC Brasil*, June 10. Accessed February 24, 2020. www.bbc.com/portuguese/internacional-36456703.

Hall, S. 2006. "The West and the Rest: Discourse and Power." In *The Indigenous Experience. Global Perspectives*, edited by R. C. A. Maaka and C. Andersen, 165–173. Toronto: Canadian Scholars' Press.

Hardoon, D. 2017. "An Economy for the 99%. It's Time to Build a Human Economy that Benefits Everyone, Not Just the Privileged Few." *Oxfam International*, January 16. Accessed February 26, 2020. www.oxfam.org/en/research/economy-99.

Haritaworn, J. 2016. *The Biopolitics of Mixing. Thai Multiracialities and Haunted Ascendancies*, 1st ed. London: Taylor and Francis.

Hasenbalg, C. A. 2005. *Discriminação e desigualdades raciais no Brasil*, 2nd ed. Belo Horizonte, Rio de Janeiro: Editora UFMG; IUPERJ.

Henley & Partners. 2019. *Henley Passport Index and Global Mobility Report*. Accessed July 7, 2020. www.henleypassportindex.com/assets/2019/HPI%20Global%20Mobility%20Report_Final_190104.pdf.

Knoblauch, H., and M. Löw. 2020. "The Re-Figuration of Spaces and Refigured Modernity—Concept and Diagnosis." *Historical Social Research* 45 (2): 263–292. doi: 10.12759/hsr.45.2020.2.263-292.

Lewis, M. W., and K. E. Wigen. 1997. *The Myth of Continents. A Critique of Metageography*. Berkeley: University of California Press.

Light, J. 2013. "The U.S. is Now More Unequal than Much of Latin America." *Moyers on Democracy*, January 29. Accessed March 2, 2020. http://billmoyers.com/2013/01/29/the-u-s-is-now-more-unequal-than-much-of-latin-america/.

Mignolo, W. D. 2006. "Islamophobia/Hispanophobia: The (Re) Configuration of the Racial Imperial/Colonial Matrix." *Human Architecture* 5 (1): 13–28.

Oxfam International. 2020. "Time to Care. Unpaid and Underpaid Care Work and the Global Inequality Crisis." January 20. Accessed July 6, 2020. www.oxfam.org/en/research/time-care.

Pe, R. 2016. "Yes, Asia Is Obsessed with White Skin." *INQUIRER.net*, October 1. Accessed February 26, 2020. https://business.inquirer.net/215898/yes-asia-is-obsessed-with-white-skin#ixzz4l29zd78T.

Quijano, A., and I. Wallerstein. 1992. "Americanity as a Concept, or the Americas in the Modern World-System." *International Social Science Journal* 44 (4): 549–557.

Shohat, E. 2017. "'Coming to America': Reflections on Hair and Memory Loss." In *On the Arab-Jew, Palestine, and Other Displacements. Selected Writings of Ella Shohat*, edited by E. Shohat, 339–355. London: Pluto Press.

Todorova, M. 2005. "Spacing Europe: What is a Historical Region?" *East Central Europe* 32 (1–2): 59–78.

Wallerstein, I. 1979. *The Capitalist World-Economy*. Cambridge: Cambridge University Press.

Wallerstein, I. 2000. *The Essential Wallerstein*. New York: New Press.

9
SPATIAL TRANSFORMATIONS IN WORLD-HISTORICAL PERSPECTIVE

Towards mapping the space and time of wealth accumulation

Roberto Patricio Korzeniewicz and Corey R. Payne

A world-historical perspective on spatial transformations

The present moment is one of dramatic social change. The wave of "globalization" characterizing the world-system since the 1980s—as well as the movements against its harshest effects—have, in the words of the call for contributions to this volume, "manifest[ed] themselves in conflicting approaches to interpreting spaces, as the Charlottesville protests and the debate about whether nation states should have more (or less) open borders show" and have been "articulated in beliefs about security and insecurity, and in processes of closures, such as the rise in initiatives to build new border walls" (Knoblauch and Löw 2017a; cf. 2017b). Such reconfigurations are the guiding subject of this book.

In this chapter, we aim to provide a world-historical perspective to this ongoing discussion of spatial transformations. We are particularly interested in addressing a guiding hypothesis of the Collaborative Research Center on the "Re-Figuration of Spaces" (CRC 1265, Berlin, Germany):

> The traditional, globally dominant model of modernity with its centralized nation states, borders and national economies conflicts with post- and late-modern transnationalization with its polycentrism, globalizing scope and breaking down of barriers. Our hypothesis is that spatial refiguration is a result of this tension.
>
> *(Knoblauch and Löw 2017a)*

Thus, the CRC calls for

> a conception of space that is no longer understood as—and simplistically reduced to—a fixed and homogeneous entity lying about somewhere out

there calling for conquest or protection, but rather as a highly complex act of configuration.

(Knoblauch and Löw 2017a)

We argue that such *reconfigurations of* space are intimately intertwined with *relocations in* space—of labor, of capital, of production, of accumulation—that have long characterized historical capitalism. By briefly examining such spatial relocations in the modern world-system, this chapter seeks to contribute a world-historical perspective to the discussion on spatial transformations. In short, we argue:

(1) Examining spatial transformations of social relations requires a unit of analysis larger than the nation-state, *no matter the time period we seek to understand*
(2) Over time, spatial transformations have interacted with what Joseph Schumpeter calls "creative destruction," yielding *spatial innovations*
(3) The "local" and the "global" are not merely distinct spheres that are now in more complex interaction, but rather interacting, longue durée geographies of social and political contestation, cooperation, and identity-formation that, precisely as a consequence of their very interactions, have constantly undergone change

The world-system as unit of analysis

For the most part, the social sciences remain trapped in a familiar centuries-old paradigm wherein social interactions are constituted by, and constitutive of, individual nation-states. Perspectives that would otherwise differ across theoretical and methodological spectrums converge under this paradigm to understand social processes and social forces as the outcome or expression of interactions that take place primarily within national boundaries (e.g., class relations in versions emphasizing distributional struggles or, in others, emphasizing social integration, the particular solidarities produced by a growing division of labor).

Throughout the twentieth century, social scientists scrutinized individual national trajectories, particularly as they manifested themselves in the wealthiest countries of the world, to extrapolate generalizable patterns of economic, political, and social development. In the study of inequality, for example, modernization scholars predicted a growing gap between urban (largely industrial) and rural (largely agricultural) populations in the transition from traditional arrangements to modernity. Such a transition was the focus of much work on stratification, with the general expectation that modernization would bring about the displacement of ascription by achievement as the main criterion shaping social hierarchies. The withering away of ascription as a basis of social hierarchy, in turn, would both allow and require enhanced social mobility (e.g., from rural to urban areas, from agriculture into industry, from tradition to modernity).

More critical approaches argue that the trajectories of wealthy nations cannot be assumed to be independent from those of poor nations, or that the specific path of wealthy nations cannot be generalized into a universal model of social development that all nations are likely to follow. But while such critical perspectives have been productive in conceptualizing social inequality, stratification, and mobility in wealthy and poor nations as inter-relational, many versions of these critical perspectives have assumed or maintained their own unverified generalizations. Often, the assessment of world-systems perspectives, for example, has come to be reduced to the inclusion of a few variables in quantitative models, as if such perspectives can be reduced simply to the notion that high levels of wealth accumulation are secured to a much greater extent by manufacturing production rather than raw material production, by production for domestic consumption rather than by production for export, or by domestic rather than foreign investment.

In short, the mainstream social sciences by and large manage to hold on to the assumption that nation-states constitute the most relevant unit of analysis for the study of the social world. But nation-states are not always the appropriate unit for theorizing social relations.

We can use a foundational text of the modern social sciences, Adam Smith's *The Wealth of Nations* ([1776] 1976), to illustrate the importance of choosing an appropriate unit of analysis. In several passages of *The Wealth of Nations*, Smith discusses wealth disparities within and between town and countryside, in ways that echo discussions of such disparities within and between wealthy and poor nations today. Rather than following the existing common sense to explain the wealth of towns and the poverty of the countryside in the late eighteenth century as the outcome of processes occurring independently within each of these bounded territories, *The Wealth of Nations* chooses an alternative unit of analysis, one that encompasses both sets of spaces (town and countryside).

In Smith's account, the citizens of towns historically used corporate association to regulate production and trade in ways that restricted competition from the countryside—useful to contrast against the assumption that towns have been built primarily around inclusive practices.

> The inhabitants of a town, being collected into one place, can easily combine together. The most insignificant trades carried on in towns have accordingly, in some place or another, been incorporated; and even where they have never been incorporated, yet the corporation spirit, the jealousy of strangers, the aversion to take apprentices, or to communicate the secret of their trade, generally prevail in them, and often teach them, by voluntary associations and agreements, to prevent that free competition which they cannot prohibit by byelaws.
>
> *(Smith [1776] 1976, I, 141)*

As a result of such exclusionary arrangements, in their dealings with the countryside ("and in these latter dealings consists the whole trade which supports and enriches every town") town-dwellers were "great gainers" able to "purchase, with a smaller quantity of their labour, the produce of a greater quantity of the labour of the country" (Smith [1776] 1976, I, 139–140). In this account, the wealth of towns and the poverty of the countryside become inextricably linked, as it was largely to regulate and shape the flows (e.g., of goods, capital, and people) constituting this very relation that territorial boundaries between town and country were constructed and enforced.

While such arrangements tended to raise the wages that town employers had to pay,

> in recompence, they were enabled to sell their own just as much dearer; so that so far it was as broad as long, as they say; and in the dealings of the different classes within the town with one another, none of them were losers by these regulations.
>
> (Smith [1776] 1976, I, 139)

What Smith thereby describes is a process of selective *exclusion*. Through institutional arrangements establishing a social compact that restricted entry to markets, town-dwellers attained a virtuous combination of growth, political autonomy, and relative equity that simultaneously transferred competitive pressures to the countryside.

Adam Smith ([1776] 1976) provides important insights into the crucial role played by opportunity hoarding in shaping the relative prevalence of wealth and scarcity in town and countryside. But these insights would have been missed if his unit of analysis in *The Wealth of Nations* had failed to encompass both sets of spaces (towns and country) and their interaction in his narrative. For example, Smith could have attributed the wealth of towns to the individual effort, frugality, and/or values of their citizens—thereby explaining the relative poverty of rural peoples as the consequence of insufficient achievement in each or any of these dimensions. But his account avoided such a naturalization of town/countryside boundaries and emphasized instead the relational processes (including the creation and enforcement of the boundaries demarcating "town" and "countryside") that in his account play a central role in explaining the uneven distribution of wealth across these spaces.

Like Smith, we find that the study of social relations most often requires a unit of analysis that is both global and historical—a perspective, moreover, that emphasizes the necessity of understanding these relations as embedded in space.

Spatial "innovations" and Schumpeter's creative destruction[1]

From a world-historical perspective, spatial transformations have been constant. Of course, the notion that "innovation" is at the heart of capitalist accumulation is deeply rooted in the social sciences and a central notion in the work of Adam Smith and Karl Marx. While Smith and Marx differed in explaining the sources of such innovation—the former emphasizing its dimensions as a response to competitive pressures, the latter focusing on the specificities of labor exploitation under capitalist production (with an emphasis on relative surplus)—they both emphasized innovation as a key outcome. This is why Joseph Schumpeter (1942, 82–3) emphasizes that, instead of a single transition from one state of equilibrium to another, we should conceive of capitalism as entailing continuous transformation:

> Capitalism is by nature a form or method of economic change and not only never is but never can be stationary. The opening up of new markets, foreign or domestic, and the organizational development from the craft shop and factory to such concerns as U.S. Steel illustrate the same process of industrial mutation—if I may use that biological term—that incessantly revolutionizes the economic structure from within, incessantly destroying the old one, incessantly creating a new one. This process of Creative Destruction is the essential fact about capitalism. It is what capitalism consists in and what every capitalist concern has got to live in.

In the Schumpeterian model, the introduction and clustering of innovations disturb existing economic and social arrangements. Over time, this is the fundamental process driving cycles of prosperity (characterized by intense investment in new productive opportunities) and depression (characterized by the broader absorption of innovative practices and the elimination of older activities). We would contend it is also key to understanding changing opportunities for mobility and experiences of social upheaval, as embodied in waves of spatial relocation of economic activities. This argument is substantially similar to what Harvey (2001) and Silver (2003) describe as capital's "spatial fix."

The assortment of populations across the world into spatial territories is linked to processes of creative destruction. For the most part, the "wealthiest" within a key particular distributional array are constituted by those who are involved in the more "creative" end of the processes of creative destruction described by Schumpeter. Deskilling and the creation of the unskilled is precisely the outcome of constant "destruction," and processes of construction of categorical inequality are linked precisely to the criteria that are used at any given historical moment to assort populations into spaces that come to be denominated as "wealthy" and "poor," "skilled" and "unskilled," "civilized" and "barbarian." Historically, entry into privileged spaces has been constrained by the regulation of competition (e.g., as in the towns described by Adam Smith). We would argue that the use of ascriptive criteria to sort populations and thereby construct "space" (e.g., town and countryside, but also women and men, Black and white, poor nations and rich nations) has been, and continues to be, constitutive of the very creation and reproduction of inequality (see Korzeniewicz and Payne 2019 for a more detailed treatment of such processes).

Schumpeter (1942) purposefully did not restrict his notion of innovation to technological change or manufacturing. He emphasized that epicenters of wealth shifted constantly and are not associated with any single particular array of products, market networks, or institutional arrangements. New forms of raw material production, the capacity to engage in innovative forms of deploying territorial or political power, or even rent-seeking behaviors are just as likely to be a source of creation and destruction as any other innovation labeled by some as more "productive." Hand-in-hand with creative destruction, processes of exclusion in some spaces both led those excluded to seek better life chances elsewhere, and at times provided opportunities for the use of inclusion by rulers and elites elsewhere as a strategy to attract greater wealth. The pursuit of inclusion, in challenge to exclusionary practices, often was a driving force in the expansion of markets. In this sense, spatial reconfigurations—yielded by spatial relocations of economic activities—are an outcome of spatial innovations in accumulation.

Blurred boundaries between the "local" and the "global"

As noted by Giovanni Arrighi (1994, 4), in turn citing Fernand Braudel (1984),

> the essential feature of historical capitalism over its *longue durée*—that is, over its entire lifetime—has been the "flexibility" and "eclecticism" of capital rather than the concrete forms assumed by the latter at different places and at different times.

In this sense, the association between wealth accumulation, industrial manufacturing, and particular geographical spaces that came to prevail in the nineteenth and twentieth centuries represented a "moment" in the development of the capitalist world-economy—a "particular input–output combination"—rather than its "true identity." Giovanni Arrighi (2001, 116) repeatedly emphasized that the constant mutation of world-economic processes generated difficulties for social science research:

> Not only is the real home of capitalism a "shadowy zone." Not only is capitalism sometimes at home (as in the course of financial expansions) and sometimes away from home (as when it plunges massively into trade and production). On top of all of that, it becomes identified with states of ever-changing form and substance. No wonder that economic sociologists focusing on specific places and specific times find it hard to turn capitalism into a meaningful object of analysis.

Thus, transformations in patterns of wealth accumulation during the late nineteenth and twentieth centuries should be understood as a unique configuration of ongoing processes of creative destruction, just as much as the late twentieth and early twenty-first centuries (or, for that matter, the sixteenth century itself) represent another unique configuration. This is perhaps another way of stating that "as the form of organization of the juxtaposed, spaces epitomize simultaneities" (Löw 2008, 25).

Constitutive of these patterns of change, there has been a recurrent tendency by those successful in business to firmly locate themselves in place and/or specific economic activities. For example, Korsch (2014, 228) indicates that the members of the Sceriman family who settled in Venice and Livorno followed the same economic strategies as the local upper classes: they had accumulated wealth through their trading activities, yet when profit margins from international commerce diminished they expanded their banking business and invested in property.

This was a general pattern, visible in all merchant communities, as illustrated by another example:

> The wool trade had first brought the Castilians to Bruges, but in the mid-sixteenth century the members of the Castilian community were buying real estate and making other local investments. Such diversification served them well and reinforced their other local ties. As a consequence, the Castilian Consulado of Bruges lasted until the beginning of the eighteenth century, long after its initial raison d'etre, the wool trade, had ceased to be fundamental for its members' economic concerns.
>
> *(Phillips 1986, 48)*

Genoa serves as another example of such relocations. The city-state had played an important role in the maritime European expansion of the sixteenth century "by seizing the opportunity for enormous gains through financing the empires of Charles V and Philip II" (Kirk 2005, 196). By the seventeenth century, Dutch and English merchants would become the ones to be on the ascendancy. Genoese financiers, moreover, while drawing significant profits from their activities, faced suspension of payments and/or bankruptcies by the Spanish Crown in 1575, 1607, and 1627, and by the late 1620s. Events such as these, and military reversals for Spain, came to be followed by gradual disinvestment—first from shipping and commercial activities, later from financing Spanish debt (Kirk 2005). Merchants and financiers came to see Dutch and English ships as providing more effective and secure protection than Genoese galleys. By the late 1650s, the main Genoese merchant companies (such as Compagnia di Nostra Signora di Libertá, the Compagnia Maritima di San Georgio, or the Compagnia delle Indie Orientali) found themselves "to be at a continual disadvantage with respect to the (by then) consolidated presence of the Dutch and, perhaps even more so, to the English" (Kirk 2005, 132). For Kirk (2005, 149), the decline of Genoa at sea demonstrated that its ruling class had become "very far removed from the reality of Liguria's seafaring men and from the day-to-day world of maritime commerce."

But, of course, locating themselves more firmly in place and/or specific economic activities made elites more exposed to potential obsolescence in ongoing processes of creative destruction. Just as in the case of black pepper and spices in the early sixteenth century, specific commodities and their chains of production, trade, and consumption were subject to shifting fortunes—and we have many contemporary examples (vide late twentieth century Detroit and its automobile industry) of such perilous outcomes. Thus, the ability to escape the constraints of obsolescence always has been unequally distributed across populations.

This is behind Pritchett's (2006, 5) "much less relentlessly happy story about the consequences of the proliferation of sovereigns and globalization of everything but labor." As geographic space is sliced into smaller nation-state units, some regions will experience large, persistent, positive shocks to labor demand and become "boom towns" with rapidly rising wages and incomes. But other regions may well experience large, persistent, negative, geographic-specific productivity shocks that reduce labor demand and lead to incipient "ghost countries." However, if outward labor mobility is limited, this will lead the adjustment to come not in changes in population but in wages, so countries will be "zombies"—the "living ghosts"—with falling wages and incomes.

Perhaps the most useful instrument to escape such fixed rigidities, avoid obsolescence, and limit the potential of confiscation was the transformation of capital into its most liquid form: finance. Despite significant changes (e.g., money in the sixteenth century did not "look" the same as it would in the nineteenth century, nor did its networks of circulation and exchange), finance has remained, since the early days of historical capitalism, a key arena of apparent safety for capital avoiding rigid investments in space or activities.

To take an example. Ehrenberg's ([1928] 1963) detailed study of finance in the sixteenth and seventeenth centuries emphasizes that state-building and war-making efforts at the time were made possible by the "pure capital companies" developed by financiers in the Italian city-states and Southern Germany. Through their

> concentration of great quantities of capital with individual intermediaries on the exchanges . . . these companies (in their earlier versions, the Bourses of the trade fairs), made large money amounts more available (for example, for rulers engaged in territorial expansion and/or preservation).
>
> *(Ehrenberg [1928] 1963, 376)*

But the further expansion of such new financial and lending instruments, promoted substantially in the seventeenth century by the large capital needs of the companies seeking to capture "trade with the East Indies" (and, most notably, in the Amsterdam Chamber of the VOC), was key to overall capitalist development. Of course, Ehrenberg in 1928 is also trying to argue that speculation is part and parcel of the very character of financial and lending institutions.

In short, when taken from a transnational and historical perspective, it becomes clear that there has been a changing relevance of various kinds of territorial and institutional networks over the longue durée. Such variegated importance of networks, associations, cultural affiliations, and political containers challenges the often-prevailing emphasis on a gradual transition, characterized by the rise of towns, to a deepening divide between the urban and the rural in the rise and growing prevalence of national states, and an eruption of the global at the end of the twentieth century. Instead, we argue, the "local" and the "global" always have interacted in complex ways, both shaping (and given shape by) specific configurations of time and space. After all, "(s)pace makes action possible and is itself the field of action" (Löw 2008, 28), so space "can be seen as a relational ordering of living entities and social goods," and specific spaces are "products of action which at the same time have structuring power" (Löw 2008, 33–5). Likewise, flows have been as constitutive of space, as spaces have been constitutive of flows.

From a historical perspective, the spatial transformations taking place today, with the deindustrialization of the formerly prosperous areas of the mid-twentieth century and the rise in inequality in many wealthy countries, together with the populist right-wing challenge to globalization, can be seen as yet another iteration of conflict between practices of exclusion and practices of inclusion, over whether institutional arrangements (such as those embedded in national identities) should selectively continue to exclude the vast majority of the world population from access to opportunity.

Conclusion

This returns us to the three core arguments of this short chapter: First, no matter the time period we seek to understand, we should make sure to use an appropriate unit of analysis for the research through which we examine space and its transformations, and we argue for a world-historical perspective—understanding transnational geographies and longue durée evolutions—as a productive lens for examining the questions at hand.

Second, historically, waves of spatial transformation have interacted in fundamental ways with what Joseph Schumpeter calls "creative destruction"—for creative destruction always has entailed, simultaneously, both the opportunities of social mobility and the constraints of social dislocation, or, just as importantly, both social inclusion and social exclusion. Such spatial relocations of economic activities—or spatial innovations—are critical to understanding capitalism over its historical evolution.

Finally, from a world-historical perspective, the more "local" and the more "global" are not merely distinct spheres that only now are coming face-to-face in more complex interaction, but interacting geographies of social and political contestation, cooperation, and identity-formation that have always been present but, simultaneously and often as a consequence of their very interactions, are constantly undergoing change. Through the extension of networks and flows of rule and wealth, time and space become mutually redefined, changing the meaning of "place"—simultaneously at the most "local" and at the most "global," and intersecting with processes of inclusion, exclusion, and contestation.

These arguments, derived from past empirical work on the development of the capitalist world-system, point to the need for more rigorous future research on the links between the socioeconomic and the cultural-symbolic dimensions of spatial transformations. It may be that spatial reconfigurations are thus sparked by spatial innovations (in the Schumpeterian sense that we described earlier). Such matters require further investigation. For now, at least, it is clear that these processes—*reconfigurations of* space and *relocations in* space—are intimately intertwined in the longue durée of the capitalist world-system.

Note

1 Several of the arguments in this section draw on previous work, such as Korzeniewicz and Moran (2009); Albrecht and Korzeniewicz (2014; 2017); and Korzeniewicz and Payne (2019; 2020).

References

Albrecht, Scott, and Roberto Patricio Korzeniewicz. 2014. "Global Wages and World Inequality: The Impact of the Great Recession." In *Structures of the World Political Economy and the Future Global Conflict and Cooperation* (World Society Studies Volume 2014), edited by Christian Suter and Christopher Chase-Dunn, 33–52. Berlin: Lit.

Albrecht, Scott, and Roberto Patricio Korzeniewicz. 2017. "'Schöpferische Zerstörung' aus Perspektive des Weltsystems: Milliardäre und die große Rezession von 2008." *Zeitschrift für Weltgeschichte* 18 (1): 79–108.

Arrighi, Giovanni. 1994. *The Long Twentieth Century: Money, Power, and the Origins of Our Times*. London: Verso.

Arrighi, Giovanni. 2001. "Braudel, Capitalism, and the New Economic Sociology." *Review* (Fernand Braudel Center) 24 (1). 107–123.

Braudel, Fernand. 1984. *The Perspective of the World*. New York: Harper & Row.

Ehrenberg, Richard. (1928) 1963. *Capital and Finance in the Age of the Renaissance: A Study of the Fuggers and their Connections*. New York: Augustus M. Kelley.

Harvey, David. 2001. "Globalization and the Spatial Fix." *Geographische Revue* 2 (3): 23–31.

Kirk, Thomas A. 2005. *Genoa and the Sea: Policy and Power in an Early Modern Maritime Republic, 1559–1684*. Baltimore: The Johns Hopkins University Press.

Knoblauch, Hubert, and Martina Löw. 2017a. "TU Berlin: Spatial Analysis of Current Transformation Processes." *Informationsdienst Wissenschaft (idw)*, December 6. https://idw-online.de/de/news685947.

Knoblauch, Hubert, and Martina Löw. 2017b. "On the Spatial Re-Figuration of the Social World." *Sociologica* 11 (2): 1–27. doi: 10.2383/88197.

Korsch, Evelyn. 2014. "The Scerimans and Cross-Cultural Trade in Gems: The Armenian Diaspora in Venice and its Trading Networks in the First Half of the Eighteenth Century." In *Perspectives in Economic and Social History: Commercial Networks and European Cities, 1400–1800*, edited by A. Caracausi and C. Jeggle, 223–239. London: Pickering & Chatto Publishers.

Korzeniewicz, Roberto Patricio, and Timothy Patrick Moran. 2009. *Unveiling Inequality*. New York: Russell Sage Foundation.

Korzeniewicz, Roberto Patricio, and Corey R. Payne. 2019. "Sugar, Slavery, and Creative Destruction: World-Magnates and 'Coreification' in the Longue-Durée." *Journal of World-Systems Research* 25 (2): 395–419.

Korzeniewicz, Roberto Patricio, and Corey R. Payne. 2020. "Rethinking Core and Periphery in Historical Capitalism: World-Magnates and The Shifting Epicenters of Wealth Accumulation." In *Economic Cycles and Social Movements: Past, Present and Future*, edited by Eric Mielants and Katsiaryna Salavei Bardos. London: Routledge.

Löw, Martina. 2008. "The Constitution of Space: The Structuration of Spaces Through the Simultaneity of Effect and Perception." *European Journal of Social Theory* 11 (1): 25–49.

Phillips, William D., Jr. 1986. "Local Integration and Long-Distance Ties: The Castilian Community in Sixteenth-Century Bruges." *The Sixteenth Century Journal* 17 (1): 33–49.

Pritchett, Lant. 2006. "Boom Towns and Ghost Countries: Geography, Agglomeration, and Population Mobility." *Brookings Trade Forum 2006*: 1–42. doi: 10.1353/btf.2007.0009.

Schumpeter, Joseph. 1942. *Capitalism, Socialism and Democracy*. New York: Harper and Row.

Silver, Beverly J. 2003. *Forces of Labor: Workers' Movements and Globalization since 1870*. Cambridge: Cambridge University Press.

Smith, Adam. (1776) 1976. *An Inquiry into the Nature and Causes of The Wealth of Nations*. Chicago: The University of Chicago Press.

10
INFRASTRUCTURES FOR GLOBAL PRODUCTION IN ETHIOPIA AND ARGENTINA

Commodity chains and urban spatial transformation

Elke Beyer, Lucas-Andrés Elsner, and Anke Hagemann

Global production networks and spatio-material infrastructures

This chapter investigates the provision of infrastructures for the processing, manufacturing, and global circulation of commodities as a mode of the transnational production of urban space. It focuses on specific architectures and infrastructures that have been developed in Ethiopia and Argentina in recent years in cooperation with international partners—such as railway lines, shipping terminals, or industrial parks. By taking a closer look at infrastructure provision and the actors involved, the chapter aims to build a deeper understanding of the spatio-material dimension of globalized production systems. Physical infrastructures of commodity processing, manufacturing, and circulation create necessary preconditions for exploiting spatial differences and thus shape and (re)produce the spatial patterns of uneven development (Sheppard 2016; Smith 1984). In the following, we chart an agenda for analyzing the provisioning of infrastructures for global production and circulation as spatial interventions that mediate and alter these dynamics, and thus contribute to the refiguration of urban spaces.

In order to study the relational and transnational constitution of spaces of production, urban and architectural research can productively build on commodity chain approaches (Gereffi and Korzeniewicz 1994; Bair 2005), especially the Global Production Networks (GPN) approach (Henderson et al. 2002). The GPN framework places emphasis on studying the dynamic supplier relations of global "lead firms," the territorial dimension of global production networks, and the role of non-firm actors on various scales. Seeking to understand the spatially dispersed organization of industrial production for global markets, proponents of this approach proclaim a strong interest in the regional embeddedness of economic activities (Coe and Yeung 2015). However, GPN research has been criticized for

DOI: 10.4324/9781003036159-12

falling short of actually "unpacking the nodes" within production networks below the scale of the region (Kleibert and Horner 2018), and also for a lack of attention to the "dark sides" of network inclusion, such as local struggles and polarization, and to disinvestment as a consequence of the constant restructuring of global production networks (Bair and Werner 2011; Werner 2016; Phelps, Atienza, and Arias 2018). If this critique is taken into consideration, the GPN approach offers valuable analytical tools for multi-sited research on the urban impacts of transnational production arrangements (Beyer and Hagemann 2018; Hagemann and Beyer 2020).

In order to fully comprehend the material and processual dimensions of infrastructural constellations on multiple scales, we suggest bringing the GPN framework into conversation with different strands of research on urban development. A valuable counterpoint to the GPN perspective is provided by work in a Marxist political economy tradition, as this strand of literature addresses and theorizes the uneven developmental benefits emerging from a place's connectivity and identifies how they are linked to the physical, built infrastructures of transport (Smith 1984; Sheppard 2016). Fruitful insights on how the provision of infrastructure networks inscribes and reinforces spatial inequalities and transforms urban landscapes and governance regimes have also been offered by recent scholarship on urban infrastructures (Rode, Tereffe, and la Cruz 2020; Kanai and Schindler 2018; Lara 2012; LeCavalier 2016; Cidell 2015; Graham and Marvin 2001), including reflections on how infrastructures transform urban space through their disposition, inscribed logics, restrictions, and possibilities, and thus may be understood as "active objects" (Easterling 2014) shaping urban development trajectories. An integration of commodity chain research and urban research has also been demanded by scholars working on the transnationality of cities (Krätke, Wildner, and Lanz 2012). In this context, Parnreiter (2012) proposes assessing the transnational constitution of urban spaces specifically with regard to the material, built environment and the transnational ways it is negotiated, planned, and constructed. In recent years, an instructive research literature on the translocal constitution of planning knowledge and practices has emerged (Harris 2013; Söderström 2014; Grubbauer 2015).

Building on this spectrum of research literature, we regard specific production environments—infrastructure complexes enabling the circulation and processing of goods within global production networks—as transnational urban spaces. In our view, different scales of analysis are required to build an understanding of how they are constituted and which actors are involved in their making:

- Global production systems, both of commodities and physical infrastructures
- National and international development agendas and policies
- Commodity hubs, i.e. spatial concentrations of industry, logistics, and infrastructure facilities, including the institutions linked to a specific GPN (Giraudo 2015)
- Specific localities and architectures in their respective urban context

In the next section, we discuss two case studies on commodity hubs and infrastructure provisioning with significant involvement of international actors, specifically from the PR China, with regard to transnational production relations and spatial transformations. In Mekelle, Ethiopia, a large export processing zone has been built with road and rail connections to international sea ports as an aspiring hub of global garment production. The Greater Rosario metropolitan area hosts Argentina's most important ports for soy export and is receiving vast investments in cargo rail and port facilities. The case studies draw on ongoing research, including site visits and stakeholder interviews in Ethiopia (2017 and 2018)[1] and Argentina (2018).

Case 1: global clothing production and infrastructure provision in Ethiopia

Ethiopia's current ambitious economic development agenda includes the goal to integrate the country into global production networks, especially of clothing and other light industries (National Planning Commission 2016, Ethiopian Investment Commission 2020). Related to this, major infrastructure developments are under way in cooperation with international partners (Map 10.1). They imply significant spatial transformations on different scales: While transport infrastructure systems of country-wide and transcontinental reach are being built, large export manufacturing zones are being established in the peripheries of major cities, in some cases in parallel to major residential development. In designing and building the physical structures enabling global manufacturing and the required connectivity, the PR China has become Ethiopia's most important international partner, as well as provider of capital and source of foreign direct investment (Jalles d'Orey and Prizzon 2017; Delz 2016; Nicolas 2017). At the time of writing, however, violent intra-regional conflicts in Ethiopia are casting doubt on the outcomes of infrastructure-led development as well as the future commitment of the notoriously volatile global clothing industry.

Ethiopia is seen as a major market for power and transport infrastructure in sub-Saharan Africa (Delz 2015; Foster and Morella 2011). The road network is being expanded, along with dry port facilities for international freight logistics (UNDP Ethiopia 2017), and a national electric railway network is envisioned. As a first leg, a new 791 km standard gauge railway between Addis Ababa and the port of Djibouti, the crucial entry and exit point of goods for land-locked Ethiopia, was built by the China Railway Construction Corporation and the China Civil Engineering Construction Corporation (CCECC), and has been operated by a Chinese–Ethiopian company since 2018. A large share of the project was financed by the China Export Import Bank, reportedly involving the import of about USD 1 billion worth of equipment and construction materials from China (Sun 2017). Construction of the second leg, extending nearly 600 km northwards to Mekelle, was taken up with engineering companies and financial backing from the PR China and Turkey. The railway construction is a strong signal of Ethiopia's commitment to state-led infrastructure development and of Ethio-Chinese cooperation, but its high cost and its actual exigency for textile export producers are subject

Infrastructures for global production **123**

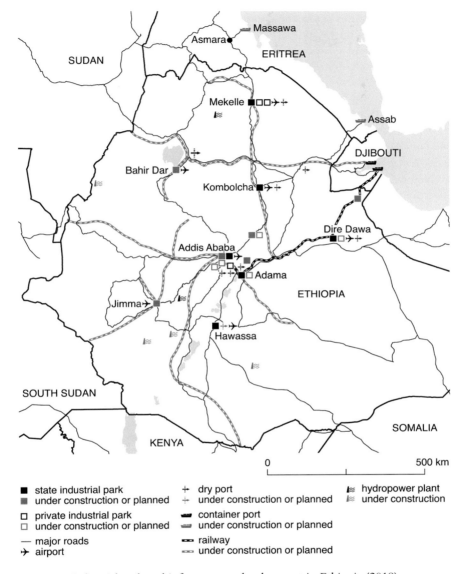

MAP 10.1 Industrial park and infrastructure development in Ethiopia (2018)

Map: Anke Hagemann, Elke Beyer, Rucha Kelkar

Sources: Google Maps, OpenStreetMap, maplibrary.org, Ethiopian Investment Commission, Industrial Parks Development Corporation, Embassy of Ethiopia (Brussels), Ethiopian Shipping Lines

to contrarian debate among transport planners (authors' interviews 2018; see also Rode, Tereffe, and la Cruz 2020).

The Ethiopian government is also staunchly pursuing the development of another type of physical infrastructure to facilitate globalized production: By late 2018, 11 large state industrial parks were commencing operations or being built in several cities across the country, mostly specialized in export-oriented clothing production (Map 10.1). These parks are developed by the Industrial Park Development Corporation (IPDC) in close cooperation with the Ethiopian Investment Commission (EIC). China's experience in special economic zone development is an important reference (UNDP and IPRCC 2015; Weldesilassie et al. 2017; Zhang et al. 2018), and for the design and construction of the parks, mostly experienced Chinese state companies such as the China Communications Construction Company (CCCC) and CCECC were commissioned. The parks offer very competitive conditions for leasing sheds or land, cheap water, and energy supply to foreign investors.[2] In addition, there are several private industrial park developments, including significant Chinese investment projects such as the Eastern Industry Zone south-east of Addis (Dannenberg, Yejoo, and Schiller 2013; Giannecchini and Taylor 2018) and major industrial zones in Adama and Dire Dawa. All these projects are located on or near the privileged rail and road connections established with Chinese financing and engineering capacities.

In terms of global clothing production networks, the industrial parks offer a physical platform attracting established suppliers to big European and US clothing brands and retailers, predominantly from South and East Asia, to move part of their sewing operations here. Transferring this segment of production requires the least amount of investment and commitment but still enables companies to profit from preferential trade frameworks with the USA and the EU, in addition to low production costs. In parallel, several big Chinese fabric producers are setting up facilities in some of the parks as potential suppliers to the sewing factories (on the importance of industry park clusters and established supplier relations, see Altenburg et al. 2020, 54–55, 60). This allows them to cut supply routes significantly while benefiting from the same incentives as export producers.

In terms of transnational actor constellations, the parks constitute arenas of collaboration between not only Ethiopian government institutions, transnational players from the clothing industry, and global construction companies, but also international banks and development agencies. Ethiopian authorities, international economic consultants, and development agencies advocate the industrial parks as high-potential locations for the labor-intensive clothing sector, as incubators for environmental sustainability and "good governance," and as profitable opportunities for investment and sourcing, as well as technology export from the agencies' home countries.[3] However, observers point out the risk that nearly no backward or forward linkages to the domestic economy are being formed at such export processing enclaves (Nicolas 2017; Staritz, Plank, and Morris 2016; Weldesilassie et al. 2017; but see Altenburg et al. 2020, 58 for a cautious revision of this assessment). Beyond offering very low-wage jobs, the value captured in Ethiopia may therefore remain very low (Whitfield, Staritz, and Morris 2020) and is subject to the extreme volatility of the global clothing industry.

Mekelle: a commodity hub in the making?

Mekelle city, capital of Tigray Regional State in northern Ethiopia, is an instructive case for studying how infrastructure provision contributes to shaping global production networks and how transnational actors become significant players in negotiating and physically transforming urban space. However, military conflict has flared up in the region in late 2020, critically affecting civilians and creating much uncertainty about the future. In late 2018, there were four large export-oriented industrial zones under construction on greenfield sites, all specializing in garment production and aspiring to employ more than 10,000 workers each (Map 10.2). In addition to the IPDC's Mekelle Industry Park (MIP), private industrial parks and major clothing production complexes were being developed by investors from India, the UAE, Bangladesh, and Italy. Similar global production relations are formed as in other Ethiopian industrial parks: Mostly suppliers of ready-made garments to global brands or retailers in Europe and North America are expanding their production from South-East Asia or Egypt to Mekelle in order to profit from preferential trade, incentives, and low costs. Initially, all supplies are imported, but some companies plan to set up vertically integrated factories. Moving production to Mekelle was supported and even pushed by major European clothing retailers with a fresh Corporate Social Responsibility strategy, seeking a new and cheap production region not yet associated with inhuman and dangerous working conditions. These retailers and brands entered notable collaborations with development agencies from European countries like Swedfund or Germany's Ministry for Development Cooperation, for example, in projects to train and educate workers.

Our research focuses on MIP as a physical infrastructure for global clothing production, developed by Ethiopian government authorities in cooperation with international partners. The regional government delineated an area of 1000 ha for textile and garment production at a site between villages in the south-west periphery of Mekelle (Map 10.2). The first development phase of 75 ha with 15 turnkey sheds, offices, road, and engineering networks was designed and built by Chinese contractor CCCC, financed by Ethiopia's government. By 2018, the park commenced operations with sewing companies from India, Bangladesh, and Pakistan among the first tenants. A second construction phase of 163 ha is to be implemented through a loan contract with the European Investment Bank. However, due to the military conflict between Ethiopia's federal government and Tigray Regional that started in late 2020, operations in the park were temporarily suspended and also the implementation of the infrastructure projects aiming at coupling Mekelle with global production networks is highly uncertain.

MIP constitutes a large monofunctional enclave of export manufacturing in a dry landscape of seasonal pasture land dotted with small village houses in traditional stone masonry, where water scarcity was already an issue before the arrival of large industrial consumers (PWC, IPE Global Triple Line, and EDRI 2017). Plugging this enclave into transport and supply networks, and establishing the urban fabric of social reproduction necessary to keep transnational commodity

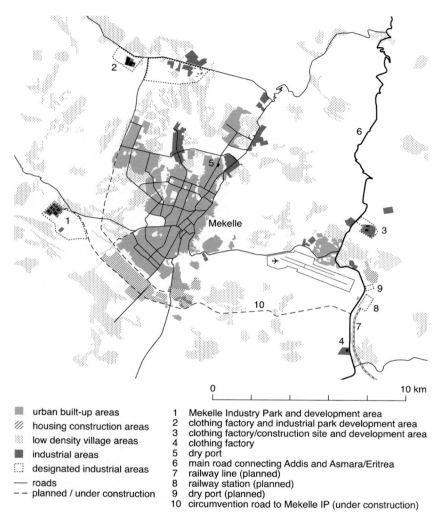

MAP 10.2 Infrastructures of manufacturing and circulation in Mekelle (2018)

Map: Anke Hagemann, Elke Beyer, Ilkim Er

Sources: Google Maps, OpenStreetMap, Industrial Parks Development Corporation

production running, emerges as a partly incremental process of spatial planning and infrastructure provision from the top down and bottom up. In conversation with the authors, local urban planners hinted at a rather retroactive integration of the industrial areas into structural planning. As in other Ethiopian industrial parks, housing for the expected tens of thousands of workers was still a matter of deliberation and improvisation: According to the park management, low-cost housing development schemes were still in search of funding, while some tenant companies had requested land on the park outskirts to build their own dormitories. At the time of our research, major transport infrastructure construction was under way in order to connect the export industry to the international ports (Map 10.2). In addition to the railway terminus planned relatively far east of the city center, adjacent to the main overland road, CCCC was building an 18 km circumvention road between MIP and the future road and rail junction. Close by, a new dry port for customs procedures and transferring containers from road to rail was in the planning stage—designed by CCCC for the Ethiopian state-owned Shipping and Logistics Service Enterprise (Kang'ereha 2017; PWC, IPE Global Triple Line, and EDRI 2017). Thus, one huge and globally active Chinese construction corporation acquired responsibility for the execution and design of most major infrastructure projects aspiring to transform the peri-urban landscape around Mekelle into an export commodity hub.

Marketing brochures for potential investors in Mekelle IP depict a high-standard manufacturing zone connected to global distribution networks by an environmentally friendly railway. Despite all the money already invested to create this physical infrastructure and conflictual land procurement negotiations, however, global supply chains to and from the emerging commodity hub might ultimately follow different routes: Railway construction was interrupted in 2019 due to financial difficulties, while the peace with Eritrea seemed to soon allow goods to be shipped through Massawa port, at a half-day truck-ride of just about 400 km, much closer to Mekelle than Djibouti at 670 km.

As large export production enclaves are built and linked to privileged transport corridors, the formation of global production networks and transnational involvement in infrastructure provisioning are closely linked and markedly impact urban development in Mekelle. We argue for a closer investigation of how urban spaces are co-produced in this asymmetrical interaction between transnational, national, and municipal actors with potentially diverse agendas as well as the workers and local residents whose changing livelihoods are fundamentally implicated in the major spatial transformations taking place.

Case 2: infrastructures for soybean processing and logistics in Argentina

Argentina's economy has been based on the export of agricultural products for more than a century. Soybeans and by-products in particular made up more than 25% of the national exports in past years, creating a critical dependency on the global market. The country is the world's third largest producer of soybeans, and the largest for processed soy-based products (Berndt and Bernhold 2017). The most important market for Argentina's grains is the PR China, receiving 96% of the country's soybean exports in 2018 (Bolsa de Comercio de Rosario 2019a). The soy industry is mostly organized in global production networks, and the sub-sectors of soybean processing and trading are dominated by a few large, vertically integrated, partly transnational companies (Gómez Lende and Velázquez 2018). The soy boom has transformed Argentina's landscape and social structure in recent decades by re-enforcing existing and creating new patterns of inequality. For instance, processes of "accumulation by dispossession" (Harvey 2006) occur in relation to the spatial expansion of industrialized soy cultivation, and its intensive pesticide use and monoculture farming cause environmental degradation. In this context, former peasants have been excluded from participating in agricultural activities, and migration to cities has increased (Lapegna 2017; Gras 2013).

Transport infrastructure development has been mired in extractivism and particularly the agroindustry in Argentina: Major road and railway corridors as well as inland waterways primarily connect growing areas to ports that provide links to global markets. The expansion of transportation networks is of great importance with regard to integrating new territories into global agro-industrial production networks (Gómez Lende and Velázquez 2018). The agroindustry is also an important player in transport operations, as large producers and traders have made the operation of port terminals, railway lines, and truck fleets part of their business. Currently, soy is mostly transported by truck (Gómez Lende and Velázquez 2018) as the railway network has eroded since the late 20th century due to neoliberal restructuring and the promotion of road-borne transport. Our research focuses on the state-run Belgrano Cargas cargo rail network. Its main corridor is currently being renovated in order to improve connectivity between the major grain ports in the Rosario area and the agrarian regions by reducing travel times. The renovation project is being financed by the Argentinean state and a USD 4 billion loan from the China Development Bank Corporation and the Industrial and Commercial Bank of China Limited. Under the direction of Argentina's federal transport ministry and coordinated by a state-owned railway infrastructure company, project implementation was commissioned to the China Machinery and Engineering Corporation (CMEC) (Ministerio de Transporte 2017). Construction work is being carried out by Argentinean companies, but the financing contract for the Belgrano Cargas project foresees the acquisition of rolling stock and construction materials from Chinese companies. In December 2019, about half of the targeted 1845 km railway line had been renovated. The project is part of larger Chinese infrastructure initiatives in Argentina, such as loans by state-owned Chinese banks for further railway projects and energy infrastructures (Inter-American Dialogue 2019).

Gran Rosario: a global center of the soy industry

Gran Rosario is the third largest metropolitan region in Argentina with about 1.3 million inhabitants. The city evolved around a port at the Paraná river and has been a center of grain trade, transport, and processing for many decades. Its urban form has been shaped by infrastructures such as railway lines, grain ports, silos, and mills, which made it the central hub connecting the vast agricultural areas of the Argentinean Pampa with global markets (Galimberti 2015). The metropolitan area of Rosario stretches more than 60 km along the bank of the Paraná river and incorporates around 20 deep-water ports that account for around 80% of the country's exports of grains and by-products (Bolsa de Comercio de Rosario 2019b). Many of these complexes also comprise processing facilities such as soy crushing plants and bio diesel refineries. Compared to other major soy-producing countries, the facilities in Argentina are characterized by large sizes and high volumes (Schweitzer 2011). Altogether, the region represents one of the world's centers for the shipping and crushing of soybeans.

On the northern fringe of the Rosario metropolitan region, the Belgrano Cargas project also implies the provisioning of new rail tracks to the ports and a large new rail yard in the small town of Timbúes (Map 10.3). This section will be financed by the three international companies operating the ports and processing facilities and those actors developing new facilities at the same location: China Oil and Foodstuffs Corporation (COFCO), Aceitera General Deheza (AGD), Renova, Dreyfus, and Asociación de Cooperativas Argentinas (ACA).[4] COFCO, a Chinese state-owned food processing and trading company, is a major actor in the context of infrastructure development in the Rosario area and has become an important player in Argentina's agroindustry in recent years through the acquisition of two large competitors operating large facilities in Rosario. At its site in Timbúes, COFCO is planning to expand its processing and logistics complex.

The companies whose terminals are being connected to the Belgrano Cargas network have been involved in the development of the project in several other ways: They are all members of the Rosario Board of Trade, a local business organization representing the interests of the agroindustry and considered to be highly influential in local, provincial, and national politics (authors' interviews 2018). In addition, most companies with facilities in Timbúes are listed as customers of Trenes Argentinos Carga, a state-owned freight railway company. Grains and by-products made up between 50 and 80% of the volume transported by the Belgrano Cargas network in the past ten years. Thus, it can be assumed that these companies generate a significant part of the cargo transported and also the future demand for which the services are planned.

The railway project and the expansion of port capacities in Gran Rosario contribute to the consolidation of the region's function as a central commodity hub within the global soy production networks, and thereby to the industry's spatial concentration. However, the railway line, which serves almost exclusively the needs of the export-oriented primary sector, and the other massive infrastructures provided for the processing and transportation of grains reinforce Argentina's extractivist development model, which produces social and environmental problems in the regions where the crops are cultivated and the urban areas where the processing and logistics facilities are located (Schweitzer 2017). In the case of Gran Rosario, the impacts of the operation and provision of infrastructures include pollution and massive traffic congestion in the suburbs as well as the displacement of small-scale fishery at the river banks (Schweitzer 2017; Cloquell et al. 2011; Roldán and Godoy 2020).

built-up areas
farms / agrarian structures
industrial areas
future development areas
—— roads
--- planned
▭▭ railway
▭▭ planned

soy processing and port facilities:
1 Renova
2 LDC
3 COFCO
4 ACA and AGD development areas

transport infrastructures:
5 Belgrano Cargas railway
6 planned railyard
7 planned railway
8 planned road

MAP 10.3 Infrastructures of manufacturing and circulation in the north of Gran Rosario (2018)

Map: Anke Hagemann, Ilkim Er, Lucas Elsner

Sources: Google Maps, OpenStreetMap, Vialidad Nacional, Trenes Argentinos Infraestructura

Spatial transformation through infrastructures of global commodity production and transnational actor constellations

It has been illustrated how the provisioning of large physical infrastructures is deeply entangled in the integration of Mekelle and Rosario in global production networks and thus the exploitation and reproduction of spatial inequalities. Looking beyond the two cases, this is not such a new insight but an aspect that has widely been neglected in GPN research. In order to position the two places within specific global production networks as a part of national developmental strategies, the urban areas of Mekelle and Rosario are currently being reconfigured as commodity hubs through the deployment of infrastructure projects that are among the largest in the respective regions. In both cases, Chinese construction engineering companies and banks play a key role among multiple international and domestic actors. They orchestrate a large network of Chinese companies from the infrastructure, transportation, and construction sector involved in the projects by acting as intermediaries for loans and by coordinating the provision of construction materials and technology as well as the respective expertise from the PRC.

The urban impact of the infrastructure projects is massive in both cases—in terms of land and resource consumption, land-use changes, social impacts including rural–urban migration, the improvisation of affordable housing for workers, and environmental externalities. The large-scale spatial interventions constitute important vectors of spatial transformation and future urbanization processes. Obviously, the spatial logics and transnational actor constellations of global clothing production and the soybean agroindustry differ in significant ways. Enhancing connectivity in Rosario promises stabilization of China's import supply with agricultural staples and qualifies the region's function as the industry's major hub. In contrast, infrastructure in Mekelle and other Ethiopian cities is set up to encourage the relocation of production capacities in the low-wage textile industry and simultaneously foster the export of commodities, industry supplies, and construction technology from China to Ethiopia. In both cases, these relations are physically inscribed in the provided infrastructures and thereby in the specific built environments constituting transnational urban spaces. The ports and railway infrastructures in Rosario are constructed according to the specific technical demands of grain shipping, and the transportation network is designed to enable unidirectional flows from the agricultural hinterlands through the ports in Rosario to global markets. In Ethiopia, large clothing production facilities are set up within reach of international ports and with advanced "green" and automated technology to meet global buyers' demands, but only basic dormitory accommodation is provided for workers arriving from distant villages to work at the lowest wages to be found among clothing exporter countries (Altenburg et al. 2020, 57). Considering the spatial transformation of the peri-urban landscapes under study, instances of "splintering urbanism" (Graham and Marvin 2001) can be observed in both cases: Niches and enclaves of globalized production benefit from infrastructure provision enabling privileged connections, while the municipalities and their inhabitants are confronted with negative externalities, such as increased water scarcity, pollution, housing needs, and high traffic volumes. At a national and regional level, the infrastructure initiatives discussed in this chapter primarily strengthen major urban centers, fostering processes of urban–rural polarization.

Although the precise roles and power relations of corporate and state actors vary, the two cases reveal instructive similarities regarding the governance of infrastructure provisioning in the context of larger bilateral cooperation initiatives with the PR China and other international partners. In both cases, the leading role of planning authorities at the national level results in challenges for planning on an urban and regional scale. Transnational enterprises are deeply involved in financing, ownership, operation, and construction of the infrastructures under study and thus in channeling the global flows of commodities (inter alia to and from China) and the value generation enabled by these structures. In this specific way, the emerging urban spaces and the modalities of spatial transformation and commodity production must be understood as transnational and relational. Studying the provision of infrastructures for global production networks substantially adds to the knowledge on the precise links that mediate and co-produce interdependent dynamics of uneven spatial development and the resulting inequalities. The discussion of the two case studies has shown that examining the transnational actor constellations of infrastructure provision is crucial for understanding the uneven spatialities of global production networks as both networks are closely entangled. We argue that an in-depth analysis of these spatialities requires an integrated approach, taking into account both the networks of commodity production and the networks of infrastructure provision in order to fully comprehend their interdependent character. Such an analysis also offers valuable insights for spatial planning, specifically when it comes to aspirations to participate in global production networks and the resulting challenges related to the (re-)production of uneven spatialities.

Notes

1. Including findings of the "Transnational Production Spaces" research project (DFG no.: MI 1893/2–1) on clothing industry sites in Turkey, Bulgaria, and Ethiopia.
2. As "renewable" power supply to manufacturing industries, giant hydropower dams are under construction on the Blue Nile and the Omo rivers.
3. We would like to thank our research partners, Melaku Tanku Gebremariam and Eyassu Kumera, for sharing their observations at the 2019 International Conference on Sustainable Industrial Areas in Addis, organized by the German Organization for the Development of Cooperation in partnership with Ethiopia's IPDC and EIC, the UK Department for International Development, and the International Finance Corporation.
4. Together these companies accounted for 43% of Argentina's exports of grains and by-products in 2018 (Bolsa de Comercio de Rosario 2019a).

References

Altenburg, Tilmann, Xiao Chen, Wilfried Lütkenhorst, Cornelia Staritz, and Lindsay Whitfield. 2020. "Exporting out of China or out of Africa? Automation versus Relocation in the Global Clothing Industry." *Discussion Paper*. Bonn: Deutsches Institut für Entwicklungspolitik.

Bair, Jennifer. 2005. "Global Capitalism and Commodity Chains: Looking Back, Going Forward." *Competition & Change* 9 (2): 153–180.
Bair, Jennifer, and Marion Werner. 2011. "Commodity Chains and the Uneven Geographies of Global Capitalism: A Disarticulations Perspective." *Environment and Planning A* 43 (5): 988–997.
Berndt, Christian, and Christine Bernhold. 2017. "Lateinamerikanischer Neostrukturalismus: Sojaboom und wirtschaftliche Konzentration in Argentinien." *Zeitschrift für Wirtschaftsgeographie* 62 (1): 30–45.
Beyer, Elke, and Anke Hagemann. 2018. "'Getting It Right from the Start'? Building Spaces of Transnational Clothing Production in Ethiopia." *Trialog* 130–131: 63–71.
Bolsa de Comercio de Rosario. 2019a. "Informativo Semanal. AÑO XXXVI—N° Edición 1898."Accessed June 28,2020. www.bcr.com.ar/es/mercados/investigacion-y-desarrollo/informativo-semanal/noticias-informativo-semanal/quienes-fueron.
Bolsa de Comercio de Rosario. 2019b. "Informativo Semanal. AÑO XXXVII—N° Edición 1921."Accessed June 28,2020. www.bcr.com.ar/es/mercados/investigacion-y-desarrollo/informativo-semanal/noticias-informativo-semanal/las-terminales.
Cidell, Julie. 2015. "The Role of Major Infrastructure in Subregional Economic Development: An Empirical Study of Airports and Cities." *Journal of Economic Geography* 15 (6): 1125–1144.
Cloquell Silvia, Roxana Albanesi, María Elena Nogueira, and Patricia Propersi. 2011. "Las localidades del sur santafesino. Factores favorables y desfavorables de la imbricación urbano-rural." *Revista Interdisciplinaria de Estudios Agrarios* 35: 5–34.
Coe, Neil M., and Henry W. Yeung. 2015. *Global Production Networks: Theorizing Economic Development in an Interconnected World.* Oxford: Oxford University Press.
Dannenberg, Peter, Kim Yejoo, and Daniel Schiller. 2013. "Chinese Special Economic Zones in Africa: A New Species of Globalisation?" *African East-Asian Affairs* 2: 4–14.
Delz, Sascha. 2015. "Development Cooperation at All Costs: How Global Actors and Concepts Influence Urban and Rural Transformation: Case Studies from Ethiopia." PhD diss., ETH Zurich.
Delz, Sascha. 2016. "Who Built This? China, China, China! Expanding the Chinese Economy through Mutual Benefit and Infrastructure Construction." In *Cities of Change—Addis Ababa. Transformation Strategies for Urban Territories in the 21st Century*, edited by Marc Angélil and Dirk Hebel, 198–206. Basel: Birkhäuser.
Easterling, Keller. 2014. *Extrastatecraft: The Power of Infrastructure Space.* New York: Verso.
Ethiopian Investment Commission. 2020. "Realizing New Productive Capacity in Ethiopia's Textiles and Apparel Sector: Strategy and Policy Recommendations." Accessed September 2020. www.investethiopia.gov.et/images/Covid-19Response/Covid-19Resources/publications_May-20/Realizing-New-Productive-Capacity-in-Ethiopia-Textiles—Apparel-Secctor—Strategy—Policy-Recommendations.pdf.
Foster, Vivien, and Elvira Morella. 2011. "Ethiopia's Infrastructure. A Continental Perspective." *Policy Research Working Paper No. 5595.* Washington, DC: The World Bank Africa Region Sustainable Development Department.
Galimberti, Cecilia. 2015. "La reinvención del Río Procesos de transformación de la ribera de la Región Metropolitana de Rosario, Argentina." PhD diss., Universidad Nacional de Rosario.
Gereffi, Gary, and Miguel Korzeniewicz, eds. 1994. *Commodity Chains and Global Capitalism.* Westport: Praeger.
Giannecchini, Philip, and Ian Taylor. 2018. "The Eastern Industrial Zone in Ethiopia: Catalyst for Development?" *Geoforum* 88: 28–35.
Giraudo, Maria Eugenia. 2015. "Commodity Hubs: Production of Space and New Geographies of Capital." *Alternautas* 2 (1): 79–87.

Gómez Lende, Sebastian, and Guillermo Velázquez. 2018. "Soybean Agribusiness in Argentina (1990–2015): Socio-Economic, Territorial, Environmental, and Political Implications." In *Agricultural Value Chain*, edited by Gokhan Egilmez, 117–136. London: InTech.

Graham, Steven, and Simon Marvin. 2001. *Splintering Urbanism: Networked Infrastructures, Technological Mobilities and the Urban Condition*. New York: Routledge.

Gras, Carla. 2013. "Agronegocios en el Cono Sur." *desiguALdades.net Working Paper Series No. 50*. Berlin: desiguALdades.net International Research Network on Interdependent Inequalities in Latin America.

Grubbauer, Monika. 2015. "Circulating Knowledge, Marketization and Norm-Making: International Developers and Construction Firms in Eastern Europe since 2000." *Global Networks* 15 (3): 288–306.

Hagemann, Anke, and Elke Beyer. 2020. "Globalizing Urban Research, Grounding Global Production Networks: Transnational Clothing Production and the Built Environment." *Articulo—Journal of Urban Research* 21.

Harris, Andrew. 2013. "Concrete Geographies: Assembling Global Mumbai through Transport Infrastructure." *City* 17 (3): 343–360.

Harvey, David. 2006. *Spaces of Global Capitalism*. London: Verso.

Henderson, Jeffrey, Peter Dicken, Martin Hess, Neil M. Coe, and Henry W. Yeung. 2002. "Global Production Networks and the Analysis of Economic Development." *Review of International Political Economy* 9 (3): 436–464.

Inter-American Dialogue. 2019. "China-Latin America Finance Database." Accessed June 28, 2020. www.thedialogue.org/map_list/.

Jalles d'Orey, Maria Ana, and Annalisa Prizzon. 2017. "An 'Age of Choice' for Infrastructure Financing? Evidence from Ethiopia." *ODI Report*, April 2017. London: ODI.

Kanai, Miguel J., and Seth Schindler. 2018. "Peri-urban Promises of Connectivity: Linking Project-Led Polycentrism to the Infrastructure Scramble." *Environment and Planning A* 51 (2): 302–322.

Kang'ereha, Dorcas. 2017. "Ethiopia's US $100m Dry Port Design Concluded." Accessed June 28, 2020. https://constructionreviewonline.com/2017/11/ethiopias-us-100m-dry-port-design-concluded/.

Kleibert, Jana M., and Rory Horner. 2018. "Geographies of Global Production Networks." In *Handbook on Geographies of Globalization*, edited by Robert Kloosterman, Virginie Mamadouh, and Pieter Terhorst, 222–234. Cheltenham: Edward Elgar Publishing.

Krätke Stefan, Kathrin Wildner, and Stephan Lanz, eds. 2012. *Transnationalism and Urbanism*. New York: Routledge.

Lapegna, Pablo. 2017. "The Political Economy of the Agro-Export Boom under the Kirchners: Hegemony and Passive Revolution in Argentina." *Journal of Agrarian Change* 17 (2): 313–329.

Lara, Juan D. de. 2012. "Goods Movement and Metropolitan Inequality: Global Restructuring, Commodity Flows, and Metropolitan Development." In *Cities, Regions and Flows*, edited by Peter V. Hall and Markus Hesse, 76–91. New York: Routledge.

LeCavalier, Jesse. 2016. *The Rule of Logistics: Walmart and the Architecture of Fulfillment*. Minneapolis: University of Minnesota Press.

Ministerio de Transporte. 2017. "El Gobierno Nacional amplió USD 1600 M el crédito para recuperar el FFCC Belgrano Cargas." Accessed December 14, 2018. www.argentina.gob.ar/noticias/el-gobierno-nacional-amplio-usd-1600-m-el-credito-para-recuperar-el-ffcc-belgrano-cargas.

National Planning Commission. 2016. *Growth and Transformation Plan II (2015/16–2019/20) Volume I: Main Text*. Addis Ababa: National Planning Commission.

Nicolas, Françoise. 2017. "Chinese Investors in Ethiopia: The Perfect Match?" *Notes de l'IFRI*, March 2017. Paris: IFRI.

Parnreiter, Christof. 2012. "Conceptualizing Transnational Urban Spaces: Multicentered Agency, Placeless Organizational Logics, and the Built Environment." In *Transnationalism and Urbanism*, edited by Stefan Krätke, Kathrin Wildner, and Stephan Lanz, 91–110. New York: Routledge.

Phelps, Nicholas A., Miguel Atienza, and Martin Arias. 2018 "An Invitation to the Dark Side of Economic Geography." *Environment and Planning A* 50 (1): 236–244.

PWC, IPE Global Triple Line, and EDRI. 2017. "Green Climate Compatible Urban Industrial Development in Ethiopia. Strategy and Projects for the Kombolcha-Mekele Industrial Corridor. Final Report." *Climate & Development Knowledge Network*. Accessed June 28, 2020. https://cdkn.org/wp-content/uploads/2018/02/Final-Reporting-Climate-Compatible-Urban-Industrial-project-development-and-Investment-Plan.pdf.

Rode, Philipp, Biruk Terrefe, and Nuno F. da Cruz. 2020. "Cities and the Governance of Transport Interfaces: Ethiopia's New Rail Systems." *Transport Policy* 91 (June): 76–94.

Roldán, Diego, and Sebastián Godoy. 2020. "Conflictos territoriales y culturales en la renovación del frente costero, Rosario (Argentina)." *EURE* 138: 95–116.

Schweitzer, Mariana. 2011. "El transporte en la producción del territorio. Corredores de transporte: La IIRSA y la hidrovía Paraná—Paraguay." *Jornadas Regionales de Información Geográfica y Ordenamiento Territorial* 2: 125–136.

Schweitzer, Mariana. 2017. "San Lorenzo y Puerto General San Martín. Territorios atravesados por dinámicas globales." *América Latina Hoy* 75: 101–124.

Sheppard, Eric. 2016. *Limits to Globalization: Disruptive Geographies of Capitalist Development*. Oxford: Oxford University Press.

Smith, Neil. 1984. *Uneven Development: Nature, Capital, and the Production of Space*. Oxford: Blackwell.

Söderström, Ola. 2014. *Cities in Relations. Trajectories of Urban Development in Hanoi and Ouagadougou*. Chichester: Wiley Blackwell.

Staritz, Cornelia, Leonhard Plank, and Mike Morris. 2016. "Global Value Chains, Industrial Policy, and Sustainable Development—Ethiopia's Apparel Export Sector." *Country Case Study. Inclusive Economic Transformation*, November 2016. Vienna: ICTSD.

Sun, Yun. 2017. "China and the East Africa Railways: Beyond Full Industry Chain Export." *Brookings*. Accessed June 28, 2020. www.brookings.edu/blog/africa-in-focus/2017/07/06/china-and-the-east-africa-railways-beyond-full-industry-chain-export/.

UNDP Ethiopia. 2017. *National Logistics Strategy*. Addis Ababa: UNDP Ethiopia.

UNDP and IPRCC. 2015. "If Africa Builds Nests, Will the Birds Come? Comparative Study on Special Economic Zones in Africa and China." *Working Paper Series No. 06*. Beijing: UNDP and IPRCC.

Weldesilassie, Alebel B., Mulu Gebreeyesus, Girum Abebe, and Berihu Aseffa Gebrehiwot. 2017. "Study on Industrial Park Development: Issues, Practices and Lessons for Ethiopia." *Research Reports No. 29*. Addis Ababa: Ethiopian Development Research Institute.

Werner, Marion. 2016. "Global Production Networks and Uneven Development: Exploring Geographies of Devaluation, Disinvestment, and Exclusion." *Geography Compass* 10 (11): 457–469.

Whitfield, Lindsay, Cornelia Staritz, and Mike Morris. 2020. "Global Value Chains, Industrial Policy and Economic Upgrading in Ethiopia's Apparel Sector." *Development and Change* 51 (4): 1018–1043.

Zhang, Xiaodi, Dejene Tezera, Ciyong Zou, Zhen Wang, Jie Zhao, and Eneyew Abera Gebremenfas. 2018. "Industrial Park Development in Ethiopia. Case Study Report." *Department of Policy, Research and Statistics Working Paper No. 21/2018*. Vienna: UNIDO.

11
SEPARATE WORLDS? EXPLAINING THE CURRENT WAVE OF REGIONAL ECONOMIC POLARIZATION[1]

Michael Storper

> Regional inequality is proving too politically dangerous to ignore.
>
> (*The Economist* 2016)

The challenge

Over the past 40 years, globalization has spread development to many parts of the world. But within countries, development has become more uneven, a phenomenon known as interregional divergence or polarization. This phenomenon poses a major challenge to theories used in economic geography and regional economics. In this chapter, I discuss some of these challenges and argue for a broader and more enriched framework moving forward. I refer mostly to the US–American case, but the phenomenon is widespread throughout the world, and the lessons for theory and evidence are similar for these other cases.

The variance of per capita personal income among US metropolitan areas was 30% higher in 2016 than it was in 1980 (Ganong and Shoag 2017). In the European Union, inequality among NUTS-2 regions, after falling in the 1990s from a high level in 1980 (prior to intensified European integration), has turned sharply up again in the new millennium. In the United States, interregional migration has dropped to half of its century-long average up to 1980, and it is more spatially selective by skill level (Kaplan and Schulhofer-Wohl 2012; Giannone 2017). At the same time, labor force participation rates have a higher interregional variance in the EU and the US than since the Great Depression of the 1930s. Intergenerational mobility increasingly differs by region (Chetty et al. 2014). The divergent new geography of employment and incomes thus seems to correspond to a divergent new geography of opportunities.

DOI: 10.4324/9781003036159-13

This polarization contrasts with the broad geographical development patterns from the middle of the 20th century. From 1940 to about 1980, variation in interstate incomes in the United States steadily narrowed, and suburbs and metropolitan hinterlands grew more in terms of population and incomes than inner-metropolitan areas. It is for this reason that we refer today to the geography of the last few decades as a 'great inversion.'

The geographical polarization of opportunity seems to be mirrored in geographical splits in political attitudes and voting behavior (Spicer 2018). In the 2016 Brexit referendum and US and French (first round) presidential elections, there were sharp divisions between urban and less urban, prosperous regions and less prosperous ones, regions with higher average levels of education and those with lower levels, and regions with less ethnic diversity and those with more. The basic density gradient of employment, income, and opportunity creates sharp cleavages in perceptions and politics. Thus, to take the US example, Hillary Clinton prevailed in just 473 of the 3144 US counties, but with supermajorities in the most densely populated areas. Trump prevailed, but with generally narrower majorities, in the vast majority of counties that were on average much less densely populated. Generally speaking, there is long-term geographical polarization of the US House of Representatives (Bishop and Cushing 2008; Sussell and Thomson 2015). It seems as if, increasingly, people from different regions within the same country are living in subjectively separate worlds.

We should be concerned about these forms of polarization for both economic and political reasons. As the *Economist* (2016) points out, 'orthodox economics has few answers to the problem of regional inequality,' and I will argue that the same could be said for the allied field of economic geography. Regional economics and economic geography together face the challenge of developing analytics that can explain these outcomes and designing better policies so as to spread prosperity because, as the same *Economist* article states, 'if economists cannot provide answers, populist insurgents will' (*The Economist* 2016).

Spatial equilibrium theories: revisiting the roles of amenities, housing, and jobs

In the past 20 years, the field of RSUE has developed a set of general equilibrium models that place factor mobility (and hence, the sorting of factors among regions) at the center of its narrative.

In the strongest standard version, households choose regions by arbitraging a wide variety of preferences, with the key ones consisting of nominal income, housing type and cost, and a variety of priced and unpriced amenities, while avoiding disamenities (Glaeser 2008). The model generates a powerful narrative about US regional development over the past 50 years. During a first wave of migration beginning as far back as the 1960s, people picked up and moved from the Northeast and Midwest Rust Belts of the USA to the Sunbelt in search of warmer winters and cheaper housing. They accepted generally lower nominal wages than in their regions of origin, but their resulting real incomes were at least equal due to access to cheaper housing, or—in an alternative version—their total utility increased due to better and more housing and amenities, such as warmer winters or lower density living and more recreation.

Spatial equilibrium researchers later turned to the selective resurgence of certain cities such as New York and Boston in the Rust Belt, as well as the strong growth of high-cost cities such as San Francisco or Seattle. These accounts center around a switch in preferences on the part of higher-skilled workers to interact in close proximity with other skilled people (Glaeser and Maré 2001). These skilled people, represented by the creative class, also wanted access to newly resurgent urban amenities, such as gyms, restaurants, parks, and hip entertainment and urban buzz in general. Notice that spatial equilibrium theory is methodologically very individualist: it focuses on choices made by individuals and households in light of their preferences. While there are some exceptions, most spatial equilibrium papers do not mention structural forces such as the shift in the location of jobs and industries or changes in income distribution, that is to say, the economic and geographical restructuring of work.

A second feature to underscore is that the key point of all the work involving spatial equilibrium is the idea of tradeoffs or arbitraging. More importantly, in order to understand the economics, this encompasses the idea that some places might have high nominal incomes and others lower nominal incomes, but that the real divergence between them is much lower, because the former are likely to have high costs of living or undesirable quality of life characteristics, while the latter will have a low cost of living. This is the difference, in these theories, between 'real income' and 'real total utility' and money income.

However, since the early 2000s, there is increasing evidence of growing divergence in not only nominal (money) wages between regions but also real terms (i.e., after adjusting for the cost of living, see Figure 11.1). Real wage convergence in the United States, a slow trend from 1880 onward, basically came to a halt sometime during the 1980s (Moretti 2012; Diamond 2016; Giannone 2017). Autor (2019), moreover, demonstrates that for college-educated workers, there were only very small gaps in wages between the regions of the US prior to 1980, on the order of 5% from the lowest to highest-wage region; but these gaps have now widened to roughly 30%. Meanwhile, for workers with less than a college education, the gaps have narrowed. Given differences in cost of living, a less-educated worker faces a much larger penalty for living in an expensive region than before, whereas an educated worker enjoys a much greater wage benefit.

Even this is likely to underestimate the total divergence, because high-income people increasingly get access to non-priced amenities such as urban buzz simply by virtue of living where they do (Diamond 2016). The converse of this is that lower-wage workers are moving to regions where their total utility or satisfaction is now lower, and increasingly different from, the average high-wage worker in a region with a high cost of living.

The stakes in these academic exercises have now become political. This objective situation may have finally become a subjective and politicized one. The Brexit and

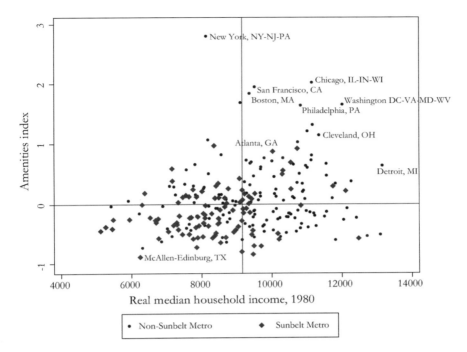

FIGURE 11.1 Amenities and real income in US metropolitan areas.

Source: Kemeny and Storper (2012).

Trump elections, as well as survey data, can be interpreted as indicating that in some regions, many people perceive their total utility to be unsatisfactory, whether or not their locations represent some type of interregional equilibrium in the distribution of people. This notion of a high level of dissatisfaction is supported by the growing literature describing how people in less prosperous regions perceive prosperous urban regions such as New York, London, Houston, Boston, and San Francisco to be better off than where they live, with the others enjoying rigged benefits, a phenomenon labeled 'the politics of resentment' (Graeber 2009; Cramer 2016; Guilluy 2016; Hochschild 2016; Isenberg 2016; Vance 2016; Gest 2016). I will return to this subjective dimension later in this chapter, when discussing values and narratives.

Slower and more selective labor mobility: is it housing and amenities?

The changing geography of wages and employment presents another challenge to urban and regional economics. If the good jobs and wages are piling up in some places rather than others, theory suggests that people will move from the low- to the high-opportunity regions. Yet, since the 1980s, there has been a significant slowdown in interstate mobility in the United States. This is coupled to more geographically selective mobility, where skilled persons migrate among high-income places and the less skilled stay in low-income places more than they have historically. The slowdown applies to virtually all age and skill categories (Kaplan and Schulhofer-Wohl 2012; Molloy, Smith, and Wozniak 2014).

Why would people not move? The mainstream literature on spatial economics turns to housing markets as the main source of the slowdown. The general backdrop for the slowdown in migration is that interregional housing price gaps have grown considerably since the 1990s. In the 1970s and 1980s, there was low demand for housing in the Northeast coastal cities, and an expansionist housing policy in the South and interior West. Since then, the major metropolitan regions in the Northeast and Pacific Coast have had big housing price increases compared to the rest of the country (Glaeser, Gyourko, and Saks 2005). This is a phenomenon found in major metropolitan areas around the world.

Mainstream urban economists mostly attribute high housing prices to over-regulation, and they tend to blame neighborhood groups who defend their privileges through zoning. They line up, in a rather odd coalition, with many self-styled progressive urban planners, who wish to promote dense transit-served neighborhoods and see homeowners as blocking agents. Their claims are sweeping. In a widely cited analysis, Hsieh and Moretti (2019) assert that if city-regions such as San Francisco, NYC, Washington, London, or Paris would open the floodgates for housing construction, then there would be a considerable increase in migration from the regions characterized by high unemployment and relatively low wages, such as the Upper Midwest of the USA, and the prosperous regions would grow through in-migration, but workers would enjoy higher real wages due to lower housing prices. Interestingly, a traditionally local debate about housing provision has, through the use of spatial equilibrium theory, been elevated to one of national importance and tied into debates about left-behind regions as well as spatial and social inequalities at large.

However, this expanded school of thought on deregulating housing construction has very weak empirical evidence. The idea that deregulating housing would substantially reshape a system of cities and solve the problems of inequality through migration and cheaper housing is not well sustained (Rodríguez-Pose and Storper 2020). A more likely explanation is the changing geography of employment and the growing inequality of wage income. Over the last few decades, there has been a great inversion in the geography of employment that continues today, such that metropolitan areas with more than 1 million people account for three-quarters of the net employment increase in the USA from 2010 to 2016. Population increases seem to match more consistently the places with growing employment—whether in expensive, dense, highly regulated metropolitan areas or in cheaper, less-regulated areas. In contrast, population does not expand in cities in either of these categories where there is little employment growth: thus, there are expensive, dense old metros with little job growth (e.g., Chicago, Philadelphia), just as there are many cheap housing cities with little job growth (in the interior West and old Rust Belt). It is very unlikely, under any housing scenario, that an unskilled worker in a left-behind region would move to an expensive region such as New York, not for lack of housing, but rather because the employment opportunities that have grown in New York are in jobs that require high levels of education and skill. In the mid-20th century, if one were a college-educated worker, location had very little impact on one's wage. Today, on average, wages for college-educated workers in America vary by about one-third between prosperous superstar cities and other regions. Meanwhile, the geography of wages for less-skilled workers has flattened. With differences in cost of living between regions, a less-skilled worker is penalized more than in the past for living in a prosperous, high-cost region. It does not make sense for the unskilled to migrate, but it does for the skilled (Autor 2019).

In other words, a structural explanation that relies on major shifts in the geography of wages and opportunity is more effective at explaining why some people move and others do not, and hence on the fundamental roots of interregional economic divergence.

Reformulation around a developmental perspective: the great inversion and the new geography of jobs, incomes, and opportunity

How can we improve our framework to better account for the divergent development patterns of the past 30 years? Kemeny and Storper (2020) propose that there are four key elements that can shape a theory and research framework in terms of both regional economics and economic geography.

1. Macro-historical perspective: waves of technological change are endogenous to the capitalist market system and regularly disrupt convergence and even reverse it. There are successive industrial revolutions that create key new, innovative production sectors with strong agglomeration economies, as emphasized by Schumpeterian economic geographers.
2. The geography of skilled labor in each industrial revolution: the geographical centers of each industrial revolution enhance divergence by maintaining their attractiveness to skilled workers.
3. Maturity and diffusion of cutting-edge industries: at certain moments in time, convergence forces can increase, through declining innovation-generated agglomeration economies as they become more routinized and the skills required to operate them decline.
4. The changing landscape of amenities and housing: amenities and housing are weaker long-term forces than the geography of nominal wages and employment in determining whether convergence or divergence dominates. As the forces of agglomeration expand, the concentration of incomes and amenities are generated endogenously in high-income places. As the forces of agglomeration weaken, the roles of housing and exogenously supplied amenities grow stronger in determining locational choices of firms and households, while the fundamental attractiveness of agglomerations weakens, thus enhancing convergence processes.

The current regional disparities were set in motion by a major wave of technological innovation that began in the 1970s—stimulating output in high technology, finance, and advanced service sectors that depend on agglomeration economies and therefore whose core, nonroutine jobs favor large metropolitan areas and draw from pools of skilled workers in high-turnover labor markets. This wave of technological change also allowed the routinization of previously dominant manufacturing sectors, thus decreasing their employment through automation, and revolutionized trade costs, allowing these forces to become more geographically dispersed (Levy and Murnane 2004). These epochal technological changes have been coupled with an expansion of world trade, itself an outcome of the ways in which such technologies have reduced trade and interaction costs and allowed global value chains to emerge due to routinization of tasks. This has hurt weaker regions and magnified the forces of divergence.

We need a framework to accommodate both times when migration contributes to divergence and when it reverses that role and contributes to convergence. In the mid-20th century United States, people left the deindustrializing regions of the Rust Belt to move to more dynamic ones, either on the coasts or in the South. This served as a safety valve and opportunity-increasing mechanism for migrants. In contrast, today we require a deeper understanding of why certain categories of workers continue to crowd into expensive metropolitan areas as well as the apparent slowdown in mobility of the less-skilled from lower-wage or lower-opportunity regions to the prosperous metropolitan areas. We can speak of groups of the workforce who are stuck in place today; it is not a matter of their underlying desires or preferences, but rather the structural labor market forces that block their path, in both the places where they are or the more prosperous places that they might dream of reaching.

The institutionalization of separate worlds

Rodríguez-Pose (2013) argues that there is a widespread consensus that 'institutions are important to development' (Acemoglu, Johnson, and Robinson 2004; Rodrik et al. 2004; Farole et al. 2010; Acemoglu and Robinson 2012). Conventionally, a broad definition of institutions includes those that are both formal and informal. Formal institutions that shape development can range from very big framework conditions, such as constitutions, laws, and governmental structures, to very specific formal rules and laws, along with organizations that apply, enforce, and interpret them. Institutions also refers to routines, in the form of manifold informal practices, norms, conventions, and beliefs, as well as informal networks of persons and organizations (North 1990; Storper and Salais 1997). Moreover, it is widely agreed that formal institutions and informal institutions (often labeled 'culture') have two-way joint effects (Alesina and Guiliano 2015).

In what follows, I discuss four possible ways that institutions are shaping current interregional economic polarization: institutions that capture and prolong agglomeration; institutionalized value systems and interactions that influence migration, skills, and sorting; set institutional structures that shape skilling and socialization; and feedback to politicians, which in turn affects divergence through policy choices.

Institutions, agglomeration, and divergence

Capturing promising new industries involves the nurturing of the entrepreneurs who come up with breakthrough innovations or products and transforming older ones involves spin-off firms who aid the major existing firms to remain dynamic (Saxenian 1994; Klepper 2009; Chatterji, Glaeser, and Kerr 2013). Kenney and Mowery (2014) emphasize the different ways that business and research institutions network in regions, as the relational infrastructures that shape innovation and entrepreneurship, so that R&D is translated into development in different manners from one place to another. Feldman and Lowe (2017) use the case of North Carolina to make a wider argument about the gradual enhancement of regional capabilities. But the field still lacks systematic, large-scale evidence, as well as structured theories, on the preconditions that enable certain regions to capture major waves of development and others to be excluded.

A related topic is why, in this wave, agglomeration-driven advantages have concentrated in certain places, and why overall divergence has thus far been so strong relative to convergence and spreading processes. Detailed studies on existing prosperous places suggest that this might be because of the endogenous coevolution of agglomeration and the local informal institutions that are specific to certain industries and places, such as Silicon Valley and London today or Detroit and Manchester in the past.

In one prominent study, Feldman and Zoller (2012) identify new types of economic intermediary agents, such as venture capitalists and deal brokers, showing that their uneven geography accompanies the growth of knowledge-intensive industries. Other recent research along these lines has quantified the value of certain kinds of local economic networks that underpin agglomeration (Kemeny et al. 2016). Another key question for such institutional approaches is how entrepreneurs emerge, what kinds of entrepreneurs emerge, where they emerge, and whether they flourish or are inhibited by the regional economic environment (Kirzner 1979; Braunerhjelm et al. 2010; Chatterji, Glaeser, and Kerr 2013; Fairlie 2013). Taking into account all these institutional forces—existing firms, innovation, networks and leadership, conventions and world views, entrepreneurship—economic sociologists speak of the emergence of 'organizational fields' or ecologies (Powell, Packalen, and Whittington 2012; Padgett and Powell 2012), referring to a complex institutionalization process. In the language of regional economics, the places that develop the institutions mentioned earlier, in tandem with the location of firms that have cutting-edge technology or knowledge endowments, develop double monopolistic advantages, from hard economies of scale to informal institutions that are difficult to imitate or transfer. This difficulty of imitation may not last forever, but it seems to prolong the advantage and hence interregional polarization in ways not fully incorporated into either RSUE superstar city approaches or NEG agglomeration modeling.

Network-embedded skills, job search, and spatial traps

Many scholars now consider that new economy skills are not just individual human capital but also are acquired and exercised through networks, which are in turn social institutions (Granovetter 2005; Owen-Smith and Powell 2012; Deming 2015; DeLong 2016; Kemeny et al. 2016). In this view, more formal skills are indeed required than ever before, but in addition to diplomas, there are also more experience skills that can only be acquired by 'being there' (De la Roca and Puga 2017). Experience itself appears to have several different components and geographies. One is simply having learned the unwritten or informal aspects of job performance. Another is that the high turnover and highly individualized work in the skilled sectors of the new economy require social networks: knowing people. The implication of this reasoning is that even those individuals who succeed at formal schooling in left-behind regions are increasingly disadvantaged by their location. They are less apt to acquire the informal experience, knowledge, and cues, and to build the networks that create advantages for individuals in the wealthier regions with similar levels of formal education. Such opportunities are scarcer and less 'in the air' in the less-developed regions than in those that are already ahead. If this is the case, then the institutions in the wealthier regions can also provide their students with better overall capacities by means of better networking and social cueing than in less-advantaged regions. Such differences then cumulate over the development cycle through the differential ability of families in the right regions to have the income and connections to afford their children such capacities. This could help us explain the observed increase in regional differences in return to education, especially among highly skilled workers, and the relative lack of migration from left-behind to superstar regions.

Research on skills, mobility, and interregional divergence should therefore consider education and experience in relation to strong and weak ties and how they affect sorting between regions and behaviors within them. It seems likely that this contributes to why less-skilled people find themselves more spatially trapped today than in previous waves of economic change.

Organizations, values, and culture: socialization and economic divergence

As noted earlier, institutions are generally broken down into formal and informal components, with the latter consisting of a variety of elements including values, norms, conventions, beliefs, and customs. Some theorists argue that all these informal dimensions should be described by the term 'culture' (Alesina and Guiliano 2015). There is increasing recognition that these forces can contribute to economic divergence.

Scholars such as Graeber (2009), Cramer (2016), Vance (2016), Hochschild (2016), and Williams (2017) call attention to different systems of values in different regions of the US. They argue that we should consider variables that capture individual characteristics in context, because it is experiences that count for people (and not just inputs such as education or outputs such as income). Operationally, two such experience-capturing variables are occupation and location. There seems to be a value split between people in manual-occupational cultures and cognitive-occupational cultures that is sharper than the splits between people at different educational and income levels (Williams 2017). Income is less closely related to many attitudes than notions of dignity and expectations of social mobility or hope about the future (see also Inglehart and Norris 2016).

These interpretations are supported by quantitative findings on voting patterns. Gelman (2008) demonstrates that the standard individual attributes adduced to explain voting—income, religious observance, race, and ethnicity—change in importance and sometimes in direction when geographically disaggregated. For example, high-income people in US blue states vote much farther to the left than their high-income counterparts in red states, and the effect of a similar degree of religious conviction varies greatly across different places. Blue counties in the USA aggregate left-wing preferences from the two ends of the income distribution spectrum, but the upper end votes overwhelmingly right-wing in less urban places. This implies that interactions within places, and not just individual characteristics (even in combination at the individual level), determine, at least to some extent, attitude formation and voting (Gordon 2018).

All of these scholars argue that individual attributes are shaped by, and mutually causal with, the collective attributes of the places in which people live and the process by which narratives are constructed based on observation and experience. The institutions of a place are in part the organizations with which people interact and that help to define and mobilize their interests and interpretations of experience. Along these lines, Hochschild (2016) reports on a detailed ethnography of Louisiana, centering on the intersection of local institutions—churches, political parties, community associations, local political and social networks—in forging narratives or world views.

The institutions of socialization are constructed by human actors, and some of them can change in relatively short periods of time. In the case of the US, the key institutions of 'CIO unionism'[2] and urban political machines have lost their force in the wake of deindustrialization in many areas of the Midwest (CIO unions were never strong in the South) (Davis 2017). CIO unionism was to the Northeast and Upper Midwest what conservative local institutions have been to the South: a key center of associational life and information for many people and their families, shaping their political choices. As CIO unions have withered due to deindustrialization and associated demographic change, other more politically and socially conservative local institutions have replaced them. As industrial cities in the Midwest have declined, those people who did not move out of the region have become more rural, and with this new rurality, their institutional attachments have changed, becoming more rural and more conservative in flavor (Cramer 2016).

An opposite form of institutional construction appears to have occurred in most major cities over the last 30 years. As noted earlier, these regions have seen the rise of a dense tissue of organizations in local civil society, associated with a high degree of social mobilization. These organizations lobby for inclusion of immigrants, for multiculturalism, for amenities such as transportation and recreation, for aiding the homeless, and for promoting urban cultural events and forums. The labor unions involved in these places are largely those of post-industrial, service-oriented workers (often non-white and female), in urban-based industries with strong immigrant constituencies. They have largely replaced industrial manufacturing unions as participants in big-city politics. Religious organizations are involved, but usually they are more concerned with justice-oriented approaches to urban problems than with religious conservatism. The civil society tissue of metropolitan areas is the source of much of the progressive politics, multiculturalism, and global outlook there, deviating substantially from the church, military, within-group, and family-dominated affinities that prevail in other areas. We could therefore say that the content of civil society organizations and networks has gone in very different directions in different regions, in a way that seems to track economic geographies and their demographic consequences. Ultimately, we need to better understand the interaction between technological change, labor market change, the geography of work and incomes, and political and institutional change.

Political and policy polarization

The fact that economic polarization gives rise to a differentiated landscape of objective interests is nothing new; this is the basis for a long line of literature on sectionalism and political choices in different regions. The current economic polarization has its version of this phenomenon. A key issue in determining the economic effects of trade is distinguishing between producer (wage, employment) impacts and consumer impacts, and determining how they interact differently across regions. These effects have been considered in the aggregate, where the evidence shows that increasing manufacturing trade has generated large net benefits from a consumer surplus (lower prices) in developed countries and net benefits in employment and wage incomes in developing countries. The greatest net consumer benefits are at lower ranges of the income distribution, because the wealthy consume more services and more locally produced goods than those with lower incomes. In geographical terms, this probably means that regions hit hardest by import competition with regard to wages and employment probably exhibit rather high consumer surpluses on the consumption side (the 'Walmart' effect). People in wealthier regions also enjoy a consumer surplus from imports, but because they consume more locally produced services, these are lower on a proportional basis. Skilled people in prosperous regions probably benefit more from the presence of low-wage immigrant labor, which provides them with labor-intensive services, more than is the case in less wealthy regions. In the latter, immigrants are likely to compete with low-skill native workers more than in metropolitan regions (Foged and Peri 2016). These structural factors will help us explain the divergent attitudes toward globalization and multiculturalism that manifest geographically today.

Rising to the challenge

I opened this chapter by noting the double challenge identified by the *Economist*: orthodox economics has few answers to the problem of regional inequality, and yet, if we do not provide some answers, populist insurgents will do so. I have attempted to propose a broader framework with which we could seek these answers. This framework would apply micro-economic analyses of employment location, wages, the role of housing and amenities, skills, and migration, and place them within a broad structural and developmental framework. This is ultimately a multi-disciplinary effort. The stakes are high because geographical polarization is a threat to social and economic stability and justice in the contemporary world.

Acknowledgements

I thank Harald Bathelt, Tom Kemeny, Henry Overman and CEP London seminar participants, as well as several anonymous referees, for their detailed and insightful critiques of two previous versions. I also benefited from comments of participants at the 'Globalization in Crisis' conference at Cambridge in July 2017.

Notes

1. Shortened and partly updated reprint: Storper, Michael. 2018. "Separate Worlds? Explaining the Current Wave of Regional Economic Polarization." *Journal of Economic Geography* 18 (2): 247–270. doi: 10.1093/jeg/lby011.
2. CIO unionism as the progressive branch of AFL–CIO, consisting of a more politicized 'European style' and class-oriented union than the AFL local unions. When the two merged, AFL 'bread and butter' unionism came to dominate in the United States, but locally, many CIO unions were already in place and played an important role in those communities long after the merger.

References

Acemoglu, Daron, Simon Johnson, and James A. Robinson. 2004. "Institutions as the Fundamental Cause of Long-Run Growth." *Working Paper 10481*. Cambridge, MA: National Bureau of Economic Research.

Acemoglu, Daron, and James A. Robinson. 2012. *Why Nations Fail: The Origins of Power, Prosperity, and Poverty*. London: Profile Books.

Alesina, Alberto, and Paola Guiliano. 2015. "Culture and Institutions." *Journal of Economic Literature* 53 (4): 898–944.

Autor, David H. 2019. "Work of the Past, Work of the Future." *AEA Papers and Proceedings* 109: 1–32.

Bishop, Bill, and Robert G. Cushing. 2008. *The Big Sort: Why the Clustering of Like-Minded Americans is Tearing Us Apart*. New York: Houghton-Mifflin.

Braunerhjelm, Pontus, Zoltan J. Acs, David B. Audretsch, and Bo Carlsson. 2010. "The Missing Link: Knowledge Diffusion and Entrepreneurship in Endogenous Growth." *Small Business Economics* 34 (2): 105–125.

Chatterji, Aaron, Edward L. Glaeser, and William R. Kerr. 2013. "Clusters of Entrepreneurship and Innovation." *Working Paper 19013*. Cambridge, MA: National Bureau of Economic Research.

Chetty, Raj, Nathaniel Hendren, Patrick Kline, and Emmanuel Saez. 2014. "Where is the Land of Opportunity? The Geography of Intergenerational Mobility in the United States" *Quarterly Journal of Economics* 129 (4): 1553–1623.

Cramer, Katherine J. 2016. *The Politics of Resentment: Rural Consciousness in Wisconsin and the Rise of Scott Walker*. Chicago: University of Chicago Press.

Davis, Mike. 2017. "The Great God Trump and the White Working Class." *Jacobin*, July 2.

De la Roca, Jorge, and Diego Puga. 2017. "Learning by Working in Big Cities." *Review of Economic Studies* 84 (1): 106–142.

DeLong, Bradford J. 2016. "Regional Policy and Distributional Policy in a World Where People Want to Ignore the Value and Contribution of Knowledge and Network-Based Returns." Accessed March 1, 2018. www.bradford-delong.com/2016/12/16/.

Deming, David J. 2015. "The Growing Importance of Social Skills in the Labor Market." *Working Paper 21473*. Cambridge, MA: National Bureau of Economic Research.

Diamond, Rebecca. 2016. "The Determinants and Welfare Implications of US Workers' Diverging Location Choices by Skill, 1980–2000." *American Economic Review* 106 (3): 479–524.

(The) Economist. 2016. "Place-Based Economic Policies as a Response to Populism." December 15.

Fairlie, Robert W. 2013. "Entrepreneurship, Economic Conditions, and the Great Recession." *Journal of Economics and Management Strategy* 22 (2): 207–231.

Farole, Thomas, Andrés Rodríguez-Pose, and Michael Storper. 2010. "Human Geography and the Institutions that Underlie Economic Growth." *Progress in Human Geography* 35 (1): 58–80.

Feldman, Maryann P., and Nichola Lowe. 2017. "The Unbearable Lightness of Effective Policy." *Unpublished Paper*. Chapel Hill, NC: University of North Carolina, School of Public Policy.

Feldman, Maryann P., and Ted D. Zoller. 2012. "Dealmakers in Place: Social Capital Connections in Regional Entrepreneurial Economies." *Regional Studies* 46 (1): 23–37.

Foged, Mette, and Giovanni Peri. 2016. "Immigrants' Effect on Native Workers: New Analysis of Longitudinal Data." *American Economic Journal: Applied Economics* 8 (2): 1–34.

Ganong, Peter, and Daniel W. Shoag. 2017. "Why Has Regional Income Convergence in the U.S. Declined?" *Working Paper 23609*. Cambridge, MA: National Bureau of Economic Research.

Gelman, Andrew. 2008. *Red State, Blue State, Rich State, Poor State: Why Americans Vote the Way They Do*. Princeton: Princeton University Press.

Gest, Justin. 2016. *The New Minority: White Working Class Politics in an Age of Immigration and Inequality*. Oxford: Oxford University Press.

Giannone, Elisa. 2017. "Skill-Biased Technical Change and Regional Convergence." *2017 Meeting Papers 190*. Society for Economic Dynamics.

Glaeser, Edward L. 2008. *Cities, Agglomeration, and Spatial Equilibrium*. Oxford: Oxford University Press.

Glaeser, Edward L., Joseph Gyourko, and Raven Saks. 2005. "Why is Manhattan So Expensive? Regulation and the Rise in Housing Prices." *Journal of Law and Economics* 48 (2): 331–369.

Glaeser, Edward L., and David C. Maré. 2001. "Cities and Skills." *Journal of Labor Economics* 19 (2): 316–342.

Gordon, Ian R. 2018. "In What Sense Left Behind by Globalization? Looking for a Less Reductionist Geography of the Populist Surge in Europe" *Cambridge Journal of Regions, Economies and Societies* 11 (1): 95–113.

Graeber, David. 2009. "Value, Politics and Democracy in the United States." *Current Sociology* 59 (2): 186–199.
Granovetter, Mark. 2005. "The Impact of Social Structure on Economic Outcomes." *Journal of Economic Perspectives* 19 (1): 33–50.
Guilluy, Christophe. 2016. *La Crépuscule de la France d'en haut* [The Twilight of France from Above]. Paris: Flammarion.
Hochschild, Arlie R. 2016. *Strangers in Their Own Land: Anger and Mourning on the American Right*. New York: The New Press.
Hsieh, Chang-Tai, and Enrico Moretti. 2019. "Housing Constraints and Spatial Misallocation." *American Economic Journal: Macroeconomics* 11 (2): 1–39.
Inglehart, Ronald F., and Pippa Norris. 2016. "Trump, Brexit, and the Rise of Populism: Economic Have-Nots and Cultural Backlash." *HKS Faculty Research Working Paper Series RWP16–026.* Cambridge, MA: Harvard Kennedy School.
Isenberg, Nancy. 2016. *White Trash: The 400-Year Untold History of Class in America*. New York: Viking.
Kaplan, Greg, and Sam Schulhofer-Wohl. 2012. "Understanding the Long-Run Decline in Interstate Migration." *Working Paper 18507.* Cambridge, MA: National Bureau of Economic Research.
Kemeny, Thomas, Maryann P. Feldman, Frank Ethridge, and Ted Zoller. 2016. "The Economic Value of Local Social Networks." *Journal of Economic Geography* 16 (5): 1101–1122.
Kemeny, Thomas, and Michael Storper. 2012. "The Sources of Urban Development: Wages, Housing, and Amenity Gaps Across American Cities." *Journal of Regional Science* 52 (1): 85–108.
Kemeny, Thomas, and Michael Storper. 2020. "Superstar Cities and Left-behind Places: Disruptive Innovation, Labor Demand, and Interregional Inequality." *Working Paper 41.* London: LSE International Inequality Institute.
Kenney, Martin, and David C. Mowery, eds. 2014. *Public Universities and Regional Growth: Insights from the University of California*. Stanford: Stanford University Press.
Kirzner, Israel M. 1979. *Perception, Opportunity, and Profit: Studies in the Theory of Entrepreneurship*. Chicago: University of Chicago Press.
Klepper, Steven. 2009. "Silicon Valley, a Chip off the Old Detroit Bloc." In *Entrepreneurship, Growth, and Public Policy*, edited by Zoltan J. Acs, David B. Audretsch, and Robert J. Strom, 79–116. Cambridge: Cambridge University Press.
Levy, Frank, and Richard J. Murnane. 2004. *The New Division of Labor: How Computers Are Creating the Next Job Market*. New York: Russell Sage Foundation.
Molloy, Raven, Christopher L. Smith, and Abigail Wozniak. 2014. "Declining Migration within the U.S.: The Role of The Labor Market." *Working Paper 20065.* Cambridge, MA: National Bureau of Economic Research.
Moretti, Enrico. 2012. *The New Geography of Jobs*. Boston: Houghton Mifflin Harcourt.
North, Douglass C. 1990. *Institutions, Institutional Change and Economic Performance*. Cambridge: Cambridge University Press.
Owen-Smith, Jason, and Walter W. Powell. 2012. "Networks and Institutions." In *The Sage Handbook of Organizational Institutionalism*, edited by Royston Greenwood, Christine Oliver, Roy Suddaby, and Kerstin Sahlin-Andersson, 594–621. Los Angeles: Sage.
Padgett, John F., and Walter W. Powell, eds. 2012. *The Emergence of Organizations and Markets*. Princeton: Princeton University Press.
Powell, Walter W., Kelley Packalen, and Kjersten B. Whittington. 2012. "Organizational and Institutional Genesis: The Emergence of High-Tech Clusters in the Life Sciences." In *The Emergence of Organizations and Markets*, edited by John F. Padgett, and Walter W. Powell, 434–465. Princeton: Princeton University Press.

Rodríguez-Pose, Andrés. 2013. "Do Institutions Matter for Regional Development?" *Regional Studies* 47 (7): 1034–1047.

Rodríguez-Pose, Andrés, and Michael Storper. 2020. "Housing, Urban Growth and Inequalities: The Limits to Deregulation and Upzoning in Reducing Economic and Spatial Inequality." *Urban Studies* 57 (2): 223–248.

Rodrik, Dani, Arvind Subramanian, and Francesco Trebbi. 2004. "Institutions Rule: The Primacy of Institutions Over Geography and Integration in Economic Development." *Journal of Economic Growth* 9 (2): 131–165.

Saxenian, AnnaLee. 1994. *Regional Advantage: Culture and Competition in Silicon Valley and Route 128*. Cambridge, MA: Harvard University Press.

Spicer, Jason. 2018. "Electoral Systems, Regional Resentment and the Surprising Success of Anglo-American Populism." *Cambridge Journal of Regions, Economy and Society* 11 (1): 115–141.

Storper, Michael, and Robert Salais. 1997. *Worlds of Production: The Action Frameworks of the Economy*. Cambridge, MA: Harvard University Press.

Sussell, Jesse, and James A. Thomson. 2015. *Are Changing Constituencies Driving Rising Polarization in the U.S. House of Representatives?* Santa Monica: RAND Corporation.

Vance, J. D. 2016. *Hillbilly Elegy: A Memoir of a Family and Culture in Crisis*. New York: Harper.

Williams, Joan C. 2017. *White Working Class: Overcoming Class Cluelessness in America*. Boston: Harvard Business Review Press.

12
SPATIAL TRANSFORMATIONS AND SPATIO-TEMPORAL COUPLING

Links between everyday shopping behavior and changes in the retail landscape

Elmar Kulke and Nina Baur

Interrelations of time and space: spatio-temporal pathways

Löw and Knoblauch (in this book) claim that since the 1970s, spaces have been refigured at a rather fast pace and within a relatively short period of time. Similarly, in accordance with most economic theories, spatial transformations should occur rather frequently and quickly—whenever production costs or consumer demands change, for example, companies should restructure their locations of production and retailing along with their value chains. However, at least for the economy, the contrary is true from an empirical standpoint. For example, Boatcă, Bhambra, Korzeniewicz, and Payne (all in this book) illustrate at the level of the world system that spatial transformations occur much more seldomly than both economic theories and the concept of refiguration of spaces suggest. Indeed, *if* they occur, spatial transformations unfold much more slowly, usually in the longue durée (Braudel 1958), and path-dependently. This is important not only as an aspect in the spatial structure of the economy but also because of the fact that the economy is a key factor in (re-)producing social inequality. Similar effects can be observed at the national and regional levels, where regional disparities of both the economic structure and social inequality have been continuously reproducing over an extended period of time (Storper in this issue; Heidenreich 2003).

Various explanations have been provided as to why the spatial structures of the economy are so slow to transform, including: power structures within the world system (Wallerstein 2004); constructions of race, nationality, and citizenship as aftermaths of colonialism (Boatcă, Bhambra, both in this book); spatial strategies of transnational elites (Korzeniewicz and Payne in this book); the agglomeration of infrastructure and institutions in regional innovation systems (Hassink, Ibert, and Sarnow 2020; Heidenreich and Baur 2015; Storper in this book); the material structure of global value chains (Beyer et al. in this book); and local economic conventions, values, and culture (Baur et al. 2014c, Storper in this book).

In this chapter, we provide an additional explanation for the sluggishness of spatial transformations, complementing these earlier accounts: the spatial and temporal coupling of institutions. The idea of "coupling" is based on the observation that space and time are inextricably entwined in both the economy and everyday life, as geography (e.g. Massey 2005) and sociology (e.g. Löw 2001; Baur 2005, 80–82, 165–172; Weidenhaus 2015) have repeatedly stressed. In this context, it is necessary to distinguish between people's spatio-temporal knowledge ("*Soziale Raumzeit*," "*Raum- und Zeitwissen*")—how people experience and interpret their living spaces ("*Lebensraum*") and their life histories ("*Lebensgeschichtlichkeit*") in their individual biographies (Weidenhaus 2015)—and their actions. With regard to people's actions in space and time, it is important to note that at any given point in time, the materiality of the surroundings determines people's actions and interactions, as each person and object (i.e. good) can only be at one location (i.e. at a specific *space-time coordinate*) at a given time. In modern economies, goods are typically transported over long distances and people commute between their homes and work spaces. Moving people and goods through (physical) space from one space-time coordinate to another takes time (Baur et al. 2014a), which is why specific *spatio-temporal pathways* ("*Raum-Zeit-Pfade*") can be observed (Cromley 1999, 64–82, 104–116).

In order to save time and facilitate coordination across time and space, different activities are often "*coupled*"—that is: combined—at the same locations. This has been demonstrated both in geography and sociology for consumers' everyday lives and in geography for economic activities. Using the example of consumer-retailer interactions when shopping for groceries in West German cities, we take this one step further in this chapter: We will not only show (a) how consumers (demand side) couple shopping with other everyday activities and (b) how retailers (supply side) couple their outlets with other retailers and social institutions but also (c) how demand and supply side are coupled and (d) how this coupling is embedded in the material urban structure, (e) which in turn is at the root of the slowness in spatial transformations.

Consumers: the driving forces behind coupling on the demand side

When analyzing consumer-retailer interactions on the demand side, one can observe that *in theory*, consumers today should both go shopping more often and spend more time on shopping than was the case 70 years ago due to increasing incomes, new lifestyles, and a new household division of labor.

First, *people's ability to afford products* has dramatically increased. Up to the 1950s in Germany, markets were characterized by insufficient supply, and a lack of food was an everyday experience. Since then, however, grocery stores have been saturated and driven by excess supply. In parallel, real household incomes have increased continuously (Ermann and Pütz 2020). As a result, in 2019, the average income was 33 times higher than 70 years ago (Destatis 2020, Figure 12.1).

Increased income encourages changes in consumption behavior, which is described by the classic Engel curves (Engel 1857; Kulke 2017): Low-income consumers can only afford to buy a limited number of goods and have to spend most of their available money on basic necessities (such as food), which therefore are not income elastic. When incomes increase, consumers both buy more goods and spend a larger share of their income on income-elastic, high-quality, or expendable goods (e.g., durable consumer goods, entertainment, electronics). Consumers typically do not buy more necessities but rather buy similar goods of a higher quality, for instance, by switching from cheap no-name articles to brand products. Regardless, in 2013, German couples with children still spent about 15% of their household income on food (Destatis 2016, 158). Higher income also equates to an increase in individual mobility, as households increasingly own private means of transportation, especially cars (Achen et al. 2008). Cars allow consumers to travel faster and to shop at more distant and varied retail agglomerations. All in all, income

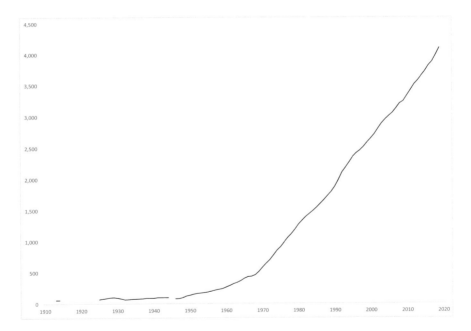

FIGURE 12.1 Average monthly gross income of German full-time employees 1913–1919 (in Euro)

Source: Own calculation based on Destatis 2020. The working population consists of the employees in production and services of the respective territory at the time, namely the German Reich 1913–1944, the American-British Bizone 1945–1949, the territory of the former Federal Republic of Germany since 1949 (without Saarland and Berlin 1950–1959, without Berlin 1960–1963, including West Berlin 1964–2006, including Berlin since 2007).

increases should impact spatio-temporal pathways, as buying more goods—at least in theory—requires more time dedicated to shopping and going to more shops.

Second, shopping behavior is only one of many daily activities needed to maintain a family. Modern urban West German families—for example, consisting of two adult partners with small children living in a single household—typically perform unpaid work (housework and care work) in addition to enjoying some leisure activities (e.g., watching TV, playing, receiving visitors) at home. If the household's adults perform their paid work outside their homes, they need to commute to/from their office. They also have to ensure that their children are transported to/from their (nursery) schools. Additional journeys result from diverse leisure activities (e.g., sports, day trips, meeting friends, eating out, visiting concerts) as well as housework and care work (e.g., shopping, seeing a doctor). In other words, the daily routines of a family's members are linked.

As people's overall time budget is limited, in order to save time, there typically is a *household division of labor* between the adult family members, which can take on different forms. From the nineteenth century to the 1950s, the "male breadwinner/female homemaker model," in which the man concentrates on work and the woman takes care of housework and carework, was common practice. Since the 1960s, due to changes in both the welfare state and social norms, the "dual career model," in which partners share these tasks evenly, has increasingly become more common (Baur 2007). This is reflected in female labor market participation: In many countries (including Germany), only 40% of women were employed in the 1960s and 1970s, while 55% were employed in 2016 (Grunow 2019, 258). Although gender ideologies have expanded since the 1950s (Baur et al. 2019; Grunow 2019), there is surprisingly little change in the general structure of the household division of labor (Grunow 2019, 260, 276): In 2012/13, men spent about 57% of their total work hours on paid work and 43% on unpaid work—for women, it was the opposite with a ratio of 35% to 65%, meaning that, on average, men spent nine hours more per week on paid and ten hours less per week on unpaid work than women, and the gender gap in overall work time has even increased still further since the early 2000s (Destatis 2016, 263).

What is rarely taken into account in debates on the household division of labor is its implications for spatio-temporal pathways: Different activities—such as cleaning and cooking, shopping, paid work, dropping off the children at school, visiting doctors, banks and public administrations—take place at different places scattered around the city: the home, shops, the office, childcare facilities, schools, government offices, etc. Consumers do not have a choice in the matter because, during the period of industrialization, the division of spheres was materially engrained in the urban structure—referred to as objectified form-investments (Hering and Baur 2019). Consumers are therefore forced to spend time *commuting between these places*.

As a result, more than half of housework is dedicated to commuting, shopping, and cooking: Of the 29.5 hours per week women dedicated to housework in 2012/13, they spent 2.7 hours per week commuting, 6.1 hours per week shopping and putting away the goods they had bought, and 6.9 hours in the kitchen, while men spent 5.7 hours per week less on these tasks. Namely, men spent 2.1 hours per week commuting, 4.9 hours per week shopping, and 3 hours per week cooking (Destatis 2016, 263). Depending on the database, in the 2010s, Germans went shopping between 3.5 times (Papastefanou and Zajchowski 2016, 120) and 4.5 times (Procher and Vance 2013, 8) per week. When Germans left their homes, two out of three trips involved some form of shopping (Destatis 2016, 343). The working population commutes much more often and over longer distances: On a given working day, nine out of ten Germans leave their homes and make an average of four journeys, mostly by car. In doing so, commuters cover about 10 to 12 kilometers per journey, requiring between 84 and 90 minutes in total (Destatis 2016, 341–342).

Due to the above-mentioned changes in the household division of labor, commuting times at least should have increased since the 1960s: In the male breadwinner/female homemaker model, commuting time is minimized as men travel to work places that are typically located in a different neighborhood or even city than the home, while women perform all tasks that can be completed in the home neighborhood, including shopping (Figure 12.2a). In contrast, in the dual career model, both partners have to travel to all places because they share all tasks, thus multiplying overall commuting time (Figure 12.2b).

Consequently, all in all, both commuting time and time spent shopping should have increased since the 1960s, due to both increasing incomes and changes in the household division of labor. However, paradoxically, since the 1980s—when mobility patterns were first systematically measured in Germany—both the percentage of commuting persons and the average time spent commuting have *not* increased but rather have stayed more or less constant (Destatis 2016, 341–342). Similarly, both men and women only spent about half an hour more shopping in the 2010s than in the early 2000s (Destatis 2016, 263).

The reason for this is that couples' overall time budget remains the same—if new tasks are added, couples have to reduce the time spent on other tasks (Hofmeister and Moen 2012). To a certain extent, working hours have been decreasing since the 1960s (Grunow 2019). However, as working hours are partly regulated nationally and partly negotiated by labor unions, couples have a limited influence on their total working hours if both want to work. Instead, couples have been saving the most time by spending less time on housework since the 1950s (Baur et al. 2019). Women's average time spent on routine housework decreased from more than four hours per day in 1965 to less than three hours in the 2000s. At the same time, men's average time spent on routine housework has only increased from 17 minutes in 1965 to 49 minutes in 2001 (Grunow 2019, 258). As a result, the total working hours—for paid work, housework, care work, shopping, and commuting—have been steadily decreasing since the 1950s and decreased further by about 45 minutes between 2001/2002 and 2012/2013 (Destatis 2016, 263).

This reduction in housework was partly driven by technological change (Baur et al. 2019). However, and more importantly, consumers have reacted to time pressure by *coupling activities in their daily life*. In the 2010s, when going shopping, only one

156 Elmar Kulke and Nina Baur

(a) Male breadwinner and female homemaker family, 19th century to 1950s

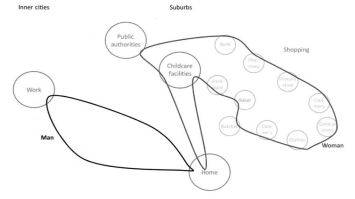

(b) Dual-earner family, 19th century to 1950s

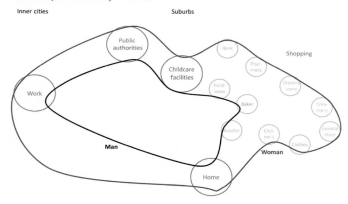

(c) Dual-earner family, 1960s to 1970

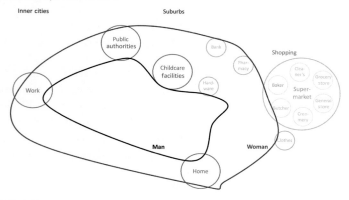

FIGURE 12.2 Typical spatio-temporal paths of couples with children on workdays depending on household division of labor and retailing structures

(d) Dual-earner family, since 1980s

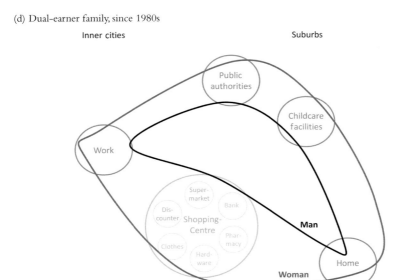

FIGURE 12.2 (Continued)

in three trips was solely dedicated to shopping, while two out of three trips *coupled shopping with other activities* (Destatis 2016, 343). In addition, consumers also couple different types of shopping activities.

In connection with rising income and mobility, motives for shopping have become increasingly differentiated (Kulke 2005; Weiss 2006). Entertainment shopping (coupling shopping with leisure activities such as visiting a restaurant), discount shopping (buying in stores with an assortment of articles at low prices), and smart shopping (buying well-known brand products for low prices) are gaining in importance. In the course of this differentiation, the connections within closest proximity—the so-called nearest-center-connections—have dissolved and more distant shopping locations are visited more often (Martin 2006).

Temporal coupling of retailing with other social institutions

It is important to note that individual people do not have much choice about how to organize their everyday lives, because when people (e.g., the members of a family) interact, their actions need to be spatially and temporally synchronized (Maurer 1992; Baur 2005). Therefore, people's spatio-temporal knowledge and spatio-temporal pathways (micro level) are embedded in spatio-temporal regimes (macro level), which are both material (objectified) and social. Although temporal and spatial regimes are obviously linked, so far, sociology has mostly focused on time regimes ("*Zeitordnungen*") and geography on material spatial orders ("*Raumstruktur*").

As sociology has shown, any social group—such as a family or a company—is synchronized by means of a time regime ("*Zeitordnung*") (Buchmann 1989; Fürstenberg 1986): Based on collective temporal knowledge ("*Zeitbewusstsein*") (Bergmann 1983), the social group defines a set of temporal rules that structure people's schedules in a typical and binding way, so that anyone can rely on the others' schedules. In Germany, for instance, the traditional working hours ("*Kernarbeitszeiten*") are 9:00 a.m. to 5:00 p.m. (Monday to Friday). Time regimes are embedded in and at the same time enforced by institutions (e.g., companies, kindergartens, schools). If different institutions do not coordinate their individual time regimes ("*Eigenzeit*") (Luckmann 1986), this might result in time conflicts ("*Zeitkonflikte*") at the individual level (Fürstenberg 1982). For example, if the employer expects an employee to be at the office from 9:00 a.m. to 5:00 p.m. but kindergartens and schools are open only between 8:00 a.m. and 1:00 p.m., this means that the same person cannot be employed and take care of the children at the same time. At the household level, this means that either only one partner can be employed or the couple cannot have children (Baur 2008).

Time conflicts are partially resolved by an implicit hierarchy that defines which institution's time regimes take precedence in cases of time clashes. In Germany, work usually takes priority over childcare which in turn takes priority over shopping, meaning that people can only go shopping when they are not working or doing carework. This institutional hierarchy means that retailers are largely forced to react to time conflicts created in other fields of social life.

An initial conflict to which retailers needed to react was the fact that shops require employees to operate and 72% of salespersons are women (BA 2020). This created a time conflict even in the 1950s, and retailing has responded to this by means of lobbying. As a result, German legislation defined a compromise in 1956 that stores may only open from Monday to Friday between 7:00 a.m. and 6:30 p.m. and on Saturdays until 2:00 p.m. (Papastefanou and Zajchowski 2016, 117), which allowed most workers to shop before or after work and salespersons to shop and do their housework at a different time. As this did not suffice to resolve the time conflicts, the strict regulations of *opening hours* have been relaxed since 1989. Since 2006, stores may open 24/6 (Monday to Saturday). This in turn had consequences for people's spatio-temporal pathways in their daily routines, as the average time people spend in stores has increased (Papastefanou and Zajchowski 2016).

A second time conflict arose as a result of changing consumer demands. As discussed previously, these have mainly been determined by three different factors (Lange 1973; Kulke 2017): first, the time available for shopping (shopping time); second, the time needed to reach the shopping locations (commuting time); and third, the transport capacity for articles. Available shopping time and commuting time (which in turn depend on the specific household division of labor) define the minimum coupling of activities needed to obtain all required articles. Transport capacity defines the maximum coupling that is possible—cars offer larger transport capacities (compared to walking or using a bike). Changing household divisions of labor and increases in income (with more articles bought) enhance the need for consumers to couple activities.

Since the 1950s, retailers have been reacting to changing consumer needs using a series of organizational innovations consisting of two elements: internal parameters of action mainly address time conflicts and change the store's characteristics; external parameters address locational choices and increasingly couple stores closer together in terms of space.

Internal parameters of action are documented in the *rising importance of larger retail formats*. These larger formats have developed because they allow consumers to buy different products at once, while at the same time enabling retailers to achieve internal economies of scale, offer more and more diverse articles, and implement different business strategies. According to the life-cycle model of retail formats (Dannenberg, Franz, and Leper 2016; Kulke 2017; Neiberger and Steinke 2020), every retail format is only competitive for a limited time span. Changing consumer preferences and changing internal cost/revenue structures drive the development of new formats, which replace older formats that no longer suit the market conditions. A retail format's life-cycle begins in the phase of market entry with only a few stores and a limited market volume of sales. If a store concept proves successful, it enters the expansion phase, during which many additional units of this format are established and the market share increases rapidly. After some time, the maturity phase is reached. The market share remains more or less constant and no additional units are opened. Finally, the format reaches the phase of decline, during which the units of this type are replaced by new formats and the market share declines.

There is strong empirical evidence for the life-cycle model. For example, in food retailing, until the 1950s, small service stores dominated the market (Figure 12.2a/b and Figure 12.3a), which were replaced by store concepts that allowed consumers to minimize their time spent shopping by combining activities, namely buying different goods in the same store and decreasing the time needed for paying and commuting: self-service stores in the 1960s and 1970s (Figure 12.2c) and later larger supermarkets (more than 400 m^2 of retail space). Since the 1990s, supermarkets have been under pressure due to the rise in discounters—which are more or less the same size as supermarkets but offer a smaller range of goods for lower prices—and hypermarkets—which are larger (more than 1,500 m^2 of retail space) and offer a wider range of products, including non-food items (such as household goods and clothing). Comparable developments can be seen in non-food retailing. The classic specialized stores have been gradually replaced by larger, self-service-based, specialized markets and discount stores.

In addition to offering a wider and deeper assortment, these larger stores position themselves on the market by employing special *internal action parameters*. To boost their competitiveness and to attract consumers, they use either the "price

(a) Closed traditional food store

(b) Modern inner-city shopping center

FIGURE 12.3 Different types of retail structures and urban structures
Source: Photos by Elmar Kulke

Price parameter:	increase attractiveness by offering articles at low prices and internal cost reductions
Assortment parameter:	increase attractiveness by optimizing/broadening the assortment of articles offered
Service parameter:	increase attractiveness by providing additional services
Distance parameter:	increase attractiveness by optimizing spatial accessibility for consumers

FIGURE 12.4 Action parameters used by retail stores

Source: Agergard, Olsen, and Allpass (1970), Kulke (2017)

parameter," the "assortment parameter," the "service parameter," or the "distance parameter" (Figure 12.4).

Spatial coupling of retailing and changes in the retail landscape

Changes in both retailing formats and action parameters result in locational changes for retailers because each format and action parameter implies specific locational preferences—and this points to the fact that institutions are coupled together not only temporally but also spatially. As there are different ways of organizing space and time collectively and socially (Baur et al. 2014b, 2014c), each city has its own rhythm (Rinderspacher 1988; Promberger et al. 1997). Over time, time regimes are engrained in a city's objectified spatial structure ("*Raumstruktur*") by constructing buildings and transport infrastructure that facilitate actions in compliance with the city's time regime and at the same time make deviant actions more difficult (Simmel 1901, 254–270; Elias [1969] 2002). In other words, both a city's rhythm and its physical spatial structure assume a specific household division of labor, and the city's spatio-temporal order is structured based on that assumption (Hering and Baur 2019). For example, since the industrialization of the nineteenth century, West German spatio-temporal regimes were organized according to the male breadwinner/female homemaker model (Baur 2008). Working time was separated from other activities, and the workspace ("*Arbeitsort*") was physically separated from the home ("*Wohnort*") (Maurer 1992).

As a result, cities were designed in such a way that the (male) workforce needed to commute to work in different quarters of the city (Hofmeister 2002). As explained earlier, women therefore performed all other tasks, included shopping, and there was an elective affinity ("*Wahlverwandtschaft*") towards coupling commuting distances and motives for shopping. In the 1950s, (female) consumers typically practiced convenience-oriented shopping, that is, women visited the shop closest to their home offering the goods needed ("nearest-center-connection") (Martin 2006). Within their neighborhood, they had to visit one shop per good—a butcher, a baker, a milk/cheese shop, a classic grocery store, etc.—which were scattered across locations close to their homes (Figures 12.2a and 3a). This resulted in a great deal of commuting time both from work to the shops and between shops, in addition to extra time spent in the shops to pay several times, for example.

As stated previously, since the 1970s, German family ideals have pluralized, and more and more people have wanted to practice a dual-career model (Baur 2008; Baur et al. 2019; Grunow 2019). In theory, this should have increased commuting time (Figure 12.2b). However, this was not the case, as retailers reacted to these changes in consumer demand by changing their external parameters.

External parameters are mainly connected to locational decisions and depend on the store's size, assortment, and strategic action. According to Nelson (1958), every retail store is able to attract a given number of consumers on its own, which is called "generative business." Large units with a diversified assortment—such as hypermarkets or large home depots—attract so many consumers on their own that they can choose locations without taking into account their proximity to other stores. However, for smaller units, their generative business is limited. Therefore, they tend to choose locations close to other stores. This proximity allows all shops to attract more customers, which is referred to as "shared business." This in turn fits consumers' need to relieve time pressure by coupling activities (Kulke 2017). More specifically, since the 1960s, retailers have reacted to the changes in consumer needs by coupling different retail formats such as supermarkets, discounters, and other stores with services, leisure, and infrastructure at a single location (Figure 12.3b): Shopping centers usually consist of several magnet stores and several smaller units, while offering many additional services (e.g., restaurants, bars, hairdressers, banks, cinemas) (Kulke and Rauh 2014). Another example is that supermarkets (such as Edeka or Rewe) and discounters (like Aldi and Lidl) are more and more often co-locating close to each other (Jürgens 2013). Consumers can save time by buying a larger number and wide range of goods with various qualities in one visit (Figure 12.2c).

In addition, external factors generating flows of people can draw additional consumers to a store. Such "higher frequencies of flows" occur at train stations, airports, or highway crossings. When stores are located at these nodes, they can profit from the flow of people, which is called "suscipient business" (Nelson 1958). For consumers, this means that—if shops are located on their way to work—they can also couple shopping with other activities and reduce commuting times. Accordingly, since the 1980s, progressively more stores have relocated to areas in proximity to other stores and close to transport nodes, resulting in a spatial concentration in the retail landscape (Figures 12.2d and 12.3b). Finally, large train stations and airports are developing structures similar to shopping centers (Jenne 2017; Korn 2006).

Objectifying spatio-temporal coupling in the urban structure

As can be seen from the previous discussion, various spheres of social life, such as family, work, and shopping, have to be coordinated and therefore are coupled together in space and time, giving a city a specific rhythm. As retailing is lowest in the institutional hierarchy, it can merely react and adapt to dominant spatio-temporal regimes and resulting consumer demands. However, in doing so, retailing may actually drive social and spatial transformations. For example, by introducing new retail formats, retailers both reacted to changing consumer demands and facilitated families practicing dual-career models. At the level of everyday life, spatio-temporal coupling reveals a paradox, namely: While people should theoretically spend more time on shopping and commuting, they are in fact doing the contrary.

By means of urban and transport design, these spatio-temporal regimes are objectified in the urban structure. This coupling in turn slows down the pace of social and spatial transformations. In fact, the case of Berlin shows that the spatio-temporal regime in place in an urban quarter's formative phase (Berking and Schwenk 2011) has an effect on the retail structure up to the present day (Fülling and Hering 2020), thus slowing down the refiguration of spaces and economic restructuring. This also explains why e-commerce does not have the strong spatial impact it should have in theory, because it offers consumers flexible hours and high coupling potential to shop: Since 2000, online shopping has offered consumers easy possibilities to see products, compare prices, and purchase merchandise from home or work (Dederichs and Dannenberg 2017; Kulke 2019). However, even in 2019, e-commerce's market share of the total retail turnover in Germany was still only 11% (HDE Online-Monitor 2019). The reason for this is partially that perishable groceries vary so much in terms of their quality that consumers want to see them in real life before they buy them. However, and more importantly, while consumers can order online, not everything can be delivered everywhere. Rather, consumers can only order goods online from the retailers in their quarter (Hering 2020).

Finally, in the long run, spatio-temporal coupling does have an effect, resulting in market and spatial concentration. A new household division of labor, income increases, limited time for shopping, better mobility, and new shopping motives have encouraged a change in the spatial distribution of demand (Kulke 2020). Small stores in scattered locations and smaller centers are facing a severe reduction in turnover and often have had to close. Larger stores with a diversified assortment of articles and shopping agglomerations with several stores have generated an over-proportional increase in turnover. In most cases, they are located in central areas of the urban agglomerations or at de-central locations with good road connections.

For future research, this means that different spheres of social life are interlocked, with the city as the unit of analysis. As there are different ways in which these spheres are interlocked, future research should compare different cities with as contrasting household divisions of labor and economies as possible. In addition, this type of research should take into account the longue durée, as many of the more important spatial transformations are taking place much more slowly than predicted by most economic theories and the concept of refiguration of spaces. Finally, in order to better understand the economy, it would be beneficial to explore in greater detail how social institutions and objectified space are entwined.

Acknowledgements

The chapter is based on our joint research within the project "Knowledge and Goods: Consumers' and Producers' Spatial Knowledge" (A03), which is part of the Collaborative Research Center "Re-Figuration of Spaces" (CRC 1265) funded by the German Research Foundation (DFG) (project number 290045248).

References

Achen, M., J. Böhmer, M. Gather, and P. Pez. 2008. *Handel und Verkehr, Mobilität und Konsum.* Mannheim: Meta GIS.
Agergard, A., P. A. Olsen, and J. Allpass. 1970. "The Interaction between Retailing and the Urban Center Structure." *Environment and Planning* 2: 55–71.
BA (Bundesagentur für Arbeit). 2020. *Statistik 7/2020.* Tabellen, Beschäftigte nach Berufen (KldB 2010) (Quartalszahlen, Stichtag 31.12.2019). Nürnberg.
Baur, N. 2005. *Verlaufsmusteranalyse.* Wiesbaden: VS-Verlag für Sozialwissenschaften.
Baur, N. 2007. "Der perfekte Vater." *Freiburger Geschlechterstudien* 21: 79–114.
Baur, N. 2008. "Konsequenzen des Verlusts des ganzheitlichen Denkens." In *Arbeitsmarkt und Sozialpolitik,* edited by O. Struck and H. Seifert, 189–229. Wiesbaden: VS-Verlag.
Baur, N., J. Fülling, L. Hering, and S. Vogl. 2019. "Die Verzahnung von Arbeit und Konsum." In *Transformationen der Arbeitsgesellschaft,* edited by S. Ernst and G. Becke, 105–132. Wiesbaden: Springer VS. doi: 10.1007/978-3-658-22712-8_5.
Baur, N., L. Hering, M. Löw, and A. L. Raschke. 2014c. "Tradition, Zukunft und Tempo im Friseursalon." In *Städte unterscheiden lernen,* edited by S. Frank, P. Gehring, J. Griem, and M. Haus, 97–124. Frankfurt am Main: Campus.
Baur, N., L. Hering, A. L. Raschke, and C. Thierbach. 2014a. "Theory and Methods." Spatial Analysis. *HSR* 39 (2): 7–50.
Baur, N., M. Löw, L. Hering, A. L. Raschke, and F. Stoll. 2014b. "Die Rationalität lokaler Wirtschaftspraktiken im Friseurwesen." In *Soziologie des Wirtschaftlichen,* edited by Dieter Bögenhold, 299–327. Wiesbaden.
Bergmann, W. 1983. "Das Problem der Zeit in der Soziologie." *KZfSS* 35 (3): 462–504.
Berking, H., and J. Schwenk. 2011. *Hafenstädte.* Frankfurt am Main: Campus.
Braudel, Fernand. 1958. "Histoire et sciences sociales: La longue durée." *Annales* 13 (4): 725–753.
Buchmann, M. 1989. "Soziale Verwaltung von Zeit." *SZfS* 15 (2): 289–299.
Cromley, E. K. 1999. "Mapping Spatial Data." In *Ethnographer's Toolkit 4,* edited by J. J. Schensul and M. D. LeCompte, 51–124. Walnut Creek: AltaMira Press.
Dannenberg, P., M. Franz, and A. Lepper. 2016. "Online einkaufen gehen." In *Online-Handel im Wandel,* edited by M. Franz and I. Gersch, 133–156. Mannheim: MetaGIS.
Dederichs, S., and P. Dannenberg. 2017. "Vom Nischenmarkt in die Expansion." In *Einzelhandel in Deutschland,* edited by P. Dannenberg, M. Willkomm, and K. Zehner, 1–8. Mannheim: Meta GIS.
Destatis. 2016. *Datenreport 2016.* Bonn: Destatis/WZB.
Destatis. 2020. *Entwicklung der Bruttoverdienste.* Accessed July 14, 2020. www.destatis.de/DE/Themen/Arbeit/Verdienste/Verdienste-Verdienstunterschiede/Tabellen/lange-reihe-frueheres-bundesgebiet-1913.html.
Elias, Norbert. (1969) 2002. *Die höfische Gesellschaft.* Frankfurt am Main: Suhrkamp.

Engel, E. 1857. "Die vorherrschenden Gewerbezweige in den Gerichtsämtern mit Beziehung auf die Produktions- und Consumverhältnisse des Königreichs Sachsen." *Zeitschrift des statistischen Bureaus des königl. sächs. Ministeriums des Inneren* 3 (8/9): 153–182.

Ermann, U., and R. Pütz. 2020. "Geographien des Konsums." In *Geographische Handelsforschung*, edited by C. Neiberger and B. Hahn, 63–74. Berlin: Springer Spektrum.

Fülling, J., and L. Hering. 2020. "Markt—Quartier—Milieu." *Arbeitsberichte des Geographischen Instituts der Humboldt-Universität zu Berlin* 197. Accessed July 17, 2020. www.geographie.hu-berlin.de/de/institut/publikationsreihen/arbeitsberichte/download/Arbeitsbericht_197.

Fürstenberg, F. 1982. "Institutionalisierung von Interessenkonflikten." In *Kultur und Institution*, edited by H. J. Helle, 175–185. Berlin.

Fürstenberg, F. 1986. "Zeit als Strukturelement soziologischer Analyse." In *Zeit als Strukturelement von Lebenswelt und Gesellschaft*, edited by F. Fürstenberg and I. Mörth, 23–36. Linz: Trauner.

Grunow, D. 2019. "Comparative Analyses of Housework and Its Relation to Paid Work." *KZfSS* 71: 247–284. doi: 10.1007/s11577-019-00601-1.

Hassink R., O. Ibert, and M. Sarnow. 2020. "Zum sich wandelnden Verhältnis von Innovation und Raum in subnationalen Innovationssystemen." In *Innovationssysteme*, edited by B. Blättel-Mink and A. Ebner, 163–185. Wiesbaden: Springer.

HDE (Handelsverband Deutschland). 2019. *Online-Monitor 2019*. Berlin.

Heidenreich, M. 2003. "Territoriale Ungleichheiten in der erweiterten EU." *KZfSS* 55 (1): 1–28.

Heidenreich, M., and N. Baur. 2015. "Locations of Corporate Headquarters in Europe." In *Transnational Corporations and Transnational Governance*, edited by S. Lundan, 177–207. Basingstoke: Palgrave.

Hering, H. 2020. "Digitales Gemüse—Wie die Materialität der Waren die Organisation des Online-Handel beeinflusst." 3. Presentation at the Workshop of the "Arbeitskreis Digitalisierung und Organisation," 05./06.03.20.

Hering, L., and N. Baur. 2019. "Die Verschränkung des Lokalen und Globalen an Einkaufsorten." In *Komplexe Dynamiken globaler und lokaler Entwicklungen*, edited by N. Burzan. http://publikationen.soziologie.de/index.php/kongressband_2018/article/view/1011.

Hofmeister, H. 2002. *Couples' Commutes to Work Considering Workplace, Household, and Neighborhood Contexts*. Ann Arbor: UMI.

Hofmeister, H., and P. Moen. 2012. "Commuting." In *Families with Futures 2*, edited by M. W. Karraker and J. R. Grochowski, 25–26. New York: Routledge.

Jenne, A. 2017. "Einzelhandelsstandort Flughafen." In *Einzelhandel in Deutschland*, edited by P. Dannenberg, M. Willkomm, and K. Zehner, 107–132. Mannheim: Meta GIS.

Jürgens, U. 2013. "Nahversorgung durch Aldi, Lidl und Co." *Geographische Rundschau* 65 (3): 50–57.

Korn, J. 2006. "Transiträume als Orte des Konsums." PhD thesis, Humboldt-Universität zu Berlin. doi: 10.18452/15509.

Kulke, E. 2005. "Räumliche Konsumentenverhaltensweisen." In *Dem Konsumenten auf der Spur*, edited by E. Kulke, 9–26. Passau: LIS.

Kulke, E. 2017. *Wirtschaftsgeographie*. Paderborn: Schöningh.

Kulke, E. 2019. "Online-Einzelhandel in Deutschland." *Praxis Geographie* 12: 9–13.

Kulke, E. 2020. "Neue Dimensionen des Konsums." *Berichte Geographie und Landeskunde* 93 (1/2): 5–10.

Kulke, E., and J. Rauh, eds. 2014. *Das Shopping Center Phänomen*. Mannheim: Meta GIS.

Lange, S. 1973. *Wachstumstheorie zentralörtlicher Systeme*. Münster.

Löw, M. 2001. *Raumsoziologie*. Frankfurt am Main: Suhrkamp.
Luckmann, T. 1986. "Zeit und Identität." In *Zeit als Strukturelement von Lebenswelt und Gesellschaft*, edited by F. Fürstenberg and I. Mörth, 135–174. Linz: Trauner.
Martin, N. 2006. *Einkaufen in der Stadt der kurzen Wege?* Mannheim: Meta GIS.
Massey, D. 2005. *For Space*. London: Sage.
Maurer, A. 1992. *Alles eine Frage der Zeit*. Berlin: Sigma.
Neiberger, C., and M. Steinke. 2020. "Dynamik der Betriebsformen." In *Geographische Handelsforschung*, edited by C. Neiberger and B. Hahn, 27–38. Berlin: Springer Spektrum.
Nelson, R. L. 1958. *The Selection of Retail Location*. New York: Dodge.
Papastefanou, G., and D. Zajchowski. 2016. "Time for Shopping." *International Journal of Time Use Research* 13 (1): 109–131. doi: 10.13085/eIJTUR.13.1.109-131.
Procher, V., and C. Vance. 2013. "Who Does the Shopping?" *Ruhr Economic Papers* #393. RWI. doi: 10.4419/86788448.
Promberger, M., J. Rosdücher, H. Seifert, and R. Trinczek. 1997. *Weniger Geld, kürzere Arbeitszeit, sichere Jobs?* Berlin: Sigma.
Rinderspacher, J. P. 1988. "Der Rhythmus der Stadt." *Difu-Materialien* 1/88. Berlin.
Simmel, G. (1901) 1996. *Philosophie des Geldes*. Frankfurt am Main: Suhrkamp.
Wallerstein, I. 2004. *World-Systems Analysis*. Durham: Duke University Press.
Weidenhaus, G. 2015. *Soziale Raumzeit*. Berlin: Suhrkamp.
Weiss, J. 2006. *Umweltverhalten beim Lebensmitteleinkauf*. Berlin: menschundbuch.

PART III
Digitization and visualization of space

PART III

13
NETWORK SPILLOVER EFFECTS AND THE DYADIC INTERACTIONS OF VIRTUAL, SOCIAL, AND SPATIAL

Marco Bastos

Does social media exist in space?

The proposition that online activity may be inconsequential to events transpiring on the ground stems from the suspicion that virtual communities are not organically tied to offline social networks. This assumption claims that online activism is ineffective, with no follow-through, as aggrieved individuals limit their outrage to online communities of acquaintances incapable of effecting change in the real world. This critique underpins much of the discussion about clicktivism and slacktivism, an assertion passionately advocated by Morozov (2013) and convincingly argued by Gladwell (2010), though a wealth of studies have since identified significant relationships between online activism and developments on the ground (Bastos, Mercea, and Charpentier 2015; De Choudhury et al. 2016; Freelon, McIlwain, and Clark 2018). While these studies found significant associations between online and offline activity, they rarely included granular spatial data accounting for the geographic dispersion of online activity.

The relative absence of granular spatial data is a perennial challenge in Internet research. Online communities are expected to operate by a set of social rules as complex as those observed offline, but multidimensional network data linking online activity to geographic areas is rarely available (Bailey et al. 2018). The literature has thus remained relatively ambiguous about the mechanisms through which online social networks interact with their offline, spatialized counterparts. These relationships are difficult to pinpoint and speak to the limited vocabulary available to address that which is social but formed largely online and that which is social but shaped largely offline. Additionally, there are situations where it may not be possible to extricate spatial social networks from online communities, including communities whose members are evenly connected to each other both online and offline (Subrahmanyam et al. 2008).

Space has thus been treated as a secondary force underpinning tie-selection and retention in online social networks, notwithstanding the large body of literature evincing the bidirectional association between geography and network formation (McPherson, Smith-Lovin, and Cook 2001). There is also evidence that geographic proximity affects tie-formation mechanisms associated both with opportunity and preferences, as physical places can be conceived of as a bundle of resources and opportunities constrained by spatial contiguity (Glückler 2007). Online communities may incorporate remote strangers who are activated and incorporated as organic members of one's social network (Rainie and Wellman 2012). Similarly, the relationship between spatial distance and social media interaction has been found to be significant (Laniado et al. 2017), with social ties on Twitter largely confined to distances shorter than 100 kilometers (Takhteyev, Gruzd, and Wellman 2012). Other studies have suggested a spillover from in-person interaction patterns to online social media, further problematizing the hypothesis about the direction of homophily (Bastos, Mercea, and Baronchelli 2018).

The overlap between ties established online and offline also depends on the criteria employed to define online activity. Face-to-face interactions invariably take place offline, but phone networks, or the graphs derived from who talks to whom on the phone, can be defined as online networks despite the physical constraints imposed by the infrastructure of telephone wires and the higher billing rate associated with long-distance landline calls. Other disputed examples include the relationship one has with parents living far away; what was previously a network with clear physical and spatial boundaries can transition to a place that is largely virtual. As such, while one may communicate with their parents online, they invariably fall into a different category compared with one's Twitter followership. Indeed, the perennial tension between spatial and social can be traced to seminal studies on dining-table partnerships coded by Moreno (1953), as the seating choices of students in a classroom were also spatially and segregationally patterned.

But the differences between face-to-face and online interaction are usually straightforward, and never so clear-cut as when social media bots are activated. Due to the high overhead involved in growing sockpuppet accounts, botnets are often set to retweet and comment on other bots' messages, thereby triggering message cascades read by absolutely no actual person. Vast portions of the social media supply chain are conceivably colonized by automated posting protocols and quasi-autonomous parasites entirely detached from the geographies inhabited by users. Conversely, influence operations often resort to zombie accounts, promptly revamped with stolen profile photos, to feed communities where online interaction may depart radically from what is observed offline (Bastos and Farkas 2019). Twitterbots are nonetheless a rather extreme case, which may include sophisticated networks combining human and automated accounts to manipulate public deliberation. The worlds of real users and automated protocols feed from each other and it is not always possible to separate them.

The sudden outbreak of the COVID-19 global pandemic has paradoxically reinforced the differences and tightened the interdependencies between online and offline social networks. The enforced policy of social distancing required businesses and governments to manage their workflow online, with e-commerce struggling to handle the unprecedented demand. As movie theaters suspended operations, Netflix and other streaming platforms registered record numbers of new customers. Universities and schools implemented measures to stream lectures and upload course materials to teaching platforms. Real life suddenly became detached from the physical world, with social relationships carried out over WhatsApp, work meetings moving to Zoom, and friends and colleagues socializing on Google Hangouts. This arrangement, however provisional, foregrounded the gregarious nature of human life and the perennial need to interact with real people in physical spaces. While the outbreak rendered network technologies instrumental in carrying out routine and critical work tasks, it also expounded the limitations of online interaction compared with the multisensorial, time-dependent, and irrevocably space-constrained social network interactions that take place offline.

Online communities are likely to continue triggering interactions that depart from those observed in face-to-face communities beyond the COVID-19 outbreak. This is particularly the case in view of the growing algorithmization of community governance implemented by social platforms. Smartphones and Internet-capable household devices continuously store individual trace data in the cloud, which is imperfectly processed by machine-learning algorithms with limited precision and recall, trained with incomplete datasets, and tailored for purposes that are indistinguishable from those of the company collecting the data. By aggregating digital trace data at individual and group levels, social platforms can offer advertisers granular targets benchmarked with incomplete data and limited precision. The business model is nonetheless sound, as imprecisions measured at the individual level are likely offset at the group level; yet, these imprecisions and incompleteness are then built into the system recursively. Eventually, social groups identified by and modeled with digital trace data can take on a life of their own on social platforms, with niche subcommunities that only partially match their physical counterparts.

Network spillover effect

The dyadic interactions between virtual ↔ spatial, virtual ↔ social, and social ↔ spatial reflect the largely unexplored connection between the online and offline dimensions of social activity. These dyads can reveal intricate relationships between physical ties and online interactions encapsulated in the problem of the directionality in social relationships, a sociological debate about the causal direction of homophily: the phenomenon that like-minded people with similar social characteristics are more likely to be connected with each other, be it online or offline. Causality may of course move in either direction, but previous research has focused mostly on the hypothesis that similarity causes interaction (McPherson, Smith-Lovin, and Cook 2001), likely a reflection of the divide separating social network analysis, leveraging social media data, and spatial analysis, exploring geographic data.

This is unfortunate because the primary and secondary effects associated with the scalable deployment of social technologies are situated at the junction of networks that are simultaneously social and spatial, but whose social/spatial relationship is not symmetric. Individuals can partake in online communities and be exposed to information diets with little similarity to their offline surroundings. At the limit, ideological orientation, identity formation, and feelings of belonging can be pieced together depending on the networks to which individuals find themselves embedded. Perceived social memberships based on age, race, income, and location can be reinforced, but also potentially rewired, as one connects with social networks online that may differ from their proximate communities. Network spillover effects happen not only when face-to-face networks are replaced with social media, but particularly when the embedding in online networks spills over to geographic communities. While these interactions are not trivial, the network spillover effect is relatively simple: seemingly unrelated social activities online and offline reinforce each other.

Network spillover is associated with neighborhood effects that were first described in the seminal studies of Butler and Stoke (1969) about the 1964 and 1966 United Kingdom General Elections. The election cycle consolidated the Labour Party's majority through a process of partisan reinforcement: the tendency of prevailing opinions to draw additional support to become dominant in local areas. The geographic or neighborhood component of network spillover was mapped by Miller (1977), for whom contact, largely structured by family, choice of friends, social characteristics, and locality such as neighborhoods, is a condition for consensus, with patterns of contact being predictive of political consensus within high-contact groups. The neighborhood effect is perhaps best described by Miller's (1977) assertion that locality is a better predictor of how people vote than their social characteristics.

Spillover effects are thus intrinsically linked to neighborhood effects due to homophilic interdependencies tying spatial and social cohesion. Locational decisions involve a considerable degree of social selection, whereby people choose to live in neighborhoods populated by people similar to themselves. This results in social networks that are geographically delimited and socially homogenous, not just in their socio-economic and demographic composition, but also ideologically, behaviorally, and culturally. Although geographic constraints and ideological homogeneity mutually reinforce each other, neighbors may come across attitudes and behaviors different from those held within the group. Particularly those holding a minority view in the group are more likely to come across new information, including new ideas, behaviors, and ideologies. New information may then rapidly break into the group majority, as social interactions are optimized to negotiate, and thereby spread, attitudes and behavior.

Johnston and Pattie (2011) provide an account of how neighborhood effects can be further amplified by other network externalities, a process that may trigger feedback loops and spillovers. For instance, if a political debate between individuals holding opposing views about the best candidate in an election can persuade people to reconsider their own positions (conversion), then any social network with a majority of the population supporting a given candidate is more likely to switch to the minority candidate than the other way around. This contradicts the assumption of research on opinion evolution, but it is conceptually accurate because voting preferences are socially structured not only by the characteristics of the voter, but also by those with whom the voter discusses politics. Contact with voters in a given area influence not only the individuals directly connected, but also others in the neighborhood (Huckfeldt and Sprague 1995). On the other hand, and perhaps paradoxically, this process would render the majority view within the network even more prevalent, as dominance would be greater than expected from knowledge of the individuals' personal characteristics alone. If neighborhood effects can be observed whenever conversation networks are spatially constrained, then the political complexion of areas should be more polarized than their social composition implies.

Spillover effects are traditionally associated with exogenous policy interventions on subjects who were not originally targeted by the intervention, but who happen to be connected to those in the target population. Social media microtargeting can thus spill over to actors in local social environments who were not targeted by the message themselves. In this scenario, the spillover effect is the contagion effect on actors due to interventions targeting their friends. In contrast, endogenous peer effects stem directly from peers. In other word, actors in a network influence each other without being subjected to any microtargeting or intervention. While the source of exogenous effects is situated outside of the network, in reality it is difficult to separate endogenous from exogenous peer effects, as many of the endogenous peer effects could originally be generated by external forces unobservable to researchers (An 2011). Likewise, an exogenous peer effect such as microtargeting can be further compounded by endogenous effects such as the neighborhood effect, so that it is not always possible to untangle nested peer effects (Duflo, Dupas, and Kremer 2011).

These problems have long been studied in research on opinion evolution that highlights the non-linear patterns through which opinions and social change emerge from system interactions. While opinion dynamics progress fairly linearly over time, they often lead to nonlinearities and complex dynamic behavior, of which clustering (i.e., "bubbles") and the polarization of opinions are common outcomes (Nowak, Szamrej, and Latané 1990; Latané 1996). In other words, while changing public opinion is a process governed by intrinsic dynamics, the transition to a new prevailing opinion is likely linked to changes in extrinsic control factors that affect intrinsic dynamics (Nowak, Lewenstein, and Frejlak 1996). The negotiation of social values offline can be reinforced online, and vice-versa, thereby triggering network spillover effects and feedback loops typical of regulatory processes with a high density of connections.

In our study on echo chambers during the Brexit debate (Bastos, Mercea, and Baronchelli 2018), we found that social media echo chambers actually reflect real-life conversations that link to the geographic locations of users. The findings contradict the prevailing narrative on echo chambers, arguing that social media interactions lead users to engage with political content that resonates with them (Sunstein 2007). The ideological clustering observed in politically homogeneous echo chambers would stand in contrast to the diversity of opinions found in offline, face-to-face interactions. Transposed to the network of tweets about the UK–EU membership referendum, and following the prevailing narrative in the literature, we would have expected to find echo chambers as a communication effect resulting from online discussions alone. Conversely, we did not expect the geographic location of users to play a significant role in politically homogenous communication, as echo chambers reportedly result from social media interactions unaffected by geographic space.

Indeed, social anxieties surrounding echo chambers posit that social media is another force driving political polarization (Bessi et al. 2015), with a substantive body of observational evidence showing the role of social media in stratifying users across information sources (Conover et al. 2011). While the rapid growth of online social networks has fostered an expectation of higher exposure to a variety of news and politically diverse information (Messing and Westwood 2014), it has also increased the appetite for selective exposure in highly polarized social environments (Wojcieszak 2010), with the sharing of controversial news items being particularly unlikely in these contexts (Bright 2016). The filter bubble hypothesis encapsulated these claims by postulating that social platforms deploy algorithms designed to quantify and monetize social interaction, narrowly confining it to a bubble algorithmically populated with information closely matching user preferences (Pariser 2012).

The results of our study show that although most interactions are within a 200-km radius, echo chamber communication predominantly takes place in neighboring areas within a 50-kilometer radius. However, the geographic trend of echo chamber communication was different between the Leave and Remain campaigns, with pro-Leave messages covering much shorter distances compared with pro-Remain tweets. The trend was also reversed for non-echo chamber communication, which covered shorter distances on the Remain side. In other words, Leave-campaign messages were chiefly exchanged within ideologically and geographically proximate echo chambers. Although echo chambers also prevailed on the Remain side, the trend was inverted: as the distance between the sender and receiver increased, echo chambers became more common and covered increasingly larger areas compared to non-echo chamber communication. This reverse trend was captured by the mean distance covered by Leave messages, at 199 km for echo chambers and 234 km for non-echo chambers ($\tilde{x} = 168$ and $\tilde{x} = 208$, respectively). For Remain tweets, inversely, the mean distance of echo chambers was 238 km versus 204 km for non-echo chambers ($\tilde{x} = 209$ and $\tilde{x} = 184$, respectively).

The study indicates that online echo chambers result from conversations that spill over from in-person interactions and call into question the assumption that echo chamber communication is driven by online interaction alone, suggesting instead that people bring their pub conversations to online debate. The findings also appear to confirm the hypothesis that similarity causes interaction, as politically homogenous network interactions would be triggered by or from geographical proximity. Correspondingly, studies have found that radicalization on YouTube stems from the same factors that persuade individuals to change their minds in real life—that is to say, absorbing and interiorizing new information, but at scale (Munger and Phillips 2019). Instead of depending on algorithms that increasingly radicalize audiences, political media on YouTube would be driven by supply and demand, with the increased supply of right-wing videos tapping a latent demand previously constrained by limited offer offline.

Online–offline coordination

The extent to which online social networks overlap with the boundaries of their offline communities is of course an empirical question hindered only by the challenges in collecting relational data that can be mapped onto geographic boundaries while also preserving metrics of online activity. In subsequent attempts to address the problem, we validated the use of social media signals to model the ideological coordinates underpinning the Brexit debate. Geographically enriched Twitter data was coupled with a machine learning algorithm that identified tweets along the ideological space of populism, economism, globalism, and nationalism. The granular spatial data amassed for this study allowed us to map the political value space of users tweeting the referendum onto Parliamentary Constituencies (Bastos and Mercea 2018).

The study required the extensive collection of Twitter data supplemented by multiple queries to Twitter API to identify the location of users tweeting the UK–EU membership referendum. After adding geographic markers to the database, we calculated the ideological inclination of users and mapped them onto voting constituencies in England, Wales, Scotland, and Northern Ireland. The research was informed by suggestions of a geographical and socio-demographic patterning of voting preferences in the referendum explored in the literature (Rennie Short 2016; Hanretty 2017). The geography of the vote, it was proposed, reflected a socio-economic imbalance between an affluent metropolitan elite clustered around London who voted to remain and parts of England and Wales that were economically worse off and voted to leave the EU. Following this line of inquiry, the political geography of the vote was unpicked at the level of local authority areas (Becker, Fetzer, and Novy 2016) to assess the extent to which users tweeting nationalist and populist content would overlap across geographic enclaves—and conversely, whether such patterns could be observed in relation to users tweeting globalist or economist content.

While we succeeded in identifying the geographic location of 60% of users who tweeted the referendum, a considerable portion of their locations could be identified only up to city level, but not postcode level. Upon identifying the location of users, we removed user accounts located outside the United Kingdom or whose location we could not identify up to postcode level. This reduced the database to 565,028 messages or 11% of all collected messages. Despite the multiple efforts to maximize the collection of geographic information about users, research seeking to explore the overlap between online and offline networks must contend with smaller data samples. In this study, the various sampling techniques applied to the data, particularly the geographic rendering of user locations up to postcode level, reduced the universe of collected tweets to only 11% of the data.

Another challenge in this type of research consists of defining the unit of analysis. In this specific case, we selected council wards and parliamentary constituencies because they provided optimal granularity relative to online and offline data sources. Twitter data was aggregated first at user level and then at constituency level, which was the unit of analysis employed in the study. The resulting dataset included multiple streams of Twitter data consolidated into a single database of online and offline activity at constituency level. A scaled Poisson regression model was applied to incorporate demographic information from lower-level geographies, thereby aggregating the results at the ward or constituency level, along with voting estimates at the level of council wards for authorities that did not disclose the results at such granular levels (Huyen Do, Thomas-Agnan, and Vanhems 2015; Hanretty 2017). The resulting referendum database was relatively granular with data down to the ward level in England, Scotland, and Wales and Local Authority District in Northern Ireland.

Mapping geographically rich social media data onto census area or electoral districts is another challenge due to the hierarchical subdivision of UK local government areas into various sub-authority areas and lower levels such as enumeration districts. As council wards comprise the most granular level to which we could retrieve results or estimates for the referendum vote, we mapped referendum-related Twitter activity to this unit of geographic analysis. User locations were geocoded and reverse-geocoded to match postcodes to wards and Parliamentary Constituencies using the database provided by National Statistics Postcode Lookup (ONS Geography 2011). Twitter users were thus simultaneously matched to the fields OSLAUA, OSWARD, and PCON11CD (Local Authority, Ward, and Constituency codes, respectively). The first field includes Local Authority District (LAD), Unitary Authority (UA), Metropolitan District (MD), London Borough (LB), Council Area (CA), and District Council Area (DCA).

Upon geocoding the self-reported location of users, we found that only 30% of them were based in the UK, with 19% of users who participated in the Brexit debate based in the United States and nearly 30% in other EU countries. This is of course another marker of the differences in political discourse online and offline, as the former allows individuals from different locations to participate, albeit in a restricted capacity, in the public discourse on an issue circumscribed to the UK. Also surprising was the large geographic spread of the British Twitter userbase, with London accounting for 14%, Lancashire 7%, Kent, Essex, West Yorkshire, and West Midlands ranging 3–4%, and South Yorkshire, Hertfordshire, Cheshire, Merseyside, Surrey, and Hampshire at 2% each. Taken together, each of these geographic groups are of comparable size to London in the share of users who tweeted the referendum.

The results somewhat upset our expectations. Apart from London, globalist messages were relatively underwhelming. Nationalism was indeed quintessential to the referendum debate, with three-quarters of messages (74%) displaying nationalist sentiments, as opposed to 26% that expressed globalist values such as international cooperation. We did not find that economically fragile northern England, an area generally supportive of Brexit, was any more likely to embrace nationalist content. In fact, it was Remain-backing Scotland that appeared as a fertile ground for nationalism. Though nearly 40% of tweets contained populist sentiments, these messages were concentrated in a small number of constituencies. In only 10% of the constituencies did populist sentiments prevail, compared with economic issues, and in less than 5% did globalist sentiments dominate. All 72 constituencies with overwhelming support for Leave presented predominantly nationalist sentiments. Conversely, only 17 of these constituencies had a Twitter debate predominantly defined by populist sentiments, with 55 of them discussing mostly the economic outlook.

Conclusions

One possible explanation for the conflicting evidence on the geography of echo chambers is that politically homogeneous communication may reflect the imprint of deliberation driven by offline social networks. These homophilic preferences can coexist with social media platforms that provide ideologically diverse networks (Barberá 2014). As such, the boundaries of one's network can be simultaneously permeated by echo chambers rooted in offline relationships while being exposed to competing opinions on polarizing topics that circulate on social media. Similar associational effects have been reported in the literature (Laniado et al. 2017), suggesting that the geographic dependence of echo chambers would result from the physical clustering of fundamentally disparate social networks.

Instead of incorporating remote strangers who are activated and incorporated as organic members of one's social network (Rainie and Wellman 2012), the results suggest a spillover from in-person conversations to online social media interaction. In other words, echo chambers connect homophilous dependencies in physical social networks that are relatively independent of social media activity. This is also consistent with the differences in echo-chambers observed in the Leave and Remain campaigns, as the demographic makeup of these subgraphs is considerably different. In other words, the significant geographic variation found in the data would be driven not only by the locations where the two groups were clustered, but also the social positions embedded in the geographical location of Leave and Remain constituencies.

The different social positions occupied by Leavers and Remainers are consistent with the geographical splintering of the country expressed in the referendum and reflect the socio-economic imbalances separating urban loci of political and economic power, clustered around London, which voted Remain, and economically fragile parts of England and Wales, where the Leave vote prevailed. With city-dwellers spending more time shopping and exploring areas outside their neighborhoods, as well as living and working in hubs of the national and global economy (Storper 2018), it is unsurprising that the resulting social networks of Remain urbanites would cover larger geographic areas. The distances covered by their interactions should likewise be lengthier compared with those inhabiting rural or low-density areas of the country. This is of course only one aspect of the intricate relationship connecting existing physical ties and online interactions, with others likely at play (Takhteyev, Gruzd, and Wellman 2012; Laniado et al. 2017).

In summary, while research on the directionality of homophily between online and offline social networks is still forthcoming, there is growing evidence for the spatial dependencies of social media. This body of work also contradicts Facebook's assumption that social platforms necessarily strengthen existing communities; that they invariably help individuals to come together online and offline; or that they enable groups to form completely new communities that transcend physical location (Zuckerberg 2018). Indeed, the assumption that social platforms merely connect individuals online to reinforce their physical communities tends to ignore the complex and multidirectional association between geography and tie-selection and retention in online networks. It also fails to consider that the diffusion of information on social media platforms may differ from patterns observed offline, and that these interactions can make or break the fabric of society. In other words, while interaction across social platforms can evolve in the absence of physical ties, the network externalities arising from interactions developed online may impinge on our very sense of what is real offline.

References

An, W. E. 2011. "Models and Methods to Identify Peer Effects." In *The Sage Handbook of Social Network Analysis*, edited by John Scott and Peter J. Carrington. London: SAGE Publications.

Bailey, M., R. Cao, T. Kuchler, J. Stroebel, and A. Wong. 2018. "Social Connectedness: Measurement, Determinants, and Effects." *Journal of Economic Perspectives* 32 (3): 259–280. doi: 10.1257/jep.32.3.259.

Barberá, P. 2014. "How Social Media Reduces Mass Political Polarization. Evidence from Germany, Spain, and the US." Paper prepared for the 2015 APSA Conference, New York University.

Bastos, M. T., and J. Farkas. 2019. "'Donald Trump Is My President!': The Internet Research Agency Propaganda Machine." *Social Media + Society* 5 (3). doi: 10.1177/2056305119865466.

Bastos, M. T., and D. Mercea. 2018. "Parametrizing Brexit: Mapping Twitter Political Space to Parliamentary Constituencies." *Information, Communication & Society* 21 (7): 921–939. doi: 10.1080/1369118X.2018.1433224.

Bastos, M. T., D. Mercea, and A. Baronchelli. 2018. "The Geographic Embedding of Online Echo Chambers: Evidence from the Brexit Campaign." *PLoS ONE* 13 (11): e0206841. doi: 10.1371/journal.pone.0206841.

Bastos, M. T., D. Mercea, and A. Charpentier. 2015. "Tents, Tweets, and Events: The Interplay between Ongoing Protests and Social Media." *Journal of Communication* 65 (2): 320–350. doi: 10.1111/jcom.12145.

Becker, S., O. T. Fetzer, and D. Novy. 2016. "Who Voted for Brexit? A Comprehensive District-Level Analysis." 1–69. Coventry: Centre for Competitive Advantage in the Global Economy, University of Warwick. www2.warwick.ac.uk/fac/soc/economics/research/centres/cage/manage/news/305-2016_becker_fetzer_novy.pdf.

Bessi, A., F. Petroni, M. D. Vicario, F. Zollo, A. Anagnostopoulos, A. Scala, G. Caldarelli, and W. Quattrociocchi. 2015. "Viral Misinformation: The Role of Homophily and Polarization." In *Proceedings of the 24th International Conference on World Wide Web*, 355–356. New York: ACM.

Bright, J. 2016. "The Social News Gap: How News Reading and News Sharing Diverge." *Journal of Communication* 66 (3): 343–365.

Butler, D., and D. Stoke. 1969. *Political Change in Britain: Forces Shaping Electoral Choice*. London: Macmillan.

Conover, M. D., J. Ratkiewicz, M. Francisco, B. Goncalves, F. Menczer, and A. Flammini. 2011. "Political Polarization on Twitter." 5th International AAAI Conference on Weblogs and Social Media (ICWSM11), Barcelona.

De Choudhury, M., S. Jhaver, B. Sugar, and I. Weber. 2016. "Social Media Participation in an Activist Movement for Racial Equality." 10th International AAAI Conference on Web and Social Media.

Duflo, E., P. Dupas, and M. Kremer. 2011. "Peer Effects, Teacher Incentives, and the Impact of Tracking: Evidence from a Randomized Evaluation in Kenya." *American Economic Review* 101 (5): 1739–1774.

Freelon, D., C. McIlwain, and M. Clark. 2018. "Quantifying the Power and Consequences of Social Media Protest." *New Media & Society* 20 (3): 990–1011.

Gladwell, M. 2010. "Small Change: Why the Revolution Will Not Be Tweeted." *The New Yorker*, 4 October 2010. www.newyorker.com/reporting/2010/10/04/101004fa_fact_gladwell.

Glückler, J. 2007. "Economic Geography and the Evolution of Networks." *Journal of Economic Geography* 7 (5): 619–634. doi: 10.1093/jeg/lbm023.

Hanretty, C. 2017. "Areal Interpolation and the UK's Referendum on EU Membership." *Journal of Elections, Public Opinion and Parties* 27 (4): 466–483. doi: 10.1080/17457289.2017.1287081.

Huckfeldt, R. R., and J. Sprague. 1995. *Citizens, Politics, and Social Communication: Information and Influence in an Election Campaign*. New York: Cambridge University Press.

Huyen Do, V., C. Thomas-Agnan, and A. Vanhems. 2015. "Spatial Reallocation of Areal Data—Another Look at Basic Methods." *Revue d'Économie Régionale & Urbaine* 1–2: 27–58. doi: 10.3917/reru.151.0027.

Johnston, R., and C. Pattie. 2011. "Social Networks, Geography and Neighbourhood Effects." In *The Sage Handbook of Social Network Analysis*, edited by John Scott and Peter J. Carrington. London: SAGE Publications.

Laniado, D., Y. Volkovich, S. Scellato, C. Mascolo, and A. Kaltenbrunner. 2017. "The Impact of Geographic Distance on Online Social Interactions." *Information Systems Frontiers*: 1–16.

Latané, B. 1996. "Dynamic Social Impact: The Creation of Culture by Communication." *Journal of communication* 46 (4): 13–25.

McPherson, M., L. Smith-Lovin, and J. M. Cook. 2001. "Birds of a Feather: Homophily in Social Networks." *Annual Review of Sociology* 27 (1): 415–444. doi: 10.1146/annurev.soc.27.1.415.

Messing, S., and S. J. Westwood. 2014. "Selective Exposure in the Age of Social Media." *Communication Research* 41 (8): 1042–1063. doi: 10.1177/0093650212466406.

Miller, W. L. 1977. *Electoral Dynamics in Britain since 1918*. London: Macmillan.

Moreno, J. L. 1953. *Who Shall Survive? Foundations of Sociometry, Group Psychotherapy and Socio-Drama*. Oxford, England: Beacon House.

Morozov, E. 2013. *To Save Everything, Click Here: The Folly of Technological Solutionism*. New York: Public Affairs.

Munger, K., and J. Phillips. 2019. "A Supply and Demand Framework for YouTube Politics." Preprint.

Nowak, A., M. Lewenstein, and P. Frejlak. 1996. "Dynamics of Public Opinion and Social Change." In *Modelle sozialer Dynamiken: Ordnung, Chaos und Komplexität*, edited by Rainer Hegselmann and Heinz-Otto Peitgen. Wien: Hölder-Pichler-Tempsky.

Nowak, A., J. Szamrej, and B. Latané. 1990. "From Private Attitude to Public Opinion: A Dynamic Theory of Social Impact." *Psychological Review* 97 (3): 362–376.

ONS Geography. 2011. "National Statistics Postcode Lookup UK." In *Office for National Statistics*. London: ONS.

Pariser, E. 2012. *The Filter Bubble: What the Internet Is Hiding from You*. London: Penguin.

Rainie, L., and B. Wellman. 2012. *Networked: The New Social Operating System*. Cambridge, MA: MIT Press.

Rennie Short, J. 2016. "The Geography of Brexit: What the Vote Reveals About Disunited Kingdom." *The Conversation*. http://theconversation.com/the-geography-of-brexit-what-the-vote-reveals-about-the-disunited-kingdom-61633.

Storper, M. 2018. "Separate Worlds? Explaining the Current Wave of Regional Economic Polarization." *Journal of Economic Geography* 18 (2): 247–270. doi: 10.1093/jeg/lby011.

Subrahmanyam, K., S. M. Reich, N. Waechter, and G. Espinoza. 2008. "Online and Offline Social Networks: Use of Social Networking Sites by Emerging Adults." *Journal of Applied Developmental Psychology* 29 (6): 420–433. doi: 10.1016/j.appdev.2008.07.003.

Sunstein, C. R. 2007. *Republic.Com 2.0*. Princeton, NJ: Princeton University Press.

Takhteyev, Y., A. Gruzd, and B. Wellman. 2012. "Geography of Twitter Networks." *Social Networks* 34 (1): 73–81. doi: 10.1016/j.socnet.2011.05.006.

Wojcieszak, M. 2010. "'Don't Talk to Me': Effects of Ideologically Homogeneous Online Groups and Politically Dissimilar Offline Ties on Extremism." *New Media & Society* 12 (4): 637–655. doi: 10.1177/1461444809342775.

Zuckerberg, M. 2018. "Building Global Community." *Facebook*. www.facebook.com/notes/mark-zuckerberg/building-global-community/10154544292806634.

14

TALKING TO MY COMMUNITY ELSEWHERE

Bringing together networked public spheres and the concept of translocal communities

Daniel Maier, Daniela Stoltenberg, Barbara Pfetsch, and Annie Waldherr

Dynamic notions of two concepts: space and public sphere

The concept of the public sphere, which ties political decision-making to (mediated) public debates, has significantly changed with the advancement of digitization. Thirty years ago, the reach of public debates was tied legally and economically to territories. Political information and opinions were broadcast almost exclusively through legacy media. The transmission of mass-mediated messages was closely related to spaces that overlapped with political and administrative units at the local, regional, or national levels. Media organizations, journalists, and socio-economic elite speakers constituted the mass-mediated arenas for these territories. Therefore, it is no surprise that, back then, most researchers investigated public spheres within national territories.

Drawing on the work of Benkler (2006) and Neuberger (2009), we refer to public spheres as heterogeneous and overlapping mediated networks of publicly communicating persons, organizations, and institutions. In contrast to the territorially aligned public spheres of the past, these mainly digital networked public spheres elude simple territorial attachments. The communicative connections among humans on the web and on social media transcend the borders of cities, regions, and nation states.

The advent of digital communication not only implies a structural change of public debate. Networked public spheres are also less centered on the communication of mass-mediated organizations (Benkler 2006). As a consequence, they are also much less centered on territories. However, their spatial dimension is no less important than that of their predecessors; it just does not fit the rigid territorial notion of space. Rather, we argue that we are better served by also thinking of public spheres in terms of the spatial figure (Löw 2020) of a network. While territorial spaces focus on actors drawing borders around

DOI: 10.4324/9781003036159-17

themselves and their social goods, network spaces shift the perspective to the connections between these elements, even across distances (Löw 2020, 154, 159; Mol and Law 1994, 643).

To understand and describe the spatial configurations of networked public spheres, we need to revisit the nature of social media communication. We argue that the concept of communities is crucial for this purpose. Moreover, we must acknowledge that the dwindling importance of the mass media and their broadcasting territories is accompanied by the increased importance of direct communicative connections between social actors, who are located in places. That is, they are located in (geographic) locations, which are ascribed meaning and identity and which relate to other places (Löw 2020, 156). Communicative relations between social actors span the distance between their places and may be considered translocal. Here, translocality refers to the communicative construction of relations between (distant) localities through media (Hepp 2009a, 330).

On the social web (i.e., on social media platforms and in other online environments where people communicate with each other), individual users and collective actors assemble into social communication networks, which form larger communities with distinct translocal interaction patterns. Communities are networks of social actors with a shared imagination of their communion (Anderson 2006). Ties among members of imagined communities are based on a common sense of identity, such as a common language and/or socio-cultural identity (e.g., ethnic communities), a shared migration history (e.g., diasporic communities), interest in a common topic or political issue (e.g., issue communities), or affective reactions to events (e.g., affective communities).

Increased mobility, Internet-based communication, and social media platforms in particular have elevated the translocal potential of communities. Thus, we argue that the study of public communication should consider the translocal potential of communities as a signifying feature of networked public spheres. This does not mean that local or national figures have become irrelevant. Rather, we argue that communities with distinct translocal and fluid interaction patterns provide a useful and augmented description for the spatial anchoring of public communication processes on the social web.

Our argument is organized into three sections. First, we explain why territorial notions have become inadequate when researching networked public spheres. Second, we argue that (imagined) communities of users constitute the spatially anchored social underpinnings of networked public spheres on the social web. Third, we explore how digitization has led communities to increase their mobility and become more translocal, and we conclude that public sphere research should integrate the translocal potential of communities as an important analytical category. We also understand the digitization-induced spatial restructuring of public spheres as one aspect of the meta-process of what Knoblauch and Löw (2017, 3) coin "spatial re-figuration of the social world" (i.e., "a fundamental shift in our understanding of space").

Territorial notions in public sphere research

In social research, the public sphere is a basic category used to understand processes of will formation in society. The public sphere denotes an open communication system in which issues and opinions are discussed publicly and which allows the members of a society to observe and participate in the deliberation of issues and the formation of public opinion (Neidhardt 1994, 7; Habermas 1996, 360). Its general functions are openness toward issues and opinions, their validation through the public exchange of arguments, and the orientation of society on what is at stake (Neidhardt 1994, 8–10). In Habermas' (1996, 356–357) writings, the public sphere is normatively bound to democracy since the issues and opinions that are processed in the public sphere stem from the lifeworlds of the citizens and are made salient through communication as an indication of what should be tackled in the political system.

Even though Habermas (1996, 360) talks about the public sphere as the "social space generated in communicative action," the term space has mostly been used metaphorically and has not been a focus in much of the public sphere research (Wallner and Adolf 2014). However, due to its normative functionality for democracy (Habermas 1996), the public sphere concept is mostly and implicitly aligned with the boundaries of national political territories (Pfetsch, Heft, and Knüpfer 2019; Volkmer 2014). This presupposed alignment may have been a consensus for traditional, mass-mediated public spheres because media systems and markets tended to be structured along political and linguistic borders. However, research into online public spheres has also adopted these national boundaries. For instance, research on social media communication often maps Twitterspheres or blogospheres at the country level (e.g., Bruns and Enli 2018; Ausserhofer and Maireder 2013).

Meanwhile, other studies have focused on urban public spheres (e.g., von Saldern 2013). Moreover, over the last two decades, the concept of transnational public spheres has been established with the progress of integration in the European Union and the search for European public spheres (e.g., Koopmans and Statham 2010).

Theoretical discussions propose that digital public spheres transcend the national scope with a potentially global reach (Castells 2008). In line with Volkmer's (2014, 6) critique that public communication has become largely "disembedded" from national territories, just like the "core assets of public 'civil' culture [and] public institutions," this body of literature moves the public sphere beyond the scope of nation states. This is done explicitly in reference to the expanded communicative possibilities provided by the Internet (e.g., Pfetsch, Heft, and Knüpfer 2019).

However, even while altering the geographic scope—shrinking it down to the level of cities or extending it to whole continents and beyond—these public sphere concepts arguably remain bound to a territorial notion of space. We argue that the merely territorial figure is no longer appropriate for grasping the shape and extent of digital public spheres. Rather, the network, with its focus on relations between distant elements (Löw 2020; Mol and Law 1994), is a more fitting spatial figure.

The nature of networked public spheres stands in stark contrast to territory-based concepts. The core features of networked public spheres are digital communicative connections among social actors, which—as we will describe in the next section—quite naturally transcend the borders of cities, regions, and nation states (Hampton and Wellman 2003).

The inclusion of social media in many people's communication patterns has changed the structure of public communication and implies a new spatiality of public debate. Findings from existing research foreground that the most significant ties in social media communication connect the cosmopolitan centers of the world (Leetaru et al. 2013; Lin, Halavais, and Zhang 2007) and constitute a global network. At the same time, we still witness that most communication takes place within relatively short distances inside the same metropolitan area (Takhteyev, Gruzd, and Wellman 2012). The literature corroborates a clear spatial pattern: metropolitan clusters of tightly connected users emerge simultaneously with long tie connections between urban centers.

Imagined communities as social underpinnings of networked public spheres

In social terms, recent literature understands digital communication networks as the outcome of community-building processes (Stephansen and Couldry 2014). Social media communication structures represent not only "interpersonal communication, but also how people orient themselves to public life" (Swart, Peters, and Broersma 2018, 4329). These networks reflect individual users' sense of belonging and may be interpreted as support structures in people's everyday lives (Gruzd, Wellman, and Takhteyev 2011).

According to Gruzd, Wellman, and Takhteyev (2011), social media networks feature the characteristics of various community concepts (Anderson 2006; Jones 1997; McMillan and Chavis 1986). As the concept of community is normative and contested (Bourke 2010; Wellman 1979), controversial debates and diverging traditions of theorizing the concept have developed (see Blokland 2017, 15–41; Jones 1995). While tracing this development goes beyond the scope of this chapter, a short conceptualization can provide clarity.

Community has traditionally been a vital category in sociology and urban studies and is marked by two features: relationality and spatiality (Bourke 2010). In terms of relationality, it denotes both the result of social interactions between individuals and a relationship between individuals and society, driven by a desire for belonging (Bourke 2010). In terms of spatiality, the concept of community was traditionally thought of as distinctly local, namely, as "a set of social relationships operating within a specific boundary, location, or territory" (Bourke 2010, 171). This territorially bound notion of community has, however, been challenged. According to Wellman (1979, 1202), the notion of community as a solidarity group in a given local territory may obscure the search for true communities in present-day societies. Instead of focusing on local and close-knit groups, Wellman (1979) proposes looking for the sociable and supportive primary ties of individuals without being preoccupied about their location. In other words, "community is based on sociable and supportive social relations, and not on physical locality" (Gruzd, Wellman, and Takhteyev 2011, 1298).

That does not mean, however, that physical localities are insignificant for communities. Empirically, people maintain multiple, highly individualized, and geographically dispersed personal community networks (Chayko 2015). At the same time, "neighborly relationships remain important, but as a minority of ties within the overall network" (Hampton and Wellman 2003, 278–279). Against this backdrop, we define communities as follows:

> Communities consist of far-flung, kinship, workplace, friendship, interest group, and neighborhood ties that concatenate to form networks providing sociability, aid, support, and social control. Communities are usually not groups, but are social networks that are sparsely knit, loosely bounded, and far flung.
>
> *(Hampton and Wellman 2003, 278)*

The advent of the digital age marks a breaking point for how we conceive of communities. The rise of digital communication has facilitated the emergence of widespread interest communities (Hampton and Wellman 2003, 281). The "space-liberating power of the Internet" allows people to connect regardless of borders and distance, potentially on a global scale (Hampton and Wellman 2003, 282). Again, this does not mean that place becomes insignificant. The potential to maintain long-distance connections must not veil the importance of physical places. Connections to others living in the same area or within close geographical reach (Gruzd, Wellman, and Takhteyev 2011; Hampton and Wellman 2003) or connections between metropolitan areas (Lin, Halavais, and Zhang. 2007) remain important parts of personal networks.

Social connections in personal networks are not fixed or given; they are invigorated in living practices and manifest in the details of everyday life (Blokland 2017, 2). These manifestations reflect that people value their communities and that "they hold imaginations of what they are" (Blokland 2017, 2). Anderson (2006) argues that shared imaginations are crucial for communities. Members of large-scale communities, such as nations, "will never know most of their fellow-members, . . . yet in the minds of each lives the image of their communion" (Anderson 2006, 6). Gruzd, Wellman, and Takhteyev (2011, 1297–1298) transfer Anderson's concept of imagined communities to social media networks; users cannot know everyone in their virtual surroundings but are aware of the presence of other users as either their imagined audience when they write a message or their sources of information when they read their timeline.

Although not usually explicitly referring to the community concept, social media studies abound with references to different kinds of cohesive networks gathering around shared identities, interests, or experiences (see, e.g., Hepp 2009b).

For example, a branch of social movement research studying new forms of collective action online has widely acknowledged the capacity of social media platforms to organize actors interested in specific topics and to create so-called issue networks (McKelvey, DiGarzia, and Rojas 2014).

Common interest in issues bears a strong potential for creating common identities and issue communities; this has been shown, for instance, in the LGBT community in London (Linfoot 2018). Likewise, although protest movements take place at specific sites (Earl et al. 2013), they are often connected translocally via social media (Bastos and Mercea 2016). Via trending hashtags, such as #MeToo (Mendes, Ringrose, and Keller 2018) or #Ferguson (Jackson and Foucault Welles 2016), these movements have formed counterpublic spheres.

As framing devices, hashtags not only focus attention on certain issues but also offer venues through which to share emotions and sentiment, creating affective publics which "assemble around media and platforms that invite affective attunement, support affective investment, and propagate affectively charged expression" (Papacharissi 2016, 308). Such affective communities have been observed in the aftermath of events, such as hurricanes (Shelton et al. 2014) or terrorist attacks (Lin and Margolin 2014), when people from all over the world connect to express their sympathy and emotional support.

Finally, in a world of digital communication and mobility, language and ethnicity are still crucial to identities and maintaining a sense of belonging in ethnic communities (Christiansen 2019); with respect to shared migration histories, they are also crucial to deterritorialized diasporic communities (Hepp 2009a).

All of these examples constitute imagined communities gathering around shared identities, interests, or experiences. Their network infrastructure bears an inscribed potential for translocality. However, communicative relationships on social media platforms often have their origin in real-world social relationships (Ellison, Steinfield, and Lampe 2007), which tend to develop among geographically proximate individuals. Proximity increases the likelihood of face-to-face interaction and communication and allows individuals to explore what they might have in common (Monge and Contractor 2003, 227–228). The proliferation of digital media led to a refiguration of communication networks, simultaneously strengthening local and distant relations. It helped "increase our global reach but also strengthen[ed] local communities and geographically distributed, but culturally contiguous, 'diasporas'" (Monge and Contractor 2003, 231). Although social media platforms such as Facebook or Twitter are not bound to geopolitical borders, a large share of the interactions between users still takes place within a proximate local or regional radius (Takhteyev, Gruzd, and Wellman 2012). Consequently, communicative relationships between users who are geographically distant from one another are comparatively rare. In the next section, we argue that the distribution of communicative relations resembles the structures of translocal communities.

Translocal potentials of communities in networked public spheres

Where public sphere theory still largely remains bound to territorial notions of space, it has much to learn from community research. This trajectory of investigation highlights that, while the local remains a powerful category, shared identities and support structures now extend into more complex, translocal patterns. Blokland (2017) argues that communities feature specific roots and routes, which means that sociable and supportive ties among people are anchored in places, while also emphasizing the connections between them. Etymologically, the term translocality denotes the continued relevance of the local, but the prefix *trans* shifts the analytical focus to connections and in-betweenness (Hepp 2004, 163).

Translocality may be interpreted as the result of both globalization and digitization. Globalization typically describes an increase in the mobility of people, goods, and services. This mobility implies growing migration, commuting, and traveling for work and leisure for individuals and those within their network. Simultaneously, digitization enables "communicative relations across certain localities" (Hepp 2009a, 330) to an unprecedented degree. While the traditional notion of community used to be more local, digital media "allow us to communicate beyond our primary location, which suggests [that] geographical distance becomes less important for the formation and maintenance of attachments" (Wehden and Stoltenberg 2019, 1402). Translocality, therefore, focuses on interlinkages between places but does not assume a diminished importance of place: "The always-on, always accessible network produces a broad set of changes to our concept of place, linking specific locales to a global continuum and thereby transforming our sense of proximity and distance" (Varnelis and Friedberg 2008, 15). Actors link relevant places communicatively, cognitively, and emotionally (Lingenberg 2014). From this follows the notion of translocal communities.

According to Hepp (2009b), communities emerge from processes of "translocal communicative thickening." In that sense, the term translocal denotes that the local continues to be the prime anchor point of an individual's lifeworld. Communicative densifications, however, are increasingly oriented toward other specific places (or individuals in other places) beyond geopolitical territories.

In line with this argument, we propose that networked public spheres often emerge from such communities. Of course, these communities are not congruent with public spheres, and many communities do not constitute public spheres per se. For a public sphere to emerge from an imagined community, in addition to a shared identification and a generalized communicative densification between its members, activation around an issue is required. However, if communities are spatially distributed following ethnic, commercial, political, and religious communitizations (Hepp 2009b), then they will strongly shape where and for whom an event becomes an issue. Through the formation of translocal ties, they therefore influence the emergence of issue-specific "communicative thickening" between particular places.

Concluding remarks

Networked public spheres provide a framework for considering the emergence, meaning, and consequences of digital public communication and connections. However, due to the lack of theorization, the concept either neglects the spatial dimension of public communication on the social web or adopts inappropriate territorial notions. We have laid out an argument for integrating the notion of translocal communities into this line of research.

Under conditions of increased global mobility and connections, translocal communities form around shared notions of identity, interest, and experience. Digital media enable this process by providing opportunity structures for members of these imagined communities to connect with and potentially support one another. We argue that these communities are the social underpinnings of many networked public spheres, as they can become activated around shared issues. Conceiving of communities as the social foundation of public spheres not only elevates the importance of space but also emphasizes that social mechanisms are a driving force of structure in networked public spheres. Thus, the underlying spatial figure of networked public spheres is better described as a translocal network of places rather than a contiguous territory.

Translocality therefore proves to be a valuable lens for the study of (networked) public spheres. It is our conviction that it can help us more fully understand spatially structured but non-locally bound communication phenomena, such as international protest movements, social media trends, or discourses on transnational political problems.

Moreover, our sketch of the spatial reformation of the public sphere concept feeds into the meta-process of the refiguration of space (Knoblauch and Löw 2017). The social web may be understood as an opportunity structure for social actors to build networks. Those actors are place-bound, locally anchored nodes that connect with others, potentially across large distances and beyond the borders of cities, nation states, or even continents. While the network structure itself bears an inscribed potential for translocality, research findings support that network-building processes are often based on homophily; shared social identities, interests, or experiences increase the likelihood of community networks to be formed among similar actors. All of these features are, of course, not independent of the local embeddings and relational positions of actors in their networks. Likewise, transforming the community into a public sphere requires the activation of the network through a shared public issue. Thus, we may conclude that the spatial features of networked public spheres strongly adhere to the social mechanisms of translocal community building.

Acknowledgements

This research has been funded by the Deutsche Forschungsgemeinschaft (DFG, German Research Foundation)—project number 290045248—SFB 1265.

References

Anderson, Benedict. 2006. *Imagined Communities: Reflections on the Origin and Spread of Nationalism*, 3rd ed. London: Verso books.

Ausserhofer, Julian, and Axel Maireder. 2013. "National Politics on Twitter: Structures and Topics of a Networked Public Sphere." *Information, Communication & Society* 16 (3): 291–314. doi: 10.1080/1369118X.2012.756050.

Bastos, Marco Toledo, and Dan Mercea. 2016. "Serial Activists: Political Twitter Beyond Influentials and the Twittertariat." *New Media & Society* 18 (10): 2359–2378. doi: 10.1177/1461444815584764.

Benkler, Yochai. 2006. *The Wealth of Networks: How Social Production Transforms Markets and Freedom*. New Haven: Yale University Press.

Blokland, Talja. 2017. *Community as Urban Practice*. Cambridge: Polity.

Bourke, Alan Gerard. 2010. "Community." In *Encyclopedia of Urban Studies*, edited by Ray Hutchison, 171–175. Los Angeles: Sage.

Bruns, Axel, and Gunn Enli. 2018. "The Norwegian Twittersphere: Structure and Dynamics." *Nordicom Review* 39 (1): 129–148. doi: 10.2478/nor-2018-0006.

Castells, Manuel. 2008. "The New Public Sphere: Global Civil Society, Communication Networks, and Global Governance." *The Annals of the American Academy of Political and Social Science* 616 (1): 78–93. doi: 10.1177/0002716207311877.

Chayko, Mary. 2015. "The First Web Theorist? Georg Simmel and the Legacy of 'The Web of Group-affiliations'." *Information, Communication & Society* 18 (12): 1419–1422. doi: 10.1080/1369118X.2015.1042394.

Christiansen, Sidury M. 2019. "'Listisimo para los #XVdeRubi': Constructing a Chronotope as a Shared Imagined Experience in Twitter to Enact Mexicanness Outside of Mexico." *Lingua* 225: 1–15. doi: 10.1016/j.lingua.2019.05.002.

Earl, Jennifer, Heather McKee Hurwitz, Analicia Mejia Mesinas, Margaret Tolan, and Ashley Arlotti. 2013. "This Protest Will Be Tweeted: Twitter and Protest Policing during the Pittsburgh G20." *Information, Communication & Society* 16 (4): 459–478. doi: 10.1080/1369118X.2013.777756.

Ellison, Nicole B., Charles Steinfield, and Cliff Lampe. 2007. "The Benefits of Facebook 'Friends': Social Capital and College Students' Use of Online Social Network Sites." *Journal of Computer-Mediated Communication* 12 (4): 1143–1168. doi: 10.1111/j.1083–6101.2007.00367.x.

Gruzd, Anatoliy, Barry Wellman, and Yuri Takhteyev. 2011. "Imagining Twitter as an Imagined Community." *American Behavioral Scientist* 55 (10): 1294–1318. doi: 10.1177/0002764211409378.

Habermas, Jürgen. 1996. *Between Facts and Norms: Contributions to a Discourse Theory of Law and Democracy*. Cambridge: Polity.

Hampton, Keith, and Barry Wellman. 2003. "Neighboring in Netville: How the Internet Supports Community and Social Capital in a Wired Suburb." *City & Community* 2 (4): 277–302. doi: 10.1046/j.1535-6841.2003.00057.x.

Hepp, Andreas. 2004. *Netzwerke der Medien. Medienkulturen und Globalisierung*. Wiesbaden: Springer VS.

Hepp, Andreas. 2009a. "Localities of Diasporic Communicative Spaces: Material Aspects of Translocal Mediated Networking." *The Communication Review* 12 (4): 327–348. doi: 10.1080/10714420903344451.

Hepp, Andreas. 2009b. "Transculturality as a Perspective: Researching Media Cultures Comparatively." *Forum Qualitative Sozialforschung/Forum: Qualitative Social Research* 10 (1). doi: 10.17169/fqs-10.1.1221.

Jackson, Sarah J., and Brooke Foucault Welles. 2016. "#Ferguson is Everywhere: Initiators in Emerging Counterpublic Networks." *Information, Communication & Society* 19 (3): 397–418. doi: 10.1080/1369118X.2015.1106571.

Jones, Quentin. 1997. "Virtual-Communities, Virtual Settlements & Cyber-Archaeology: A Theoretical Outline." *Journal of Computer-Mediated Communication* 3 (3). doi: 10.1111/j.1083-6101.1997.tb00075.x.

Jones, Steven G. 1995. "Community in the Information Age." In *Cybersociety. Computer-Mediated Communication and Community*, edited by Steven G. Jones, 138–163. Thousand Oaks: Sage.
Knoblauch, Hubert, and Martina Löw. 2017. "On the Spatial Re-figuration of the Social World." *Sociologica* 11 (2): 1–27. doi: 10.2383/88197.
Koopmans, Ruud, and Paul Statham, eds. 2010. *The Making of a European Public Sphere: Media Discourse and Political Contention*. New York: Cambridge University Press.
Leetaru, Kalev H., Shaowen Wang, Guofeng Cao, Anand Padmanabhan, and Eric Shook. 2013. "Mapping the Global Twitter Heartbeat: The Geography of Twitter." *First Monday* 18 (5). doi: 10.5210/fm.v18i5.4366.
Lin, Jia, Alexander Halavais, and Bin Zhang. 2007. "The Blog Network in America: Blogs as Indicators of Relationships Among US Cities." *Connections* 27 (2): 15–23. www.insna.org/Connections-Web/Volume27-2/Lin.pdf.
Lin, Yu-Ru, and Drew Margolin. 2014. "The Ripple of Fear, Sympathy and Solidarity During the Boston Bombings." *EPJ Data Science* 3: 31. doi: 10.1140/epjds/s13688-014-0031-z.
Linfoot, Matthew. 2018. "Queer in Your Ear: Connecting Space, Community, and Identity in LGBT BBC Radio Programs, 1992–2000." *Journal of Radio & Audio Media* 25 (2): 195–208. doi: 10.1080/19376529.2018.1473402.
Lingenberg, Swantje. 2014. "Mobilisiert-mediatisierte Lebenswelten und der Wandel des öffentlichen Raums." In *Medienkommunikation in Bewegung*, edited by Jeffrey Wimmer and Maren Hartmann, 69–86. Wiesbaden: Springer VS. doi: 10.1007/978-3-531-19375-5.
Löw, Martina. 2020. "In welchen Räumen leben wir? Eine raumsoziologisch und kommunikativ konstruktivistische Bestimmung der Raumfiguren Territorialraum, Bahnenraum, Netzwerkraum und Ort." In *Grenzen der Kommunikation—Kommunikation an den Grenzen*, edited by Jo Reichertz, 149–164. Weilerswist: Velbrück.
McKelvey, Karissa, Joseph DiGrazia, and Fabio Rojas. 2014. "Twitter Publics: How Online Political Communities Signaled Electoral Outcomes in the 2010 US House Election." *Information, Communication & Society* 17 (4): 436–450. doi: 10.1080/1369118X.2014.892149.
McMillan, David W., and David M. Chavis. 1986. "Sense of Community: A Definition and Theory." *Journal of Community Psychology* 14 (1): 6–23. doi: 10.1002/1520-6629(198601)14:1<6::AID-JCOP2290140103>3.0.CO;2-I.
Mendes, Kaitlynn, Jessica Ringrose, and Jessalynn Keller. 2018. "#MeToo and the Promise and Pitfalls of Challenging Rape Culture Through Digital Feminist Activism." *European Journal of Women's Studies* 25 (2): 236–246. doi: 10.1177/1350506818765318.
Mol, Annemarie, and John Law. 1994. "Regions, Networks and Fluids: Anaemia and Social Topology." *Social Studies of Science* 24 (4): 641–671. doi: 10.1177/030631279402400402.
Monge, Peter R., and Noshir S. Contractor. 2003. *Theories of Communication Networks*. New York: Oxford University Press.
Neidhardt, Friedhelm. 1994. "Öffentlichkeit, öffentliche Meinung, soziale Bewegungen." In *Öffentlichkeit, öffentliche Meinung, soziale Bewegungen*, edited by Friedhelm Neidhardt, 7–41. Opladen: Westdeutscher Verlag.
Neuberger, Christoph. 2009. "Internet, Journalismus und Öffentlichkeit. Analyse des Medienumbruchs." In *Journalismus im Internet*, edited by Christoph Neuberger, Christian Nuernbergk, and Melanie Rischke, 19–105. Wiesbaden: Springer VS.
Papacharissi, Zizi. 2016. "Affective Publics and Structures of Storytelling: Sentiment, Events and Mediality." *Information, Communication & Society* 19 (3): 307–324. doi: 10.1080/1369118X.2015.1109697.
Pfetsch, Barbara, Annett Heft, and Curd Knüpfer. 2019. "Transnationale Öffentlichkeiten in der Digitalen Gesellschaft: Konzepte und Forschungsperspektiven." In *Politik in der*

digitalen Gesellschaft, edited by Jeanette Hofmann, Norbert Kersting, Claudia Ritzi, and Wolf J. Schünemann, 83–101. Bielefeld: transcript.

Shelton, Taylor, Ate Poorthuis, Mark Graham, and Matthew Zook. 2014. "Mapping the Data Shadows of Hurricane Sandy: Uncovering the Sociospatial Dimensions of 'Big Data'." *Geoforum* 52: 167–179. doi: 10.1016/j.geoforum.2014.01.006.

Stephansen, Hilde C., and Nick Couldry. 2014. "Understanding Micro-Processes of Community Building and Mutual Learning on Twitter: A 'Small Data' Approach." *Information, Communication & Society* 17 (10): 1212–1227. doi: 10.1080/1369118X.2014.902984.

Swart, Joëlle, Chris Peters, and Marcel Broersma. 2018. "Shedding Light On the Dark Social: The Connective Role of News and Journalism in Social Media Communities." *New Media & Society* 20 (11): 4329–4345. doi: 10.1177/1461444818772063.

Takhteyev, Yuri, Anatoliy Gruzd, and Barry Wellman. 2012. "Geography of Twitter Networks." *Social Networks* 34 (1): 73–81. doi: 10.1016/j.socnet.2011.05.006.

Varnelis, Kazys, and Anne Friedberg. 2008. "Place: The Networking of Public Space. In *Networked Publics*, edited by Kazys Varnelis, 15–42. Cambridge, MA: MIT Press.

Volkmer, Ingrid. 2014. *The Global Public Sphere: Public Communication in the Age of Reflective Interdependence*. Cambridge: John Wiley & Sons.

von Saldern, Adelheid. 2013. "Großstädtische Kommunikation im Wandel—Das 20. Jahrhundert." In *MediaPolis—Kommunikation zwischen Boulevard und Parlament*, edited by Barbara Pfetsch, Janine Greyer, and Joachim Trebbe, 23–50. Konstanz: UVK.

Wallner, Cornelia, and Marian Adolf. 2014. "Räume und Kontexte öffentlicher Kommunikation." In *Medienkommunikation in Bewegung*, edited by Jeffrey Wimmer and Maren Hartmann, 87–101. Wiesbaden: Springer VS.

Wehden, Lars-Ole, and Daniela Stoltenberg. 2019. "So Far, Yet So Close: Examining Translocal Twitter Audiences of Regional Newspapers in Germany." *Journalism Studies* 20 (10): 1400–1420. doi: 10.1080/1461670X.2018.1520609.

Wellman, Barry. 1979. "The Community Question: The Intimate Networks of East Yorkers." *American Journal of Sociology* 84 (5): 1201–1231.

15
ANNOTATING PLACES

A critical assessment of two hypotheses on how locative media transform urban public places

Eric Lettkemann and Ingo Schulz-Schaeffer

Locative media and their impact on urban public places

This chapter investigates social implications of a new form of media-facilitated transformation of places, which is arising from an increased merging of urban places with digital information, driven in particular by locative media. Locative media is an umbrella term used to describe a new form of mobile apps that utilize a device's location awareness (e.g., GPS, WiFi triangulation) to retrieve digital information annotated to a particular physical location (Frith 2015, 2). For example, a mobile recommendation app displays a map of restaurants located in the vicinity, including their menus, experience reports, and ratings from previous customers. A much-debated implication of using locative media is that public places no longer appear the same to all people present, because their perceptions of these places are now based on additional information, which is represented only digitally. Depending on which apps are used and which personalized settings are selected, users may receive quite different information on the same physical location. Our chapter discusses whether the increasing use of locative media leads to the creation of new inclusive meeting places or—on the contrary—reinforces the tendency towards urban segregation by creating exclusive places of retreat. The discussion is based on the results of a pilot study on locative media users in Berlin.[1]

Public places: physical, virtual, and hybrid

By places, we refer to distinctive locations in space defined by their physical settings as well as by the people who frequent these locations and ascribe some sort of meaning to them (see Gieryn 2000, 466–467). Places nest in larger social territories, transcending immediate experience. In the case of urban places, this larger social territory is usually conceptualized as the "public space" (Lofland 1973). We

DOI: 10.4324/9781003036159-18

follow Lofland's definition that the public space of cities consists of freely accessible places in which large numbers of mutual strangers pursue their activities—sometimes together, often in parallel (ibid., 19). These activities are expressions of different social worlds populating the city. According to Anselm Strauss (1978), social worlds organize around core activities, concerned, for example, with the production of certain goods or collective identities. Large cities in particular are a mosaic of the most diverse cultural, ideological, occupational, or leisure time–oriented social worlds. Each social world is a relatively independent "universe of discourse" assembled from specific symbols, lifestyles, and stocks of knowledge. All social worlds have some kind of spatial reference points where participants share knowledge and perform activities, making them a recognizable place.

One of the reasons why the diverse social worlds within a city coexist mostly without conflict is that just a few places in the public space are frequented equally by all social worlds. Only in subway stations, on city plazas, in shopping malls, and other such areas does the entire spectrum of social worlds meet and mingle. In contrast, most places in the public space are accessed de facto only by small portions of the city population. Examples of such places of retreat are churches, cafés, sports venues, parks, or similar sites, which serve as places of encounter for one or very few social worlds. Although access is not restricted legally, there is little probability that outsiders would seek out the dedicated meeting places of other social worlds. According to Anselm Strauss, this is due to the fact that urban places are endowed with different meanings, attracting some social worlds while repelling others (Strauss 1961, 59–67). These meanings establish a spatial order that determines which locations act as places of encounter or retreat for which segments of an urban society.

Numerous activities that give a public place its specific meaning make use of media. The consumption of mobile media such as newspapers or the Walkman have long been commonplace in public life, but digital media did not play a role until recently (de Souza e Silva and Frith 2012, 59–74). In the early days of the digital revolution, the virtual space of the Internet was largely separated from the physically experienced reality of urban life. Digital information was accessible only intermittently and temporarily—via the computer workstation at home. In other words, people experienced virtual space as a reality of its own, as a separate universe of discourse and as an experimentation site for new (digital) lifestyles (Turkle 1995). This separation has undergone a drastic change within the past decade. With the emergence of Internet-capable mobile devices, particularly smartphones, digital information is now accessible at any time and anywhere. Instead of drifting further apart, physical and virtual space are increasingly converging (Löw, Steets, and Stoetzer 2008, 81).

The mobilization of the Internet is a core element in the current phase of mediatization of space, which is increasingly permeating our everyday life. The continuously accessible digital information infrastructures result in an increasing superimposition and merging of virtual and physical realities to form so-called cyber-physical systems (Rajkumar et al. 2010). One of the observable consequences resulting from the proliferation of cyber-physical systems is that the strict distinction between online and offline communication loses its practical relevance in the everyday life of many smartphone users. In particular, today's younger "hyperconnected digital media users" (Parisi 2015, 6) quite naturally integrate social media communication as part of their daily routine into a number of physical activities. In this way, new forms of cyber-physical reality arise that are currently spreading in urban life, predominantly through the adoption of locative media.

The term locative media arose in the 2000s within the context of location-based computer games. The original aim of merging virtual and physical reality was to turn public urban places (back) into playgrounds (see de Souza e Silva and Sutko 2009). This genre of locative media is presently enjoying great popularity, as in the commercial variant Pokémon Go. In the meantime, the same basic process of the location-based merging of virtual and physical reality is taking place in many other smartphone apps as well, which are also referred to collectively as location-based services (LBS). Today, these services include navigation, search, and advertising as well as tracking, dating, and many more.

The potential of locative media to transform places gains plausibility in ethnographic studies focusing on the microlevel of social interaction. These illustrate how the smartphone screen becomes a sensory extension: The melding of virtual and physical spaces takes place on the screen of the smartphone; here, cyber-physical reality becomes visually accessible. As conveyed on the screen, a "hybrid space" (de Souza e Silva 2006, 261) arises, whose constitution is equally physical and virtual, and which links the social media communication online back to the current physical location. In this hybrid space, the boundaries between physical and virtual reality and between face-to-face interaction and media-based interaction become blurred. For example, the Waze navigation app provides information on traffic congestion and alternative routes by automatically tracking the movements of all mobile devices on which Waze is installed, aggregating this data, and displaying it in real time as traffic flows on a digital map. At the same time, users can also manually enter information, showing other users on the app's map where they have seen construction work, accidents, or other traffic obstacles. Based on this information, Waze users navigate through a hybrid space constructed of physical, social, and virtual elements.

This cyber-physical merging has many consequences for how people experience public places. Popular locative media include navigation apps as well as recommendation services like Foursquare and Yelp or hybrid reality games like Ingress and Pokémon Go. Via the screens of their smartphones, users have access to digital annotations attached to their environments. From a technical standpoint, the term annotation refers to the linking of GPS coordinates with digital information such as ratings, photos, or comments. From a sociological point of view, annotations add new layers of meaning to public places (de Souza e Silva and Frith 2012, 94–96; Frith 2015, 81–95). Annotations make use of a broad spectrum of media-based forms of expression. For example, users check in at places, showing their friends where they currently are. Others annotate personal experiences, photos, and opinions at a place.

Presently, discussion is underway as to the extent to which the advancing diffusion of locative media in urban everyday life is altering the interaction between strangers in public places. Two predominant strains of discussion can be identified here, which we term inclusion hypothesis and exclusion hypothesis. The typical proponents of the inclusion hypothesis assume that the use of locative media increases the de facto accessibility of public places and leads to more encounters and to more participation in public life. Locative media are considered to encourage the playful and participative reshaping of public places because they circumvent urban rules of civil indifference and facilitate communicative exchange between strangers (Keijl, Klaassen, and op den Akker 2013, 10–11). According to the inclusion hypothesis, locative media increase sensitivity for the urban environment and stimulate communication within neighborhoods as the users carry the "participative culture" of the Internet into public urban places (Hamilton 2009, 393).

In contrast, the exclusion hypothesis maintains the position that the de facto accessibility of public spaces is decreased and the decline of urban public life is accelerated. Mechanisms of social closure, already familiar from social media as "filter bubbles," are thought to fragment everyday reality into customized experiences of a "splintered space" (Frith 2015, 140f.). The filtered, selective perception and appropriation of places could result in a further intensification of urban tendencies towards social segregation. Instead of promoting socialization and the emergence of new forms of public life, locative media are considered to simply foster dialog between those city dwellers who already share common interpretive patterns and lifestyles (Crawford 2008, 91). It is expected that locative media contribute to the emergence of subcultural and private places of retreat within the public urban space, invisible to outsiders.

From an empirical standpoint, the question currently remains open in which direction—inclusion or exclusion—the use of locative media will transform urban life as a whole. To date, no systematic investigations have been conducted to more accurately determine the implications of the two hypotheses and to describe the mechanisms of inclusion and exclusion. Though locative media is a recent phenomenon, the number of corresponding apps is already too large to examine the field as a whole. Hence, we propose investigating typical forms and consequences of the use of locative media. In this chapter, we focus on two popular annotation apps. The results will serve as a reference point for comparative case studies on mobile gaming, dating, and more. Naturally, the results unveiled by our research are influenced by how broadly or narrowly we define the terms inclusion and exclusion. No empirical research is necessary to demonstrate that locative media do not perform inclusion in the sense of integrating society as a whole. In view of the future of urban life, we deem it more interesting to pose the question of to what extent the digital native generation of hyperconnected users itself is impacted by the inclusive or exclusive effects of locative media. Although the members of this generation are bonded through their affinity with locative media, they also inhabit different social worlds, some of which are quite heterogeneous, each with its own lifestyle. In reference to Hitzler, Bucher, and Niederbacher (2001), these various social worlds can also be designated "scenes." Our primary focus of interest is on how the users of locative media, as inhabitants of their specific social worlds, their scenes, appropriate public places and how they perceive the hybrid space of annotations.

Two case studies: Foursquare City Guide and Swarm

In our research, we have approached the phenomenon of digital annotations using a mix of qualitative methods to investigate how smartphone users receive, create, and share spatial annotations. Inspired by the "walkthrough method" of Light, Burgess, and Duguay (2016), we carried out auto-ethnographic self-observations to explore the affordances and restrictions of two apps: Foursquare City Guide and Swarm. Furthermore, we interviewed different types of users.[2] The sample of interviewees ranged from experienced fans of the apps to inexperienced users. The latter group tested both apps for about four weeks, documenting their experiences in the form of digital diaries. The aim of the analysis was to obtain a typology of using annotations with regard to their inclusive or exclusive effects.

Swarm and City Guide are good examples for studying the effects of digital annotations. As both apps are developed by Foursquare Labs company, they can be used either in combination or independently. Foursquare Labs is a pioneer in the field of annotation services, exceeding over 50 million registered users in 2014 (further information is available from Frith 2015, 96–111). A comparison of City Guide and Swarm is worthwhile because the two apps represent contrasting design principles of locative media:

Foursquare City Guide contains mainly search-and-recommendation functions. The app collects location-based information, which is annotated in the forms of comments, ratings, and photos. This information is freely accessible to all registered users.

Foursquare Swarm combines a location-based social network with gaming elements. The app offers the option of connecting and competing with friends for in-game rewards. The users of Swarm also annotate information such as their current location ("check-ins") or location-based comments.

Given the fast pace of digital media markets, it is not yet clear whether these apps will prevail in the long term. Social media platforms such as Google and Facebook, however, increasingly integrate similar annotation functions into their app versions, imitating the interface design of Foursquare's apps. Therefore, an analysis of Swarm and City Guide promises more readily generalizable insights into the use of annotations, regardless of whether these specific apps will survive in the long run or will be supplanted by larger platforms.

Foursquare City Guide: lurking and editing

Foursquare City Guide suggests two complementary forms of use. When you open the app, the City Guide screen initially offers various search-and-discovery options. For example, users can search maps, categories, or lists to obtain information on their GPS location. In contrast to similar services, there is also the option of making full text searches within the archived annotations. After a brief period of familiarization, City Guide is a suitable tool for what is termed "lurking." Within the context of social media, lurkers are typically considered users of an Internet platform who retrieve content but do not actively participate in generating it.

An eye-catching interface feature that makes lurking easy is called the Foursquare score. Every location that is created in Foursquare is rated by the app with a score from 1 to 10. This Foursquare score is derived from various pieces of information, such as user ratings or the total number of check-ins. The score helps the mobile user to quickly assess the popularity of a location at a glance. In our interviews, experienced users considered a score above 8.0 to be a sure indication that a location is worth visiting. Lurkers, who spend more time searching for interesting locations, can read the comments left by other users. These comments, which City Guide calls tips, typically consist of one or a few sentences (see Figure 15.1). They

FIGURE 15.1 Screenshots of Kollwitzplatz in Berlin as displayed in Foursquare City Guide: the score of 8.1 is shown on the left; on the right is a selection of annotated tips

are often complemented by photos intended to convey an impression of the location's atmosphere. In contrast to purely digital communication, the constitutive point of reference for annotations is the physical location. Therefore, the credibility of tips increases in the perception of many users when the app shows that the writers have already checked in to the location several times.

Although the City Guide uses pop-up windows to repeatedly prompt the user to rate the locations visited and to leave comments, the majority of users belong to the lurker category. For the smaller group, which is willing to share their experiences with a public audience of users, City Guide offers various options for generating content. Aside from rating locations with emoticons and uploading photos and short texts, users can create lists of similar locations or add new locations to a GPS point. In the language of experienced users, these activities are referred to as editing. The most important contribution of the so-called editors to the success of the app is the continuous writing of tips. From conversations with regular writers of tips, we learned that they consider the work of editing to be an authentic form of reporting. Although theoretically conceivable, users are not interested in endowing locations with new meanings or making public places more exotic. The objective of most editors is to share practical everyday knowledge and positive experiences.

Although it is technically possible to explore any location in the environment and to create new meeting places, in practice this is hardly the case. The predominant motivation for using City Guide seems to be the desire to find more places that reflect a user's personal preferences. Instead of looking for unfamiliar or different places, users set the various search filters such that most of the locations in their environment are made invisible. Many interviewees confirm that they only search for places that resemble those that they already know and that match their lifestyle. For example, users report that they always search for vegan products, free WiFi, or special brands of coffee. Even though the majority of interviewees insisted that they were definitely interested in discovering new places, their use of the app was mainly motivated by the desire to find more of the places they already favored than by the desire to discover completely different places. The sheer curiosity to obtain access to unknown locations is not a very common motivation for using City Guide—at least not in our sample.

However, we also found indications in our empirical material of increased accessibility to public places. The fact that many experienced users have "blind faith" in high Foursquare scores is a source of surprising encounters from time to time. For instance, a tax consultant who is a longtime fan of the app reported that while searching for pancakes he ended up in a restaurant with an unusually high score that he had hitherto avoided:

> A restaurant, from the outside it looks like a rocker bar. So I probably wouldn't have gone in there. But on the inside it looked like my grandma's living room and they had delicious pancakes! [Laughter] Well, I really would never have gone in there. I had based my search on the score as well.
>
> *(Experienced user, age 37)*

Repeatedly, our interviewees referred to City Guide as a "window" that allows them to look behind the walls of unfamiliar places. For example, a young historian reported that she often feels uncomfortable entering new places. Normally she enters unfamiliar places only in the company of friends. But reading the annotations of other users also helps her to overcome social barriers:

> Places you don't otherwise go into, it's a kind of barrier, I don't really know what would make me go in there, especially not alone, and I think the app does give you a different feeling about what you can expect there. And so it can kind of remove the barrier a little, or you just see, yes, no, it confirms my impression, but in a certain way, sure, it also takes over the role of people who might say to you in such a case, "hey, it's worth going in there", but they aren't always around and not all your friends have been everywhere. . . . So I do believe that it [the app] is a door opener.
>
> *(Inexperienced user, age 25)*

In other words, comments and pictures on City Guide make it easier for users to slip into the role of explorers discovering unknown places within their close environment. They reduce uncertainty about what to expect.

Swarm: lifelogging and following

Turning to Swarm, we notice that the user interface of the app has little in common with the design used for City Guide. In Swarm, everything revolves around the check-in function. As soon as a user clicks on the check-in button in the bottom center of the user interface, Swarm displays a list of possible locations that share the current GPS coordinates. Every time a check-in is performed, the user is prompted by the app to enter a brief comment or upload a photo. However, users can easily bypass this prompt. For each check-in, users receive points, referred to in the app as coins, and stickers. First-time and periodic check-ins are rewarded with additional coins. The stickers relate to the function of a location. For example, users receive a gas tank sticker for their first check-in at a gas station, a shopping bag sticker for a shopping mall, a cocktail sticker for a bar, etc. Users can collect up to 100 stickers that reflect the variety of the places they have visited (see Figure 15.2).

Swarm offers two options for using check-ins. First, Swarm offers a new location-based form of lifelogging. A digital lifelog is a detailed chronicle of a person's everyday activities that typically encompasses large volumes of technically protocolled data. Originally, lifelogging apps recorded fitness- and health-related data. In the case of locative media, lifelogging involves protocolling the locations visited. For instance, Swarm can show its users a list of their check-ins in chronological order or make them visible on a map. In this way, users can track how often and on which days they checked in to a health club or a supermarket, for example. In tandem with the comment function, this list becomes a digital journal and photo album. The purpose of this function is not to exchange information with other

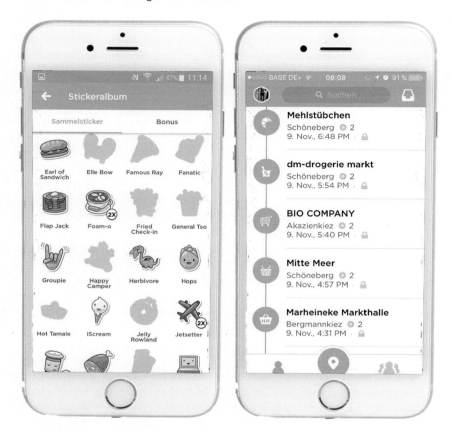

FIGURE 15.2 Screenshots of stickers available in Foursquare Swarm (left) and a list of places checked in

users or to augment the accessibility of a location. Rather, our interviewees were motivated primarily by their personal desire to preserve fleeting recollections of locations visited and to retain such memories. For instance, an insurance agent who visits many places on his business trips told us that he greatly appreciates the lifelogging functions of Swarm:

> For me it's a kind of memory function. A type of localization that tells me: You've already been here. And I've checked in to locations where I could swear I'd never been before, but then it seems I actually had been there before! And checked in there.
>
> *(Experienced user, age 36)*

Aside from lifelogging, Swarm offers a second function typical of social networks: following the activities of other users. As in social network websites similar to

Facebook and Instagram, users can send messages to befriended members. Far more important, however, is the fact that the users of Swarm can follow check-ins in order to keep track of their friends' current locations. As in conventional social networks, the number of Swarm friends normally extends beyond the close circle of personal acquaintances to include other users whom they rarely if ever meet face to face. The inclusive potential remains low, however, as users generally follow people who share their same lifestyle and tastes. In her interview, an experienced user reported how she chooses friends and what constitutes her community of Swarm friends:

> Interviewer: "Do many of your friends use Foursquare [Swarm], too?" Interviewee: "Nah, not many. I have my friends and my Foursquare [Swarm] friends. I mean, my friends from the office or my boyfriend's friends and people I know. And then I have Foursquare friends, and they think like me. They have similar tastes. And I trust their taste. So I wouldn't consider them to be friends, but rather acquaintances. But I trust their opinions. And that's why I follow what they say and I believe in their ratings. But the communities are separate. Not all of them. My boyfriend is a Foursquare fan, too. And other friends, who I would consider friends. But not all of them. Some are very 'random'. And I know them through Foursquare and not through anything else."
>
> *(Experienced user, age 34)*

In short, the emphasis of the functions in Swarm is on personal life and the network of contacts that encompasses either personal friends or acquaintances with similar preferences. Thus, the app has more potential for intensifying exclusive social interaction constellations because it emphasizes and strengthens existing social bonds and lifestyles. It offers only a few opportunities for interaction with unknown users in the immediate vicinity.

The future of urban public places: neither inclusion nor exclusion

Our two case studies, presented earlier, show that neither the inclusion hypothesis nor the exclusion hypothesis can adequately describe social reality. Both apps, City Guide and Swarm, encourage the exploration of unknown places. City Guide's annotated pictures and tips as well as the check-ins of Swarm friends display nearby places that are worth visiting. In accordance with the inclusion hypothesis, these apps tempt users to extend their own mobility radius and to visit new places. Contrary to the inclusion hypothesis, users rarely encounter representatives of unknown social worlds when they visit these places. Filtering digital annotations and following the check-ins of like-minded friends increase the likelihood that users remain within the borders of their own social worlds. With respect to this effect, the use of locative media is more in line with the exclusion hypothesis. For the future of public space, this could mean that the places where certain scene worlds meet no longer need to concentrate in certain streets or neighborhoods to ensure social exchange between like-minded people. With the help of locative media, it is conceivable that the meeting places of urban scene worlds will become more scattered physically across public space.

In the first step of our analysis, we successfully demonstrated that the City Guide app supports the location-based use forms of lurking and editing. Although these forms of use have the potential to increase accessibility to public spaces because they make it easier for users to obtain information on their physical surroundings firsthand, many users filter the annotated information according to lifestyle-related criteria, with the result that they rarely cross the boundaries of their own social worlds. Empirical reality (presently) seems far removed from the expectation of earlier studies that digital annotation might contribute to social inclusion by creating cyber-physical arenas that make the diverse voices of urban life heard. The proponents of the inclusion hypothesis took the fact that more and more public places are being annotated to draw the premature conclusion that users receive this information unfiltered. But, just as something as trifling as legal access to public places is sufficient to make them into urban meeting places, general accessibility of annotated information alone is equally insufficient to counteract the segregation of social worlds. On the contrary, many users apply the annotated information in order to maneuver more unerringly within their own urban scenes.

The results of our second analytical step, which focused on the social network functions of annotation services using Foursquare Swarm as an example, also seem to indicate that it would be wise to exercise caution with respect to the expectations reported in the literature regarding the inclusive potential of locative media. The primary purposes of location-based lifelogging and following are private recollection and the communicative exchange between like-minded people. However, we do not view Foursquare Swarm or other similar services as a significant motor of social exclusion. In fact, lifelogging and following reflect the already existing lifestyle of users who create social-spatial distance and distinctions independently of their media use. Swarm and other similar services offer tools to more strongly emphasize the location-based aspects of its users' lifestyle. In this way, the physical contours of social world lifestyles can be stabilized and may become more obvious. However, as we have demonstrated, existing social barriers are not raised, either. Based on these statements, it becomes clear that the inclusion and exclusion hypotheses denote extreme poles of social development trends that outline a space of possibility within which the actual development takes place. Both the fears of the exclusion hypothesis and the euphoria of the inclusion hypothesis seem exaggerated. In fact, locative media tend to modify the existing physical pattern of public space. The spatial segregation of social worlds is likely to decrease, but that does not mean that the social boundaries of different scene worlds will become more permeable than before.

Notes

1 We performed this study as part of the project "Locative Media: Inclusion and Exclusion in Public Spaces" (B04), which is part of the Collaborative Research Center "Re-Figuration of Spaces" (CRC 1265) funded by the German Research Foundation (DFG) (project number 290045248). Aside from the authors, student project team members Nina Meier and Johanna Weirauch also participated in the collection and evaluation of data, and we are indebted to them for their support.
2 We recruited users via the project website. The sample consisted of fourteen users, six of whom were female and eight male. Six users had years of experience with Foursquare apps, while the others had little or no experience. The users ranged in age from 21 to 43; the average age was 29 years.

References

Crawford, Alice. 2008. "Taking Social Software to the Streets: Mobile Cocooning and the (An)erotic City." *Journal of Urban Technology* 15 (3): 79–97.
Frith, Jordan. 2015. *Smartphones as Locative Media*. Cambridge: Polity Press.
Gieryn, Thomas F. 2000. "A Space for Place in Sociology." *Annual Review of Sociology* 26: 463–496.
Hamilton, Jillian G. 2009. "Ourplace: The Convergence of Locative Media and Online Participatory Culture." In *The Proceedings of OZCHI 2009, 23–27 November 2009*, 393–396. Melbourne, Victoria: The University of Melbourne.
Hitzler, Ronald, Thomas Bucher, and Arne Niederbacher. 2001. *Leben in Szenen: Formen jugendlicher Vergemeinschaftung heute*. Opladen: Leske + Budrich.
Keijl, Edwin, Randy Klaassen, and Rieks op den Akker. 2013. "The Influence of Locative Media on Social Information Sharing: A Review." *CTIT Technical Report Series, no. TR-CTIT-13–05*. Enschede: Centre for Telematics and Information Technology (CTIT).
Light, Ben, Jean Burgess, and Stefanie Duguay. 2016. "The Walkthrough Method: An Approach to the Study of Apps." *New Media & Society* 20 (3): 881–900.
Lofland, Lyn H. 1973. *A World of Strangers: Order and Action in Urban Public Space*. New York: Basic Books.
Löw, Martina, Silke Steets, and Sergeij Stoetzer. 2008. *Einführung in Die Stadt- Und Raumsoziologie. 2., Aktualisierte Auflage*. Opladen & Farmington Hills: Barbara Budrich.
Parisi, Lorenza. 2015. "'Where 2.0.' Exploring the Place Experience of 'Hyperconnected' Digital Media Users." *Sociologica* 3: 1–23.
Rajkumar, Ragunathan, Insup Lee, Lui Sha, and John Stankovic. 2010. "Cyber-Physical Systems: The Next Computing Revolution." In *Design Automation Conference 2010*. Anaheim, CA.
Souza e Silva, Adriana de. 2006. "From Cyber to Hybrid: Mobile Technologies as Interfaces of Hybrid Spaces." *Space and Culture* 9 (3): 261–278.
Souza e Silva, Adriana, de, and Jordan Frith. 2012. *Mobile Interfaces in Public Spaces: Locational Privacy, Control, and Urban Sociability*. New York: Routledge.
Souza e Silva, Adriana, de, and Daniel M. Sutko, eds. 2009. *Digital Cityscapes: Merging Digital and Urban Playspaces*. New York: P. Lang.
Strauss, Anselm L. 1961. *Images of the American City*. New York: Free Press.
Strauss, Anselm L. 1978. "A Social World Perspective." *Studies in Symbolic Interaction* 1: 119–128.
Turkle, Sherry. 1995. *Life on the Screen: Identity in the Age of the Internet*. New York: Simon & Schuster.

16

REPRESENTATIONAL AND ANIMATIC CORPOREALITY

Refiguring bodies and digitally mediated cities

Gillian Rose

Introduction: mediating posthuman embodiment

This chapter approaches the contemporary refiguration of urban space by exploring how embodiment is being reconfigured in digitally mediated cities. For Kember and Zylinska (2012, 40), mediation is 'a multiagential force that incorporates humans and machines, technologies and users, in an ongoing process of becoming-with'. Hence,

> mediation becomes a key trope for understanding and articulating our being in, and becoming with, the technological world, our emergence and ways of interacting with it, as well as the acts and processes of temporarily stabilizing the world into media, agents, relations, and networks.
>
> (Kember and Zylinska 2012, xv)

This chapter focuses specifically on how the flows of data that now saturate so many cities are mediating (post)human embodiment, and in particular how a specific form of spatiality is part of that mediating stabilisation of corporeality—a spatiality that also refigures urban space.

The chapter assumes that corporeality is a process and that different embodiments are co-produced with different kinds of technologies. Visual technologies are especially important in this process, particularly in cities that are full of people looking at images of other people, on digital screens, in that city or somewhere else. Data that become images of various kinds are a significant part of the immense streams of digital data flowing through and beyond cities, including images of cities and their inhabitants (McQuire 2016). Created and processed, distributed and redistributed, some will materialise as figurative images like photorealistic advertisements, news videos or selfies. Some will be converted into types of data visualisations: a symbol

DOI: 10.4324/9781003036159-19

on a map, a node in a network, a category in a graph. These many image types are seen variously in their turn, studied, glanced at, swiped through (Rose and Willis 2019; Krajina 2014). Made somewhere and uploaded, travelling somewhere else, being reconfigured, analysed, or multiplied, and then being downloaded, perhaps to the same device, perhaps to many others, in the same place or elsewhere: these are the distributed circuits of many forms of visual media now (Browne 2015; Casetti 2015). And at the interface between a digital image and its viewers, particular kinds of bodies coagulate.

In urban studies, most of the attention given to digital mediation has focused on the 'smart city' and its flows of big digital data (key references include Greenfield 2013; Hollands 2016; Hollands 2008; Kitchin 2014; Marvin, Luque-Ayala, and McFarlane 2016; Karvonen, Cugurullo, and Caprotti 2018). The term 'smart' refers to the use of digital data to improve urban governance. For example, city authorities and commercial providers suggest that smart policies and technologies can enhance environmental sustainability by enabling more efficient use of resources, especially energy and water; or that traffic flow or air pollution can be improved by using real-time environmental data; or that economic growth can be increased by innovating new products and markets based on digital data. Attention has also been given to the range of commercial platforms that collate and integrate urban data, such as Airbnb, Uber, and Mobike (Barns 2020). As various feminist critics have pointed out, however, most of this work focuses on the agency of digital infrastructure and the political economy of its data extraction (Leszczynski 2019; Rose 2017). Inspired by decades of intersectional feminist work, this chapter instead asks how to see bodies in this context.

This is an important question to ask since much of the data circulating through urban spaces are related to bodies. Corporations and city authorities produce, analyse, and visualise data about populations, citizens, commuters, taxpayers, users, residents, and consumers, among others (Rose et al. 2020). Residents and tourists take and look at selfies, influencer videos, video chats, and GIFs on WhatsApp, Instagram and TikTok. That is, much of the data that circulate through and about cities materialise as images on some kind of screen, showing and being seen by specific bodies. The chapter approaches this visuality as a form of technosociality. Ways of seeing are co-constituted by the affordances of technologies, the social practices in which those technologies are embedded, their discursive framings and affective dispositions (see Gordon 2010; Otter 2008; Wilson 2014). The phrase 'ways of seeing' was coined by John Berger (1972). The chapter follows his use of the term to refer not only to what is seen but also to the body doing a particular kind of visualising. 'Though obviously one who sees, an observer is more importantly one who sees with a prescribed set of possibilities, one who is embedded in a system of conventions and limitations' (Crary 1990, 6). Berger was also attentive to (some of) the ways in which the relation between seer and seen is always riddled with power. If visual images 'body forth' corporeality (Copier and Steinbock 2018, 924), these are of specific kinds, in particular relations.

Many digital images mimic visual genres with long histories, which shape their making and viewing. Maps generated by geographical information systems may use the same data and be seen in the same way as earlier hand-drawn maps of census data, for example; three-dimensional digital models of urban morphology may be used in the same way as the physical architectural models. But the chapter suggests that these ways of seeing and constituting bodies are being joined by other ways of seeing other forms of embodiment, which are caught up with the specific dynamics of data circulation. Specifically, the chapter suggests that *animatic* embodiment is part of the digital refiguration of urban bodies and space.

To make this argument, it draws on Deborah Levitt's (2018) account of animation. Animation brings things to life. For Levitt (2018, 1), animation is 'the dominant medium of our time', moving us from 'questions about ontology, category, and being to ones of appearance, metamorphosis, and affect' (Levitt 2018, 2). Animation is both a medium and a contemporary cultural condition, according to Levitt. Its logic is not based on correspondence with a real; instead, animations envision metamorphosis, erasure, and resurrection rather than ontological presence. Schematically, the chapter argues that the spatial organisation of bodies in cities is also shifting between representational and animatic forms—and so, too, are city spaces.

Animation, softimages, and urban bodies

For Levitt, 'new forms of life and vitality emerge at the spectator–screen intersection as this transforms over time' (Levitt 2018, 3). While not directly determined by technological changes in the spectator–screen intersection, animatic life is enabled by some of the specific dynamics of digital images. It is important, therefore, to say a little more about how digital visual imagery is different from previous image forms. Hoelzl and Marie's (2015, 7) discussion of what they term the 'softimage' is useful here:

> As a program, the image, while still appearing as a geometrical projection on our screens, is inextricably mixed up with the data (physical and digital) and the continuous processing of data. What was supposed to be a solid representation of a solid world based on the sound principle of geometric projection (our operational mode for centuries), a hard image as it were, is revealed to be something totally different, ubiquitous, infinitely adaptable and adaptive and intrinsically merged with software: a softimage.

A defining element of that merger is the software that allows digital images to be networked images (Munster and MacKenzie 2019; Rubinstein and Sluis 2008). The shift from analogue to digital popular photography was enabled by not only digital cameras but also increasingly seamless connections between cameras, other viewing devices such as computers, and then phones and social media platforms. Social media is saturated with images, of course, and design professionals create elaborate computer-generated images via a global division of labour (Chung 2018; Rose, Degen, and Melhuish 2014). Images appear on multiple screens, in different forms, at different sites. They are shared and favourited, liked or deleted, copied and posted, circulated and recirculated. There are nonhuman agencies at play here, too. Many visual data are processed algorithmically; indeed, Steyerl (2017, 47) suggests that 'contemporary perception is machinic to a large degree. The spectrum of human vision covers only a tiny part of it'. The speed of image production, processing, and circulation is enacting a shift to 'something more akin to live transmission' (Rubinstein and Sluis 2008, 22). The speed and scale of image production and analysis suggests not so much a network as a vast

> stratified constellation of technical memory matter, composed of resources that shape political and cultural imaginaries . . . with depth, height, scale, extensiveness and duration . . . moving in different directions. . . . Its forms may change and its content migrate, accruing or shedding textures in the process.
>
> *(Withers 2015, 17)*

Softimages, then, are networked, processed, live, and distributed (cf. Rose 2016). So, how are bodies visually mediated by softimages? The chapter will now sketch two visual regimes: the *representational* and *animatic*. Representational and animatic ways of seeing are not completely distinct, nor do they map neatly onto different technologies (as Levitt [2018] notes). Technologies, practices, discourses, and affects all contribute to each visual regime. Many digital images mimic the appearance of non-digital images and are observed in ways that those have long been observed, as representations of particular forms of urban life: closed circuit-television footage taken with digital cameras, for example, can be seen in the same way as video-taped CCTV. *Animatic* refigurations of urban environments and inhabitants, however, invite a different way of seeing—emergent, distributed, transformational—whether they are hand-drawn cartoons of urban superheroes or real-time maps of Twitter sentiment.

Seeing cities representationally

With those caveats in mind, the chapter now indicates how bodies and cities continue to be visualised through *representational* ways of seeing. Drawing on Barad, Kember and Zylinska (2012, 31) describe representationalism as the conviction that what is represented exists independently of all practices of representation. Representational ways of seeing assume that there is a real that images—no matter how selective and distorted—re-present to the viewer. In terms of visuality, cinema and photography have both been understood as media that are themselves representational but are also parts of a wider representational visual culture, which Levitt calls the 'cinematic regime' composed of 'light, the machine, and an analytic eye' (Levitt 2018, 12). In Levitt's account, as in that of many others, this is not the only visuality enacted by cinema. However, the dominant representational cinematic regime sees bodies in particular ways. What we see when we see bodies cinematically are 'autonomous, massy entities' (Levitt 2018, 12) that refer to a pro-filmic real. Twentieth-century traditions of urban documentary photography, for example, are usually cinematic.

For Levitt, then, the representational cinematic regime entails the seeing of massy bodies by an analytic eye. In terms of thinking about bodies in urban space, seeing bodies as fleshy entities to be analysed is part of the 'productive, biopolitical dimensions of cinema in the discourse of reflection, representation, and reality' (Levitt 2018, 11). That is, the representational cinematic regime is aligned with Foucauldian biopower (Levitt 2018, 28). This is a crucial step in understanding representational regimes of urban visuality. Representational urban visuality sees bodies as masses: as epidermal volumes with surfaces that can be analysed and categorised.

In biopolitical regimes, ways of seeing analyse bodies through discursive codes and, in so doing, enact a range of social categories such as sex, gender, and race (along with distinguishing between bodies that are human and not [Butler 2007]). Feminist, critical race, and crip scholarship have been particularly attentive to this process. From hooks (1992) and Bordo (1993) to Weheliye (2014), Browne (2015), and Benjamin (2019), the ways in which bodies' surfaces are marked with, and interpreted through, signs of social difference have been described. And this analytical, biopolitical way of seeing continues in the digitally mediated city. 'Visual technologies and racial taxonomies fashion each other' (Benjamin 2019, 99). Corporeal bodies are rendered (as the) real surface on which particular social categories are visible. Facial 'recognition' software can identify the gender, sex, race, and even sexuality of bodies, we are told (though their failures are also regularly reported [Leszczynski 2019]). The notion of 'recognition' here exemplifies the representational regime in which a reality is there to be recognised; and also obscures the process by which algorithms are trained to produce that 'recognition' by human operators (Benjamin 2019). We might also consider the ways in which big urban data are converted into conventional demographic or geospatial categories and then into dashboard displays (Ruppert 2012).

Urban spaces are also visualised representationally in the cinematic regime. Visual technologies of many kinds are put to work to identify truths about the city. Images—photographs, maps, diagrams, graphs—are understood to represent some aspect of an urban reality. From creating and mapping data to photographing housing defined as slums, visual techniques for seeing cities and their inhabitants became part of understanding and governing urban spaces.

Understanding the digital mediation of bodies and cities as representational produces a particular form of critique. Much criticism of the algorithmic production of urban code/space (Kitchin and Dodge 2011) is based on the representational assertion of a 'radical incommensurability between embodied and represented life' (Agostinho 2018, 143). Assuming that incommensurability exists between a real and its representation, this way of seeing is challenged because it 'renders some things more visible than others, yielding new parameters of visibility that determine who or what dis/appears' (Agostinho 2018, 132). Thus, planners' and developers' digital images of new urban developments are criticised for their inaccuracy: too clean, too sunny, too wealthy. In this regime, the who and the what exist before they are brought into, or excluded from, visibility.

It is this assumption of a pre-existing real that animatic ways of seeing abandon. Levitt's (2018) account of the representational cinematic regime and the animatic apparatus is careful not to assume a recent and complete transition from a film-based regime to a software-based apparatus. She is also careful not describe specific visual technologies as either representational or animatory. As she notes, films can be animated and animations can be representational. She does suggest, however, that a new technological and discursive dispositif is emerging in which 'it doesn't matter so much what life is, as rather you can do with it' (Levitt 2018, 20). She suggests that this is a wider cultural shift, and, like Clough (2018), she references the life sciences where bodies are increasingly understood less as corporeal masses and more and more as information that—ever since gene-splicing, DNA mapping, and transgendered bodies became possible—can be transformed and recombined.

Animatic embodiment

The mediation of bodies into data happens in a great number of everyday urban contexts, as noted in the introduction to this chapter. And while some of that mediation may take representational forms, animation also occurs, more and more often. Deleuze (1992) famously argued that the biopolitical was being displaced by what he termed 'societies of control'. In societies of control, the social is constituted through constantly mediated data and there is no sense of an incommensurability between that data and a real. (Incommensurability remains but is better thought of as glitches within and between different data flows, as Leszczynski [2019] argues.)

If animation is a cultural condition, then one of its central dynamics is the circulation and recombination of data: 'big data sorting that is designed to collate seemingly unrelated sets with the intention of producing novel relations' (Clough 2018, 107). Emergent patterns within and between data replace correspondence between image and reality and between sign and category. As Rouvray (2013) points out, this algorithmic logic 'spares [humans] the burden and responsibility of transcribing, interpreting and evaluating events of world. It spares them the meaning-making processes of transcription or representation'. Animatic embodiment in a smart city is configured by such emergent, algorithmic constellations of data. The boundary between the corporeal body and the network no longer holds. 'Embodiment cannot be contained within the organic skin' when traces of digital data now so fundamentally compose what has to be called the posthuman (Clough 2018, xxxii). Bodies are turned into data and the algorithmic analysis of big data produces new corporeal entities (Rose et al. 2020).

Gabrys's (2014) discussion of smart citizenship is exemplary here. Gabrys explores the notion of smart citizenship assumed by a smart city design proposal and suggests that the production of digital data produces smart citizens as 'ambividuals': citizen-subjects whose emergence is contingent on events, articulated through the technologies and practices of computational urbanism. Citizenship, she suggests, can thus become less an individualised subjectivity and more a digitally mediated distribution, configuring 'ambient and malleable urban operators that are expressions of computer environments' (Gabrys 2014, 42–43).

But what does this animated embodiment in a smart city look like? If the bodies in digitally mediated cities are not all configured as the 'body-as-organism', the body that we see pictured, the massy body bounded by skin, if some forms of embodiment do not look like that anymore, then how do we see them?

Levitt's (2018) response is to look at a range of visual animations differently. She looks and reads a range of films and books not as representations but as animations. In animations, says Levitt, things are only erased, mutated, or resurrected; things are not categorised but transformed. Her methodology is therefore to read animations not for their correspondences, references, and presences, but rather for their transformative generation of novel sensations. Animation must be seen as an enactment; it exemplifies, not signifies; it must be looked at less for what and more for how. She turns her gaze to dolls, automata, cyborgs, and robots, and other urban inhabitants that have long featured in films as not-quite-human. These are figures, she says, that continue to look human enough for viewers to relate to them but that are also different enough to suggest other forms of lively animation. They retain 'just enough resemblance so that its potentials—if not the extent of its "dimensions, depths, and distances"—become graspable' (Levitt 2018, 51). This potential is the animatory vitality of recombinant invention and other forms of emergent embodiment.

Here we might turn to semi-autonomous technologies such as food delivery robots, trundling alongside other pedestrians, or driverless cars; we might consider the 'data doubles' that shadow corporeal bodies in city streets (Cheney-Lippold 2017). But we might also turn to the viewer in animatic ways of seeing. Rather than the cinematic regime's positioning of the analytical spectator as separate from the screen, animations tend to merge and exchange image space and body space (Levitt 2018, 83). The screen is now an interface. 'A user is not consolidated in identity but rather . . . consist[s] of roving populations of action in the network' (Halpern 2015, 240). No longer a single point of view framed by perspectival techniques, the spectator becomes a constantly mobile point of view, decentred, zooming and hovering through an environment that seems to have no frame. Elsaesser (2013, 240) describes this unanchored viewing, tracking seamlessly through spaces from the nano to the planetary, as 'the default value of digital vision' (and points to its non-digital precedents in a range of efforts to create convincing three-dimensional films).

This suggests that looking for animatory embodiments means being particularly attentive to erasure, mutation, re-emergence, mobility, and this is a vocabulary that is as much spatial as visual.

Refiguring city spaces as animatory

If animatory bodies are organised as emergent, combinatory patterns of data, then so too are the spaces of digitally mediated cities. Geographers have been particularly attentive to the various dynamics through which city spaces are digitally refigured (Rose 2017; 2018; Wilmott 2016; Wilson 2014). Here, the plethora of digital visualisations that now bring urban spaces into visibility are particularly relevant (Halpern 2015). Cities now are insistently visualised through multiple interfaces, in different formats, genres, and media. There is no single frame, no nest of scales, no coherent territory. Different images merge and blend, and the same image reappears in different contexts. Rather like Steinbock's (2019) trans account of cinema, this is a way of seeing cities through cuts and layers, disjunctures and recombinations, mutations and excrescences. References to a real become references to multiple reals, which become a seamless dissolution of one real into another, which in turn becomes more visual flow, exemplified in videos evoking the smart city that seamlessly mutate between multiple types of visualisations of city spaces (Rose 2018). Cities are thus also constantly transformed in the 'mixed-space effect' of animation (Levitt 2018, 68).

An example, paradoxically, is the smart city control centre. As the site for visualising many kinds of data regarding a city, a smart control centre without doubt works in part on a representational logic: what truth is this data representing, and how therefore should the city be managed? However, as Luque-Ayala and Marvin (2016; Marvin and Luque-Ayala 2017) point out in their accounts of Rio de Janeiro's smart operations centre, the centre is also a site that generates multiple spatialities through which Rio materialises differently. It enacts an infrastructure through which all sorts of things move—people, electricity, rainfall, traffic—but which may also fail at any moment. The operations centre produces a network of logistical circulation but is also a nodal site for maintenance and incident control. Through the operations centre, 'the city is reconfigured as a space of agility, efficiency, modularity, flexibility and configurability' (Marvin and Luque-Ayala 2017, 92), and these spaces of the digitally mediated urban operating system may not align. The city as bricolage morphs between these configurations as the data from all kinds of urban sensors flicker across its screens.

Re-refiguring digitally mediated cities and bodies

So, if we think about the digitally mediated city and ask—where are the bodies?— this chapter has suggested that there are several ways to answer the question. Drawing on Levitt's (2018) work, the chapter has sketched a regime of *representation* and what it makes *visible*, and a regime of *animation* and how it makes things *live*. The chapter has discussed how bodies in the digitally mediated city can be thought of representationally in terms of features distributed across epidermal surfaces, which represent certain pre-existing social categories and can be analysed. Animatic bodies, on the other hand, are seen and sensed as constantly emergent, mobile, fluid, and mutating. These two configurations are constitutive of not only how embodiments are made visible but also different regimes of seeing. Moreover, they constitute different organisations of urban space. Representational and animatic bodies are constituted through different kinds of spatial organisation, and so too are the cities they inhabit. Urban representational regimes proffer a city about which some truths can be known. Animatic cities, on the other hand, are fluid and emergent.

The question of power in this visual culture remains, as always. Representational and animatic regimes of urban embodiment have different accounts of power. In representational regimes, power consists of the ability to analyse, identify, and label bodies and spaces; to misrepresent; to exclude and render invisible. The power of animatic regimes also rests in the power to analyse and define, but also to extract, transfigure, morph, and assimilate corporealities and cities. Each requires different actions, engagements, resistances, and ethics. Urban scholars often seek resistance to exclusion. But animation demands a different critique. If the animatic apparatus

> reorders the self as data . . . then it is important to continue opening out the question of the self and its constituent, relational others in order to see what kinds of relations are facilitated and prohibited in the process and what consequences various enactments of relationality will have, for 'us' and 'the world' at large.
>
> *(Kember and Zylinska 2012, 112)*

The challenge, then, is to calibrate potentials for other transformations and potentials (Clough 2018), and other recombinations (Rose 2017), in urban data circulations.

References

Agostinho, Daniela. 2018. "Chroma Key Dreams: Algorithmic Visibility, Fleshy Images and Scenes of Recognition." *Philosophy of Photography* 9 (2): 131–155.
Barns, Sarah. 2020. *Platform Urbanism: Negotiating Platform Ecosystems in Connected Cities*. Basingstoke: Palgrave Macmillan.
Benjamin, Ruha. 2019. *Race After Technology: Abolitionist Tools for the New Jim Code*. Cambridge: Polity Press.
Berger, John. 1972. *Ways of Seeing*. London: BBC with Penguin.
Bordo, Susan. 1993. *Unbearable Weight: Feminism, Western Culture, and The Body*. Berkeley: University of California Press.
Browne, Simone. 2015. *Dark Matters: On the Surveillance of Blackness*. London: Duke University Press.
Butler, Judith. 2007. "Torture and the Ethics of Photography." *Environment and Planning D: Society and Space* 25 (6): 951–966.
Casetti, Francesco. 2015. *The Lumière Galaxy: Seven Key Words for the Cinema to Come*. New York: Columbia University Press.
Cheney-Lippold, John. 2017. *We Are Data: Algorithms and the Making of Our Digital Selves*. New York: New York University Press.

Chung, Hye Jean. 2018. *Media Heterotopias: Digital Effects and Material Labor in Global Production*. London: Duke University Press.
Clough, Patricia Ticineto. 2018. *The User Unconscious: Affect, Media and Measure*. London: University of Minnesota Press.
Copier, Laura, and Eliza Steinbock. 2018. "On Not Really Being There: Trans★ Presence/Absence in *Dallas Buyers Club*." *Feminist Media Studies* 18 (5): 923–941.
Crary, Jonathan. 1990. *Techniques of the Observer: On Vision and Modernity in the Nineteenth Century*. Cambridge, MA: MIT Press.
Deleuze, Gilles. 1992. "Postscript on the Societies of Control." *October* 59: 3–7.
Elsaesser, Thomas. 2013. "The 'Return' of 3-D: On Some of the Logics and Genealogies of the Image in the Twenty-First Century." *Critical Inquiry* 39 (2): 217–246.
Gabrys, Jennifer. 2014. "Programming Environments: Environmentality and Citizen Sensing in the Smart City." *Environment and Planning D: Society and Space* 32 (1): 30–48.
Gordon, Eric. 2010. *The Urban Spectator: American Concept Cities from Kodak to Google*, 1st ed. Hanover, NH: Dartmouth College Press.
Greenfield, Adam. 2013. *Against the Smart City*. London: Do Projects.
Halpern, Orit. 2015. *Beautiful Data: A History of Vision and Reason since 1945*. Durham NC: Duke University Press.
Hoelzl, Ingrid, and Rémi Marie. 2015. *Softimage: Towards a New Theory of the Digital Image*. Bristol: Intellect Books.
Hollands, Robert G. 2008. "Will the Real Smart City Please Stand Up?" *City* 12 (3): 303–320.
Hollands, Robert G. 2016. "Beyond the Corporate Smart City? Glimpses of Other Possibilities of Smartness." In *Smart Urbanism: Utopian Vision or False Dawn*, edited by Simon Marvin, Andrés Luque-Ayala, and Colin McFarlane, 169–185. London: Routledge.
hooks, bell. 1992. *Black Looks: Race and Representation*. Boston: South End Press.
Karvonen, Andrew, Federico Cugurullo, and Federico Caprotti, eds. 2018. *Inside Smart Cities: Place, Politics and Urban Innovation*, 1st ed. London: Routledge.
Kember, Sarah, and Joanna Zylinska. 2012. *Life After New Media: Mediation as a Vital Process*. Cambridge, MA: MIT Press.
Kitchin, Rob. 2014. "The Real-Time City? Big Data and Smart Urbanism." *GeoJournal* 79 (1): 1–14.
Kitchin, Rob, and Martin Dodge. 2011. *Code/Space: Software and Everyday Life*. Cambridge, MA: MIT Press.
Krajina, Zlatan. 2014. *Negotiating the Mediated City: Everyday Encounters with Public Screens*. London: Routledge.
Leszczynski, Agnieszka. 2019. "Glitchy Vignettes of Platform Urbanism." *Environment and Planning D: Society and Space* 38 (2): 189–208. doi: 10.1177/0263775819878721.
Levitt, Deborah. 2018. *The Animatic Apparatus: Animation, Vitality, and the Futures of the Image*. Winchester: Zero Books.
Luque-Ayala, Andrés, and Simon Marvin. 2016. "The Maintenance of Urban Circulation: An Operational Logic of Infrastructural Control." *Environment and Planning D: Society and Space* 34 (2): 191–208.
Marvin, Simon, and Andrés Luque-Ayala. 2017. "Urban Operating Systems: Diagramming the City." *International Journal of Urban and Regional Research* 41 (1): 84–103.
Marvin, Simon, Andrés Luque-Ayala, and Colin McFarlane, eds. 2016. *Smart Urbanism: Utopian Vision or False Dawn?* Abingdon: Routledge.
McQuire, Scott. 2016. *Geomedia: Networked Cities and the Future of Public Space*. Cambridge: Polity Press.

Munster, Anna, and Adrian MacKenzie. 2019. "Platform Seeing: Image Ensembles and Their Invisualities." *Theory, Culture & Society* 36 (5): 3–22. doi: 10.1177/0263276419847508.

Otter, Chris. 2008. *The Victorian Eye: A Political History of Light and Vision in Britain, 1800–1910*. London: University of Chicago Press.

Rose, Gillian. 2016. "Rethinking the Geographies of Cultural 'Objects' through Digital Technologies: Interface, Network and Friction." *Progress in Human Geography* 40 (3): 334–351.

Rose, Gillian. 2017. "Posthuman Agency in the Digitally Mediated City: Exteriorization, Individuation, Reinvention." *Annals of the American Association of Geographers* 107 (4): 779–793.

Rose, Gillian. 2018. "Look Inside™: Visualising the Smart City." In *An Introduction to Geomedia: Spaces and Mobilities in Mediatized Worlds*, edited by Karin Fast, André Jansson, Johan Lindell, Linda Ryan Bengtsson, and Mekonnen Tesfahuney, 97–113. London: Routledge.

Rose, Gillian, Monica Degen, and Clare Melhuish. 2014. "Networks, Interfaces, and Computer-Generated Images: Learning from Digital Visualisations of Urban Redevelopment Projects." *Environment and Planning D: Society and Space* 32 (3): 386–403.

Rose, Gillian, Parvati Raghuram, Sophie Watson, and Edward Wigley. 2020. "Platform Urbanism, Smartphone Applications and Valuing Data in a Smart City." *Transactions of the Institute of British Geographers* 1–14. doi: 10.1111/tran.12400.

Rose, Gillian, and Alistair Willis. 2019. "Seeing the Smart City on Twitter: Colour and the Affective Territories of Becoming Smart." *Environment and Planning D: Society and Space* 37 (3): 411–427.

Rouvroy, Antoinette. 2013. "The End(s) of Critique: Data Behaviourism versus Due Process." In *Privacy, Due Process and the Computational Turn: The Philosophy of Law Meets the Philosophy of Technology*, edited by Mireille Hildebrandt and Katja de Vries, 143–167. Abingdon: Routledge.

Rubinstein, Daniel, and Katrina Sluis. 2008. "A Life More Photographic: Mapping the Networked Image." *Photographies* 1 (1): 9–28.

Ruppert, Evelyn. 2012. "Category." In *Inventive Methods: The Happening of the Social*, edited by Celia Lury and Nina Wakeford, 36–47. Abingdon: Routledge.

Steinbock, Eliza. 2019. *Shimmering Images: Trans Cinema, Embodiment, and the Aesthetics of Change*. London: Duke University Press.

Steyerl, Hito. 2017. *Duty Free Art: Art in the Age of Planetary Civil War*. London: Verso.

Weheliye, Alexander G. 2014. *Habeas Viscus: Racializing Assemblages, Biopolitics, and Black Feminist Theories of the Human*. Durham NC: Duke University Press.

Wilmott, Clancy. 2016. "In-between Mobile Maps and Media: Movement." *Television & New Media* 18 (4): 320–335.

Wilson, Matthew W. 2014. "Continuous Connectivity, Handheld Computers, and Mobile Spatial Knowledge." *Environment and Planning D: Society and Space* 32 (3): 535–555.

Withers, Deborah. 2015. *Feminism, Digital Culture and the Politics of Transmission*. London: Rowman & Littlefield International.

17

REFIGURING SPACES

Transformative aspects of migration and tourism

Stefanie Bürkle

This visual essay explores the issue of "spatial transformation" through photographs of various places in Berlin (Alexanderplatz, Gendarmenmarkt, Lustgarten, Dong Xuan Center), Korea (Dogil Maeul, Seoul, Songdo), and China (Shenzhen, Window of the World), in which very different cultural ideas of urban space can be found.

In this case, "refiguring spaces" refers to an ongoing transformation of urban space, which is defined by means of the cultural concepts of center and rim, outer and inner spatiality. My photographs often capture spatially marginal situations, which offer a behind-the-scenes peek into these ideas of space. The shift from living urban spaces to empty stages, where the city appears to be nothing more than a backdrop, was not solely caused by the lockdown during the corona outbreak in spring 2020.

The selection of photographs in this essay covers a time frame from 2006 to 2020 and in part originated within the context of the art project "Migrating Spaces and Tourism" (a subproject of the Collaborative Research Center 1265 "Re-Figuration of Spaces"), which explores the overlapping of migration and tourism in physical urban space. I have arranged the single images into a series, a continuous band of images. The absence of captions frees the viewers from a purely content-based classification of the images, transforming them into travelers between the spaces. Isolated motifs reappear in the preceding or following image, thus creating new compositional and content-related connections beyond the images. Objects and perspectives link the pictures and form a new visual texture. Connections and transitions are the focus of the observation. Single images become interrupted, only to be continued when flipping to the next page. Hence, this series of images sheds light on the complex spatial overlapping of tourism and migration and their polycontexturality.

DOI: 10.4324/9781003036159-20

Art and research project: MIGRATOURISPACE | Space Migration and Tourism
Director: Stefanie Bürkle
Assistant director: Janin Walter
Scientific assistance: Ilkin Akpinar, Berit Hummel, Tae Wong Huur, Aaron Lang
This visual essay was produced as part of the DFG-financed project "Migrating Spaces and Tourism." The project is part of the CRC 1265 "Re-Figuration of Spaces" (project number 290045248).
www.migratourispace.de
www.kunst.tu-berlin.de
www.stefanie-buerkle.de
Photography © Stefanie Bürkle/VG Bild-Kunst, Bonn 2021

PART IV
Imagining, producing, and negotiating space

Part IV

Imagining, producing, and negotiating space

18
ONTOLOGICAL SECURITY, GLOBALIZATION, AND GEOGRAPHICAL IMAGINATION

Ilse Helbrecht, Janina Dobrusskin, Carolin Genz, and Lucas Pohl

Globalization anxieties from a geographical perspective

In the year 2016, the majority of the British people voted in a referendum to leave the European Union. The results of the national election in 2019 strongly reaffirmed this Brexit vote, and by now, the UK has already left the EU. At the same time, Donald Trump governs the United States of America with a new policy of "America First," thereby shaking up the geopolitical order and demanding new foreign, trade, and military politics from most of its partners around the globe. On the same note, the global corona pandemic has provoked a widespread closing of national borders and a preliminary end of globalization "as we know it." While many states and governments are predominantly engaged in reorienting their geopolitical positioning as a result, people from various crisis regions are increasingly claiming political asylum in areas such as the United States or Europe. Civil wars and both social and democratic uprisings in Syria, Sudan, Afghanistan, and Iran have created a global refugee population, caused and accompanied by enormous human suffering through war crimes and forced displacement. Hence, millions of refugees are attempting to come by foot, boat, bus, or train in a desperate effort to enter the EU and the US—risking their lives at the harsh, ever more militarized borders of the West. And even more refugees live in "indefinite exile" in refugee camps across the global South, only poorly provided by the UNHRC like in Jordan or Kenya (Hyndman and Giles 2016, 2).

Yet, whereas Western countries are viewed as safe havens from the perspective of international refugees, within Europe and North America new anxieties are being stirred against economic and political globalization as well as international migration. A strong right-wing populism has arisen, with populist (party) leaders like Marie Le Pen in France, Matteo Salvini in Italy, or Björn Höcke in Germany, who are promising safety for "their" people. Based on empirical evidence, the latter can even legally be called a "fascist," as ruled recently by a German court (Verwaltungsgericht Meiningen 2019). This national populism has been institutionalized, either in new political parties all over Europe like the "Front National" in France, the "Lega Nord" in Italy, or the "Alternative für Deutschland" in Germany, or it has captured traditional, established parties like the "Republicans" headed by Donald Trump. Sadly enough, racism, sexism, homophobia, and islamophobia are (back) on the agenda. And it is through mechanisms of fear, of rising anxiety towards "the stranger" or "the other"—which can be the refugee, the migrant, or your neighbor next door—that new waves of nationalism and territorial security policies are legitimized. Hence, whereas the 20th century ended with the hopeful fall of the Berlin Wall and the termination of the Cold War, the beginning of the 21st century is marked by revanchist movements of right-wing populism, the erection of new (state and cultural) borders, and the return of xenophobia, of fear towards the stranger.

We argue that what seems like a paradox at first glance—the simultaneous existence of consummate globalization, on one hand, and the rise of xenophobic nationalism, on the other hand—is structurally linked. After all, it is not by accident that (economic) globalization irritates national identities or even deeply unsettles personal identities (Anselmi 2018; Steger and James 2019). Quite the opposite, we suggest, it is in fact the personal and deeply emotional level of the subject that is strongly affected by globalization, i.e. processes of increasing exchange and interaction on a global scale (Nagar et al. 2002; Kinnvall 2004; Matthews and Sidhu 2005; Sassen 2013; Dirksmeier and Helbrecht 2015a). It is the basic trust of people in the continuity of their identity, the continuity of their life, and the continuity of their environment—in a nutshell: their ontological security (Laing 1990; Giddens 1991)—that is challenged and at times even highly at risk through globalization. Thus, rising ontological insecurity can partially contribute to the emergence of new nationalist populist currents, besides other factors such as political persuasions.

These far-reaching effects of globalization on personal affects and identities have to be scrutinized (Dirksmeier and Helbrecht 2015b) if we are to understand the sweeping changes of national sentiment and international resentment that can be observed in many countries worldwide. Thus, we uphold the argument that it is only through a multiscale analysis, combining the most intimate scale of personal development and psychological processes, on one hand, with broader national political discourses and/or global formations, on the other hand, that we can fully understand the (re)emergence of nationalism, racism, and xenophobia. Certainly, this is exactly what feminist scholars have long argued for: applying an embodied, feminist perspective to geopolitics and political geography (Hyndman 2004; 2019).

Therefore, in this chapter, we aim to explore some of the geographical depth in these anxieties. What are we afraid of in times of globalization? Which kind of insecurity is raised through the continuously intensifying processes of economic exchange, international migration, and communication? And, more importantly, how do we reassure ourselves in times of disorienting societal dynamics? Which spatial routines, practices, places, and imaginations help us to stabilize our own identities and the positioning of self in such a dynamically changing world? Because fully understanding the complete picture of the globalization-anxiety complex is required in order to grapple with it, address it politically and culturally, and, thus, help overcome the fatal return of xenophobia, racism, and their likes.

It was Anthony Giddens who first addressed these pressing questions. As early as 1991, he argued that late modernity is characterized by intense processes of globalization and disembedding, which strongly influence the institutional composition of modern societies, as well as the very personal dispositions, emotions, and self-identities of each and every individual: "The reorganisation of time and space, plus the disembedding mechanisms, radicalize and globalize pre-established institutional traits of modernity; and they act to transform the content and nature of day-to-day social life" (Giddens 1991, 2). Giddens goes on to argue that it is a particularly demanding task of late modernity, that the self—as well as institutions and the state—has to reflexively construct an identity "amid a puzzling diversity of options and possibilities" (Giddens 1991, 3).

In this chapter, we will scrutinize the modern task of identity building in times of globalization through the lens of ontological security. We argue that the concept of ontological security helps us to understand some of the more fundamental dimensions and dynamics of identity challenges caused by globalization. Yet, although extensive literature on ontological security is available in the fields of sociology and psychology, there is barely any geographical scrutiny or application of the concept in debates on globalization. This is all the more surprising as spatial questions are at the very core of processes of globalization and ontological security and insecurity, likewise, as we will explain further on.

Hence, in this chapter we will apply a specific geographic reading to the literature on ontological security. We thereby achieve a spatialization of the concept of ontological security, which is helpful in comprehending the role and workings of ontological (in)security in the face of globalization. Furthermore, we draw on empirical findings from our Berlin case study on ontological (in)security and geographical imaginations. Between the years 2018 and 2020, we applied the method of photo-elicitation and conducted 60 qualitative interviews and three focus groups in Berlin (Germany). In terms of the composition of our respondents, we strove for a fairly mixed sample, representing different age groups (aged 15 to 70) and gender identities equally (30 female, 30 male respondents). Only in the social composition did we strive for a rather polarized profile, capturing the geographical imaginations of globalization from 32 people with a rather marginalized background, on the one hand, in order to compare them with 28 people who can be considered elite due to their high income and cultural and social capital, on the other hand. In these interviews, we examined subjective notions of ontological security on various scales from the body to the global.[1]

Based on our empirical findings, we propose three spatial modes for how individuals aim to attain ontological security by geographical means: a) geopolitical positioning, b) home-making, and c) nature-related routines. The geographical imaginations are hereby central to the ways in which ontological security can be achieved. Hence, we argue, it is only through a spatialized, geographic understanding of ontological security that we fully grasp the complex relationships between globalization, self-identity, and ontological security. We pay particular attention to the manners in which ontological security is attained. In order to be accountable to society, the field of social sciences must not limit itself to identifying problems, but rather contribute to solving them.

What is ontological security?

Humanist psychiatrist Ronald D. Laing first developed the concept of "ontological security" in order to grasp what it takes to be, to become, and to stay mentally healthy. Having observed and treated mentally ill persons professionally, he claims that it is a certain characteristic feature that distinguishes the mentally healthy (for example non-schizophrenic) person: "ontological security" (Laing 1990, 39).

> A man (sic) may have a sense of his presence in the world as a real, alive, whole, and, in a temporal sense, continuous person. As such, he can live out into the world and meet others: a world and others experienced as equally real, alive, whole, and continuous. Such a basically ontologically secure person will encounter all the hazards of life, social, ethical, spiritual, biological, from a centrally firm sense of his own and other people's reality and identity.
>
> *(Laing 1990, 39)*

Using the schizophrenic as a counterpoint, Laing carves out a quintessential characteristic of mental health and personal autonomy: an existential and thus ontological posture, where an individual feels secure about her own identity, the role of other persons as counterparts in life, and the existence of a continuous environment, a (material) world around them. Thus, it is the very being-in-the-world of the subject in a "real, alive, whole, and continuous" way that the concept of ontological security grasps. Without it, mental instability or even madness lurks around the corner. Hence, ontological security is a "basic need" (Mitzen 2006a).

Anthony Giddens complements this psychological insight from a sociological perspective. He elucidates that, in our current state of late modernity, a heightened need for self-reflexivity, positioning, and identity formation is needed due to the disorienting dynamics of what geographer David Harvey has coined "time-space compression" (Harvey 1989, 4ff) and Giddens calls time-space distanciation:

> Transformations in self-identity and globalization, I want to propose, are the two poles of the dialectic of the local and the global in conditions of high modernity.... the level of time-space distanciation introduced by high modernity is so extensive that, for the first time in human history, "self" and "society" are interrelated in a global milieu.
>
> *(Giddens 1991, 32)*

Almost everyone is immersed today in a globally connected world and has to position themselves within.

This "global milieu" through which self and society now navigate their ways confronts the individual—and as other authors in political geography and international relations have argued, also the state (Huysmans 1998; Mitzen 2006a; 2006b; Hyndman and Giles 2016)—with the pressing task of (re)considering, (re)inventing, (re)building, or (re)affirming the feelings and notions of ontological security. For Giddens, this implies providing answers to existential "questions about ourselves, others, and the object-world" (Giddens 1991, 37). The less ontological security exists, the less agency is possible. Because it is only if we know who we are, and in which world we live, that we can know and decide what to do—and why. The threat of meaninglessness has to be countered by the construction of a reassuring identity. "Armed with ontological security, the individual will know how to act and therefore how to be herself" (Mitzen 2006a, 345).

Yet, if ontological security is partial, volatile, or not fully achieved by an individual, then—as Laing argues from a psychological perspective and Giddens from a sociological standpoint—anxieties are bound to arise. These anxieties are existential, because they concern the very relationship between self and world. Moreover, they are ontological, because they are rooted in the mode of being in the world. In contrast to fear, anxiety is "free floating: lacking a specific object" (Giddens 1991, 44). Hence, the very amorphous character of globalization processes, their disperse, fluid, and abstract dynamics, make them prone to stir anxieties. While fear relates to an "objective danger" that can be located in the world "out there," anxiety has no object that could be located in a particular place. "Anxiety is characterized by the fact that what threatens is nowhere" (Heidegger 2001, 231). Anxiety confronts us with our self, our being-in-the-world.

Consequently, reflecting back on some of the phenomena discussed in the introduction, such as Brexit, America First, and the rise of right-wing parties, we come to understand that these political currents, which are heavily based on nationalist identity politics, are strongly (but of course not exclusively) linked to ontological insecurity. Voting for national independency, strengthening national borders, and stirring feelings of fear towards strangers are practices of navigating the self and society through a global milieu. It involves taking a spatialized (i.e. often nationalized) stance towards global challenges and thereby fostering ontological security of the self through—equally social and territorial—exclusion.

Thus, besides other important factors such as political persuasions and racism, ontological insecurity helps to understand the multidimensional roots of right-wing populism. It particularly adds the existential dimension of the subject, its self-identity, and being-in-the-world to the discourse. Long before Brexit and similar nationalist identity movements occurred, Catarina Kinnvall was already arguing in 2004 that globalization destabilizes and even threatens self-identities and, thereby, nationalism and religious orthodoxies become "simple answers" (Kinnvall 2004, 742). She claims that people who are "uprooted from their original social milieu" and feel overwhelmed and confronted by the uncertainties of a globalized world could tend "to 'de-modernize,'" by which she means essentializing their own national or religious identity and even: "Going back to an imagined past" (Kinnvall 2004, 744). Such a backward-oriented, essentializing securitization of subject identities is as powerful as it is costly for those constructed as the inferior "Other." "Increasing ontological security for one person or group by means of nationalist or religious myths and traumas is thus likely to decrease security for those not included in the nationalist and/or religious discourse" (Kinnvall 2004, 763).

Therefore, the pressing personal and societal task of searching for ontological security in a globalized world is never innocent. It is highly power-loaded. And on that account, it bears an enormous responsibility for self and other. It is here, we argue, that a spatialized, intrinsically geographic perspective on ontological security can deeply enhance and complement the existing psychological reflections on the self and sociological reflections on late modernity. In what follows, we argue that there are particular geographical imaginations that people hold that help them to establish ontological security in a globalized world.

A spatialized approach: how to achieve ontological security in a globalized world

In our empirical research, we found particular spatial strategies that are deployed to achieve ontological security in the face of globalization in the 21st century. Drawing on insights from our interviews and inspired by a geographic reading of the relevant literature, we suggest three ways by which individuals can attain ontological security by spatial means. For this purpose, the notion of a "geographical imagination," which was profoundly conceptualized by David Harvey, is central to our argument. Because Harvey's notion of the geographical imagination elaborates what is truly at stake: the geographical imagination

> enables the individual to recognize the role of space and place in his (sic) own biography, to relate to the spaces he sees around him, and to recognize how transactions between individuals and between organizations are affected by the space that separates them. It allows him to recognize the relationship which exists between him and his neighborhood, his territory, or, to use the language of the street gangs, his "turf." It allows him to judge the relevance of events in other places (on other peoples' "turf")—to judge whether the march of communism in Vietnam, Thailand and Laos is or is not relevant to him wherever he is now. It allows him also to fashion and use space creatively and to appreciate the meaning of the spatial forms created by others.
>
> *(Harvey 1973 quoted in Harvey 2005, 212)*

This geographical imagination becomes central when we reassure ourselves in times of disorienting societal dynamics. In geographical imaginations, we enunciate spatial practices and routines that help us stabilize our own identities and position ourselves in the changing world. Imaginations evoke power—they shape practices and social orders. Moreover, imaginations are influenced by the subject's embodied intersectionality (Gieseking 2017). In what follows, we present three particular dimensions of geographical imaginations that help our interviewees to feel ontologically secure in a globalized world: through imaginations and practices of a) geopolitical positioning, b) home-making, and c) nature-related routines.

Geopolitical positioning

A fundamental task that has to be surmounted in order to establish ontological security is designing and developing a subjective understanding of the world in which the individual is living. Individuals have to situate themselves in the world. For this purpose, they require a conception of the social order in which they are living. Furthermore, an understanding of the world in the broader sense of a *Weltbild* helps to situate, locate, position, and thus anchor individuals in their lives. The literature often stresses the relevance of developing a notion of a *social* order, referring to a general idea about the normative and symbolic order of society, which helps the individual to remain ontologically secure (Huysmans 1998, 242). However, we argue that this rather non-spatial contemplation of social order does not fully address the particularly spatial identity challenges posed by globalization—neither for the individual nor for the state.

The ability to "judge the events in other places" and relate them to the spaces we see around us, as Harvey (2005, 212) puts it, is a truly spatial positioning of the self and a consistent topic running through our interviews in Berlin (Genz et al. 2021). We encountered many narratives of geographical imaginations—for example, Ukraine and the Russian occupation of the Crimea, the Syrian war and its consequences for the situation of refugees in Germany—where Berlin citizens of all ages, genders, and class backgrounds tried to make sense of the new world order, Berlin's situation, and their own place therein. Through photo-elicitation interviews, where representations of various spatial settings were provided as visual stimuli for narration and interpretation, it became crystal clear how extensive people's efforts were to try to make sense of major geopolitical shifts in order to achieve ontological security in their everyday lives.

In one of our interviews, a 50-year-old man who lives in a small apartment on the outskirts of Berlin provided us with his account of the 'Berlin truck attack' in the year 2016, when a truck driver deliberately drove into a Christmas market in Berlin, leaving 12 people dead and 56 injured. This assault was vividly debated in the German media, primarily in the context of rising Islamist terrorism in Europe and the United States. Our interviewee expressed his concerns in the form of a geopolitical reading and positioning of the event.

> Uncertainty, ambiguous, it's both. . . . I am just saying how much has happened since the attack here [in Berlin] last year or two years ago, the Christmas market. You can understand other countries that are handling these issues differently, of course, where that doesn't happen, but as I said, we haven't had

a war since 1945. . . . And I don't want to experience one either, but we . . . don't know where we are heading, and there is this political uncertainty. And that was also a reason why I wanted to stay here in Germany.

(Interview B5, 143)

The perceived uncertainties and ambiguity of the new geopolitical order become visible in the interviewee's wish to attain ontological security by geographical means, geopolitical positioning, for instance: his desire to "stay here in Germany." As the interview quote illustrates, it is the very spatial dimension of our positionality and being in the world that requires reinterpretation. Particularly, the identity question has returned in its most spatial sense. This is also what the rise of nationalist populism signifies (Steger and James 2019).

Thus, as feminist dialectical thinking has argued all along, it is important to understand international politics and geopolitical events as always "co-constituted with the local, the intimate and private subjectivities" (Botterill, Hopkins, and Sanghera 2019, 468). The literature on feminist geopolitics has convincingly shown how important it is—in these uncertain and confusing times even more so—to attend to the embodied geopolitics of everyday life, and thus to scrutinize and understand the struggles and perceptions of ordinary people as part of the geopolitical (Botterill, Hopkins, and Sanghera 2019; Dowler and Sharp 2001; Hyndman 2004, 2019; Pain and Smith 2008). The interconnectedness of multiple scales related to (ontological) security run through our interviews and the narrative presentations of self as a recurring topic.

Anthony Giddens has posited that ontological security is primarily based on conceptions of social order that are part of the unconscious and practical consciousness, and enlivened in routines. Based on our research, we claim that the opposite holds true as well: people also struggle consciously and cognitively to make sense of the complex shifts in our contemporary geopolitical situation. Being reflexive and conscious about the social order and our own positioning therein creates the opportunity to reflect on privileges (being held, how they are distributed, or being lost); it could also bear the potential of an empowering moment, with the discovery of people in the same (deprived) geopolitical position. In any case, ontological security can only be attained if individuals achieve a trustworthy and reliable geographical imagination that frames and supports their positioning. To more fully understand these relations, much further feminist geopolitical research is necessary.

Home-making

Making yourself at home is yet another highly important spatial practice that is strongly linked with procuring ontological security. In our interviews, deep, subjective, emotional meanings of "home" were often brought up by the respondents as a necessary precondition for their ontological security (Pohl et al. 2020). In fact, it was often the first place they mentioned when thinking about their well-being and feeling secure. Of course, there is a variety of different factors that can enable the home to be a builder of ontological security. Additionally, what makes for a home has been widely discussed in the literature on housing studies and geographies of home (Blunt and Dowling 2006). The following main characteristics recur in various studies: having a private space free of surveillance; having space to live one's identity and establish it on a daily basis through recurring routines; decorating and creating one's own space in a way that reflects one's sense of belonging and identity (Dupuis and Thorn 1998, 33). Furthermore, this all strongly depends on individual characteristics, such as age, social status, gender, and cultural background. Yet, the very need for a home in order to feel secure echoes through all our interviews. The home becomes a haven to retreat to and nurture one's subjective sense of identity.

Nevertheless, feelings of being at home do not necessarily correlate with the material place of living. People refer to places they have never been as their "home" or that they have lost after moving somewhere else. Thus, for most people, a profound sense of security does not involve living at their material home as a place of residence, but rather is connected to the feeling of belonging. With regard to a more abstract understanding of home as the imagined place of belonging, we aim to sensitize present for wider notions of home through imaginations.

In urban studies, home has long since been considered a space of individualization and intimate personal development (Bahrdt 1961). Thus, it is not surprising that the home also plays a major role in shaping ontological security. Interestingly enough, though, the form of tenure is not a determining factor whatsoever. Home owners are by no means more inclined to be ontologically secure (Hiscock et al. 2001). Although the ideology of a homeowner society suggests (Saunders 1990) that homeowners feel more secure in their lives, this does not hold true when tested empirically (Behring and Helbrecht 2002; Elsvinga et al. 2007).

It was Ronald D. Laing who observed early on: "When there is uncertainty of identity in time, there is a tendency to rely on spatial means of identifying oneself" (Laing 1990, 109). Ever since, numerous studies involving homeowners, social renters, and even homeless people have confirmed that "housing can provide a fundamental building block for ontological security" (Padgett 2007, 1937). Hence, ontological security is "strongly linked to the material environment" (Dupuis and Thorn 1998, 30) and the material practices of building oneself a home—a critical source of ontological security that tends to be overlooked in most sociological or political discussions. An embodied way of expressing the own being in the world is of great importance (Giddens 1991, 53ff).

For this embodiment to take place, it is crucial to insist that no material environment can "in-itself" bring about ontological security. What it requires is a subject who feels emotionally attached to their environment—the subject has to "occupy" this place both physically and mentally.

> If we narrow our home down to only one place, then there should be free space and room for oneself. Space in which you are not so restricted and can simply let your thoughts flow freely, for example. . . . but otherwise, it is also

connected strongly with feelings and people. The feeling that, if you are in this room with your best friends or your boyfriend, it can feel like home.
(Interview B20, 39)

Therefore, home is not limited to "the physical structure of a house"; rather, it relates to the moment "when such spaces are inscribed with meaning" (Easthope 2004, 135). Hence, home always involves the subjective labor and process of home-making in order to create a sense of ontological security through being at home.

Nature-related routines

Routines are per se a common denominator for the production of ontological security (Mitzen 2006a; 2006b, 349; Kinnvall 2004). Through the establishment of (daily) routines, frightening questions and fundamental doubts about ontological insecurity are kept at bay. In the literature, it is disputed whether these routines are rather unconscious practices, which in Giddens' terminology are enlivened as part of the practical consciousness (Giddens 1991), or whether people consciously try to establish routines in order to tackle ontological insecurity (Dupuis and Thorn 1998, 30). In any case, routines and customs are created over time. It is this trust in one's routines and habits in particular that can act as a buffer:

> In the unstable world of endless change characterized by the trust deficit, the trust in habit offers a very powerful proposition on how to manage the discontinuity, how to enhance the predictability of surroundings through compressing action and how to train for embracing progression and change.
> *(Misztal 2019, 57)*

Based on our Berlin case study, it is clear that people establish a routine in their everyday life by visiting certain places, which are often in nature. To frequent a certain walk through a park, along a river bank, a lake, or a forest path can help people to reassure themselves of where they are, who they are, and what they want to do. In doing so, this (re)assurance is often experienced through a moment of freedom and independence from social relationships with others, such as friends or family. For instance, in a quote from one of our interviews, a person talked about the reason behind his passion for lonely walks in the woods: "Because I am alone and I can breathe in nature or the smells there and I am shielded from the noise of the city" (Interview B14, 36).

Giddens already foresaw the special role nature might play in the formation of ontological security today. In spaces of nature, he claimed, people could feel at ease with their being-in-the-world (Dupuis and Thorn 1998, 28). Our interviewees in Berlin confirm this assumption. People from various age groups, genders, and social backgrounds reported that it is in spaces of nature—in the woods, at the seaside, in the mountains, or wherever personal preferences take them—where they root, regain, and recharge their ontological security. "It is calm and also alive. I love green. And I love nature anyway. I feel very connected, I can relax. So, I can thaw there" (Interview B13, 41). It is reasonable to assume that places in nature function as counterspaces to the highly engineered, urbanized, and fast-moving environment most of our interviewees experience in their globalized everyday lives. The possibility to see, smell, and feel utterly emerged in "pristine nature" becomes a rare opportunity against the backdrop of planetary urbanization. Especially in the Anthropocene, where it becomes increasingly difficult (if not impossible) to view nature as being separated from humanity, a new quest for nature and natural habitats might begin.

Global anxieties, global identity, and global citizenship

Globalization has changed just about everything. Through processes of international marketization, migration, communication, colonization, and economic and cultural exchange, the world has shrunk while expanding at the same time. Globalization processes have connected and uprooted, disembedded, and transformed the lives and perceptions of people around the globe. From Calcutta to Cologne, from Helsinki to Hong Kong, from Johannesburg to Rio de Janeiro: we are witnessing "the making and unmaking of new models of global citizenship" (Roy 2016, 27). This implies the many ways that people in different places, from different generations and with different social backgrounds, imagine themselves to be "empowered global citizens" who live in and shape a global milieu (Roy 2016, 27). However, in contrast to hopes for a global cosmopolitanism, in the UK, on the European continent, and in the United States, nationalism and religious orthodoxy are on the rise again (Kinnvall 2004).

In this chapter, we have used the concept of ontological security to explore the depth and extension of globalization anxieties. When we speak of ontological security, existential questions are always implied. If we scrutinize globalization anxieties as the emergence of ontological *in*security, and thus as an intrinsic dynamic in the relationship between the subject and the world, we can start to find answers to questions surrounding the new ontological positioning of the self in relation to processes of globalization and time-space compression.

Therefore, we argue that a spatialized understanding of ontological security—in other words, the use of a geographical imagination—not only will allow us to understand the immense irritations and uncertainties that are stirred up by globalization (and the fundamental spatial transformations that are evoked in turn), but also becomes an alley of thought that helps us understand how to build ontological security in times of globalization. Based on our empirical research in Berlin and a geographic reading of the literature, we have shown how immensely important a spatialized understanding of globalization anxiety is. Spatial phenomena are of utmost importance in order to understand how ontological security can be attained.

The empirical evidence from our Berlin case points towards three modes of spatial practices that people deploy to personally deal with the fundamental anxieties stirred by spatial transformations: a) by developing geographical imaginations of new geopolitical positionings; b) by establishing imaginative practices of home-making and attaching meaning to home; and c) by routinely seeking out spaces in nature that help root as well as regain and charge ontological security through the reassertion of one's self-identity. We have shown how a spatial approach can help to understand these modes as particular strategies to resist the insecurities emanating from (economic) globalization. These spatial practices and strategies are ways to achieve ontological security in a globalized world with which we want to engage in the future. Our empirical research is comprised of a comparative study, in which we will also compare our Berlin findings with interviews from Singapore and Vancouver. A future task of ours will be to compare the geographical imaginations of nature, home, and geopolitical positions and their particular role for the projection of ontological security in different geographic settings.

Yet, we can already surmise from our Berlin interviews that the spatial transformation called "globalization" poses a significant challenge to most people's sense of ontological security. Though our Berlin interviewees have established for themselves meaningful geographical imaginations that help them feel ontologically secure, none of our respondents have deliberately declared themselves a "global citizen." Nobody saw their self-identity connected to cosmopolitanism or referred to themselves as *Weltbürgerin* (i.e. global citizen). Hence, if we reflect on the paradox that nationalist and xenophobic attitudes are on the rise in spite of globalization, it seems reasonable to argue that the spatial transformation called globalization has been fairly limited thus far. It has not achieved or led to a global identity of the (late) modern subject. The many spatial transformations and refigurations implied by globalization to date seem only to have adhered to a rather one-dimensional refiguration of institutional spaces in politics and the capitalist economy (Helbrecht et al. 2021): the establishment of tariff unions, international supply chains, immigration policies, new branches of the United Nations, and the like. Yet, at the level of the subject, limited answers to this worldwide economic and political transformation prevail, such as walking in nature, making a home, and geopolitical reasoning and repositioning. Therefore, we would argue, it is the one-sidedness of current globalization processes, i.e. their economic and political reductionism, that hinders the formation of a subjective global identity.

All things considered, since spatiality is an integral part of globalization and time-space compression, it is also within the realm of the spatiality of self, society, and world that we can find constructive answers to the current challenges and threats of ontological insecurity. To include the perspective of the everyday and the subject into research on globalization has long been an important demand of feminist scholars (Hyndman 2019). Particularly on issues of security and insecurity, the contributions from feminist geopolitics have been numerous (Williams and Massaro 2013). If we want to prevent a relapse to nationalist populist sentiments in Germany (and elsewhere) and achieve ontological security in times of globalization, it seems mandatory that we continue our move towards feminist geopolitical research. Only if we address the existential, ontological, and spatial identity challenges posed by economic globalization can we tackle the dangerous nationalist and xenophobic currents—on a personal as well as on a social scientific basis. This shift in perspective towards a feminist geopolitics is at least twofold. First, it includes a focus on the embodied subjects and the everyday. Second, a "feminist understanding of globalization requires substantial conceptual, analytical, and epistemological shifts" (Nagar et al. 2002, 279). By this, we mean the necessity to address globalization and the ontological insecurity it stirs as truly spatial processes that can only be fully understood through the deployment of a geographic perspective.

Acknowledgements

This research has been funded by the Deutsche Forschungsgemeinschaft (DFG, German Research Foundation)—project number 290045248—SFB 1265. We are grateful to Miro Born, Ylva Kürten, and Yannick Ecker for conducting the interviews we refer to in this chapter and to Henning Füller for inspirational theoretical debates in the early stages of the research project.

Note

1 For a detailed account of our research method, see Dobrusskin et al. (2021).

References

Anselmi, Manuel. 2018. *Populism: An Introduction*. New York, London: Routledge.
Bahrdt, Hans P. 1961. *Die moderne Großstadt: Soziologische Überlegungen zum Städtebau*. Opladen: Verlag für Sozialwissenschaften.
Behring, Karin, and Ilse Helbrecht. 2002. *Wohneigentum in Europa. Ursachen und Rahmenbedingungen unterschiedlicher Eigentumsquoten im Vergleich*. Ludwigsburg: Wüstenrot Stiftung.
Blunt, Alison, and Robyn Dowling. 2006. *Home*. London: Routledge.
Botterill, Kate, Peter Hopkins, and Gurchathen S. Sanghera. 2019. "Young People's Everyday Securities: Pre-emptive and Pro-active Strategies towards Ontological Security in Scotland." *Social & Cultural Geography* 20 (4): 465–484.
Dirksmeier, Peter, and Ilse Helbrecht. 2015a. "Everyday Urban Encounters as Stratification Practices: Analysing Affects in Micro-situations of Power Struggles." *City* 19 (4): 486–498.
Dirksmeier, Peter, and Ilse Helbrecht. 2015b. "Resident Perceptions of New Urban Tourism: A Neglected Geography of Prejudice." *Geography Compass* 9 (5): 276–285.
Dobrusskin, Janina, Ilse Helbrecht, Miro Born, and Carolin Genz. 2021. "Bildgestützte Interviews in der Raumforschung: Potenziale der Foto-Elizitation." In *Handbuch qualitativer Methoden der Raumforschung*, edited by Anna J. Heinrich, Séverine Marguin, Angela Million, and Jörg Stollmann, 209–221. Bielefeld: transcript.
Dowler, Lorraine, and Joanne Sharp. 2001. "A Feminist Geopolitics?" *Space and Polity* 5 (3): 165–176.
Dupuis, Ann, and David C. Thorn. 1998. "Home, Home Ownership and the Search for Ontological Security." *The Sociological Review* 46 (1): 24–47.
Easthope, Hazel. 2004. "A Place Called Home." *Housing, Theory and Society* 21: 128–138.

Elsvinga, Marja, Jannike Toussaint, Gudrun Tegeder, and Ilse Helbrecht. 2007. "Security and Insecurity of Housing. Comparing the Netherlands and Germany." *European Journal of Housing Policy* 7 (2): 173–192.

Genz, Carolin, Lucas Pohl, Janina Dobrusskin, and Ilse Helbrecht. 2021. "Geopolitical Caesuras as Time-Space-Anchors of Ontological (In)security: The Case of the Fall of the Berlin Wall." *Geopolitics* (online first). doi: 10.1080/14650045.2021.1912021.

Giddens, Anthony. 1991. *Modernity and Self-Identity*. Stanford: Stanford University Press.

Gieseking, Jen J. 2017. "Geographical Imagination." In *International Encyclopedia of Geography: People, the Earth, Environment and Technology*, edited by Douglas Richardson, Noel Castree, Michael F. Goodchild, Audrey Kobayashi, Liu Weidong, and Richard A. Marston. Oxford: Wiley-Blackwell.

Harvey, David. 1973. *Social Justice and the City*. Athens: University of Georgia Press.

Harvey, David. 1989. *The Condition of Postmodernity: An Enquiry into the Origins of Cultural Change*. Oxford: Blackwell.

Harvey, David. 2005. "The Sociological and Geographical Imaginations." *International Journal of Politics, Culture, and Society* 18 (3): 211–255.

Heidegger, Martin. 2001. *Being and Time*. Oxford: Blackwell.

Helbrecht, Ilse, Lucas Pohl, Carolin Genz, and Janina Dobrusskin. 2021. "Imaginationen der Globalisierung." In *Am Ende der Globalisierung*, edited by Martina Löw, Volkan Sayman, Jona Schwerer, and Hannah Wolf, 307–336. Bielefeld: transcript.

Hiscock, Rosemary, Ade Kearns, Sally MacIntyre, and Anne Ellaway. 2001. "Ontological Security and the Psycho-Social Benefits from the Home: Qualitative Evidence on Issues of Tenure." *Housing, Theory and Society* 18 (1): 50–66.

Huysmans, Jef. 1998. "Security! What Do You Mean? From Concept to Thick Signifier." *European Journal of International Relations* 4 (2): 226–255.

Hyndman, Jennifer. 2004. "Mind the Gap: Bridging Feminist and Political Geography through Geopolitics." *Political Geography* 23 (3): 307–322.

Hyndman, Jennifer. 2019. "Unsettling Feminist Geopolitics: Forging Feminist Political Geographies of Violence and Displacement." *Gender, Place & Culture* 26 (1): 3–29.

Hyndman, Jennifer, and Wenona Giles. 2016. *Refugees in Extended Exile*. London, New York: Routledge.

Kinnvall, Catarina. 2004. "Globalization and Religious Nationalism: Self, Identity, and the Search for Ontological Security." *Political Psychology* 25 (5): 741–767.

Laing, Ronald D. 1990. *The Divided Self: An Existential Study in Sanity and Madness*. London: Penguin Books.

Matthews, Julie, and Ravinder Sidhu. 2005. "Desperately Seeking the Global Subject: International Education, Citizenship and Cosmopolitanism." *Globalisation, Societies and Education* 3 (1): 49–66.

Misztal, Barbara A. 2019. "Trust in Habit: A Way of Coping in Unsettled Times." In *Trust in Contemporary Society*, edited by Masamichi Sasaki, 41–59. Leiden and Boston: Brill Academic Publishers.

Mitzen, Jennifer. 2006a. "On Ontological Security in World Politics: State Identity and the Security Dilemma." *European Journal of International Relations* 12 (3): 341–370.

Mitzen, Jennifer. 2006b. "Anchoring Europe's Identity: Habits, Capabilities and Ontological Security." *Journal of European Public Policy* 13 (2): 270–285.

Nagar, Richa, Victoria Lawson, Linda McDowell, and Susan Hanson. 2002. "Locating Globalization: Feminist (Re)readings of the Subjects and Spaces of Globalization." *Economic Geography* 78 (3): 257–284.

Padgett, Deborah. 2007. "There's No Place like(a)Home: Ontological Security among Persons with Serious Mental Illness in the United States." *Social Science & Medicine* 64 (9): 1925–1963.

Pain, Rachel, and Susan J. Smith, eds. 2008. *Fear: Critical Geopolitics and Everyday Life*. Burlington: Ashgate.
Pohl, Lucas, Carolin Genz, Ilse Helbrecht, and Janina Dobrusskin. 2020. "Need for Shelter, Demand for Housing, Desire for Home: A Psychoanalytic Reading of Home-Making in Vancouver." *Housing Studies* (online first). doi: 10.1080/02673037.2020.1857708.
Roy, Ananya. 2016. "Encountering Poverty." In *Encountering Poverty: Thinking and Acting in an Unequal World*, edited by Ananya Roy, Genevieve Negrón-Gonzales, Kweku Opoku-Agyeang, and Clare Talwalker, 21–50. Oakland: University of California Press.
Sassen, Saskia, ed. 2013. *Deciphering the Global: Its Scales, Spaces, and Subjects*. London, New York: Routledge.
Saunders, Peter. 1990. *A Nation of Home Owners*. London: Unwin Hyman.
Steger, Manfred, and Paul James. 2019. "Making Sense of the Populist Challenge to Globalization." In *Globalization Matters: Engaging the Global in Unsettled Times*, edited by Manfred Steger and Paul James, 187–208. Cambridge: Cambridge University Press.
Verwaltungsgericht Meiningen. 2019. "Judgement from September 26, 2019." Reference number (Aktenzeichen) 2 E 1194/19 Me. http://www.thovg.thueringen.de/webthfj/webthfj.nsf/$$webservice?openform&vgmeiningen&entscheidungen
Williams, Jill, and Vanessa Massaro. 2013. "Feminist Geopolitics: Unpacking (In)Security, Animating Social Change." *Geopolitics* 18 (4): 751–758.

19

WHERE WE TURN TO

Rethinking networks, urban space, and research methods

Talja Blokland, Daniela Krüger, Robert Vief, and Henrik Schultze

To whom do we turn for support, and *where*?

Activists and policymakers often assume that neighborhoods are significant for social support. Sociologists have a strong tradition of studying how social support develops and sustains in physical proximity of "neighborhoods." They study mobility as *interfering* with networks, neighborhoods, and an assumed warmth and strength of urban communities. Public concerns with individualization, lost community, and urban loneliness (Blokland 2017) reflect a re-assessment of personal ties in European cities in particular. Moreover, with the retreat of welfare states, Europeans have had to adjust to a rescaling of citizenship to the urban dimension (Blokland et al. 2015) and to state reorganization (Le Galès 2002).

Organizing non-state support was always standard in most cities worldwide (Swaan 1990). A comparative gesture (Robinson 2006) immediately highlights that beyond the state, getting things done may take different paths than fixed forms of social, cultural, and economic capital (Schilling, Blokland, and Simone 2019). Indeed, improvisations produce unplanned exchanges: urban ways of organizing resources are not often included, directly or routinely, in network-based sociology (Schilling, Blokland, and Simone 2019). Additionally, while cities have always attracted arrivals, globalization made routes longer. The *network society* (Castells 1996) refigures space in new ways (Knoblauch and Löw 2017). Translocal mobility has increased and distance no longer poses a significant hindrance to staying in touch. Thus, support *cannot* be simply assumed to be local.

Social capital, ties, closeness

Social capital, mostly defined as people's possibilities to get by or ahead (Briggs 1998) by virtue of embeddedness in social networks (Bourdieu 1986; Putnam

DOI: 10.4324/9781003036159-23

2000; Portes 1998; Granovetter 1973), is central for measuring support. Scholars have mapped people's networks and investigated how neighborhood ties provide social capital (Völker and Flap 2007; Forrest and Kearns 2001; Middleton, Murie, and Groves 2005) in poverty concentration areas (Marques 2012; Wilson 2012; Rankin and Quane 2000; Osterling 2007) or mixed neighborhoods (Blokland and van Eijk 2010; Musterd and Andersson 2005; Galster 2007). Others asked whether moving from deprived neighborhoods produces new capital (Goering and Feins 2003; Curley 2010; Barwick 2016; Briggs, Popkin, and Goering 2010). Most studies share two ideas. First, they differentiate between strong, weak, and (sometimes) absent or invisible ties (Felder 2020). Second, they imply similar notions of how inequalities operate within those ties.

The usual differentiation between strong/weak/absent ties draws on Granovetter (1973). While absent ties—"'nodding' relationship between people living on the same street" (Granovetter 1973, 1361)—have long been seen as a non-relationship, social scientists have demonstrated that strong ties to close neighbors, kin, and friends help meeting needs and overcoming crises. In this context, scholars have not always clearly stated whether "closeness" is spatial or emotional, and what defines "emotional closeness." The strength of ties has been perceived as a "(*probably* linear) combination of the amount of time, the emotional intensity, the intimacy (mutual confiding), and the reciprocal services which characterize the tie" (Granovetter 1973, 1361; our italics). Therefore, studies typically measure closeness by *frequency* and reciprocity of help (e.g., Wellman and Wortley 1990; Kornienko et al. 2018) or by how many people respondents know, and how they perceive the tie's strength, then *assuming* an exchange of support (Marsden and Campbell 1984; McCarty 2002). Weak ties expand close-knit ("core") networks and provide information on important subjects such as job opportunities (Granovetter 1995). Scholars generally consider those ties to be unrelated to emotional, intimate support and instrumental, non-affective (Wegener 1991). Low interaction frequency becomes an indicator of weakness. Proximity, moreover, is generally measured by where network members *live* in relation to anchors (Mollenhorst 2015).

All this assumes that frequency creates intimacy, and that closeness means both disclosing secrecy and meeting often. While, practically, spatial closeness—living not far apart—influences interaction frequency even in digital times, especially for concrete forms of transferring things between people, emotional closeness does not depend on proximity. Lending sugar cannot be done over an app with far-away persons, but how far we (digitally) travel for emotionally supporting others may vary greatly. Closeness is curiously underdeveloped as a concept.

Another set of arguments regarding ties raises a similar issue. Sociologists acknowledge that the networked society provokes new kinds of relationships, but their research designs have not changed. A strong body of research has provided evidence that the internet boosts existing, face-to-face ties rather than new ones. Rainie and Wellman (2012) speak of a network revolution, characterized by a shift from group embeddedness (in families, work units, neighborhoods, or other groups) to networked individuals who knit together loosely connected or unrelated social circles. If digital technology has changed how people interact (Rainie and Wellman 2012), and online communication has expanded the reach, number, and velocity of ties (McEwen and Wellman 2013), did we also, maybe, change where and how we seek support? If how we interact has changed, has this also affected the closeness of ties? If group embeddedness has become less essential, is this true for all, or does spatiality affect ties in different ways, depending on agents' access to mobility?

Methodological discussions thus far have, firstly, often concentrated on whether people can recall names in name-generating questions, whether potential support is also activated, and whether weak ties are less commonly noted (see Brewer 2000). Few researchers methodologically discuss the role of space in distinctions between strong, weak, and absent ties.

Secondly, the division between strong/weak ties has been widely adopted in studies on urban inequalities. As poverty is so often studied in geographical pockets, a focus on local ties has developed since classics such as Stacks (1975) or Gans (1962). Studies of poor people start at where they live (e.g., Brisson and Usher 2007; Curley 2010), studies of middle-class people start with what they do, where they travel, and their elective belongingness (Andreotti, Le Galès, and Moreno-Fuentes 2014), and recent work on the super-rich focuses on enclaves (Atkinson 2019; Smithsimon 2010). Literature addressing the value of social mix for poor neighborhoods assumes that weak and strong ties benefit poor urbanites (Kleit 2008; Campbell and Lee 1992; Oliver 1988), suggesting that poor residents only live locally with networks of people residing in the same area, in contrast to affluent residents.

This research perspective prioritizes where we reside over where we spend time. Specific localities can become resource foci (Small 2009)—but this does not imply that network-ties exist close to each other or that all exchanges between residents "grow" into close network ties that name generators can catch. With changing ideas of what social networks are and how they operate, how we study them must also change (Wellman 1996). So, what happens when we do not follow the common ideas of weak/strong/absent ties and do not make "localness" a characteristic of a tie based on where network-members live? In other words: if being in each other's physical presence in a moment of need is an important yet overlooked element of how people organize resources (Small and Sukhu 2016), then where do people receive support?

A focus on practices

While other scholars have also challenged conventions of support and social and spatial proximity (Arbter 2016; Blokland and Nast 2014), Small (2017) formulated the strongest critique on the conceptualization of support in survey-based research. Small and his team conducted two interview rounds with first-year American graduate students. The students' graduate school was often located far away from former networks, thus creating new demands, systems, and sociability. Instead of tracing network ties and then their supportiveness, Small asked what challenges students faced and who supported them. The students often did not turn to strong ties and even kept troubles secret from them. They confided in people with whom they had weak ties: professionals, acquaintances, or strangers "who happened to be there." Small methodologically and empirically dismantled the assumptions that people have a fixed, durable set of people to whom they talk, and that kin and friends equate closeness and intimacy (also: Blokland 2019). It is not that strong ties do not matter, but rather that weak ties have been underestimated. Furthermore, how and why we avoid strong ties has been undertheorized. Small's interview partners give up secrecy (Simmel 1906) by revealing feelings like anxieties and fears. We intuitively tend to say that we share these feelings with closest friends and family. In practice, we do not always do so.

Small (2017) eloquently illustrated that, due to the fact that sociologists have measured (especially emotional) support rather non-reflexively from one research project to the next because variables "worked," we may have failed to see what happens in practice. From a different angle, we have argued in a similar direction (Blokland 2017; Blokland and Nast 2014) by showing that the division between strong/weak/absent ties neglects the contextual or spatial dimension of tie formation and maintenance. Whereas Small (2017) shows that in whom we confide depends partly on who happens to be there, we argued that support must not per definition come from strong or even weak ties. Instead, urban sociologists should pay special attention to absent ties. Neighborhood use patterns or running into the same people locally does not automatically result in fixed sets of ties that show up in network surveys, but can establish public familiarity (Blokland and Nast 2014, 1146). While moving with ease in such zones, we can engage casually with people who do not fit into categories of weak/strong ties (Blokland and Nast 2014, 1146). Yet, casual encounters may result in support and information. The extent to which they do so is not known: how sociologists study support has not included absent ties extensively (exception: Arbter 2016). Could public familiarity facilitate resourceful exchanges? Do only resources resulting from embeddedness in social networks constitute social capital, or can access to resources be acquired, maintained, or situationally negotiated more fleetingly (see Blokland et al. 2016)?

Part of the problem is confusion about the role of networks in social capital definitions—an overall connectivity of individuals, a web of affiliations (Simmel 1955)—with their meaning in survey measurements—names egos give. An in-depth understanding of work with social capital requires understanding it as more than bonds/bridges. We may want to move away from a preoccupation with ties to one with practices (Blokland and Nast 2014; Blokland et al. 2016).

When we map people's networks and then measure their actual/potential support, we assume that we only get help from people we know, that ties must exist before being activated, and that gifts follow from ties. Starting with practices opens new perspectives. A gift may initiate a tie (Mauss 2002). Confiding can start a relationship, so that a person does not appear on a strong ties list when researchers ask their questions. Confiding in people we do not know well may have low risks of sanctions or debts. Seeking support in crises with close ties assumes shared norms. For some LGBTQ people coming out, religious people leaving their faith, seeking support with family and friends may not be an option. Less emotional labor may be involved when confiding in non-close ties: we do not have to think as much about what meaning personal concerns carry for others. If sociologists rely on (and reify) categories like friends, family, or neighbors and assume social qualities (e.g., intimacy, proximity, availability), we may forget that ties change and are never fixed (Blokland 2017, 65; Mollenhorst, Volker, and Flap 2014). Thus, we direct attention to potential productivity of interactions outside personal networks.

For this purpose, like Small (2017), we must incorporate contexts. The context of Small's students, however, was particular: they had institutionalized meeting moments. Elsewhere, Small (2009) also strongly argued that organizations may provide support. However, not all organizations do so equally: organizations with a high degree of institutionalized interactions like courts or emergency departments may do so differently than those with low routines, such as cafes, bars, clubs (Oldenburg and Brissett 1982), or bus stops (Desmond 2012). As such, the spatiality of meeting moments matters and provides people with different opportunities for "meeting and mating" (Small and Adler 2019).

Studies with qualitative research designs have already made these points. Most network researchers work with quantitative data for good reason. To bridge this, we thus must construct context-based but not context-specific surveys. Rather than asking issue-based questions to inquire into social networks (examples: Petermann 2015; Pfenning and Schenk 2014; Fischer 1982; Wellman and Wortley 1990), we may ask people, first, about which challenges they have recently faced, then who supported them, and finally where they and their supporter physically were at the moment of interaction.

Moreover, a great deal of literature emphasizes in situ face-to-face conversation for support. But increasing mobility and technological change may refigure the networks' spatiality, as noted earlier. We agree that the spatial dimension "is not just an accidental aspect but a basic feature of sociality" (Knoblauch and Löw 2017, 11) and, in order to be able to thoroughly analyze processes of refiguration in social support, quantitative studies of social networks need to acknowledge the importance of the spatial dimension in survey tools. We may recognize, more than is currently the case in research on support, the relevance of spatiality and materiality for unequal access to social support.

Bringing practices to the quantitative study of social support

Qualitative analyses of people's personal challenges could suggest that more open approaches are not quantifiable (or not comparable), or that surveys (by definition) do not allow for more reflexive measurements (Wyly 2011). We think they do and propose measuring personal networks in urban settings by inverting several common survey logics. While studies on place-based social capital and neighborhood effects studies address neighborhoods to measure social relations, we propose only using the residence of people as a starting point to follow their practices. It is common practice in survey research to pre-define what support means. Surveys typically inquire about events that supposedly matter most for respondents. Many of these surveys are inspired by Fischer (1982) and revise, extend, and modify individual items. In doing so, surveys construct a set of fixed, hypothetical events (see ISSP 2000, 11–12): "Who would be the person taking care of your apartment when you're not in town," "Who would you get help from if you had the flu," or "Who are you going to go to when you want to borrow some money?" Other typical questions cover social actions within defined timespans (Mollenhorst, Volker, and Flap 2014; Pfenning and Schenk 2014; Fischer 1982; Bernard et al. 1990; Bien, Marbach, and Neyer 1991; Marsden 1987): "Who did you invite for dinner at your apartment over the last three months?"

Most ego-centered network surveys focus on social exchanges (e.g., sociability, emotional trust or functional daily help), mixing questions about real and hypothetical social actions and meetings (Burt 1984). This raises four issues:

1) Hypothetical assessment ("Who would do XY for you?") has a cognitive bias (Small and Sukhu 2016) and does not mean that respondents would actually receive support if the scenario were to occur ("A/B/C did XY for me").

2) Some surveys ask about events and encounters without inquiring about support: contacts are measured, not what actually happens. For example, persons invited for dinner over the last few months may have accepted the invitations for various reasons. What happens over dinner depends on who else is there, what the occasion was, whether kids joined the dinner table, etcetera. Was the dinner a moment of support? Dinners can be gaining (discussing emotional problems over a good plate of food in a relaxed setting) or draining (the socially desirable invite of parents-in-law sparks old conflicts). All in all, the names of who came for dinner feed equally on the social capital indicator; yet they reveal little more than the fact that people ate together.

3) Surveys often pre-define communication modes, reproducing 1980s ideas of valuable support without considering digitalization. Is it always more important to talk to someone face-to-face when having dinner than texting on the subway? Are voice messages less resourceful than a pub chat? Does seeing each other matter for all support? And if not, for which scenarios?

4) Existing research makes assumptions on how respondents use space to get support. Survey questions mapping networks tend to require or imply spatial proximity of the alter/ego. They specifically construct encounters in households or nearby facilities (such as bars and restaurants). Such constructs may overlook new (digital) forms of where we turn to others.

In short, many survey-based studies of ego-centered networks assume that researchers know which scenarios matter most to people, in what spatial context, and through what communication mode.

This contradicts, remarkably, studies on globalization and transnationalism. Analyses of life-style pluralization, mobility, individualization, and increasing life-stage development varieties (Beck and Beck-Gernsheim 2010; Bauman 2013; Giddens 2013; Brüderl 2004; Knoblauch and Löw 2017) suggest that it is increasingly less accurate to assume a priori what forms of support people may need (or are able to provide). Hence, we should follow Small's (2017) openness to support scenarios.

Figure 19.1 summarizes our alternative survey design. We asked participants in face-to-face interviews to tell us about challenges that then became provisional labels. We invited respondents to think of anything from long-term burdens to everyday challenges.[1]

Using the scenario labels, we allow respondents to define their support and where they were when receiving it. We do not assume that ego and alter have met in person, even knew each other previously, or had informal ties: we only seek to learn to whom people turned when facing a challenge. A geocoding tool then recorded where respondents and supporters were and hence the geography of their support. When aggregated, this data assesses the neighborhood relevance: not as a rather un-defined or administratively defined concept, but as a set of possible "hubs" where residents interact to develop and maintain forms of support. While shortcomings exist,[2] this measurement answers the lack of attention to spatiality in network data. The data structure makes it possible to analyze whether social support is local or translocal. It allows us to see whether mobility and migration influence support sites. Finally, we can analyze whether sites where people meet for support form neighborhood hubs, and whether (if at all) neighborhood organizations serve as sites where resources are exchanged between persons.

Concluding thoughts on how our approach addresses support networks differently

Research on support networks so far has worked with certain assumptions that require rethinking of how we measure. Many studies reify the importance of "tie strength" and an understanding of ties that equates closeness with intimacy.

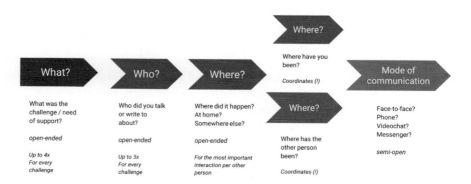

FIGURE 19.1 Alter-ego social support questions: alternative survey design

Source: Robert Vief

This carries a Global North bias (Blokland 2019). We outlined an alternative approach.

Firstly, we suggest employing an open quantitative social network analysis to people's range of supportive interactions. Our tool moves from (strong/weak/absent) ties (and their assumed qualities) to practices. Getting support does not always follow a clear intentionality of contacting certain ties. Our approach incorporates often overlooked fluid encounters and durable engagements.

Secondly, our tool provides new possibilities to map relations, spatial distances, and clusters. By means of spatial references, we can analyze social and spatial variability and inequality in support scenarios (for example, how space mediates support access for poor vs. affluent urbanites).

Thirdly, our tool acknowledges that there are different ways in which people communicate with each other. We should not assume that one form of communication is "right" and more substantially supportive. We can ask respondents to evaluate this for themselves. Gravity binds people to the ground (Gans 2002) but does not define what they mean to others. Mobility and digitalization may produce new networking routes, which we can now capture.

Finally, we reiterate the plea to turn network research upside down (Small 2017) with an appeal to integrate it into spatial contexts. Not only "who we turn to" but also where we turn to others matters for support.

Acknowledgements

This research has been funded by the Deutsche Forschungsgemeinschaft (DFG, German Research Foundation)—project number 290045248—SFB 1265.

Notes

1 "We are interested in where people get their support in the face of great, but also everyday challenges. Challenges are concerns, problems and obstacles that have to be overcome. This can concern work, family, school, health, emotional stress, but also completely different areas. What is or has been a challenge in your everyday life in the last 12 months?" We noted keywords of up to four challenges and used these scenarios in successive questions. People could name up to three alters with whom they talked about a challenge.
2 Like mapping fixed coordinates for scenarios where alter and ego moved (chat during a car ride) or enforcing choice of "most important" interaction when respondents had several important interactions in different contexts.

References

Andreotti, Alberta, Patrick Le Galès, and Francisco J. Moreno-Fuentes. 2014. *Globalised Minds, Roots in the City*. Chichester, UK: John Wiley & Sons.

Arbter, Rebecca. 2016. "Social Ties and the Moral Orientation of Sharing." In *Creating the Unequal City*, edited by Talja Blokland, Carlotta Giustozzi, Daniela Krüger, and Hannah Schilling, 137–156. London: Routledge.

Atkinson, Rowland. 2019. "Necrotecture." *International Journal of Urban and Regional Research* 43 (1): 2–13. doi: 10.1111/1468-2427.12707.

Barwick, Christine. 2016. *Social Mobility and Neighbourhood Choice*. New York: Taylor and Francis.
Bauman, Zygmunt. 2013. *Liquid Modernity*. Hoboken: Wiley.
Beck, Ulrich, and Elisabeth Beck-Gernsheim. 2010. *Individualization*. London: SAGE.
Bernard, H. Russell, Eugene C. Johnsen, Peter D. Killworth, Christopher McCarty, Gene A. Shelley, and Scott Robinson. 1990. "Comparing Four Different Methods for Measuring Personal Social Networks." *Social Networks* 12 (3): 179–215. doi: 10.1016/0378-8733(90)90005-T.
Bien, Walter, Jan Marbach, and Franz Neyer. 1991. "Using Egocentered Networks in Survey Research." *Social Networks* 13 (1): 75–90.
Blokland, Talja. 2017. *Community as Urban Practice*. Malden, MA: Polity Press.
Blokland, Talja. 2019. "Someone to Talk to, by Mario L. Small." *Journal of Urban Affairs* 41 (6): 881–883. doi: 10.1080/07352166.2018.1547548.
Blokland, Talja, Carlotta Giustozzi, Daniela Krüger, and Hannah Schilling, eds. 2016. *Creating the Unequal City*. London: Routledge.
Blokland, Talja, Christine Hentschel, Andrej Holm, Henrik Lebuhn, and Talia Margalit. 2015. "Urban Citizenship and Right to the City." *International Journal of Urban and Regional Research* 39 (4): 655–665. doi: 10.1111/1468-2427.12259.
Blokland, Talja, and Julia Nast. 2014. "From Public Familiarity to Comfort Zone." *International Journal of Urban and Regional Research* 38 (4): 1142–1159.
Blokland, Talja, and Gwen van Eijk. 2010. "Do People Who Like Diversity Practice Diversity in Neighbourhood Life?" *Journal of Ethnic and Migration Studies* 36 (2): 313–332. doi: 10.1080/13691830903387436.
Bourdieu, Pierre. 1986. "The Forms of Capital." In *Handbook of Theory and Research for the Sociology of Education*, edited by John G. Richardson, 241–258. New York: Greenwood Pr.
Brewer, Devon D. 2000. "Forgetting in the Recall-based Elicitation of Personal and Social Networks." *Social Networks* 22 (1): 29–43. doi: 10.1016/S0378-8733(99)00017-9.
Briggs, Xavier de Souza. 1998. "Doing Democracy Up-Close." *Journal of Planning Education and Research* 18 (1): 1–13. doi: 10.1177/0739456X9801800101.
Briggs, Xavier de Souza, Susan J. Popkin, and John M. Goering. 2010. *Moving to Opportunity*. New York: Oxford University Press.
Brisson, Daniel, and Charles L. Usher. 2007. "Conceptualizing and Measuring Bonding Social Capital in Low-Income Neighborhoods." *Journal of Social Service Research* 34 (1): 1–11. doi: 10.1300/J079v34n01_01.
Brüderl, Josef. 2004. "Die Pluralisierung partnerschaftlicher Lebensformen in Westdeutschland und Europa." *Aus Politik und Zeitgeschichte* (19): 3–10.
Burt, Ronald S. 1984. "Network Items and the General Social Survey." *Social Networks* 6 (4): 293–339. doi: 10.1016/0378-8733(84)90007-8.
Campbell, Karen E., and Barrett A. Lee. 1992. "Sources of Personal Neighbor Networks." *Social Forces* 70 (4): 1077–1100. doi: 10.1093/sf/70.4.1077.
Castells, Manuel. 1996. *The Rise of the Network Society*. Oxford: Blackwell.
Curley, Alexandra M. 2010. "Relocating the Poor." *Journal of Urban Affairs* 32 (1): 79–103. doi: 10.1111/j.1467-9906.2009.00475.x.
Desmond, Matthew. 2012. "Disposable Ties and the Urban Poor." *American Journal of Sociology* 117 (5): 1295–1335. doi: 10.1086/663574.
Felder, Maxime. 2020. "Strong, Weak and Invisible Ties." *Sociology* 54 (4): 675–692. doi: 10.1177/0038038519895938.
Fischer, Claude S. 1982. *To Dwell Among Friends*. Chicago: University of Chicago Press.
Forrest, Ray, and Ade Kearns. 2001. "Social Cohesion, Social Capital and the Neighbourhood." *Urban Studies* 38 (12): 2125–2143. doi: 10.1080/00420980120087081.

Galster, George. 2007. "Neighbourhood Social Mix as a Goal of Housing Policy." *European Journal of Housing Policy* 7 (1): 19–43. doi: 10.1080/14616710601132526.
Gans, Herbert J. 1962. *The Urban Villagers*. New York: Free Press.
Gans, Herbert J. 2002. "The Sociology of Space." *City & Community* 1 (4): 329–339. doi: 10.1111/1540-6040.00027.
Giddens, Anthony. 2013. *Modernity and Self-Identity*. Hoboken: Wiley.
Goering, John M., and Judith D. Feins, eds. 2003. *Choosing a Better Life?* Washington: Urban Institute Press.
Granovetter, Mark S. 1973. "The Strength of Weak Ties." *American Journal of Sociology* 78 (6): 1360–1380.
Granovetter, Mark S. 1995. *Getting a Job*. Chicago: University of Chicago Press.
ISSP. 2000. "Social Relations and Support Systems (Social Networks II)." Accessed August 09, 2021. https://dbk.gesis.org/dbksearch/file.asp?file=ZA3680_bq.pdf.
Kleit, Rachel G. 2008. "Neighborhood Segregation, Personal Networks, and Access to Social Resources." In *Segregation*, edited by James H. Carr and Nandinee K. Kutty, 237–260. London: Routledge.
Knoblauch, Hubert, and Martina Löw. 2017. "On the Spatial Re-Figuration of the Social World." *Sociologica* 11 (2): 1–27. doi: 10.2383/88197.
Kornienko, Olga, Victor Agadjanian, Cecilia Menjívar, and Natalia Zotova. 2018. "Financial and Emotional Support in Close Personal Ties among Central Asian Migrant Women in Russia." *Social Networks* 53: 125–135.
Le Galès, Patrick. 2002. *European Cities*. New York: Oxford University Press.
Marques, Eduardo. 2012. *Opportunities and Deprivation in the Urban South*. Farnham: Ashgate.
Marsden, Peter V. 1987. "Core Discussion Networks of Americans." *American Sociological Review* 52 (1): 122–131. doi: 10.2307/2095397.
Marsden, Peter V., and Karen E. Campbell. 1984. "Measuring Tie Strength." *Social Forces* 63 (2): 482–501. doi: 10.1093/sf/63.2.482.
Mauss, Marcel. 2002. *The Gift*. London: Routledge.
McCarty, Christopher. 2002. "Measuring Structure in Personal Networks." *Journal of Social Structure* 3 (1): 1–29.
McEwen, Rhonda, and Barry Wellman. 2013. "Relationships, Community, and Networked Individuals." In *The Immersive Internet*, edited by Robin Teigland and Dominic Power, 168–179. New York: Palgrave Macmillan. doi: 10.1007/978-1-137-28302-3_15.
Middleton, Alan, Alan Murie, and Rick Groves. 2005. "Social Capital and Neighbourhoods that Work." *Urban Studies* 42 (10): 1711–1738. doi: 10.1080/00420980500231589.
Mollenhorst, Gerald. 2015. "Neighbour Relations in the Netherlands." *Tijdschrift Voor Economische En Sociale Geografie* 106 (1): 110–119. doi: 10.1111/tesg.12138.
Mollenhorst, Gerald, Beate Volker, and Henk Flap. 2014. "Changes in Personal Relationships." *Social Networks* 37: 65–80.
Musterd, Sako, and Roger Andersson. 2005. "Housing Mix, Social Mix, and Social Opportunities." *Urban Affairs Review* 40 (6): 761–790. doi: 10.1177/1078087405276006.
Oldenburg, Ramon, and Dennis Brissett. 1982. "The Third Place." *Qualitative Sociology* 5 (4): 265–284. doi: 10.1007/BF00986754.
Oliver, Melvin L. 1988. "The Urban Black Community as Network." *The Sociological Quarterly* 29 (4): 623–645.
Osterling, Kathy L. 2007. "Social Capital and Neighborhood Poverty." *Journal of Human Behavior in the Social Environment* 16 (1–2): 123–147. doi: 10.1300/J137v16n01_09.
Petermann, Sören. 2015. *Persönliches soziales Kapital in Stadtgesellschaften*. Wiesbaden: Springer Fachmedien.

Pfenning, Uwe, and Michael Schenk. 2014. "Namensgeneratoren für egozentrierte soziale Netzwerke." Accessed August 09, 2021. https://zis.gesis.org/pdfFiles/Dokumentation/Pfenning%20Namensgeneratoren%20fuer%20egozentrierte%20Netzwerke.pdf.

Portes, Alejandro. 1998. "Social Capital." *Annual Review of Sociology* 24 (1): 1–24.

Putnam, Robert D. 2000. *Bowling Alone*. New York: Simon & Schuster.

Rainie, Lee, and Barry Wellman. 2012. *Networked*. Cambridge, MA: MIT Press.

Rankin, Bruce H., and James M. Quane. 2000. "Neighborhood Poverty and the Social Isolation of Inner-City African American Families." *Social Forces* 79 (1): 139–164. doi: 10.2307/2675567.

Robinson, Jennifer. 2006. *Ordinary Cities*. London: Routledge.

Schilling, Hannah, Talja Blokland, and AbdouMaliq Simone. 2019. "Working Precarity." *The Sociological Review* 67 (6): 1333–1349. doi: 10.1177/0038026119858209.

Simmel, Georg. 1906. "The Sociology of Secrecy and of Secret Societies." *American Journal of Sociology* 11 (4): 441–498. www.jstor.org/stable/2762562.

Simmel, Georg. 1955. *Conflict and the Web of Group-Affiliations*. New York: Free Press.

Small, Mario L. 2009. *Unanticipated Gains*. New York: Oxford University Press.

Small, Mario L. 2017. *Someone to Talk to*. New York: Oxford University Press.

Small, Mario L., and Laura Adler. 2019. "The Role of Space in the Formation of Social Ties." *Annual Review of Sociology* 45 (1): 111–132.

Small, Mario L., and Christopher Sukhu. 2016. "Because they Were There." *Social Networks* 47: 73–84.

Smithsimon, Gregory. 2010. "Inside the Empire." *Urban Studies* 47 (4): 699–724. doi: 10.1177/0042098009351940.

Stack, Carol B. 1975. *All Our Kin*. New York: Harper & Row.

Swaan, Abram d. 1990. *In Care of the State*. Cambridge: Polity Press.

Völker, Beate, and Henk Flap. 2007. "Sixteen Million Neighbors." *Urban Affairs Review* 43 (2): 256–284. doi: 10.1177/1078087407302001.

Wegener, Bernd. 1991. "Job Mobility and Social Ties." *American Sociological Review* 56 (1): 60–71. doi: 10.2307/2095673.

Wellman, Barry. 1996. "Are Personal Communities Local?" *Social Networks* 18 (4): 347–354. doi: 10.1016/0378-8733(95)00282-0.

Wellman, Barry, and Scot Wortley. 1990. "Different Strokes from Different Folks." *American Journal of Sociology* 96 (3): 558–588. doi: 10.1086/229572.

Wilson, William J. 2012. *The Truly Disadvantaged*. Chicago: The University of Chicago Press.

Wyly, Elvin K. 2011. "Positively Radical." *International Journal of Urban and Regional Research* 36 (3): 889–912. doi: 10.1111/j.1468-2427.2011.01047.x.

20
RECONFIGURING THE SPACES OF URBAN POLITICS

Circuits, territories, and territorialization

Jennifer Robinson

Introduction

The need to rethink urban politics arises in response to empirical developments in urbanization—such as the vast expansion and fragmentation of urban settlements, the dispersal of urban forms over extended urban regions or corridors, and the expanded role of globalized circuits shaping urbanization (such as policy circuits, networks of urban actors, and investment flows). The provocations for urban studies that have come from the insights of "planetary urbanization" represent an important articulation of this challenge (Brenner and Schmid 2015). But so do the insights developed from international urban development policy, which remind us that most people moving to cities arrive to live in self-constructed housing, often on the peripheries of cities and often facing a life-threatening lack of infrastructure (Mitlin and Satterthwaite 2013). In addition, if those contexts that have not historically informed urban studies serve as starting points for theorization (for shorthand, we might label these as "the Global South"—Parnell and Oldfield 2014), different political issues and formations emerge: the politics of access to and titling of land (Gough and Yankson 2000); the diverse interests of state actors, or state effects, as opposed to "the state" (Eriksen 2017); varied forms of political authority (Beall, Parnell, and Albertyn 2015); violent and ongoing coloniality (Porter and Yiftachel 2018); emergent associational forms of regulation, coordination of everyday life, and mobilization (Diouf and Fredericks 2014).

This sits against a backdrop of theories of urban politics based on an earlier era and on a limited range of contexts (Lauermann 2018). The classic Cox–Harvey approach to understanding the urban politics of local economic development focused on municipalities competing for footloose capital (Cox and Mair 1988; Harvey 1989). This flowed from the US context, where locally dependent municipalities and firms configured a certain range of localized political formations. Regime theory extended these insights to a nuanced assessment of how actors with different local interests might assemble a growth coalition, often informal, establishing a stable and consistent growth path (Logan and Molotch 1987; Stone 1989). These accounts traveled poorly to Europe (Harding 1994; Ward 1996), and thus wider analyses, such as that of Kantor, Savitch, and Vicari (1997), expanded the range of concerns to consider municipalities in relation to their national political context and the place of cities in relation to a range of international economic relationships. However, even approaches such as these have little purchase in situations where local governance systems are more strongly centralized, local regimes might be more collective and redistributive (Le Galès 2002), or the institutional basis and scope for the operation of local government is weak, highly informalized, or interwoven with traditional/communal forms of land ownership and governance (Parnell and Pieterse 2014; Beall, Parnell, and Albertyn 2015). In addition, a proliferation of transnational actors, such as resource extraction companies (oil, minerals), sovereign investors and development agencies, international NGOs, and actors such as the World Bank, bring a very different configuration to urban politics in many poorer country contexts. Some new starting points are needed for the theorization of urban politics in the 21st century.

The second era and approach that frames the horizon of thinking in urban politics is that of neoliberalization and, more recently in a similar idiom, financialization (Aalbers 2017). This approach takes us away from the territorially based competitive zero-sum game to attract investment, as articulated in the US-style formulation of urban entrepreneurialism. It also highlights the agency of localized political formations in potentially shaping globalizing circuits of policy, governance, and investment (see Buckley and Hanieh 2014; González et al. 2018). What is relevant for our concerns is the spatial imagination underpinning these analyses of neoliberalization. Peck, Theodore, and Brenner (2009) bring forward the idea of a "syndrome" of neoliberalization in which there is no original or pure neoliberalism, but rather circuits of policy innovation and emergent contradictions shaped by numerous local contexts that constantly generate variegated outcomes, in turn reshaping neoliberalized policy circuits.

To some extent, these analyses have self-consciously addressed a US–EU bias and have attended to the dispersed origins and circuits of neoliberal policies and practices (Peck, Theodore, and Brenner 2009). However, the experiences of poorer contexts are less commonly considered in urban studies, where neoliberalization takes place within often coercive policy circuits (Dobbin, Simmons, and Garrett 2007) in the name of structural adjustment policy or good governance. Furthermore, there are situations where a neoliberal state roll-back has not been possible as state-led institutions have never been present, are differentially present (as a result of colonial inheritance), or are long absent (McDonald 2007). At times, neoliberal innovations have enabled developmental interventions (Ferguson 2010; Parnell and Robinson 2012). In addition, in many contexts, local hybridizations of circulating processes, policy imaginaries, and governance experimentations do not necessarily contribute to the syndrome of "neoliberalism," as the outcomes may be very different. In the face of policy dead ends, personal appropriation, and counter-hegemonic or even developmental outcomes, scholars need to be able to assess "when is it no longer neoliberalization" (Leitner et al. 2007, 10).

These debates have demonstrated that urban politics is to be located at least partly in the prolific circuits and transnational networks that frame global urbanization. But a wider range of circuits and networks of urban development processes and urban policy could be brought into view. The entwining of global circuits and local economic development politics has formed a key terrain within urban studies—from place competition to world city analysis (Friedmann and Wolff 1982) and global city formation (e.g., Firman 1998). Here I wish to consider the more routine ways in which urban politics is always "more than local," encompassing a range of different transnational circuits (Allen and Cochrane 2014), agendas, actors, and types of relationships. It is with this landscape of urban politics in mind that John Lauermann (2018), in his critical assessment of the US growth coalition model of competitive inter-urban politics, observes that "entrepreneurial cities navigate geographies of inter-urban competition *and* cooperation. . . . The expansion of entrepreneurial practices to multiple governance agendas (in parallel to growth) reflects *the formation of extra-territorial political coalitions*" (Lauermann 2018, 3, italics added). He suggests that, as a result, "there remains a pressing need to trace how alternative urban politics operate alongside the growth politics of the contemporary entrepreneurial city" (Lauermann 2018, 15). The most important examples of such alternative urban politics have been seen in relation to networks of cities exploring urban bases for climate change action and transnational coalitions of urban actors promoting the UN's urban sustainable development goals (Acuto 2013; Bulkeley 2010; Parnell 2016).

Urban politics therefore needs to be theorized from different starting points than the territorialized politics of competitive local governments, the circuits of capitalist economic globalization, and their intersection. In his foundational analysis, Harvey (1989) already noted the significance of state-led circuits of investment in shaping competitive urban behavior, in which cities compete for military contracts or to secure state projects such as health or education. Kantor, Savitch, and Vicari (1997) expand this to a wider range of national and international circuits that are relevant for city development politics. Moreover, the more recent focus on the prolific policy circulations shaping urban politics (McCann and Ward 2011) invites us to see these circuits themselves as sites of urban politics. This draws attention to the national and supranational formations that shape global urban "reason" (Gonzales et al. 2018): the circuits of policy makers and city governments (Acuto 2013), collective developmental and political initiatives, and municipal networks and associations (Parnell 2016). But it also highlights informal associational connections, including those of trade and migration (Simone 2010), and the complex spatial formations associated with those who direct or switch flows of finance into the built environment, including states, sovereign fund managers, asset managers, or investment advisors (Bassens and van Meeteren 2015; Kanai and Schindler 2019).

Focusing on the circuits and networks of urban politics calls for more attention to different kinds of actors, as well as the various kinds of associations and relationships that emerge across urban settings and in circuits. Thus, policy mobilizers, development agencies, charitable organizations, think tanks, networking managers, and national, bilateral, and multinational institutions are clearly part of the landscape of the urban political. Earlier theorizations of local economic development politics were closely attentive to the constitution of political interests on an urban scale, exploring the territorial basis for the distinctive interests and motivations of different actors: "local dependence" of businesses, electoral success of governments, the emergent territorially defined interests of growth coalitions in attracting global economic investment or expanding employment, fiscal income streams, or other goals, including acting to secure their interests on regional or national scales (Cox and Mair 1988). An expanded understanding of urban politics, in the wake of analyses of neoliberalization and policy mobilities, points to the need for much more attention to the complex intersections between "locally dependent" actors, "urban" actors whose institutional bases might well be regional or national, and the circulating processes or wider networks framing "urban politics." Here, research on the spatialities of policy mobilities that entrain both circuits and localities (McCann and Ward 2011) as well as the analysis of the politics of international development policy focused on the power relations operative at the interface of international agendas and actors and national/local actors (Dobbin, Simmons, and Garrett 2007) both open up this crucial agenda.

Thus, theoretical insights need to be developed across a much wider array of urban contexts, circuits, and actors than those indexed by the US model or its critical comparative engagement with the European experience. Here, a reformatted urban comparativism can support initiatives to draw a much wider range of urban contexts into consideration (Robinson 2011a; 2015). On the one hand, comparative analyses can be enabled through a focus on circuits that entrain and involve many different urban contexts, often quite promiscuously as policy circulation, or as part of expanding transnational coalitions or municipal networks. Many different urban situations are brought into analytical proximity through their being involved in the same circuits (Porto d'Oliviera 2017; Robinson 2018b; Kanai and Schindler 2019). Attending to a greater diversity of circuits (as processes of urbanization) and the different ways in which relationships among actors are navigated across circuits and localized urban concerns opens up urban political analysis to a wider range of experiences. On the other hand, urban territories can be compared directly. While territorially based comparisons of local governments are notoriously challenging (Kantor and Savitch 2005), the complex, extended, and fragmented nature of contemporary urbanization invites urban political analysis to begin with other types of territories and territorializations. For example, the proliferation of large-scale urban developments across many urban contexts makes it possible to directly compare political formations emergent around similar kinds of long-term, multi-jurisdictional, and transcalar developments (Shatkin 2017; Robinson et al. 2020). Such developments are also frequently interconnected through circuits of policy, financial, and material flows which expand opportunities for comparative analysis. On this basis, a diversity of local governments and other urban actors come into view as part of the variation to be explained across many different developments.

Through both these methodological maneuvers, an analytical conversation across quite divergent forms of urban politics becomes possible and can form the basis for developing wider conceptualizations of urban development. We can now consider some examples of how reconfiguring the spaces of urban politics in these ways—in terms of circuits and territories—can substantially expand the repertoire of analyses.

Circuits

Connections themselves are sites of the urban political, as observed in relation to neoliberalization, which is constituted not only through the variegated formations in (urban) territories but also through international arenas, agencies, and actors. Urban politics happens in the circuits as much as in the territories (Roy and Ong 2011; Acuto 2013). More concretely, the politics of circuits constitutes new "territories" of urban politics, including, for example: networks and associations of municipalities inserting their interests into global policy agendas, such as the SDGs; processes of disseminating the urban agendas of global agencies (such as "rolling out the SDGs"—Kanuri et al. 2016); forming associations on many different topics from climate change to resilience (Bulkley 2010); or more collaborative advocacy-based initiatives such as the Cities Alliance, which is discussed later in this chapter. Thus, the power relations and dynamics of globalized circuits and networks are "urban" politics and necessarily involve actors from a wide range of urban contexts.

From the perspective of particular urban contexts, distinctive formations of politics, agents, and interests are often already part of globalized connections and networks—localized formations are intrinsically framed through circulating ideas, practices, and relationships. Thus, "local" actors arrive at policies in the midst of already present "circulating" ideas (Robinson 2016a). Urban agents are territorialized as already networked and connected; networks and global platforms are created as competitive and collaborative formations of (localized) urban actors. Hence, networks become platforms for both constituting and staging urban politics. Networked interactions might be cross-cut with the dynamics of whatever the globally "competitive city" might be concerned with—competing for the personal success of city leaders, visibility in donor circuits, potential economic expansion, or ambitions to seek developmental global change. They might be sites for inter-referencing different urban experiences or carefully learning from fellow practitioners (Roy and Ong 2011; Robinson 2018a). But these networks can equally be sites of invisibility as exclusions and uneven power relations mean that network-generated policy innovations and investments can evade the influence of municipal actors from poorly resourced contexts (Bulkeley 2010).

Important questions for further investigation include: what are the varied politics of global platforms of urban agency? How do transnational dynamics shape and in turn get shaped by the interests and activities of urban actors? How is urban politics simultaneously networked and territorialized? Questions also arise about the nature of the "relationalities" that make up networked global urban politics, that is, the interactions and influences achieved in these globalized or networked territories of urban politics. It would be helpful to consider more carefully circuits associated with the largely developmental interventions shaping poorer country contexts, which have received far less attention in urban studies (Porto D'Oliviera 2017). Here, analyses of urban agency need to focus more strongly on the exteriorized nature of the interests and capacities of ostensibly local actors and the diverse types of strategic agency that such actors bring into shaping networks.

We already know well that a certain kind of spectrality, or specular politics, inhabits the zone of local economic development—primarily in the marketing relationships that promote cities through visualizations at odds with their realities; or the silences, deceptions, evasions, or occlusions that have been a central feature of the "models" or stylized best practices that support policy circulations (Wood 2014). In relation to some developmental circuits, such spectralities are effective and impactful. There is scope for both ideas and resources to be mobilized for reasons other than those that are apparent, to be siphoned off or captured for achieving entirely different projects and divergent outcomes than initially envisaged, or for significant decisions to be based on what are known to be inaccurate assumptions.

In Lilongwe, Malawi, an ad hoc city strategy was formulated in 2009 through close cooperation with the City of Johannesburg, which had gained a strong reputation for preparing city strategies (Robinson 2011b; 2018a). The collaboration was initiated and partly supported by the United Cities and Local Governments (UCLG: an international network of municipalities) and partly by the Cities Alliance, an advocacy organization with partners including governments, inter-governmental organizations, and residents' movements. However, the ensuing collaboration was also substantially self-financed by Johannesburg and to some extent by Lilongwe. This exchange attracted my attention, as I was intrigued by the developmental focus of the policy circulation and the slow, engaged person-to-person process of policy learning—quite at odds with the "fast policy" analyses that are currently dominant (Peck and Theodore 2015). The Johannesburg–Lilongwe cooperation to produce a city strategy illuminates the transnational nature of urban politics. In this case, the capacity of Lilongwe municipal employees to act both locally and in the global arena was founded on strong and direct engagement from a series of international actors—Johannesburg municipality, the Cities Alliance, UCLG, the Gates Foundation, JICA, and many other international organizations, donors, and NGOs active in the city (Robinson 2018a).

The production of the city strategy leveraged some much-needed investment in upgrading services in settlements from the Gates Foundation as well as some earlier low-key implementations supported by Johannesburg at the end of the strategic planning process. Once the substantial funding was secured, however, Johannesburg actors were excluded, with informants cynically assuming that this might have been to avoid scrutiny and open up opportunities for personal benefit on the part of local actors. While this lengthy, committed developmental process of strategic policy formulation, which stretched over more than three years, had come forward with a number of feasible suggestions for effective development in a well-researched document, the partnership was abandoned. This was also a result of political change and ongoing governance irregularities, which Johannesburg officials felt undermined the possibility for securing "good governance," a prerequisite for their involvement. The value of this work in an administratively challenged context is reflected in the fact that a newly elected mayor was still able to refer to the 2009 City Strategy as a valid future-oriented program of work in 2017 (Robinson 2018a).

We gain some insight into aspects of the transnational dynamics of urban politics in the way in which the city strategy was specularized for personal and institutional benefit. This occurred most obviously in a process of international recognition of the institutional collaboration. Led by a new CEO who had not been involved in the city strategy process, the Lilongwe partners applied for and won a Chinese-sponsored local governance award for this work without involving Johannesburg. The city strategy was also "banked" as organizational capital for major transnational actors, including the Cities Alliance and the UCLG. The collaboration was widely cited as a success story (Cities Alliance 2010), part of the ongoing international city-to-city networking programs promoted by the CA and UCLG (UCLG 2013). And the analysis offered in the Lilongwe City Strategy supported decisions in the Cities Alliance to invest together with the Gates Foundation in settlement upgrading in Lilongwe, despite unfavorable assessments of urban governance capacity and integrity (interview, city official and consultant, 2013). Thus, substantial investments in infrastructure and housing in Lilongwe—the core business of international urban development—flowed from spectral/specular and informalized circuits of transnational urban politics.

Specular and informal dynamics of urban politics can therefore be core features of globalized circuits of urban development. It is not enough to see local variegation adding up to yet another case of an already defined global circuit (such as neoliberalization) through assumed processes of policy transfer, planning, or investment calculations. As the Lilongwe City Strategy case illustrates, there are a variety of circuits to consider, with different dynamics. And there is no inevitability as to what a globalizing circuit ends up producing, what the networked politics of urban development might lead to, or through what kinds of relationality transnational urban political processes and outcomes might be shaped.

Territories and territorialization

Reconfiguring analyses of urban politics can alternatively begin from the diverse territorializations of multiple circuits and urbanization processes. The previous section highlighted circuits and networks as intrinsic elements in any reconfiguration of the spaces of urban politics. In addition, it is important to consider the implications for urban politics of the territorial formations of the urban under planetary urbanization as extended, fragmented, sprawling, operational (Brenner and Schmid 2015), and the transnational politics of a "scramble for infrastructure" currently shaping territorial reconfigurations of urbanization as global (Kanai and Schindler 2019). I draw attention here to an approach that can potentially speak to a wide range of emergent territorialized urban formations in the midst of globalized and interconnected but also often dispersed and fragmented urban outcomes: what Ludovic Halbert calls "Transcalar Territorial Networks" (Halbert and Rouanet 2014). In my view, this analysis offers a way forward to revisit the territories of urban politics beyond municipal-based global competition or the entrepreneurial state.

Multiple globalizing circuits shape the future trajectories of urban settlements and, more generally, the extended and fragmented territories that are the outcomes of urbanization processes (Keil 2017; Schmid et al. 2018). An iconic understanding of this sees globalized processes of investment (financialization) producing repeated, seemingly identical urban forms—the serially reproduced satellite city, the repetition of "iconic" architecture, the endlessly borrowed concept or design. However, our research in London suggests that each of these apparently identical buildings requires two to three years of almost weekly meetings between planners and developers to negotiate the details of financing, planning gain, social and hard infrastructure provision, and the detailed design of buildings (Robinson et al. 2020). Actors with varying global reach and different capacities to localize, together with conventions and calculative devices (Christophers 2014) as much as a vast array of legislation and policy are at stake in each negotiated outcome. More generally, I appreciate the Deleuzian formulation in which repetition is always a differentiation, a distinctive "singularity" emergent from the shared/interconnected genetic processes: one of a kind but perhaps also *one of a series* of outcomes (Jacobs 2012; Robinson 2016b). Thus, while attending to the multiplicity of connections that shape urban outcomes, the *repeated instance* comes into view (Robinson 2018b).

A repeated instance might be the buildings or large-scale developments in which certain forms of financialized capital are implicated, such as asset management of low-income rental housing products. Or the production of new cities or infrastructure that result from numerous globalizing or translocal circuits—of policy, planning visions, globally competitive economic development strategies, financial investment, or local populations positioning themselves to benefit in some way from planned developments, perhaps long in advance of anything ever being built (van den Broeck 2017; Kanai and Schindler 2019).

In these settings, then, a range of transcalar actors and networks are territorialized in the cooperation, contestation, and creative production of new urban territories. Halbert and Rouanet's concept of transcalar territorial networks takes seriously this complexity of circulations, extensions, and territorializations:

> The concept of transcalar territorial networks (TTN) is suggested to explain how resources from multiple horizons are pulled together in a given business

property development, from a fixed plot of land to capital allocated in distant investment committee boardrooms.

(2014, 472)

Allen and Cochrane's (2007) conceptualization of "regional assemblages" is also helpful here—different "scales" are flattened into a patchwork of overlapping territorializations of different institutional agency. This opens up new lines of investigation for thinking about urban politics.

Thus, across a range of territories—extended and city-regional configurations, corridors, dispersed fragments of the urban—political formations are assembled out of diverse actors operating with varied reach, capacity, and transcalar competencies. It is important to also layer in the specific regulatory pathways that emerge in urban contexts, perhaps around jurisdictions or governance structures, such as municipalities, metropolitan areas, countries, regions. We can take a cue here from a regulationist idea of a *rapport territorial*—territorial relations of regulation emergent in different metropolitan contexts:

> The territorial relationship generates a contradictory and complex system of dependencies, jurisdictions and rules . . . it consists not only of laws, bylaws and prescriptions, but also of diverse unwritten, implicit rules; as a result it is often barely comprehensible to outsiders—and even so to insiders.
>
> *(Schmid 2015, 297)*

Thus, the territorial grounds for urban politics could be conceived as emergent territorializations, embracing transcalar territorial networks that constellate around designated urban projects and programs, as well as the complex formations associated with territorialized regulatory assemblages. Rather than competing municipalities and footloose capital, we can acknowledge the emergence of (new) territories on which urban politics emerges, such as large-scale development projects, satellite cities, extensive infrastructural developments, or the transcalar regulatory contexts that establish pathways of development. In these settings, a diverse cast of actors with differently configured interests and concerns emerge, varying from context to context (even within the same city, region, or country).

In this light, the interests and practices of actors may be surprising: "global" developers and architects whose local reputations and relationship inspire more modest goals for developments may be at odds with states whose commitment is to intensify extraction to support their own ambitions. Or developmental state interests in securing an adequate housing supply might be aligned with new processes of globalized investment—financialization or "build to rent" (Robinson and Attuyer 2020; Todes and Robinson 2020). Thus, we need to take seriously the territorial embeddedness of both (global) developers and states.

We also can see how, within the scope of these territorialized formations, openings for effective state agency might not depend on building strong institution-wide agency but could involve having some capacity to shape decision-making and negotiations in relation to specific developments. This potentially opens up a significant perspective on questions of African governance, for example, where analysts and development organizations have been perplexed by, and highly critical of, the extensive investments in large-scale urban developments across the continent (Watson 2014; Murray 2017; van Noorloos and Kloosterboer 2018). Here, a determinedly scalar developmental imagination of government/governance could be enriched by a view of transcalar governance and the overlapping circuits (private, developmental, sovereign) shaping African cities. Rather than a good governance agenda focused on improving hierarchical interjurisdictional arrangements (Pieterse, Parnell, and Haysom 2018), close attention to the transcalar territories of urban development might indicate targeted opportunities to improve outcomes (planning gain, application of international law). Improved understanding of the actors, interests, and scope for intervention in these developments could yield stronger public benefit from investments (Turok 2016; Goodfellow 2020).

More generally, the shared features of large-scale developments (multi-jurisdictional, of long duration, with a complexity of interests and shifting governance arrangements) allow them to be fruitfully compared across a very wide range of contexts, potentially contributing to wider theorizations of urban politics (Robinson et al. 2020). In these settings, the nature of the future city is negotiated, and urban politics is revealed. For this, though, it is important not to treat the variety of outcomes as so many different "contexts" making residual contributions to wider circuits (van Loon, Oosterlynck, and Aalbers 2018). Rather, comparative analysis of the (transcalar) territories (Halbert and Rouanet 2014) of large-scale urban developments could build new theoretical insights across a diversity of urban politics rather than framing these as "variegated" cases of wider processes or circuits.

Gavin Shatkin's (2016; 2017) comparative study of three large-scale urban development projects in Asia is especially helpful in this regard. He insists that these cases can be treated as starting points for new theoretical analyses, emergent from Asian experiences and appropriate to contemporary global urbanization. In his view, theorizations of urban politics need to encompass "state capitalism," as well as the land grabs characteristic of peremptory states, and the often exuberant and informalized political contestation associated with democratic but poorly capacitated states. He summarizes his analytical insights in relation to the dimensions of more or less autonomy of state land managers, and more or less state control of land markets.

Starting from this theorization inspired by the Asian context, a closer focus emerges on the interests of the state itself in urban development (Shen, Luo, and Wu 2020). This has been occluded in favor of a focus on the politics of financialization, neoliberalization, and the role of global developers (Aalbers 2017; Robinson and Attuyer 2020). In a recent comparative research project (London–Johannesburg–Shanghai),[1] we focused on three large-scale development projects and identified significant territorializations of urban politics at the scale of the "project" (Pinson 2009). Our study expands Shatkin's insights from the Asian context, bringing into view a wider diversity of ways in which states and other urban actors manage land value extraction to enable new urban developments. Across the three cases, we identified a common state interest in extracting rents from different aspects of the newly constructed urban environment, at least partly in order to pay for the development itself (Robinson et al. 2020). However, rather than interpreting these as reflecting variegated forms of financialization or neoliberalization, our comparative analysis identified three business models (distinctive configurations of governance and financing arrangements) with diverse practices for generating and capturing urban value through urban development (Theurillat 2015). On this basis, we were able to explore the implications of different business models for the outcomes in each case.

Our cases highlight the difference made by these business models. In London, direct value capture on a one-off basis at the point and time of construction (through negotiated planning gain) put great pressure on built form to generate income, leading to dense and high-rise developments with low levels of affordable housing. A more metropolitan scale and dynamic property tax system in Johannesburg enabled a redistributive emphasis on providing well-located, low-income housing. And the even wider accounting of the potential returns on urban development through taxation of new enterprises and generalized economic growth supported transformational economic policies of industrial upgrading in Shanghai. The scope to understand the interests and roles of different actors, and to inform critical analysis of different business models, comes into view through comparative analysis. Thus, state actors might be motivated by electoral concerns to promote redistributive outcomes (Harrison et al. 2019), or by securing consent for (or at least compliance with) the processes of removal and development (Wang and Wu 2019), maximizing income streams (Robinson and Attuyer 2020), or effectively managing developmental growth agendas across complex institutional spaces, in part through market mechanisms (Shen, Luo, and Wu 2020; Wu 2020).

As international actors ranging from sovereign wealth funds to transnational private firms or developmental agencies turn to the urban built environment to realize both profit and potential public benefit, including in some of the poorest urban contexts (Turok 2016), it is important to be aware of the range of ways in which urbanization can be secured, governed, and financed. The business models of large-scale urban developments are diverse and the role and interests of different actors involved in securing urban developments are highly specific, even as transnational processes and actors are key in most large-scale urban developments. While enhancing land value as well as securing other value streams through development is often the foundation for financing urban development, the different ways of mobilizing resources and realizing value to enable the development make a significant difference to outcomes—in terms of the physical form of the development, the types of activities supported, and the relative distribution of benefits to different agents of development and to the wider society (Robinson et al. 2020).

Conclusion: reconfiguring urban politics

This chapter has explored the rich potential to reconfigure the spaces of urban politics. This involves expanding the territories from which urban politics might be theorized and encouraging urban scholars to take into account a much richer array of actors and more varied explanations for their actions and interests. I have suggested that a diversity of transnational networks and circuits represent new territories of urban politics, which convene a range of different kinds of political interests and dynamic relationships involving urban actors from across the globe. In addition, by starting with the fragmented and dispersed territories that characterize contemporary processes of (planetary) urbanization, such as large-scale urban developments, direct comparisons can be drawn across highly diverse urban settings, expanding and enriching insights into the interests of urban actors and the nature and outcomes of urban development politics. On the basis of such a reformatted comparative analysis, places like London can become destinations for theory from elsewhere, for example, learning from analyses of state interests in land development from Asia. More generally, in a world where all cities might be thought of as "ordinary" and thus assumed to contribute to wider theorizations (Robinson 2006), understandings of the spaces and nature of urban politics can be reconfigured through comparative analysis of the diverse territories and circuits of global urbanization.

Note

1 With Phil Harrison and Fulong Wu, I acknowledge funding from the ESRC for an Urban Transformations grant ES/N006070/1, "Governing the Future City: A comparative analysis of governance innovations in large-scale urban developments in Shanghai, London, Johannesburg."

References

Aalbers, M. B. 2017. "The Variegated Financialization of Housing." *International Journal of Urban and Regional Research* 41 (4): 542–554.

Acuto, M. 2013. "The New Climate Leaders?" *Review of International Studies* 39 (4): 835–857.

Allen, J., and A. Cochrane. 2007. "Beyond the Territorial Fix: Regional Assemblages, Politics and Power." *Regional Studies* 41: 1161–1175.

Allen, J., and A. Cochrane. 2014. "The Urban Unbound: London's Politics and the 2012 Olympic Games." *International Journal of Urban and Regional Research* 38: 1609–1624.

Bassens, D., and M. van Meeteren. 2015. "World Cities under Conditions of Financialized Globalization: Towards an Augmented World City Hypothesis." *Progress in Human Geography* 39 (6): 752–775.

Beall, J., S. Parnell, and C. Albertyn. 2015. "Elite Compacts in Africa: The Role of Area-Based Management in the New Governmentality of the Durban City-region." *International Journal of Urban and Regional Research* 39 (2): 390–406.

Brenner, N., and C. Schmid. 2015. "Towards a New Epistemology of the Urban?" *City* 19 (2–3): 151–182.

Buckley, M., and A. Hanieh. 2014. "Diversification by Urbanization: Tracing the Property-Finance Nexus in Dubai and the Gulf. *International Journal of Urban and Regional Research* 38 (1): 155–175.

Bulkeley, H. 2010. "Cities and the Governing of Climate Change." *Annual Review of Environment and Resources* 35: 229–253.

Christophers, B. 2014. "Wild Dragons in the City: Urban Political Economy, Affordable Housing Development and the Performative World-making of Economic Models." *International Journal of Urban and Regional Research* 38 (1): 79–97.

Cities Alliance. 2010. *Cities Alliance in Action: Johannesburg-Lilongwe Partnership Leads to a Robust City Development Strategy*. www.citiesalliance.org/resources/knowledge/cities-alliance-knowledge/cities-alliance-action-johannesburg-lilongwe.

Cox, K., and A. Mair. 1988. "Locality and Community in the Politics of Local Economic Development." *Annals of the Association of American Geographers* 78 (2): 307–325.

Diouf, M., and R. Fredericks. 2014. *The Arts of Citizenship in African Cities: Infrastructures and Spaces of Belonging*. London: Palgrave MacMillan.

Dobbin, F., B. Simmons, and G. Garrett. 2007. "The Global Diffusion of Public Policies: Social Construction, Coercion, Competition, or Learning?" *Annual Review of Sociology* 33: 449–472.

Eriksen, S. 2017. "State Effects and the Effects of State Building: Institution Building and the Formation of State-Centred Societies." *Third World Quarterly* 38 (4): 771–786.

Ferguson, J. 2010. "The Uses of Neoliberalism." *Antipode* 41: 166–184.

Firman, T. 1998. "The Restructuring of Jakarta Metropolitan Area: A 'Global City' in Asia." *Cities* 15 (4): 229–243.

Friedmann, J., and G. Wolff. 1982. "World City Formation: An Agenda for Research and Action." *International Journal of Urban and Regional Research* 6: 309–344.

González, S., S. Oosterlynck, R. Ribera-Fumaz, and U. Rossi. 2018. "Locating the Global Financial Crisis: Variegated Neoliberalization in Four European Cities." *Territory, Politics, Governance* 6 (4): 468–488.

Goodfellow, T. 2020. "Finance, Infrastructure and Urban Capital: The Political Economy of African 'Gap-Filling'." *Review of African Political Economy*. doi: 10.1080/03056244.2020.1722088.

Gough, K., and P. Yankson. 2000. "Land Markets in African Cities: The Case of Peri-Urban Accra, Ghana." *Urban Studies* 37 (13): 2485–2500.

Halbert, L., and H. Rouanet. 2014. "Filtering Risk Away: Global Finance Capital, Transcalar Territorial Networks and the (Un)Making of City-Regions: An Analysis of Business Property Development in Bangalore, India." *Regional Studies* 48 (3): 471–484.

Harding, A. 1994. "Urban Regimes and Growth Machines: Towards a Cross-National Research Agenda." *Urban Affairs Quarterly* 29 (3): 356–382.

Harrison, P., M. Rubin, A. Appelbaum, and R. Dittgen. 2019. "Corridors of Freedom: Analyzing Johannesburg's Ambitious Inclusionary Transit-Oriented Development." *Journal of Planning Education and Research* 39 (4): 456–468. doi: 10.1177/0739456X19870312.

Harvey, D. 1989. "From Managerialism to Entrepreneurialism: The Transformation in Urban Governance in Late Capitalism." *Geografiska Annaler. Series B, Human Geography* 71 (1): 3–17.

Jacobs, J. 2012. "Commentary: Comparing Comparative Urbanisms." *Urban Geography* 33 (6): 904–914.

Kanai, J. M., and S. Schindler. 2019. "Peri-Urban Promises of Connectivity: Linking Project-Led Polycentrism to the Infrastructure Scramble." *Environment and Planning A: Economy and Space* 51 (2): 302–322.

Kantor, P., and H. V. Savitch. 2005. "How to Study Comparative Urban Development Politics: A Research Note." *International Journal of Urban and Regional Research* 29 (1): 135–151.

Kantor, P., H. V. Savitch, and S. Vicari. 1997. "The Political Economy of Urban Regimes: A Comparative Perspective." *Urban Affairs Review* 32 (3): 348–377.

Kanuri, C., A. Revi, A. Espey, and H. Kuhle. 2016. "Getting Started with the SDGs in Cities." *Sustainable Development Solutions Network*. Accessed November 24, 2020. https://resources.unsdsn.org/getting-started-with-the-sdgs-in-cities.

Keil, R. 2017. *Suburban Planet: Making the World Urban from the Outside In*. Cambridge: Polity.

Lauermann, J. 2018. "Municipal Statecraft: Revisiting the Geographies of the Entrepreneurial City." *Progress in Human Geography* 42 (2): 205–224.

Le Galès, P. 2002. *European Cities: Social Conflicts and Governance*. Oxford: Oxford University Press.

Leitner, H., E. Sheppard, K. Sziarto, and A. Maringanti. 2007. "Contesting Urban Futures: Decentering Neoliberalism." In *Contesting Neoliberalism*, edited by H. Leitner, J. Peck, and E. Sheppard, 1–25. New York: Guilford.

Logan, J., and H. Molotch. 1987. *Urban Fortunes: The Political Economy of Place*. Berkeley: University of California Press.

McCann, E., and K. Ward. 2011. *Mobile Urbanisms*. Minneapolis: University of Minnesota Press.

McDonald, D. 2007. *World City Syndrome: Neoliberalism and Inequality in Cape Town*. New York: Routledge.

Mitlin, D., and D. Satterthwaite, eds. 2013. *Urban Poverty in the Global South: Scale and Nature*. London: Routledge.

Murray, M. 2017. *The Urbanism of Exception: The Dynamics of Global City Building in the Twenty-First Century*. Cambridge: Cambridge University Press.

Parnell, S. 2016. "Defining a Global Urban Development Agenda." *World Development* 78: 529–540.

Parnell, S., and S. Oldfield, eds. 2014. *Handbook for Cities of the Global South*. London: Routledge.

Parnell, S., and E. Pieterse, eds. 2014. *Africa's Urban Revolution*. London and New York: Zed Books.

Parnell, S., and J. Robinson. 2012. "(Re)theorising Cities from the Global South: Looking beyond Neoliberalism." *Urban Geography* 33 (4): 593–617.

Peck, J., and N. Theodore. 2015. *Fast Policy: Experimental Statecraft at the Thresholds of Neoliberalism*. Minneapolis: Minnesota University Press.

Peck, J., N. Theodore, and N. Brenner. 2009. "Neoliberal Urbanism: Models, Moments, Mutations." *SAIS Review* XXIX (1): 49–66.

Pieterse, E., S. Parnell, and G. Haysom. 2018. "African Dreams: Locating Urban Infrastructure in the 2030 Sustainable Developmental Agenda." *Area Development and Policy* 3 (2): 149–169.

Pinson, G. 2009. *Gouverner la ville par projet: Urbanisme et gouvernance des villes européenes*. Paris: Presses de la fondation national des sciences politiques.

Porter, L., and O. Yiftachel. 2018. "Urbanizing Settler-Colonial Studies: Introduction to the Special Issue." *Settler Colonial Studies* 9 (2): 177–186. doi: 10.1080/2201473X.2017.1409394.

Porto de Oliviera, O. 2017. *International Policy Diffusion and Participatory Budgeting*. Basingstoke, UK: Palgrave Macmillan.

Robinson, J. 2006. *Ordinary Cities*. London: Routledge.

Robinson, J. 2011a. "Cities in a World of Cities: The Comparative Gesture." *International Journal of Urban and Regional Research* 35: 1–23.

Robinson, J. 2011b. "The Spaces of Circulating Knowledge: City Strategies and Global Urban Governmentality." In *Mobile Urbanism: Cities and Policymaking in the Global Age*, edited by E. McCann and K. Ward, 15–40. Minneapolis: University of Minnesota Press.

Robinson, J. 2015. "Comparative Urbanism: New Geographies and Cultures of Theorizing the Urban." *International Journal of Urban and Regional Research* 40 (1): 219–227.

Robinson, J. 2016a. "'Arriving At' Urban Policies: The Topological Spaces of Urban Policy Mobility." *International Journal of Urban and Regional Research* 39 (4): 1468–2427.

Robinson, J. 2016b. "Thinking Cities through Elsewhere: Comparative Tactics for a More Global Urban Studies." *Progress in Human Geography* 40 (1): 3–29.

Robinson, J. 2018a. "The Politics of the (Global) Urban: City Strategies as Repeated Instances." In *The City as a Global Actor*, edited by S. Oosterlynck, D. Bassens, L. Beeckmans, B. DeRudder, L. Braeckmans, and B. Segaert, 100–131. London: Routledge.

Robinson, J. 2018b. "Policy Mobilities as Comparison: Urbanization Processes, Repeated Instances, Topologies." *Revista de Administração Pública* 52 (2): 221–243. doi: 10.1590/0034-761220180126.

Robinson, J., and K. Attuyer. 2020. "Extracting Value, London Style: Revisiting the Role of the State in Urban Development." *International Journal of Urban and Regional Research*. doi: 10.1111/1468-2427.12962.

Robinson, J., P. Harrison, J. Shen, and F. Wu. 2020. "Financing Urban Development, Three Business Models: Johannesburg, Shanghai and London." *Progress in Planning*. doi: 10.1016/j.progress.2020.100513.

Roy, A., and A. Ong. 2011. *Worlding Cities*. Oxford: Wiley-Blackwell.

Schmid, C. 2015. "Specificity and Urbanization: A Theoretical Outlook." In *The Inevitable Specificity of Cities*, edited by C. Diener, J. Herzog, M. Meili, P. de Meuron, M. Herz, C. Schmid, and M. Topalovic, 287–307. Zurich: Lars Müller Publishers.

Schmid, C., O. Karaman, N. Hanakata, P. Kallenberger, A. Kockelkorn, L. Sawyer, M. Streule, and K. P. Wong. 2018. "Towards New Vocabularies of Urbanization Processes: A Comparative Approach." *Urban Studies* 55 (1): 19–52.

Shatkin, G. 2016. "The Real Estate Turn in Policy and Planning: Land Monetization and the Political Economy of Peri-Urbanization in Asia." *Cities* 53: 141–149.

Shatkin, M. 2017. *Cities for Profit: The Real Estate Turn in Asia's Urban Politics*. Ithaca: Cornell University Press.

Shen, J., X. Luo, and F. Wu. 2020. "Assembling Mega-Urban Projects Through State-Guided Governance Innovation: The Development of Lingang in Shanghai." *Regional Studies*. doi: 10.1080/00343404.2020.1762853.

Simone, A. 2010. *City Life: From Dakar to Jakarta*. London: Routledge.

Stone, C. 1989. *Regime Politics: Governing Atlanta, 1946–1988*. Lawrence: Kansas University Press.

Theurillat, T. 2015. "The Creation of Urban Value in China: The Case of the Modernization of Qujing City in Yunnan." *Working Paper 1*, MAPS, University of Neuchâtel. Accessed June 3, 2020. www.unine.ch/files/live/sites/maps/files/shared/documents/wp/WP-1_2015_Theurillat.pdf.

Todes, A., and J. Robinson. 2020. "Re-Directing Developers: New Models of Rental Housing Development to Re-Shape the Post-Apartheid City? *Environment and Planning A: Economy and Space* 52 (2): 297–317.

Turok, I. 2016. "Getting Urbanization to Work in Africa: The Role of the Urban Land-Infrastructure-Finance Nexus." *Area Development and Policy* 1 (1): 30–47.

UCLG. 2013. *Peer Learning: UCLG Mentoring Stories, Johannesburg and Lilongwe, 2008–2012.* Accessed March 6, 2018. https://issuu.com/uclgcglu/docs/jb_lilongwestory.

Van den Broeck, J. 2017. "'We Are Analogue in a Digital World': An Anthropological Exploration of Ontologies and Uncertainties around the Proposed Konza Techno City Near Nairobi, Kenya." *Critical African Studies* 9 (2): 210–225.

Van Loon, J., S. Oosterlynck, and M. Aalbers. 2018. "Governing Urban Development in the Low Countries: From Managerialism to Entrepreneurialism and Financialization." *European Urban and Regional Studies* 26 (4): 400–418.

Van Noorloos, F., and M. Kloosterboer. 2018. "Africa's New Cities: The Contested Future of Urbanisation." *Urban Studies* 55 (6): 1223–1241.

Wang, Z., and F. Wu. 2019. "In-Situ Marginalisation: Social Impact of Chinese Mega-Projects." *Antipode* 51: 1640–1663. doi: 10.1111/anti.12560.

Ward, K. 1996. "Rereading Urban Regime Theory: A Sympathetic Critique." *Geoforum* 27 (4): 427–438.

Watson, V. 2014. "African Urban Fantasies: Dreams or Nightmares?" *Environment and Urbanization* 26 (1): 215–231.

Wood, A., 2014. "Moving Policy: Global and Local Characters Circulating Bus Rapid Transit through South African Cities." *Urban Geography* 35 (8): 1238–1254.

Wu, F. 2020. "The State Acts through the Market: 'State Entrepreneurialism' beyond Varieties of Urban Entrepreneurialism." *Dialogues in Human Geography*. Advance online publication. doi: 10.1177/2043820620921034.

21
APPROPRIATING BERLIN'S TEMPOHOMES

Ayham Dalal, Aline Fraikin, and Antonia Noll

The appropriation of refugee camps: a growing research agenda

Flags, logos of humanitarian organizations, textiles, barbed wire, electricity cables, concrete blocks, swamps, zinco sheets, tents, and appropriated shelters are a few of the things that one would expect to see in a refugee camp. Since the early 2000s, not only has knowledge about the spatialities of refugee camps increased (cf. Agier 2016), but their designs and layouts have also diversified. In a previous study, we examined how the need to plan "better" camps in Jordan and Berlin has led to the creation of new camps and shelter designs that seek to foster control over refugees (Dalal et al. 2018). In this chapter, we will expand on this debate by showing how refugees find ways to subvert the initial designs and appropriate the camp for the purpose of dwelling (Heidegger 1971).

In the literature, the appropriation of physical space is linked to the ways in which social space is perceived and theorized (Bourdieu 2018; Lefebvre 1991). In studies involving refugee camps, however, the appropriation of space is never addressed explicitly. Instead, it is perceived through two concepts: urbanization and agency. For instance, it is generally suggested that appropriations would eventually lead to the urbanization of camps (Agier 2002; Misselwitz 2009; Herz 2013; Dalal 2014). This would also underline the refugees' agency (Sanyal 2010; Ramadan 2013), in contrast to their theoretical passiveness (Agamben 1998), which presents appropriation as a political action (Maqusi 2017). In our research, we extend this argument by demonstrating that the appropriation of these camps is driven by a conflict in the understanding and use of space:

1 Humanitarian technocratic planning seeks to produce manageable camps (using handbooks, manuals, and standardized regulations), so that refugees are protected and contained safely in shelters

DOI: 10.4324/9781003036159-25

2   Refugees seek to create social spaces of meaning, to inhabit the space or, precisely, to dwell

This argument was portrayed earlier in the Zaatari refugee camp, where appropriations were explained as a result of the conflictual relationship between a humanitarian "far order" and a local and socio-cultural "near order" (Dalal 2014). In this chapter, we explore this relationship in the newly designed and built Tempohomes in Berlin.

To understand how spaces are being planned and subsequently appropriated in the camp, we use grounded theory and combine various methods of data collection, namely qualitative interviews and "co-mapping" (Dalal 2020), which allow both researchers and interviewees to map the changes within a certain space over time, often accompanied by sketches seeking to document socio-spatial constellations that are difficult to understand solely based on oral descriptions. Moreover, participatory observations allow the researchers to directly address particular appropriations within the space of the container, while observing how the space is being used. In addition, we conducted 18 interviews and mappings of the camp on different scales, which helped to understand the spatial arrangements of various Tempohomes in Berlin (Columbiadamm, Alte Jakobstraße, Wollenberger Straße, Quittenweg, Ostpreußendamm, and Refugium Buch) between 2018 and 2019, and Karl-Marx Straße in 2020; to explore how appropriations are linked to refugee backgrounds and family conditions (single travelers, extended families, or women-headed families); and to consequently understand the Tempohome planning and observe appropriations. It also allowed us to conduct theoretical samplings (Charmaz 2006), from which the case study was selected.

Tempohome: a new type of camp

A "Tempohome" is a specific type of camp that emerged in Berlin as a response to the comparatively large influx of refugees to the city in 2015. It was designed by a special task force at the Berlin State Office for Refugee Affairs (Landesamt für Flüchtlingsangelegenheiten, or LAF) to accommodate 200 to 500 refugees, supervised locally by an operator (a for-profit or non-profit organization). Inside the camp, refugees are housed in rows of adjacent container units. Each container unit is composed of three identical containers (2.3 × 5.9 meters) attached to each other. The unit is accessed from the middle: a shared space used as a small lobby, entered through a porch and cantilever, and equipped with a small kitchenette and washroom. The two adjacent rooms are equipped with standardized furniture, which can differ slightly from one Tempohome to the next, yet generally include: two beds, two mattresses, two wardrobes, one fridge, one table, and two chairs. When fully furnished, however, a container room in a Tempohome leaves its inhabitants with only 7 m^2 of space to move (Darweesh 2019). This affords refugees a very limited space in which to live and to share with others.

Moreover, a Tempohome is conditioned by strict safety regulations such as "fire protection." These regulations apply to all housing in Germany. In a Tempohome, however, they pose a major challenge for refugees due to the scarcity of space and the design of the container. For instance, gardening boxes or other refugee belongings cannot be placed in front of the windows outside the container since they would hinder refugees' exit in case of fire. Curtains, which are usually hung on the porches to increase privacy, cannot be attached to the metal structure of the container as they would block the main door. Curtains and carpets inside the container are also frowned upon as they might cause a fire if they touch the heaters for an extended period of time. Nor is inserting screws or nails into the container walls permitted. The furniture should remain inside the container and be protected, and the space inside the container should be cleaned. "It is like a hotel room," said a camp operator, to underline the fact that these containers are meant as temporary accommodations and thus not suitable for *dwelling* (interview in Karl-Marx Straße, July 2020). But how do refugees appropriate the container under these strict and minimal conditions?

Leila's family: converting a group of containers into a dwelling

When visited in August 2019, Leila, her husband, and their three sons had been living in a Tempohome for three years. Leila is a 48-year-old Palestinian from Syria who left the Yarmouk camp in December 2012. Between 2012 and 2016, her family lived between Syria and Lebanon, until her young sons fled to Europe. In August 2016, they settled in a Tempohome in Berlin, and, for about six months, they moved between rooms until they settled down when their parents arrived at the same Tempohome.

According to regulations, the family was eligible for one full container unit. Living inside three containers of about 40 m², the five-member family had to appropriate the space and rearrange it anew. Unlike other camps where appropriations can be practiced extensively and are thus easy to spot, appropriating Tempohomes occurs within the clearly demarcated boundaries of the container and are therefore subtle and less visible. This does not mean that a visitor to a Tempohome would not notice new elements that have been added to the containers by refugees, but the way these appropriations are linked to each other and the rationale behind them is less obvious. As such, we aim to illustrate how these appropriations are linked to each other, and how they are intended to create a dwelling that transcends the initial design of the Tempohome as a standardized shelter.

The transition from a group of containers into a dwelling began with symbolic gestures such as cooking, re-organizing space, and adding carpets. As the eldest son explained:

> When mom arrived, the first thing I noticed was that we started to use the oven in the kitchen and that she started to organize things around.

Using the kitchen to prepare meals is an important dimension that is deeply intertwined with the socio-spatial dynamics of dwelling (Bourdieu 1970). Bringing a carpet into the rooms not only adds more warmth but also makes them multifunctional when needed. For instance, food can be placed on the floor atop a plastic sheet to keep it clean, and mattresses can be arranged on it to create seating corners when needed. In a normal context, adding a carpet to one's own house is not a surprising practice. However, in a Tempohome, it requires negotiations with the camp managers since it contradicts the rules: a carpet inside the container can be dangerous as it could ignite quickly in case of fire. Luckily, Leila and her family managed to convince the operators of the Tempohome and were allowed to add a few carpets to beautify the space and increase its adaptability.

Of course, appropriations within the container often include other practices of personalization, such as adding photos and decorations. But the significance of this case is its ability to show how the sum of the various spatial practices results in a "dwelling arrangement" in contrast to the initial "shelter design." For instance, one of the rooms was appropriated to carve out a private space used as a sleeping space for Leila and her two youngest sons. Initially, the room was furnished to temporarily accommodate two refugees using a bunk bed and two wardrobes. Instead, the family dismantled the bunk bed—a practice that Leila's sons had learned during their stay in the emergency centers—and placed the single beds next to one another. Since they are five members, the family was eligible for an additional single bed. The bed was added and placed next to the other two, creating a longer bed used by Leila and her younger sons during the night, and as a space for napping when the husband and the eldest son returned from work during the day. The rest of the room was appropriated as a storage space with a larger fridge composed of the two small fridges initially installed in each of the rooms. This practice was also observed in other containers, especially among families.

As argued elsewhere (Dalal 2020), refugees tend to dismantle the standardized elements of the humanitarian technocratic planning, reassembling the objects differently in order to create spaces for dwelling. In the same room, a small table with a TV and a gaming console was added to entertain the youngest sons during the day. A smaller table was added in the kitchen, providing Leila with additional space to prepare the meals.

While not all family members were able to sleep in one room, the other remaining room was utilized as a multi-functional space: a "living space" during the day and a "living room" during the night. Having been sheltered in limited spaces that often fail to accommodate extended family structures, this practice was observed in other camps in Jordan and Lebanon as well (see, for instance, Oueishek 2018; Dalal 2020). To make use of the space, the bunk bed was not dismantled in this room, but rather pushed towards the edge. Next to it, the wardrobes were placed facing each other, creating a transitional space to the beds, and leaving enough space for the lower bed to be used for seating during the day. The remaining part of the room is used occasionally for gathering and receiving guests, and primarily as a dining area. Initially, each room is furnished with a small table and two chairs

Appropriating Berlin's Tempohomes **289**

for the two refugees to be sheltered within. In Leila's case, however, the physical dimensions of the shelter posed an "invisible" challenge for the family to gather at one table. As she explained:

> As you can see, the room is very small. When I cook, we push the table to the center, and try to squeeze five chairs around it, otherwise, we won't all fit . . .

After having meals, the table is pushed against the wall, freeing up a bit of space for several chairs or a mattress to be put on the ground, either for receiving guests or sleeping. As the eldest son who sleeps on the upper bunk explained:

> Every day, you need to go up and down [the bunk bed], and I barely can jump because the ladders are hidden behind the wardrobes. . . . Sometimes when I don't have the energy, I get the mattresses down and I sleep on the ground.

While functioning as a bedroom for the father and his son at night, the mattress is removed in the morning and placed on the bunk bed again to facilitate the use of the room as a "living space" during the day.

One of the main challenges faced by refugees while trying to dwell in a Tempohome, or in any camp shelter in general, is the lack of space for storing personal belongings. In humanitarian designs, refugees are often imagined to be escaping drastic conditions, therefore arriving to camps with few or no belongings at all. Although this holds true for some, this is not the case for all. In fact, when performing fieldwork in the Tempohomes, the lack of space for storing personal belongings was evident, with many wardrobes packed full of clothes, leaving little space for other activities. Luckily, in Leila's case, the family was able to utilize an adjacent room entirely for that purpose. As she explained:

> We are five in two rooms, so we are eligible for one more. Thus, they [the management] gave the children one . . . since no one lives there, we use it for storage . . . and if we want to fry something, we fry it in the kitchen there since it is empty to avoid the smell of frying oil in our own living space.

This means that the resulting dwelling arrangement was not only limited within the container unit that they initially received, but extended to practically four containers in which the functions and furniture were redistributed and rearranged (see Figure 21.1).

Finally, and to ensure that the newly formed dwelling space has become a private space for its inhabitants, curtains were added to the windows and door. Hanging curtains in Tempohomes is one of the most practiced appropriations, according to observations. In some Tempohomes, these practices even extend to the porch, where sheets are added to close it off fully, thus enclosing it as a dwelling space, or

290 Ayham Dalal, Aline Fraikin, Antonia Noll

FIGURE 21.1 The conversion of the standardized container into a dwelling space
Source: Authors

partly covering its sides with sheets so that it can be closed and opened as needed, thus functioning as a semi-private space. Curtains are so commonly used in dwellings that we sometimes fail to recognize their significance. Nonetheless, it is only within shelter—an abstract humanitarian space where social relations are vaguely represented—that their significance for creating privacy appears. In a camp such as Zaatari in Jordan, producing a gradient of social spaces where the private space of the dwelling is well demarcated and, above all, protected is one of the main processes that steered the transition from shelters to dwellings (Dalal 2020). Similarly, in an informal tented settlement in Lebanon, refugees built covered porches or "balconies" in order to create a transition from the very private space of the tent to the public area outside (Oueishek 2018). The reason behind this is that, in contrast to the shelter where notions of privacy are not necessarily present, a "dwelling" is first and foremost a space where a human's existential need for privacy, safety, and peace are ensured (Heidegger 1971). In order to add curtains and sheets for their spaces, refugees had to overcome further "invisible" challenges posed by the containers. Particularly, the structures of the container cannot be amended, and therefore installing screws or nails in its sheets is not allowed. In the Tempohome where Leila lived, a local technique employed to overcome this obstacle emerged: refugees used spoons or other metal elements to wedge objects such as sheets, curtains, or threads between the cracks of the containers. Because the shutters of the

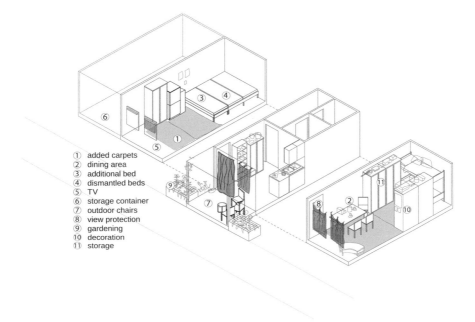

FIGURE 21.2 A perspective showing the rearrangement of elements and furniture to produce new spaces within the containers

Source: Authors

sleeping room are often closed, curtains were only added to the windows in the living space and to the kitchen where privacy and light are needed during the day. To overcome the challenging thermal conditions in the container, especially on hot summer days, the family added a curtain to the main door leading to the kitchen as well. This way, the kitchen could remain a private space, while the door could be opened to let a cool breeze into the container on hot days. Thus, a specific curtain also serves as an important element to regulate the transition between the private space of the "dwelling" and the appropriated porch (see Figure 21.2).

The spatial transformation of camps

This chapter sheds light on how refugees appropriate space in Berlin's Tempohomes. Subtle practices—such as hanging curtains, placing carpets, dismantling beds, assembling fridges, storing luggage, and relocating mattresses, chairs, and tables—showed how the standardized layout of the container was subverted. Although the main structure of the container and its furniture remained, refugees managed to produce an alternative design that maximized the use of the space for the purpose of dwelling. By doing so, we have contributed to the debate on appropriating camps in particular and to spatial transformation in general.

These findings have shown that changes within the physical space clearly reflect refugees' attempts to produce new social spaces. Moving beds, or squeezing them to the edge of the room, indicates an attempt to either create a "sleeping space" or a "multi-functional living room." Here, it should be noted that our observations are limited to the short periods of visits, and thus refugees' practices and uses of space extend far beyond what we have presented. Yet, our findings reveal that the factors of scale, power relations, and politics must not be disregarded when producing new social spaces within the containers. By articulating and comparing how Leila appropriated their three containers, we demonstrated that the sum of these appropriations produced a new space at a meta level: the dwelling. This means that spatial appropriations cannot be understood solely based on their immediate scale (physical space); their multi-scalar impact must be addressed as well. Changing the position of a wardrobe or adding a curtain are indeed changes to physical space that aim to create privacy and diversify the use of space. However, the sum of these practices led to the creation of a comprehensive, complex, and dynamic space, namely a dwelling, which the original container failed to offer and even hindered with its limiting regulations. This underscores the importance of scale and the connectedness between appropriations in physical space. Research needs to take into account the multiple scales on which appropriations occur, both inside and outside camps.

The second contribution of this chapter relates to the notion of spatial transformation and, in general, to the "refiguration of space" (Knoblauch and Löw 2017). The case of Tempohomes in Berlin clearly illustrates that refugees' appropriation of space is not only an interplay between physical and social spaces, but first and foremost a political act. Through a series of "tactics" (De Certeau 2013), refugees have overcome the challenges imposed on them by the limited design of the containers and their strict regulations. Hanging curtains, placing rugs, or planting flower beds are not simple acts of personalization, for they require constant negotiations with the operator, who might knock on their door and demand that these changes be removed or placed back inside the container. The container space becomes a field of spatial negotiations—a contestation of forces and power relations. Wedging a spoon between the sides of the container to hang curtains is therefore an act of resistance to disciplinary power, a demand to dwell. A better understanding of how space is transformed or "refigured," therefore, cannot be established without taking into consideration how space is disciplined and politically shaped; how it is permeated by power relations; and, most importantly, how appropriations, though sometimes "subtle" or "random," contribute to the erosion of disciplinary powers through space. In our case, this led to the emergence of a new hybrid spatial constellation: namely, a dwelling inside a shelter.

Acknowledgments

This research has been funded by the Deutsche Forschungsgemeinschaft (DFG, German Research Foundation)—project number 290045248—SFB 1265. The authors would like to thank the editors and Toby Parsloe for commenting on earlier drafts of this chapter.

References

Agamben, Giorgio. 1998. *Homo Sacer: Sovereign Power and Bare Life*. Stanford: Stanford University Press.
Agier, Michel. 2002. "Between War and City: Towards an Urban Anthropology of Refugee Camps." *Ethnography* 3 (3): 317–341.
Agier, Michel. 2016. "Afterword: What Contemporary Camps Tell Us about the World to Come." *Humanity: An International Journal of Human Rights, Humanitarianism, and Development* 7 (3): 459–468.
Bourdieu, Pierre. 1970. "The Berber House or the World Reversed." *Social Science Information* 9 (2): 151–170.
Bourdieu, Pierre. 2018. "Social Space and the Genesis of Appropriated Physical Space." *International Journal of Urban and Regional Research* 42 (1): 106–114.
Charmaz, Kathy. 2006. *Constructing Grounded Theory: A Practical Guide Through Qualitative Analysis*. London: SAGE Publishers.
Dalal, Ayham. 2014. "Camp Cities between Planning and Practice: Mapping the Urbanisation of Zaatari Camp." Unpublished Master thesis. Stuttgart and Cairo: Universität Stuttgart & Ain Shams University.
Dalal, Ayham. 2020. "From Emergency Shelters to Dwellings: On the Construction of Dwellings in Zaatari Refugee Camp, Jordan." Unpublished PhD thesis. Berlin: Technische Universität Berlin.
Dalal, Ayham, Amer Darweesh, Philipp Misselwitz, and Anna Steigemann. 2018. "Planning the Ideal Refugee Camp? A Critical Interrogation of Recent Planning Innovations in Jordan and Germany." *Urban Planning* 3 (4): 64–78.
Darweesh, Amer. 2019. "Planning for Asylum Accommodation in Berlin." Unpublished Master thesis. Berlin: Technische Universität Berlin.
De Certeau, Michel. 2013. *The Practice of Everyday Life*. Translated by Steven Rendall. 2. print. Berkeley: University of California Press.
Heidegger, Martin. 1971. "Building Dwelling Thinking." In *Poetry, Language, Thought*, translated by Albert Hofstadter. New York: Harper Colophon Books.
Herz, Manuel. 2013. *From Camp to City: Refugee Camps of the Western Sahara*. Edited by Eidgenössische Technische Hochschule Zürich. Zürich: Lars Müller Publisher.
Knoblauch, Hubert, and Martina Löw. 2017. "On the Spatial Re-Figuration of the Social World." *Sociologica* 11 (2): 1–27. doi: 10.2383/88197.
Lefebvre, Henri. 1991. *The Production of Space*. Translated by Donald Nicholson-Smith. Oxford: Blackwell Publishing.
Maqusi, Samar. 2017. "'Space of Refuge': Negotiating Space with Refugees Inside the Palestinian Camp." *Humanities* 6 (3): 60.
Misselwitz, Philipp. 2009. "Rehabilitating Camp Cities: Community Driven Planning for Urbanised Refugee Camps." Unpublished PhD thesis. Stuttgart: Universität Stuttgart.
Oueishek, Alina. 2018. "Features of the Home in the Refugee Camp: Applied Study on Al Jarahiya Camp." In *Different Perspectives on the Syrian Reality*, edited by Ettijahat, 17–70. Stuttgart: ibidem Verlag.
Ramadan, Adam. 2013. "Spatialising the Refugee Camp." *Transactions of the Institute of British Geographers* 38 (1): 65–77.
Sanyal, Romola. 2010. "Squatting in Camps: Building and Insurgency in Spaces of Refuge." *Urban Studies* 48 (5): 877–890.

22

"I SPY WITH MY LITTLE EYE"

Children's actual use and experts' intended design of public space

Ignacio Castillo Ulloa, Angela Million, and Jona Schwerer

Introduction: *intuitive* versus *calculated* uses of public space

In this chapter, we examine the tension between children's use and experts' design of public space, based on the assumption that children actually use it in manners deviating from those originally intended by experts (Reicher et al. 2015; Hendricks 2011). We explore the discrepancies arising therefrom through the concepts of: affordance (the uses space enables by its material and constituent elements as well as the interactions among them and with the environmental settings); relational space (rather than existing independently of objects, persons, and events, space results from their interactions); spatial knowledge (the ways space is perceived, thought of, used, and acted out); and spatial pedagogization (the spatialized rationale buttressing space's topology and asserting specific discernments and uses). By conceiving public space here as a socially constructed arrangement of multiple material objects (with certain qualities) and actors (with varying degrees of spatial knowledge as well as physical qualities) that is ostensibly accessible to everyone, we pose the question: how can the spatial knowledge of children, objectified in their uses of spatial arrangements, be substantively integrated into the design process? Against this backdrop, we discuss the intervention of a public space located on the outskirts of the city of Lima, which has followed a fairly unorthodox approach toward child participation and seems to have moved from a "prescriptive" to a "responsive" posture regarding what uses to infuse into public space.

Deeming space in "four acts": affordance, relationality, knowledge, and pedagogization

Substances, surfaces, and individuals: intrinsic qualities and latent affordances

James J. Gibson first introduced the concept of "affordance" in his 1977 article "The Theory of Affordances" and further developed it in his book, *The Ecological Approach to Visual Perception* (1979). Gibson (1977, 67; italics in the original) sustains that "*the affordance of anything is a specific combination of the properties of its substance and its surfaces taken with reference to an animal.*" Such a definition of affordance points out all action possibilities that, while "concealed" in the surroundings (whether built or natural), exist regardless of the individual's (or, as Gibson puts it, "the animal's") ability to recognize them. Hence, potential actions that something may support only become palpable in relation to a specific individual and its agency as well as competences. In its initial acceptation, affordance, to Gibson, denotes a "material disposition, the consequent of which is specified in human terms"; thus, any given "material thing may have a great many different possible ways in which it can be used. Each one is an affordance" (Harré 2002, 27). These lurking affordances, moreover, are dependent on not only the aforementioned object-individual's agency plus knowledge relationship, but also on environmental circumstances. As cultural sociologist Terrence McDonnell (2010, 1806) points out, the "latent set of possible actions that environments and objects enable . . . are relationally tied to the capabilities of the person interacting with" them. In this regard, a distinction between *qualities* and *affordances*, McDonnell suggests, ought to be made: whereas the former are "inherent and independent characteristics of objects and places," the latter "are made manifest through interactions between audiences, objects and context" (2010, 1806). In this sense, affordances can be seen as the interchanges among the qualities of objects, of immediate settings, and the individuals interacting with both of them. Out of these intersections, in the specific case of public space, emerges a wide array of actions. Individuals, according to their subjective interpretations, establish particular linkages with the elements that make up public space and its immediate surroundings, then giving way to "hidden" affordances. To sum up, in public space substances, surfaces, and individuals coalesce by way of intrinsic qualities and latent affordances—this, we believe, happens inasmuch as public space, far from being absolute and static, results from constant interrelations and their synthetizing among objects, groups thereof, and environments.

Not absolute, but interrelated and synthesized: deeming space relationally

For the purpose of our discussion, space is deemed as being deeply entangled with sociality, and, as such, understood as a social product. More specifically, we draw on the *relational* take Martina Löw (2001; 2016) developed on space, in which it is conceptualized as "*a relational arrangement of living beings and social goods*" (Löw 2016, 131; italics in the original). Social goods, according to Löw, can be primarily *material* and *symbolic*, which in turn underpins the analytic differentiation between one form of social goods and the other (Löw 2016, 130). Furthermore, space is not, in and of itself, a relational arrangement of persons and goods—individuals have to link these elements actively to compose a space. Therefore, "*space is constituted by two processes that must be analytically distinguished: spacing and the operation of synthesis*" (Löw 2016, 135; italics in the original). Spacing, on the one hand, refers to the placing of the social goods and persons in relation to other placements and the operation of synthesis, while on the other, it describes the process through which these elements are turned into one coherent whole; as Löw writes, "an *operation of synthesis* is required for the constitution of space, that is, goods and people are amalgamated to spaces by way of processes of perception, imagination, and memory" (Löw 2016, 135). While Löw accurately highlights the relevance of both living beings and social goods for the process of the constitution of space, we will focus, in our argument, mainly on the social goods—that is to say, chiefly material goods as the material objects *affording* certain actions in space. In addition to this, the process of the constitution of space is mediated through the individuals' spatial knowledge, for it comprises how space is perceived, imagined, and remembered. Thus, given the several affordances that crop up, while spacing and the operation of synthesis simultaneously unfold, the way space is effectively conceived and thus constituted varies from one individual to another. In other words, the subjective knowledge of individuals not only renders space relevant and meaningful in variegated manners but also shapes the (inter)action established with its material constituent elements. Consequently, the veiled affordances of material objects (i.e., ensembles of social goods) involved in any given process of space constitution theoretically allow different spaces, made out of the same material components, to be constituted. Space, in brief, is interrelated and synthesized through the individuals' spatial knowledge.

Experiential, sensory, and motoric bodily practices: the bedrock of spatial knowledge

Drawing on the sociology of knowledge, knowledge can be understood "as socially mediated meaning" (Knoblauch 2019, 26). Hence, "action is dependent on and defined by knowledge" (Knoblauch 2019, 26). To put it another way, our worldviews are strongly defined by what we know. Spatial knowledge, in that regard, comprises "the subjective or individual experiences and perceptions of space" as well as "imaginations, emotions and affective reactions related to space" (Löw and Knoblauch 2019, 11). Moreover, it is usually, though not exclusively, acquired by dint of sensorimotor systems as individuals move around, through, and experience the world. It develops, sequentially, in three phases: (i) *landmark knowledge* (based on characterizing and unique spatial features); (ii) *route knowledge* (the habitual movements and paths that order and unite landmarks); and (iii) *survey knowledge* (quantitative in nature, it responds to the ability to simultaneously interrelate diverse locations characterized by landmarks; as a result, one becomes capable of shortcutting and detouring) (Siegel and White 1975; Montello 2001). In the midst of such landmark–route–survey sequences, institutional knowledge resources—such as those produced and conveyed in and by families, science, schools, standardized rule systems, or art—are fed into the constant production of spatial knowledge.

Likewise, there is arguably a parallelism between the construction of landmark–route–survey sequences and the process by which hidden affordances of the elements making up space are disclosed. While moving through and within spaces, individuals not only associate spaces (to create routes) but also, through interactions with their material elements, show their concealed affordances. Provided that spatial knowledge is, in and of itself, subjective, it ought to physically, linguistically, or materially become objectified in order for it to be analyzed. To that end, it should be taken into consideration that spatial knowledge conflates single spaces ("referential locations") and systems that are built thereof ("landmark-based routes") while also deriving "from actual experience within a space" (Pick Jr. 2001, 9682). Spatial knowledge, to wit, arises, by means of experiential, sensory, and motor aspects of bodily practices, from the entire host of actions that are performed in, on, from, with space: appropriating, using, interacting, traversing. The myriad actions that individuals perform, particularly regarding public space, are mediated by their capacity to spot latent affordances embedded in its material components, which, as aforementioned, enables different spaces to be concurrently constituted. Material arrangements of public space—and their concomitant affordances—are likewise swayed by the rationale with which they are imbued, which attempts to assert specific perceptions and uses: that is to say, the spatial pedagogization of public space.

Curbing perceptions, uses, and sentiments: spatial pedagogization

The pedagogy that underpins space refers to the spatialization of the rationale that advances arrangements in order to establish specific perceptions and uses of space—at times in a subtle manner, at others, more bluntly. Eventually, space is subject to a "pedagogization." This term stems from the educational sciences and has been employed to, by and large,

> indicate the steady expansion and increased depth of educational action during the nineteenth and particularly the twentieth centuries . . . [which] not only concerned the increase in the number of child-raising and educational governmental bodies and the greater range of child-raising and educational processes but also encompassed the ever-increasing central role of the pedagogical in the society.
>
> *(Depaepe et al. 2008, 14–15)*

The influence that "the pedagogical" has exerted is not limited to the formal processes and arenas (e.g., school curricula and classrooms). Contrariwise, it cuts across all strata of society and, as such, public space has been ostensibly instrumental to pedagogizing societies in addition to being seen as a setting for learning and co-education (Pike 2011; Visscher and Bouverne-De Bie 2008; Rodó-de-Zárate and Baylina 2014). This is seen in the case of children growing up in countries throughout the so-called Global North and their forms of play in urban areas, which, as Kathrin Hörschelmann and Lorraine van Blerk (2012, 104–105) explain, have undergone the effects of, on the one hand, commodification, rendering "objects, places and even relationships or less tangible aspects of life . . . 'purchasable'" and, on the other hand, "the increasing institutionalization of afterschool leisure time." Moreover, the spatial pedagogy of public space seeks to establish not only acuities and usages but also feelings. For example, the "development of managed adventure playgrounds and parks mean (sic) that, through the constructed nature in the city, children are being encouraged to engage with the natural at the same time as removing parental fears and anxieties" (Hörschelmann and van Blerk 2012, 103). All things considered, the spatial pedagogization of public space seems to neglect aspects of affordances and therefore the simultaneous constitution of spaces. Uses are prominently defined through the discipline of design and are often meant to be pervasive and univocal. Be that as it may, the "disruptive" uses that children make of public space suggest otherwise. We next look into the tension between children's actual use and experts' intended projection of public space.

Children's advertent spatial knowledge vis-à-vis experts' pedagogical design of public space

As our research hypothesis, we propose that children, in their interaction with the material constitutive elements of public space, make diverse latent affordances visible and relevant, thereby objectifying their spatial knowledge. Moreover, the diverse interactions between children and the material elements that constitute public space and its immediate context tend, markedly, to diverge from the underlying spatial pedagogization of experts' designs. From a general standpoint, as shown in Figure 22.1, at one of the poles along the continuum of the affordances of the material elements that make up public space, design experts objectify their spatial knowledge and intended uses in their yet-to-materialize *abstract* designs. Experts thus attempt to predetermine not only the way in which each individual element of public space is to be perceived and used, but also the combination among them and in conjunction with the surrounding settings. Therefore, public space embodies a spatial pedagogization that is ultimately asserted, once designs are materialized, in the realm of *concrete* space. At the opposite end of the continuum, children begin to interact with the already materialized pedagogization of public space and consequently enable potential affordances to come into play. Thus, the spatial knowledge of design experts signals an understanding of public space as something that, by being malleable, fixable, and tamable, makes it possible to establish a specific topology and its *exact* perception and use. The spatial knowledge of children, on the other hand, indicates, via *advertent*, intuitive practices

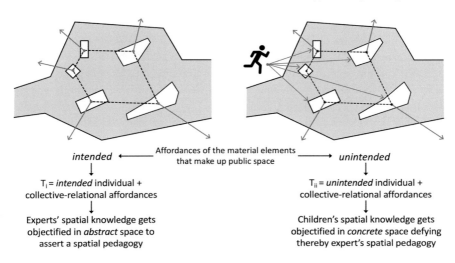

FIGURE 22.1 A continuum from intended (by design and planning experts) to unintended (prompted by children) affordances of public space

Source: © the authors

and appropriations an open-ended imagination of public space and any given topological (pre)disposition thereof. All in all, children, by using public space as they see fit, constitute a different space than that of the experts, depending on different stocks of spatial knowledge. In the next section, we explore, in the wake of a progressive intervention of a public space on the outskirts of the city of Lima, Peru, how children can be integrated into a participatory design process in such a way that experts' intended design and children's actual use of public space come closer together.

Tahuantinsuyo Park: experts and children meet halfway

Tahuantinsuyo Park is a section of a larger central public space in the neighborhood of La Balanza, located within the district of Comas in northern Lima, Peru. Both the park and its immediate surroundings have been gradually developed parallel and around the redesign and refurbishment of the *Comedor Comunal San Martín* (a community dining hall)—an institution best described as a mixture of a self-organized neighborhood kitchen (run by a group of women called "the mothers of the *Comedor San Martín*"), a public cafeteria, a multi-purpose room, and a small library, situated in the heart of La Balanza. The dining hall was first adapted based on initiatives put together by the mothers of the *Comedor San Martín* and the members of the artistic association *Fiteca*, who had been reclaiming public spaces throughout the barrio over the years with the aim of promoting cultural activities (theater, dance, and plastic arts) for children and young people. As of 2012, the Coordinadora de la Ciudad (en Construcción) (CCC), a Lima-based architectural studio founded and headed by Peruvian architects Javier Vera and Eleazar Cuadros Choque, has been leading the growing intervention of the dining room, the park, and its adjacent settings (planned in two phases: 2012–2014 and 2015–2017).

Once the dining hall had been revamped and expanded, its encircling spaces started to be transformed, drawing upon the input of children through a fairly unorthodox strategy. In a first step, called "*Proyecto Semilla*" ("seed project"), wooden sticks were brightly painted and placed right outside the main entrance of the dining room, to "entice" children to come around and see what they would do with them: children started to climb up and down the poles and, eventually, attempted to move boldly from one to another. In addition, benches made out of painted tires were made available to children and a fence was replaced by a dirt ramp leading up to a nearby greenery (see Figure 22.2).

The wooden sticks, benches, and dirt ramps are envisioned not as fixed and definitive, but rather as adaptable and changeable elements making up public space (anew) and thus providing a wide array of "dormant" affordances. In doing so, they not only offer alternative ways for children to devise their practices of play but also invite (or even pedagogize) parents and neighbors to alter their views on, and the ways in which they make use of, the public space right next to the dining hall:

> In order to avoid the irruption of automobiles, instead of a fence, a labyrinth of wooden high sticks, where children climb up and down and think up their own games, was used. To keep "potheads" away, rather than policemen, children are keeping them at bay by simply playing with used tires, which they've painted themselves. Adults may sit on benches, made out of worn tires and located at the foot of the dining hall, to wait while their children play. Is a green area without a spike fence unthinkable? A small slope proves otherwise.
>
> *(Vera 2018, 87; own translation)*

FIGURE 22.2 The "seed project": colorful wooden poles were installed using a worn tire filled with concrete and brightly painted as well. In addition, used colored tires were set right next to each other (to form a "bench") and at intervals for children to play. Moreover, dirt slopes (in the background) were sown with grass

Source: © CCC Archive

Also central to the argumentation underpinning the CCC's design principles is the belief that, in order to design public space in Lima,

> previous experience . . . allows to see that public space is first appropriated and then occupied. Thus, rather than "physical seizure", what is at issue is its symbolic resignification, provided that, once the function of public space has been transgressed, it becomes a sort of creative device. To that end, prior to recover a space, the sense of what is public must be both redefined and reclaimed; that is, producing public space implies setting positive conflicts off.
>
> *(Vera 2018, 89; own translation)*

Bearing such aims in mind, designers and planners alike combine aspects of affordance (also in a sense of being surprised by what children are actually capable of doing), designedly knowing (Cross 2006) (having experienced the materiality and design of some of the elements before—here, in particular, the wooden sticks), and spatial pedagogization (prompting change in people's ways of thinking of and using public space).

Over a period of three to four years (2015–2018), the space was increasingly intervened upon and, as children took it over, adapted as accordingly as possible. (It is worthwhile underscoring that, while teenagers and adults started to signal preferences, they were not as straightforward and upfront as those of children—though members of the CCC did not, at all, disregard them.) The wooden climbing poles were eventually replaced by more durable metal structures (some of them are now climbing frames, and swings were added here and there), the benches put together using tires are now parallelepiped elements made out of concrete, and the surface adjacent to the community dining hall entrance was refurbished, integrating mosaics co-designed with children, which somewhat hint at a distinction between where to play and where to walk by. Furthermore, members of the CCC, when asked about the most striking disjuncture between what they had envisioned and what children have displayed in situ, were surprised by children's marked preference for using dirt slopes for climbing and sliding and, in so doing, wrecking newly planted green grass and flowers (Lima's weather is extremely dry and green areas are therefore highly cherished, particularly in settlements throughout its disenfranchised periphery). As a result, the intention of proving, as pointed out by Javier Vera earlier, that a green area could stand alone without a "protective" fence had to be revised and ultimately modified—the green areas were substantially reduced to give way to concrete slanted surfaces that were equipped with climbing ropes or turned into ramps (see Figure 22.4). Such "gymnastic" and incremental material transformations of the public space continued, and a couple of new "concave pipes," encouraging skateboarding, emerged alongside several stands meant to create a small amphitheater (where small concerts and theater plays are organized periodically). In addition, a third concave surface has been constructed opposite the stands as a sort of backdrop. The park will eventually be connected to the main entrance of a nearby elementary school through a set of stairs, which are also envisioned to function as potential stands.

The steady and piecemeal intervention on and transformation of Tahuantinsuyo Park, when seen through the threefold lens of affordance, relational space, and spatial knowledge, reveals more than meets the eye with regard to its process of spatial pedagogization—which in turn arguably constitutes a catalyzer for the refiguration of public space. First of all, designers of the CCC imprint the diverse constitutive elements with specific affordances (for instance, the poles are suggestively "offered" to children to climb up and down) and their spatial knowledge is synthetized a priori in the form of the "coherent" overall redesign of the park (see Figure 22.3)—though such a process of spacing and synthesizing, as has been explained, is susceptible to the enhancements children may provide. Hence, the spatial knowledge of children, chiefly their "performative" articulation, could be integrated, not without suffering adaptions, into the future phases of implementation. To put it another way, children's actual enactment of their spatial knowledge—which could be regarded as their spacing and synthetizing—revealed the pitfalls underlying the design experts' pedagogization of the park inasmuch as they challenged its imbued—and brought to the fore other "hidden"—affordances. This becomes particularly clear in the case of the aforementioned dirt slopes: instead of caring for, or even nursing, the newly planted grass and flowers, children identified a possibility for sliding and climbing, thus expressing a different perception of space (and, more specifically, of the affordances offered by its material constitutive elements) than that of the members of the CCC. In effect, children constituted another, quite distinctive space than the one imagined and projected onto the abstract space of the initial design. Interestingly enough, despite being somewhat pitted against the expert's pedagogical design of Tahuantinsuyo Park, the children's advertent spatial knowledge provided for other demands that would normally be entailed in the intervention of any given public space (e.g., budget, timeline, mix of interests, etc.). Far from being downplayed as a delaying or even irrelevant factor, this was seriously considered by the CCC designers. Consequently, children's relational take on public space (by climbing up and down the poles, using the dirt slopes to slide, and running aimlessly throughout the park, children were producing *their* space through experiential, sensory and bodily practices) has been aptly—for it is not definitive—drawn upon to develop the space further, all the while trying to inscribe the unintended affordances the children made visible into its actual materialization.

The case of Tahuantinsuyo Park, rather than being exclusively the outcome of professional design expertise, embodies an iterative process of materializing, appropriating, and adapting, along with a course of action underpinned by a trial-and-error principle, whereby both designers and children willingly learn from each other. Moreover, the redesign of the park, as already stated, has not yet been completed. In fact, it may well be said that it has reached an open-ended stage. Moreover, among various fairly unexpected upshots, other users have responded quite well to the physical alteration to which the park has been subjected thus far. For example, the metal structure that the wooden poles were turned into is used by teenagers to exercise, while adults have also grown fond of the park's transformation and have made it their stomping ground (to be sure, as members of the CCC commented during our fieldwork, there are neighbors who criticize these actions, though a number of bystanders were ultimately won over by the whole process). The park furthermore seems to already represent a referential location within the landmark-based routes of people living nearby (most likely due to the existence of the communal dining hall) and, as such, is imbued in their spatial knowledge. However, spatial knowledge comprises not only implicit and habituated practices (such as traversing the park every day), but also, as the children boldly demonstrated, an array of sensory and motor aspects embedded in bodily practice. Including it as a central factor in redesigning and intervening upon the park meant paying attention and reacting to what the children exhibited was feasible using the constitutive material elements of public space. All things considered, the tension between the children's ability to foresee, seize, and disclose dormant affordances by means of their singular spacing and synthetizing, and design experts' explicit and implicit pedagogical design of public space, seems to have given rise to a third, alternative course, which has allowed designers and children to meet halfway.

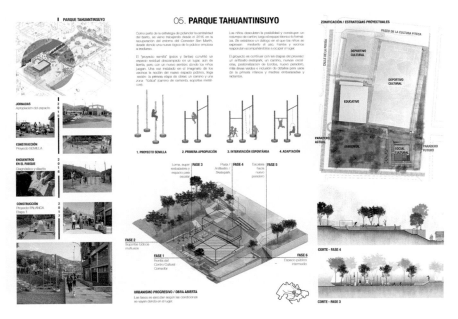

FIGURE 22.3A Poster showing the location of Tahuantinsuyo Park (top left), a picture documentation (bottom left) and an isometric display (bottom center) of the different phases of intervention, a diagrammatic representation of the evolution of the "seed project" (above the isometric drawing), a zoning and overall site design (top right), and two sections of the design (bottom right)

Source: © CCC Archive

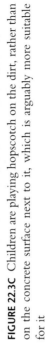

FIGURE 22.3B The picture evinces how children bring to the fore hidden affordances of the holes dug out to erect metal, instead of wooden, poles, yet again testing the limits of the envisaged design and its gradual materialization

Source: © CCC Archive

FIGURE 22.3C Children are playing hopscotch on the dirt, rather than on the concrete surface next to it, which is arguably more suitable for it

Source: © CCC Archive

"I spy with my little eye" **305**

FIGURE 22.4A Children sledding on one of the concave concrete surfaces next to the stands

Source: © the authors

FIGURE 22.4B Metal poles and frames: a more durable stage of the "seed project"

Source: © the authors

FIGURE 22.4C Children climbing up and down slanted concrete surfaces

Source: © the authors

Conclusion: learning to spy with their little eye—toward a "child-responsive" design process of public space

In this chapter, we have examined the relation between children's use and experts' design of public space through the concepts of affordance, relational space, spatial knowledge, and spatial pedagogization. As children use the constitutive material elements of public space in divergent and unexpected fashions—often quite differently than intended by design and planning experts—we pose two questions: (i) how can children's spatial knowledge be more substantially and meaningfully integrated into the design process, and (ii) how can the notion of spatial pedagogization, which is intrinsic to the planning and design of public space, be taken into account more consciously by planners and designers?

Children and young people show through their set of bodily actions that they not only perceive space differently but also see other qualities in its material objects and thus potentially use them in a manner that was not expected by designers and planners. The many "dormant" affordances children are able to "awaken" indicate that there is never just one predetermined, univocal, and unequivocal use of public space, but rather that the ambiguity of material objects—and thus of the resulting spaces—always allows for other uses and spatial constitutions. After all, public space is, par excellence, the domain of multiplicity. The unforeseeable uses of spaces, made visible through the affordances children render relevant, compose a dimension that designers and planners cannot fully foresee as they undertake their professional work, more often than not departing from a quite distinct knowledge base—one that regards space as malleable, fixable, and tamable. The designing and planning of public space are therefore always faced with the conundrum of finding a middle ground between being able to make proposals for its use, based on experts' knowledge, and actively incorporating how people may eventually use the material objects of which public space is composed together with any arrangements thereof. We also have to acknowledge, in this regard, that the described tension between the spatial knowledge of children and young people and that of design and planning experts very much applies to other social groups in public space (e.g., the elderly, homeless, street vendors, etc.). Furthermore, children and young people obviously do not share an entirely common spatial knowledge. Rather, stocks of spatial knowledge among children and young people (as well as other social groups) are shaped by categories such as age, class, and gender. It goes without saying that all of them possess a distinct form of spatial knowledge, with which other hidden affordances are brought to the fore. While it is virtually impossible to anticipate and accordingly stipulate every single potential affordance the diverse users of public space may render significant during the design and planning phase, such an "impossibility" may well be tackled theoretically through the concepts of affordance, relational space, spatial knowledge, and spatial pedagogization. In practical terms, as the case of Tahuantinsuyo Park shows with a focus on children, it would then be feasible to open up a different pathway to the design and implementation of projects of public space intervention.

"I spy with my little eye"   **307**

To that end, it must be acknowledged that the formalization of public space is predominantly based on experts' spatial knowledge. This knowledge gets objectified and spatializes all the while a pedagogy. Every form of design and planning—and their materialization—is therefore a kind of "pedagogization." As reviewed in the case of Tahuantinsuyo Park, planners and designers "invite children to play" with enticing elements to see how children react and what they make of and with them. Modifications to the originally envisioned design are undertaken subsequently, seeking to adapt the materialities and arrangements of public space accordingly. During this process, the choice of sticks at the beginning also creates certain possibilities and generates tension between an a priori spatial pedagogization and the children's "obstinate" uses, which render other affordances. In addition, there is the question of further concealed or conspicuous spatial pedagogical intentions and aims planners and designers have and how they are made operative within the planning and designing process. Designers and planners of the CCC, for example, intended specific uses and came up with corresponding spatial arrangements for "public life" to thrive organically. Yet, the understanding of "public life" designers and planners possess will surely differ, to a lesser or greater extent, from that of everyday users of public space. For children, public life may well simply mean the freedom to do what they please. Hence, both the legibility and limits of spatial pedagogy's goals are, in effect, challenged—the trick is then to devise mechanisms to respond to, and not deter, such challenges. In this case, experience functions as a catalyst: members of the CCC had already tried out similar actions in other locations and projects in Lima (e.g., the wooden poles). As a result, designers and planners build up over time and through iterative experimentation an epistemological basis that translates into child-responsive design decisions (as opposed to head-on and blatant *prescriptive* spatial pedagogization).

All in all, the analytical added value of critically assessing, through the lens of affordance, relational space, spatial knowledge, and spatial pedagogization, planning and design processes fosters a user-responsive design and planning of public space. That is to say, a change in the posture of design and planning practitioners toward a praxis more strongly connected to material elements, users' interactions with them, and the interplay between the arrangements of the constitutive material objects in public space and the (immediate and larger) context in which they are set up. This would require, among other things, giving up masterplan-concept thinking, refraining from focusing almost solely on qualities of objects and places as though they were inherent and independent entities, and revisiting the dictum "form follows function," which designers and planners reverse all too often in practice. Therefore, the myriad hidden and overt affordances of space becomes an integral part of designing and planning processes, which in turn prompts a shift of emphasis from an approach based on an expert's vision of a fixed product to an open-ended sequence of possibilities. Furthering such a shift is far from an easy task, for it would involve, on the one hand, reconsidering the language and means of design and planning communication (e.g., 3-D renderings and illustrations tend to present a ready and finished vision of conceived projects). On the other hand, for research purposes, it would require promoting accompanying research, instead of a post-reconstructing process of planning and designing. At the same time, interventions in as well as alterations of public space, led and propelled by participatory design and planning processes, need to be reexamined, as spatial refigurations and also as a mutual synergic learning process for participants and experts alike, since they are "not only an institutional phenomenon (sociogenesis) but also [affect] subjects themselves (psychogenesis)" (Knoblauch and Löw 2017, 11). When the "affected subjects" happen to be children, designers and planners may well lead the participatory process according to the children's game precept "I spy with my little eye"; rather than guessing, have children, as in the case of Tahuantinsuyo Park, physically display what it is that they can see that neither designers nor planners ever could.

Acknowledgements

This research has been funded by the Deutsche Forschungsgemeinschaft (DFG, German Research Foundation)—project number 290045248—SFB 1265.

References

Cross, Nigel. 2006. *Designerly Ways of Knowing*. London: Springer.
Depaepe, Marc, Frederik Herman, Melanie Surmont, Angelo Van Gorp, and Frank Simon. 2008. "About Pedagogization: From the Perspective of the History of Education." In *Educational Research: The Educationalization of Social Problems*, edited by Paul Smeyers, and Marc Depaepe, 13–30. Dordrecht: Springer.
Gibson, James J. 1977. "The Theory of Affordances." In *Perceiving, Acting and Knowing: Toward an Ecological Psychology*, edited by Robert Shaw and John Bransford, 67–82. Hillsdale, NJ: Erlbaum.
Gibson, James J. 1979. *The Ecological Approach to Visual Perception*. Hillsdale, NJ: Erlbaum.
Harré, Rom. 2002. "Material Objects in Social Worlds." *Theory, Culture & Society* 19 (5–6): 23–33.
Hendricks, Barbara E. 2011. *Designing for Play*, 2nd ed. Burlington, VT: Ashgate.
Hörschelmann, Kathrin, and Lorraine van Blerk. 2012. *Children, Youth and the City*. London: Routledge.
Knoblauch, Hubert. 2019. "The Communicative Turn in German Sociology of Knowledge." *Society Register* 3 (1): 23–38. doi: 10.14746/sr.2019.3.1.02.
Knoblauch, Hubert, and Martina Löw. 2017. "On the Spatial Re-Figuration of the Social World." *Sociologica* 11 (2): 1–27. doi: 10.2383/88197.
Löw, Martina. 2001. *Raumsoziologie*. Frankfurt am Main: Suhrkamp.
Löw, Martina. 2016. *The Sociology of Space: Materiality, Social Structures, and Action*. New York: Palgrave Macmillan.
Löw, Martina, and Hubert Knoblauch. 2019. "The Re-Figuration of Spaces: Introducing the Research Programme of the Collaborative Research Centre 'Re-Figuration of Spaces'." *SFB 1265 Working Paper No. 2*. Berlin. doi: 10.14279/depositonce-9236.
McDonnell, Terence E. 2010. "Cultural Objects as Objects: Materiality, Urban Space, and the Interpretation of AIDS Campaigns in Accra, Ghana." *American Journal of Sociology* 115 (6): 1800–1852.

Montello, Daniel R. 2001 "Spatial Cognition." In *International Encyclopedia of the Social & Behavioral Sciences*, edited by Neil J. Smelser and Paul B. Baltes, 14771–14775. Oxford: Pergamon Press.

Pick Jr., Herbert L. 2001. "Mental Maps, Psychology of." In *International Encyclopedia of the Social & Behavioral Sciences*, edited by Neil J. Smelser and Paul B. Baltes, 9681–9683. Oxford: Pergamon Press.

Pike, Susan. 2011. "'If You Went out It Would Stick': Irish Children's Learning in Their Local Environments." *International Research in Geographical and Environmental Education* 20 (2): 139–159. doi: 10.1080/10382046.2011.564787.

Reicher, Christa, Silke Edelhoff, Päivi Kataikko, and Angela Million. 2015. *Kinder_Sichten: Städtebau und Architektur für und mit Kindern und Jugendlichen*. Oberhausen: assoverlag.

Rodó-de-Zárate, Maria, and Mireia Baylina. 2014. "Learning in/through Public Space: Young Girls and Feminist Consciousness-raising." In *Informal Education, Childhood and Youth: Geographies, Histories, Practices*, edited by Sarah Mills and Peter Kraftl, 244–256. Palgrave Macmillan. doi: 10.1057/9781137027733_16.

Siegel, Alexander W., and Sheldon H. White. 1975. "The Development of Spatial Representations of Large-Scale Environments." *Advances in Child Development and Behavior* 10: 9–55.

Vera, Javier. 2018. "Arquitectura como (pequeña) provocación." In *Ludantia: I Bienal Internacional de Educación en Arquitectura para a Infancia e a Mocidade*, edited by Virginia Navarro Martínez, Jorge Raedó Álvarez, and Xosé Manuel Rosales Noves, 83–89. Colexio Oficial de Arquitectos de Galicia.

Visscher, Sven De, and Maria Bouverne-De Bie. 2008. "Recognizing Urban Public Space as a Co-Educator: Children's Socialization in Ghent." *International Journal of Urban and Regional Research* 32 (3): 604–616. doi: 10.1111/j.1468–2427.2008.00798.x.

INDEX

Note: Page numbers in italics indicate a figure or a diagram and page numbers in bold indicate a map or a table on the corresponding page.

Abyssinia 36
acceleration 21, 38, 40, 46–48, 61, 76
Aceitera General Deheza (AGD) 129
Achaemenid Empire 32
"acidification" 42
activism, online 169
Aeschylus 29
affordances 10–12, 196, 205, 294–298, *299*, 301–302, *303*, 303, 306–307; dormant 11, 300, 303, 306; latent 295, 297–298
Afghanistan 243
AFL–CIO 147n2
Africa 21, 29–30, 35, 90, 101–102, 104–105, 278; North 101; sub-Saharan 122
agglomeration 141–143, 151, 153, 163; economies 141–142; urban 79, 163
agroindustry 128–129, 131
Airbnb 205
Alexander the Great 31–32
Alexander VI, Pope 35
algorithmization 171
'ambividuals' 210
America First 243, 247
animal symbolicum 39
animatic cities 212
animation(s) 80, 206, 209–212
Annales School 28
Anthropocene 41, 253
"Anthropogeography" 35

apartheid 100–101
appropriation 10, 12, 30, 32, 35, 195, 271, 285–289, 292, 299
architectural design 74, 79
architectural form 76, 79–80
Architecture Principe 6, 73–74, 76, 78–81; magazine 74; theory of the oblique function 6, 73–74, *73*, 78–81
Argentina 7, 91, 120, 122, 127–129, 132n4; Gran Rosario 128–129, **130**, 131
Aristotle 39
arrangements 2, 4, 110–113, 117, 121, 278–279, 297, 306–307; institutional 112–113, 117; social 113; *see also* spatial arrangements
Arton Capital 102–103
ascription 104, 110
Asia 21, 29–30, 41, 99, 102–103, 105, 278, 280; Northern 34; *see also* East Asia; South Asia; South-East Asia
assimilation 33, 212
asylum 87, 94; political 243
asylum seekers 87, 94, 243
Athens (ancient) 41
Augustus 33–34
Austria-Hungary 92
automated posting protocols 170
"Axial Age" 31
Aztec Empire 106

Index

Babylon (ancient) 31–33
Bakhtin, Mikhail 63
"Ballad of Early Heroes" 31
Bangladesh 125
beggars 49; *see also* rough sleepers
begging 49–50
Belgrano Cargas project 128–129
Berlin 22, 75, *75*, 80, 109, *153*, 163, 192, *197*, 216, 245, 249, 252–254, 285–292; Alexanderplatz 215; Dong Xuan Center 215; Gendarmenmarkt 215; Lustgarten 215; *see also* Berlin Wall
Berlin Wall 244
big data 209
billionaires 102–104; non-Western 103
Black Lives Matter movement 106
Blackness 105
blogospheres 183
bodies 18, 20, 77, 205, 209–210; animatic bodies 9, 211–212; animatory bodies 211; corporeal 210; homeless 51; representational 9; urban 206–209; *see also* body conduct
body conduct 52–53
Brazil 5, 48, 54–55, 57, 91–92, 99, 102, 104; Rio de Janeiro 211, 253; *see also* São Paulo
Brexit 22, 137–138, 173, 175–177, 243, 247
Britain *see* Great Britain
British Empire 32, 36
Bruges 115
Bulgaria 103, 132n1

capital 63, 90, 100, 106, 114, 116, 122, 259, 269, 275–277; cultural 258; economic 258; human 144; public 94; *see also* footloose capital; social capital
capitalism 40, 54, 64, 98, 101, 106, 110, 113–114, 116–117, 278; "digital" 23; state 278
capitalist world-economy 97–99, 101, 106, 114
capitalist world-system 117–118
Carolingian Empire 34
Carthage (ancient) 33
cartography 21, 65
Certeau, Michel de 63–64
Charles V (Habsburg) 32, 115
children 49, 144, 153–154, *156*, 158, 289; homeless 54; socialization of 24; use of public space by 11–12, 294–308, *299*, *300*, *303*, *305*
China, People's Republic of (PRC) 20, 33–34, 42, 93, 102, 104, 106, 122, 124, 127, 131–132, 216; Shanghai 278–279; Shenzhen 216; Window of the World 216; *see also* Hong Kong
China Civil Engineering Construction Corporation (CCECC) 122, 124
China Communications Construction Company (CCCC) 124–125, 127
China Development Bank Corporation 128
China Export Import Bank 122
China Machinery and Engineering Corporation (CMEC) 128
China Oil and Foodstuffs Corporation (COFCO) 129
China Railway Construction Corporation 122
Chinese Empire 34, 106
chronological tables 65, *66*, 68
chronotope 63
cinematic regime 207–210
'CIO unionism' 145, 147n2
circuits 269–275, 278, 280; developmental 274; digital mobility 47; distributed 205; global 271; globalized 269, 273, 275; globalizing 270, 276; informalized 275; overlapping 278; policy 269–270, 272; politics of 273; state-led 271; translocal 276; transnational 271, 280
circulating policies 10
circulation 5–6, 18, 22, 24–26, 73–74, 80–81, 116, 120–121, **126**, **130**, 206–207, 209, 211–212, 276; policy 271–272, 274; transnational 7; urban 9
Cities Alliance (CA) 273–275
citizenship 6–7, 33, 88–90, 93–94, 103–104, 151, 209–210, 258; differentiated 6, 93; global 103, 253; premium 104; smart 209–210
City Guide 9, 194, 196–199, *197*, 201–202
city-regions 10, 140, 277
class 12, 102, 112, 306; backgrounds 249; capitalist 100; creative 138; differences 88; economic 89; global 40; leadership 33; middle 260; -oriented union 147n2; relations 110; ruling 115; social 7; struggle 41; transnational capitalist 99, 102; ultra-rich transnational 103; under- 97; upper 115; working- 36
Clelland, Don 98–100, 102, 104–106, 107n1
clicktivism 169
climate change 271, 273
Clinton, Hillary 137
clothing production 122–127, 131
coalitions 140, 271–272; growth 270–272; political 271; transnational 271–272

Cold War 36, 244
Collaborative Research Center 17, 25, 109, 216
colonialism 6, 34–35, 91, 93–94, 151; settler 91
coloniality 269
colonial settlers 92
colonisation 92–93
commodity chain 7, 120–121; approaches 120
commodity hubs 121–122, 127, 129, 131
communication(s): devices 41, 78; digital 9, 20, 181, 184–186, 198; face-to-face 186; interpersonal 184; medium 23; modes 263; networks 20, 182, 184, 186; offline 194; online 8, 194, 260; patterns 184; phenomena 188; processes 182; public 182–184, 188; sciences 2; social media 9, 182–184, 194; structures 184; system 183; technologies 10, 20, 23; tele- 72; theorists 23
communism 64, 248
communitizations 187
community(ies) 181–188; affective 182, 186; associations 145; building 188; commercial 187; concept of 182, 184–185; definition 185; diasporic 182, 186; ethnic 182, 186; face-to-face 171; geographic 172; imagined 182, 184–188; interest 185; issue 182, 186; LGBT 186; local 186; lost 258; merchant 115; offline 175; online 169–172; physical 178; political 33, 187; proximate 172; religious 47, 187; sub- 171; translocal 9, 186–188; urban 258; virtual 169
commuting time 154–155, 158, 162
consumers 8, 90, 125, 152–157, 159, 161–163, *161*, 205
container (home) 127, 286–292, *290*, *291*
control rooms 18, 23
convergence 2, 138, 141–143
Coordinadora de la Ciudad (en Construcción) (CCC) 299, 301–303, 307
cores 7, 97–99, 106
coronavirus *see* COVID-19
corporeality 39–40, 204–212; animatic 204; representational 204
cosmopolitanism 21, 32, 184, 253–254
coupling: spatial 8, 152, 161–162; spatio-temporal 151–163; temporal 8, 152, 157–161
COVID-19 8, 17, 20, 22, 24, 37–38, 46–48, 170–171, 216, 243
"creative destruction" 110, 112–115, 117

Crimea 249
cultural syncretism 40
cultures: cognitive-occupational 145; hydraulic 41; literal 23; manual-occupational 145; oral 23
cyber-physical reality 194
cyber-physical systems 193–194
cycles 4, 6, 113
Cyprus 101, 103
Cyrus the Great 31–32
Czechoslovakia 99

"dangerous zones" 10
Darius 32
decentralization 9, 18, 22
deindustrialization 117, 145
Deleuze, Gilles 209, 276
democracy 183; social 88
Denmark 104
"desertification" 42
destruction 28–42; creative 110, 112–115, 117
deterritorialization *19*, 25
development projects 7, 10, 277–278
diachronicity 61
digital age 185
digital annotations 194, 196, 201–202
digital communication 9, 20, 181, 184–186, 198
digital data 204–205, 209–210
digital images 205–207, 209
digital infrastructure 205
digitalization 18, 22–24, 60, 263, 265
digital lifelog 199
digitally mediated cities 9, 204, 208, 210–212
digital media 23, 186–188, 193–194, 196
digital mediation 205, 208
digital mediatization 23
digital revolution 193
digitization 8–10, 167, 181–182, 187
discrimination 6, 106
disembedding *19*, 245
divergence 136, 138, 141–144
Divine Right of Kings 31–32
dromology 72–73, 79
dual-career model 162–163
Dunaway, Wilma 98–100, 102, 104–106, 107n1
duration 3, 51, 62, 65, 207, 278; *see also* longue durée
dyadic interactions 171

early modern period 60
East Asia 21, 124

e-commerce 163, 171
economic geography 8, 136–137, 141
economic polarization 7, 142, 146
economies of scale 143, 159
economism 175
economy 4, 6–8, 12, 20, 23, 38, 85, 92, 151–152, 163; capitalist 7, 254; domestic 124; global 178; national 91, 178; new 144; political 106, 121, 205; regional 8; urban 8; world 101, 105; *see also* capitalist world-economy
Egypt 29, 31, 41, 103, 125
Einstein, Albert 63–64, 70, 72, 78
election cycle 172
Elias, Norbert 4, 18–20, 28–29, 34, 47, 101
embodiment 9, 204, 206, 210, 212, 251; animated 9, 210; animatic 206, 209–210; animatory 210; (post)human 204; urban 212
emigrationist colonialism 91, 94
Engel curves 153
Engels, Friedrich 88–89
England 23, 93, 175–178; London 48, 139–140, 143, 175–178, 186, 276, 278–280; Manchester 143
enslavement 40, 90–91
entrepreneurs 143
entrepreneurship 143
Espace (Space) group 76
Ethiopia 7, 120, 122–127, **123**, **126**, 132n1; Addis Ababa 122, **123**, 124; Mekelle 122, **123**, 125–127, **126**, 131
Ethiopian Investment Commission (EIC) 122, 124
ethnicity 12, 19, 106, 145, 186
ethnicization 102
Etruria 41
Europe 4, 20, 25, 35–36, 40, 87, 93–94, 97, 101–103, 105–106, 125, 243–244, 249, 270, 287; Central 40, 42; Eastern 101, 105; Southeast 34; Western 105
European Investment Bank 125
Europeanness 106
European Union 19, 22, 103–104, 124, 136, 175, 183, 243
Eusebius 65, *66–67*
exclusion 6, 9, 12, *19*, 22, 111, 114, 117, 195, 201–202, 212, 247, 273; selective 112; social 117, 202; *see also* exclusion hypothesis
exclusion hypothesis 195, 201–202
exploitation 34, 90, 93, 100–101, 112, 131
extractivism 128

Facebook 178, 186, 196, 201
feedback loops 172–173
Ferguson 186
feudalism 34–35, 64
"feudalization" 34
"figuration" 4, 18–19, 21, 47; centralized 47; "spatio-communicative" 2
filter bubble hypothesis 173–174, 195
finance 116, 122, 125, 128–129, 142, 271, 274, 279
financialization 270, 276–279
financial recession 103
Finland 104
First World War 36, 78
footloose capital 269, 277
Foucauldian biopower 208
Foucault, Michel 2, 208
Foursquare *see* City Guide
Foursquare Labs 196
Foursquare Swarm *see* Swarm
France 19–20, 22, 34–36, 72, 76, 104, 243–244; "Front National" 244; Lyon 63; Paris 48, 74, 140
Franco-Prussian war 92
functional differentiation 18, 21, 25, 34

gaming 195–196, 288
Gates Foundation 274–275
gender 12, 153, 208, 245, 249, 251–252, 306; gap 154; trans- 209
gentrification 6
"geodeterminism" 39
geographical imagination 243, 245, 248–250, 253–254
geographic space 116, 174
geopolitics 35–37, 244, 250; feminist 250, 254–255
German Empire 36
Germany 20, 22, 36, 40, 104, 109, 116, 125, 152, 154–155, 158, 163, 243–245, 249–250, 254, 287; "Alternative für Deutschland" 244; Cologne 25, 253; Ministry for Development Cooperation 125; Nazi 36, 78; *see also* Berlin; West Germany
Giddens, Anthony 2, 10, 62, 245–247, 250, 252
Gini coefficient 97
global distributive justice 6, 95
global inequality 6–7, 87–88, 91, 94–95, 99, 101, 103
globalism 40, 175
"globality" 40

globalization 1, 4, 10, 18, 21–22, 38, 40, 47, 60, 109, 116–117, 136, 146, 187, 243–255, 258, 264, 271
global milieu 246–247, 253
Global North 6, 90–91, 265, 298
global poverty 89–90
Global Production Networks (GPN) 120–122, 125, 127, 131–132
Global South 6, 21, 91, 243, 269
global stratification 104
global warming 42; *see also* climate change
"glocalization" 22, 37
Google 196; Google Earth 41; Google Hangouts 171; Google Street View 41
GPS 192, 194, 197–199
Great Britain 19, 35–36, 93, 97
Great Depression 136
Greece 103; ancient Greece 39, 41; Hellenistic 33
Groupe International d'Architecture Prospective (GIAP) 76
Gulf states 90

Habermas, Jürgen 39, 183
Habsburg Monarchy 36
Hägerstrand, Torsten 61–62
Hammurabi 31–32
Harvey, David 113, 246, 248–249, 269, 271
hashtags 186
Haushofer, Karl 36
Heine, Heinrich 37
Herodotus 29
Hess, Rudolf 36
heterarchies 18, *19*, 20–21
heterogeneity 18, 20–21
heterosexuality 54, 105
hierarchy *19*, 20, 158; institutional 158, 163; social 110; structural 100; world-system 99
historical dating 51, 55
historical determinism 51
historical maps 68–69
historical poly-temporality 52, 56
historicity 5, 39, 46–47, 50–52, 55–57, 61, 63–64; bitemporal 56; of mankind 51; societal 46
historiography: Marxist 64; history of 65
Hitler, Adolf 36
Höcke, Björn 243
homelessness 5, 47–50, 57
homemaking 10, 252, 254
homo erectus 30
homogeneity 18, 20, 172
homophily 8, 170–171, 178, 188
homophobia 244

homosexuality 105
Hong Kong 102, 104–105, 253
household division of labor 152, 154–155, *156*, 158, 161, 163
household income 152–153
housework 154–155, 158
humanitarian designs 289
humanitarian space 290
Hungary 103; *see also* Austria-Hungary
Huns 34

identity building 245
identity politics 10, 247
images 9, 32, 54, 63, 204–208, 211, 216; computer-generated 207; figurative 204; networked 206; spatial 9; visual 205–206; *see also* digital images; Softimage
immigrants 33, 91, 146
immobility 50, 52–53, 55, 57
imperialism 101
Inca Empire 106
inclusion 9, 12, *19*, 111, 114, 117, 146, 184, 195, 201–202; network 121; social 117, 202; *see also* inclusion hypothesis
inclusion hypothesis 195, 201–202
income differential 88–89
income inequality 97
indentured labour 90–91
India 21, 34, 93, 102, 106, 125
Indian subcontinent 33
individualization 21, 251, 258, 264
Industrial and Commercial Bank of China Limited 128
industrialization 38, 154, 161; *see also* deindustrialization
Industrial Revolution 37, 141
inequality 88–89, 91, 97–103, 106, 110, 113, 117, 128, 140, 265; economic 97; ethnic 98, 100–102; global 6–7, 87–88, 90–95, 97, 99, 101, 103; racial 98, 100–102; regional 136–137, 147; structures of 12; *see also* social inequality
inequity 6
infrastructures 7, 22–23, 120–132, **126**, **130**, 151, 162, 170, 211, 269, 275–276; development 122, **123**, 128–129; digital information 193; energy 128; hard 276; material 22, 24; mobility 22; network 186; physical 120–121, 123, 125, 127, 131; power 122; railway 128, 131; relational 143; social 24, 276; state-led 122; transport 122, 127–128, 161; urban 121
Ingress 194

innovation(s) 4, 112–114, 141, 143; breakthrough 143; neoliberal 270; organizational 159; policy 270, 273; regional 151; spatial 110, 114, 117; technical 75; technological 142
Instagram 201, 205
institutions 3, 8, 13, 24, 36, 40, 64, 98, 121, 142–145, 151–152, 158, 161, 181, 245, 272, 275, 277, 299; business 143; financial 7, 116; formal 142; government 124; informal 142–143; lending 116; local 145; multinational 272; public 183; research 143; social 8, 144, 152, 163; of socialization 145; state 92; state-led 270
integration 22, 33, 54–55, 76, 93, 110, 121, 126, 131, 136, 183; social 54, 110
interaction(s): asymmetrical 127; consumer–retailer 8, 152; dyadic 171; face-to-face 4, 170, 174, 186, 194; frequency 259; historicity of 51; homeless 50; in-person 170, 174; institutionalized 262; media-based 194; network 175; networked 273; (non-)verbal 47, 50, 52, 55–56; online 170–171, 174, 178; patterns of 50–51, 57; rules of 53–54; social 5, 47, 50–51, 56–57, 110, 172, 174, 184, 194, 201; social media 8, 170, 174, 177; social network 171; spatialities of 50–51, 54–56; spatialization of 50–51; spatialized 56; system 173; translocal 182; *see also* social exchanges
interconnectedness 3, 250
internal action parameters 159, 161, *161*
interregional divergence/polarization 136, 141–144
interregional housing price gaps 140
Iran 243
Islamist terrorism 249
islamophobia 244
Israel 102
Italy 36, 104, 125, 243–244; Genoa 115; "Lega Nord" 244; Livorno 115; Venice 115

Japan 22, 34, 102, 104, 106
Jefferson, Thomas 68
Jews 32, 106
JICA 274
Jim Crow 90
Joachim of Fiore 37
Jordan 243, 285, 288, 291

Kant, Immanuel 1
Kenya 243
Knoblauch, Hubert 4–5, 8, 17–26, 46–47, 60, 73, 88, 98, 101, 109–110, 151, 182
knowledge: children's spatial 294, 298, 302, 307; everyday 198; institutional 297; landmark 296; route 296; spatial 3, 10–11, 294, 296–299, 302, 303, 306–307; spatio-temporal 152, 157; subjective 296; survey 296; temporal 158; Western 99–100
Korea *see* North Korea; South Korea

labor unions 146, 155
Laing, Ronald D. 10, 246–247, 251
Laos 248
late modernity 245–246, 248
Latin America 36, 47, 97, 102
Lebanon 103, 287–288, 290
Le Corbusier 24, 73–74, 80
Lefebvre, Henri 5, 37, 50–52, 54–56, 63–64
Le Pen, Marie 243
Lesotho 104
lifelogging 199–200, 202
Lithuania 103
"living space" (*Lebensraum*) 35, 152
local government/governance 176, 270–275
localization 3, 200; *see also* glocalization; translocalization
location-based services (LBS) 194
locative media 9, 23, 192, 194–196, 199, 201–202
longue durée 3, 5–7, 11, 28–29, 39, 101, 110, 114, 116–118, 151, 163
Louis XIV 33–34
Löw, Martina 2, 4–5, 8, 17–26, 38, 46–47, 60–61, 73, 88, 98, 101, 109–110, 151, 182, 295–296
Luhmann, Niklas 34, 36–39
lurking 196–197, 202, 295

Macedonia 32–33, 103
Malawi 274; Lilongwe 274–275
Malaysia 105
"maloca" ("indigenous hut") 48–56, *49*
Malta 103
Mann, Thomas 40
Marduk 32
marginalization 54–55, 98, 245
Martignoni, Girolamo Andrea 68–69, *69*
Marx, Karl 21, 35, 46, 51, 64, 88–89, 93, 112, 121, 286–287
mass media 23, 182

materiality(ies) 10, 12, 23–24, 29, 33, 152, 262, 301, 307
media 23, 38, 62, 65, 73, 87, 182, 186, 202, 207; global 38; legacy 181; mobile 193; networks 38, 184–185; organizations 181; political 175; systems 23, 183; visual 205; *see also* digital media; locative media; mass media; new media; social media
mediated cities 9, 204, 208, 210–212
mediatization 4–5, 18, 22–25, 47, 74, 193
medieval Christendom 106
Mediterranean Sea 29–30, 35
Melbourne, Australia 48
Mendelsohn, Erich 75–76, *75*, 78
mental health 54, 246
Merleau-Ponty, Maurice 80
Mesopotamia 32
MeToo 186
Middle Ages 4, 60, 65
Middle East 35, 104–105
migrant labour 90
migrants 11, 89–90, 92–94, 104, 142
migration 8–10, 30–31, 54, 87–89, 91–94, 104, 128, 136, 142, 144, 147, 182, 186–187, 253, 264, 271; interregional 136; national 92; transformative aspects of 216; urban 131; *see also* international migration
Milanovic, Branko 87–90, 92–94
millionaires 103–104
Ming dynasty 34
Minkowski, Hermann 72, 75
Mobike 205
mobility 5, 10, 18, 22, 50, 52–53, 55–57, 89, 98–99, 111, 113, 139–140, 142, 144, 153, 155, 157, 163, 182, 186–187, 201, 210, 258, 260, 262, 264–265; circulation and 24–26; digital 47; economic 104; global 104, 188; intergenerational 136; interstate 139; labor 116; racial 104; translocal 258; *see also* immobility; social mobility
modernity 2, 20–22, 25, 37, 47, 88, 98, 109–110, 245–246; high 246; *see also* late modernity; postmodernity
Mommsen, Theodor 29
mondialization 37
Mongols 34
monthly gross income *153*
Mossehaus (Berlin) 75, *75*
Mughal Empire 34, 106
multiculturalism 8, 19, 36, 146
Muslims 106
Mussolini, Benito 30, 36

Namibia 104
national heritage 90, 93
nationalism 21, 175, 177, 244, 247, 253; methodological 93; *see also* transnationalism
nationality 151; *see also* transnationality
national patrimony 92
nation-building 4, 35–37
nation states 7, 11, 18–19, 21, 36, 101, 109–111, 116, 181, 183–184, 188
natural resources 22, 41
Nazi Germany 36, 78; Aryanization 40; "SS Plan East" 40
Nebuchadnezzar 31
neighborhood 10, 55, 140, 155, 172–173, 258, 261, 264, 299; effects 172–173, 262; ties 185, 259, 261
neoliberalism 40, 88, 90, 94, 128, 270
neoliberalization 270–273, 275, 278–279
Netflix 171
Netherlands, the 35
networks 4, 10, 18, 20–22, 24–26, 37, 73, 81, 116–117, 204–212, 258–265, 269, 271–277; communication 20, 182, 184, 186; community 185, 188; data 10, 169, 264; ego-centered 263; face-to-face 172; flat 18; global 184; global media 38; institutional 116; issue 186; local 10; market 113; mediated 181; offline 176–177; online 170, 172, 175–176, 178; personal 185, 262; social media 184–185; society 18, 23, 258; spatial 26; territorial 116; translocal 10, 188; transnational 271, 280; transportation 128, 131; *see also* Global Production Networks (GPN); network spillover effect; social networks; transcalar territorial networks (TTN)
network spillover effect 169–178
new media 23
New World 35, 87, 92, 249
non-Western states 99–100
non-white(ness) 101, 104–105, 146
norms 87, 89, 92, 105, 142, 144, 262; cultural 89; neoliberal 90; social 154
North America 30, 91, 101–102, 125, 243
Northern Ireland 175–176
North Korea 99

oblique function, theory of 6, 73–74, *73*, 78–81
Old Testament 32
Old World 29, 31
ontological insecurity 244–245, 247, 252–255

ontological security 10, 243–255; definition 246–248; and geopolitical positioning 245, 249–250; and home-making 245, 250–252; and nature-related routines 245, 252–253; *see also* ontological insecurity
open borders 87–95, 109
operational landscapes 10
oppression: ethnic 100; hierarchies of 99; racial 100
Orient 105
Orientalism 105
"Other," the 248
Ottoman Empire 36, 106
Out-of-Africa theory 30
Oxfam International 97, 102–103

Pakistan 125
Pan-Africanism 101
Parent, Claude 6, 73–74, *73*, 76–81, *81*
Parthians 31, 34
Pascal, Blaise 28
Pax Romana 34
pedagogization 297–298, 302, 306–307; materialized 298; spatial 11, 294, 297–298, 301–302, 303, 306–307
pedestrian city 79
peer effects 173
People's Republic of China (PRC) *see* China, People's Republic of (PRC)
peripheries 7, 33, 52, 55, 63, 97–99, 102, 106, 122, 125, 269, 301; *see also* semiperipheries
Persian Empire 29, 31–32
personal autonomy 246
Peru 299–300; Lima 11, 294, 299–301, 307
Philip II 115
Philippines, the 105
photo-elicitation 245, 249
Plessner, Helmuth 39–40
pluralization 264
Pokémon Go 194
polarization 7–8, 99, 103, 121, 136–137, 146, 173; economic 7, 142, 146; geographical 8, 137, 147; interregional 143; political 174; urban–rural 132
"Political Geography" 35, 72, 175, 244, 247
polycentrism/polycentricity *19*, 109
polycontexturalization 4, 22–24, 47
poly-linear acceleration 47–48
populism 175; national 244; nationalist 250; right-wing 243–244, 247
Portugal 35, 103
positionality 250; "eccentric" 39
postcolonial reparative action 94–95

posthuman 209
postmodernity 21
power relations 12, 35, 37, 132, 272–273, 292
power structures 5, 31, 151
power struggles 12
Priestley, Josef 68, *68*
procedurality 61
processuality 28
prosumption 23
public opinion 173, 183
public space(s) 9, 11, 22, 24, 38, 47, 56–57, 192–193, 195, 202, 294; accessibility of/to 195, 202; children's use of 11–12, 294–308, *299*, *300*, *303*, *305*; immobile 52; (im)mobile 56; offline 12; online 12; spatial pedagogization of 297–298; spatial pedagogy of 298; urban 49, 56
public spheres 8–9, 12, 181–188; counter- 186; digital 183; European 183; mass-mediated 183; networked 181–182, 184–188; offline 12; online 12, 183; traditional 183; transnational 183; urban 183; *see also* public spaces

race 29, 40, 97–106, 145, 151, 172, 208
racial colonial matrix 106
racialization 98, 105–106
racism 7, 98–102, 105–106, 244–245, 247
Raleigh, Sir Walter 35
rapport territorial 277
reality games 194
Reconquista of Andalusia 34
refiguration(s): animatic 207; of space(s) 3–5, 7–8, 11–12, 17, 21–24, 26, 28, 46–48, 50–51, 56–57, 73, 98, 109, 151, 163, 188, 216, 292; spatial 12, 47, 98, 109, 254, 308
refugee camps 243, 285–286; spatiality of 285
refugee crisis 87
refugees 11–12, 22, 30, 87, 94, 227, 249, 285–292
regional assemblages 277
regional economics 136–137, 139, 141, 143
regional inequality 136–137, 147
regressive–progressive method 5, 51–52, 56
relationality 18, *19*, 28, 39, 184, 212, 275, 295
relational space 2, 11, 47, 294, 302, 306–307
relativity, theory of 63, 72
religious orthodoxies 247, 253
Renova, Dreyfus, and Asociación de Cooperativas Argentinas (ACA) 129
resentment, politics of 139

retail(ing) formats 159, 161–163
Roman Church 35
Roman Empire 32, 34, 41
Roman Republic 33, 41
Rome, ancient 29, 31, 33, 41
rough sleepers 49
rough sleeping 48–50; *see also* homelessness
Russia 36, 102–103, 106, 249; Moscow 74; *see also* Soviet Union
Russian Empire 36, 106

Sainte-Bernadette du Banlay, church of 80, *81*
Salvini, Matteo 243
São Paulo 5, 46–57, *49*; homeless pedestrians 467, 51–52, 56–57
Sargonian Empire 31
Scharoun, Hans 80–81
Schengen zone 103
Schmitt, Carl 35–36, 40
Schöffer, Nicolas 76–80, *77*
Schumpeter, Joseph 110, 113, 117, 141
Schwarz, Rudolph 25
Scotland 175–177
Scythians 34
Second World War 25, 76, 98
sectionalism 146
seed project 300, *300*, *303*, *305*
segregation 101, 170; social 195, 202; spatial 202; urban 9, 192
self-identity 246–247, 254
semiperipheries 97–106, 107n1
sequentiality 61
serfdom 106
sexism 98, 106, 244
shopping 8, 25, 152, 154–155, 157–159, *160*, 161–163, 178, 199; behavior 154; center *160*, 162; malls 25, 193, 199; time 158
Silicon Valley 143
Simmel, Georg 35, 38
Singapore 48, 104, 254
skin-bleaching 105
skin-whitening 105
slacktivism 169
slavery 55, 90, 106
smart city(ies) 21, 23, 205, 209–211
smart control centre 211
smart operations centre 211
smartphones 171, 193–194, 196
Smith, Adam 111–113; *The Wealth of Nations* 111–112
social acceleration 46–47
social capital 245, 258–263
social dislocation 5, 117

social exchanges 202, 263
social inequality 4, 6–7, 12, 41, 57, 97, 111, 151
social media 8–9, 170–178, 181–186, 188, 194–197, 206; bots 170; communication 9, 182–184, 194; data 171, 176; echo chambers 173–174, 177; microtargeting 173; networks 184–185; platforms 177–178, 182, 186, 196, 206
social mobility 110, 117, 145; global 104; racialized 98
social networks 144–145, 169–178, 185, 196, 200–202, 258, 260–262, 265; offline 8, 169, 171, 177–178; online 8, 169–170, 174–175, 178; spatial 169
social transformations 3, 5, 23–24, 26, 51
social web 18, 22, 182, 188
social worlds 55, 70, 111, 182, 193, 195–196, 201–202
societies of control 209
sociospatial process 46, 51, 56–57
softimage 206–207
software 206, 209; animation 80; facial 'recognition' 208
South Africa 99–101; Johannesburg 253, 274–276, 279
South America 21, 35
South Asia 104, 124
South-East Asia 125
South Korea 20, 25–26, 104–105, 216; Dogil Maeul 216; Seoul 216; Songdo 25–26, 216
Soviet Union 36
soybean industry 127–129
space(s): appropriated 12; colonial 25; concrete 298; container 18, 20, 292; culturality of 63; culturally created 29; definition 61; geo-physical 29; historicity of 63; "hybrid" 21, 194, 196; mediatization of 18, 193; network 26, 182; physical 5, 8, 10, 29, 55, 72, 80, 171, 193–194, 285, 292; planned 12; polycontexturalization of 4; production of 5, 10, 46–47, 51–52, 56–57, 63; refiguration of 3–5, 7–8, 11–12, 17, 21–24, 26, 28, 46–48, 50–51, 56–57, 73, 98, 109, 151, 163, 188, 216, 292; socially constructed 35, 37, 62, 294; sociology of 38, 61, 64; soft 11; splintered 195; temporalization of 62; temporary 11; territorial notion of 181, 183; visualization of 8–9, 167; *see also* geographic space; humanitarian space; "living space" (*Lebensraum*);

public space(s); relational space; space-time entanglements; space-time, theory of; territorial space; time; trajectorial space; urban spaces; virtual space
space-time, theory of 60, 64–65, 70
space-time entanglements 11
spacing 2, 38, 61, 296, 302, 303
Spain 19, 35–36, 103, 115
Sparta 41
spatial arrangements 11, 60, 286, 294, 307
spatial constitution 12, 306
spatial economic polarization 7–8
spatial equilibrium theory 138, 140
spatial experience 3
spatial fragments 24
spatial innovations 110, 114, 117
spatiality(ies) 1–2, 10, 12, 21, 39, 50–52, 56, 132, 184, 204, 211, 254, 260, 262, 264; dating 54–55; and economy 6–8; identifying 53–54; inner 216; of interaction 55–56; outer 216; of policy mobilities 272; of refugee camps 285; of self 254; and social inequality 6–8; and temporality 3–6, 60–62, 69; of time 65
spatialization of interaction 50–52
spatialization patterns 50–51, 57
spatialization processes 57
spatial knowledge 3, 10–11, 294, 296–299, 302, 303, 306–307
spatial logics 4, 18–19, *19*, 21, 25, 131
spatial occupation 28–42
spatial pedagogization 11, 294, 297–298, 301–302, 303, 306–307
spatial pedagogy 298, 307
spatial perception 9
spatial refiguration 12, 47, 98, 109, 254, 308
spatial relocations 110, 113–114, 117
spatial transformations 18, 23, 30, 47, 109–118, 216, 253–254; analysis of 28–30; through the refiguration of spaces 1–13; of refugee camps 291–292; and spatio-temporal coupling 151–163; urban 120–132; world-historical perspective on 109–110
"spatial turn" 1, 18, 39, 61–62, 69
spatio-temporal coupling 151–163
spatiotemporal entanglements 60–70
spatio-temporality 5–6
spatio-temporal knowledge 152, 157
spatio-temporal order 161
spatio-temporal pathways 151–152, 154, *156–157*, 157–158

spatio-temporal regimes 157–158, 161, 163
"SpatioTemporal Studies" group 60, 62–63
spectator–screen intersection 206
spectrality 274
specular politics 274
state-building 116
stratification 34, 104–105, 110–111
structuration theory 61
subordination 33, 56, 90
succession 61
Sudan 243
"suscipient business" 162
Swarm 9, 196, 199–202, *200*
Sweden 104
synthesizing 2, 302
Syria 29, 243, 249, 287

Tahuantinsuyo Park 299–308, *303*
Tempohomes 285–292
temporality 3–6, 37, 50, 60–62, 64, 69, 70n1; poly- 52, 56; *see also* spatio-temporality
temporal patterns 3, 57; *see also* cycles; trajectories; turning points
tenancy 106
territoriality 25
territorialization 10, *19*, 272, 275–279; de- 25
territorial space 20, 25–26, 181
territories: border 91; bounded 21, 111; geopolitical 187; globalized 274; imperial 32; local 184; national 9, 20, 181, 183; networked 274; political 183; regional 20; social 192; spatial 113; transcalar 278; urban 272–273, 276; *see also* transcalar territorial networks (TTN)
Thailand 104, 248
Third World 98, 100–101
Thirty Years' War 40
TikTok 205
time: conflicts 158–159; -geography 61; layers 3, 5, 11; regimes 157–158, 161; -space compression 246, 253–254; -space distanciation 246–247; spatiality of 65; spatialization of 62; *see also* commuting time; shopping; space-time entanglements; space-time, theory of; working time
Tocqueville, Alexis de 36
Toronto, Canada 48
tourism 9; transformative aspects of 216–217
trace data 171

trajectorial space 25–26
trajectories 3–4, 21, 24–25, 110, 121, 276
transcalar territorial networks (TTN) 276–277
translocal communities 9, 181, 186–188
translocality 25, 182, 186–188
translocalization 4, 22–26, 47
transnational elites 6, 40, 151
transnationalism 21, 264
transnationality 121
transnationalization 19, *19*, 109
Trente Glorieuses (The Glorious Thirty) 76
Trump, Donald 137, 139, 243–244
Turkey 122, 132n1
turning points 4
Twitter 25, 170, 175–177, 186, 207
Twitterbots 170
Twittersphere 18, 22, 183

UAE 125
Uber 205
Ukraine 249
UNHRC 243
United Cities and Local Governments (UCLG) 274–275
United Kingdom 22, 100, 172, 174–176, 243, 253; Labour Party 172; *see also* England; Great Britain; Northern Ireland; Scotland; Wales
United Nations 36, 42, 254, 271
United States 7, 22, 36, 90–92, 97, 103, 124, 136–140, 142, 145, 147n2, 176, 243–244, 249, 253; Boston 138–139; Chicago 140; Detroit 115, 143; House of Representatives 137; Houston 139; Los Angeles 48; Louisiana 145; Midwest 137, 140, 145; New York City 48, 74, 138–141; Northeast 137, 140, 145; Pacific Coast 140; Philadelphia 140; "Republicans" 244; Rust Belt 137–138, 140, 142; San Francisco 138–140; Seattle 138; South 90, 140, 142, 145; Sunbelt 137; Washington, D.C. 140; West 140, 243
urban data 9, 205, 208, 212
urban design 74, 79–80
urban development 10, 121, 127, 209, 269, 271–273, 275, 278–280
urban entrepreneurialism 270
urbanization 37, 63, 131, 253, 269, 271–272, 275–276, 278–280, 285
urban loneliness 258

urban politics 10, 269–280; Cox–Harvey approach 269–270; regime theory 270; *see also* financialization; neoliberalization
urban public places 48, 192, 201–202; *see also* public space(s); public spheres
urban-rural divide 116
urban space 9, 12, 24, 64, 74, 120–121, 125, 127, 132, 195, 204–205, 208, 211–212, 216, 258; transnational 121, 131; *see also* public space(s); public spheres; urban public places
urban spatial transformation 120–132
USA *see* United States
U.S. Steel 113

value chains 142, 151–152
Vandals 33
Vatican 36
vertical hierarchical order 18, 21, 25
Vietnam 248
Ville cybernétique (Cybernetic City) 76–78, *77*, 80
Virilio, Paul 6, 72–74, 76, 78–80
virtualization 28–42
virtual space 42, 193
visual culture 207, 212; and power 212
visualizations 12, 274; of space 8–9
visual technologies 204–205, 208–209

Wales 175–176, 178
Wallerstein, Immanuel 29, 98–99, 101–102
war-making 116
ways of seeing 205–210; animatic 207, 209–210; representational 207–209
Waze navigation app 194
wealth accumulation 100, 104, 111, 114
wealth disparities 111
Weber, Max 29, 92
welfare state 89, 154, 258
West, the 47, 89, 93, 101, 104–105; Western states 104; non- 99–100
West Germany 8, 152, 154, 161
WhatsApp 171, 205
whiteness 93, 101, 104–106; 'methodological' 93
white supremacy 99–102, 104
WiFi triangulation 192
Wilhelm II 36
will formation 183
working hours 155, 158
working time 161

World Bank 88, 99, 270
world trade 142
world-system 6–7, 11–12, 97–103, 105–106, 109–111, 117–118, 151
World War I *see* First World War
World War II *see* Second World War

xenophobia 106, 244–245, 254–255
Xerxes 29

Yahweh 32
Yarmouk camp 287
Yelp 194
Yokohama International Port Terminal 80, *81*
YouTube 175
Yugoslavia 102

Zaatari refugee camp 286, 290
zombie accounts 170
Zoom 171

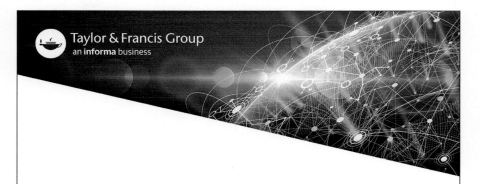